MW01631400

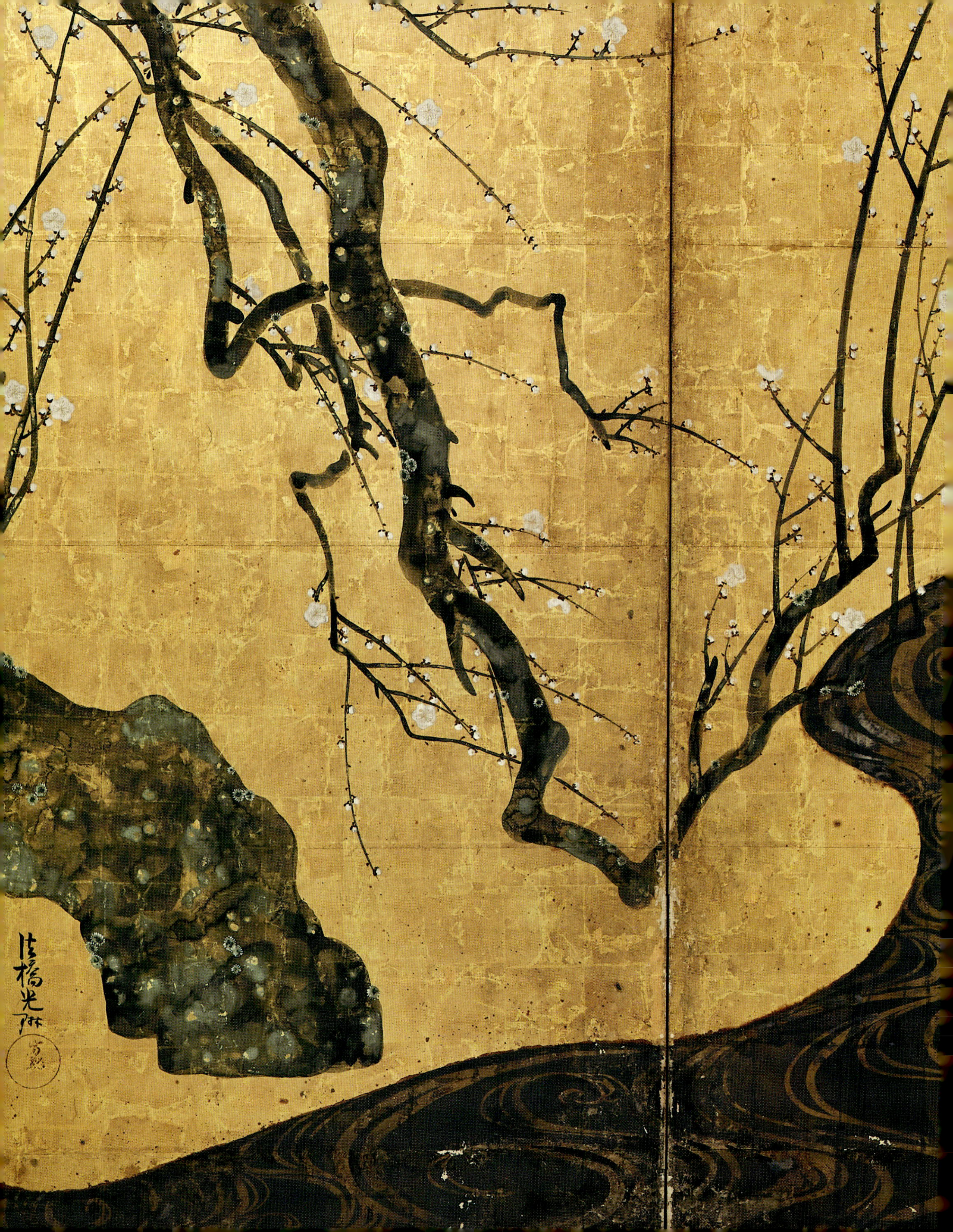
法橋光琳

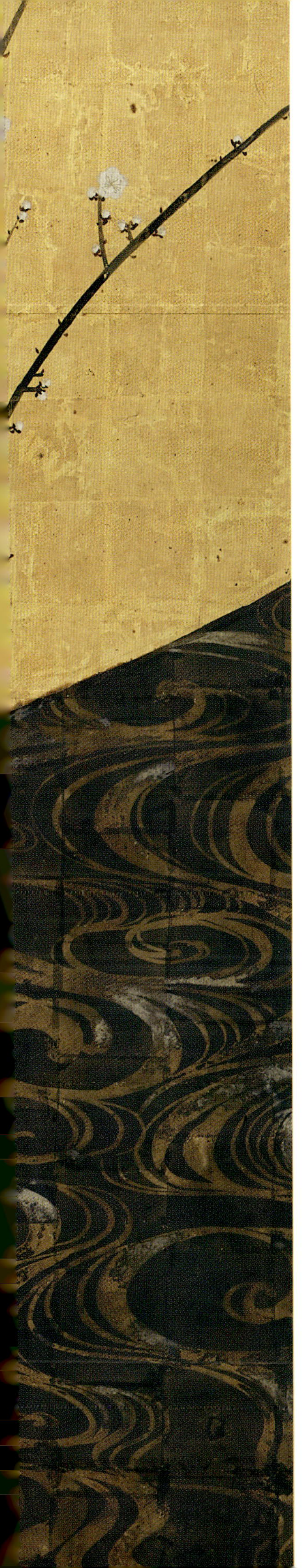

Frank Feltens

OGATA KŌRIN

Art In Early Modern Japan

YALE UNIVERSITY PRESS, NEW HAVEN AND LONDON

Published with assistance from the Annie Burr Lewis Fund.

Publication of this book has been aided by a grant from the Millard Meiss Publication Fund of CAA.

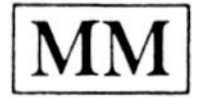

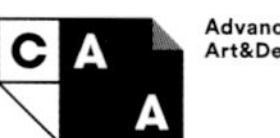

This publication received support from the Mary Griggs Burke Center for Japanese Art, Department of Art History and Archaeology, Columbia University.

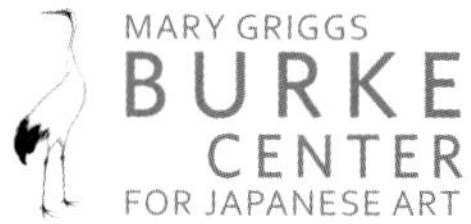

yalebooks.com/art

Designed by Leslie Fitch and Julie Allred
Jacket and cover designed by Daisuke Yajima
Set in Crimson and Source Sans Pro type by Julie Allred, BW&A Books
Printed in China by Regent Publishing Services Limited

Library of Congress Control Number: 2020946750
ISBN 9780300256918

A catalogue record for this book is available from the British Library.

This paper meets the requirements of ANSI/NISO Z39.48-1992 (Permanence of Paper).

10 9 8 7 6 5 4 3 2 1

Jacket illustration: Ogata Kōrin, *Irises at Yatsuhashi (Eight-Plank Bridge), from the Tales of Ise* (details of fig. 25)

Frontispiece: Ogata Kōrin, *Red and White Plum Blossoms* (detail of fig. 114)

Page vi: Ogata Kōrin and Ogata Kenzan, *Square Dish with Design of Eight-Plank Bridge, from the Tales of Ise* (detail of fig. 88)

Page 1: Ogata Kōrin, *Irises at Yatsuhashi (Eight-Plank Bridge), from the Tales of Ise* (detail of fig. 25)

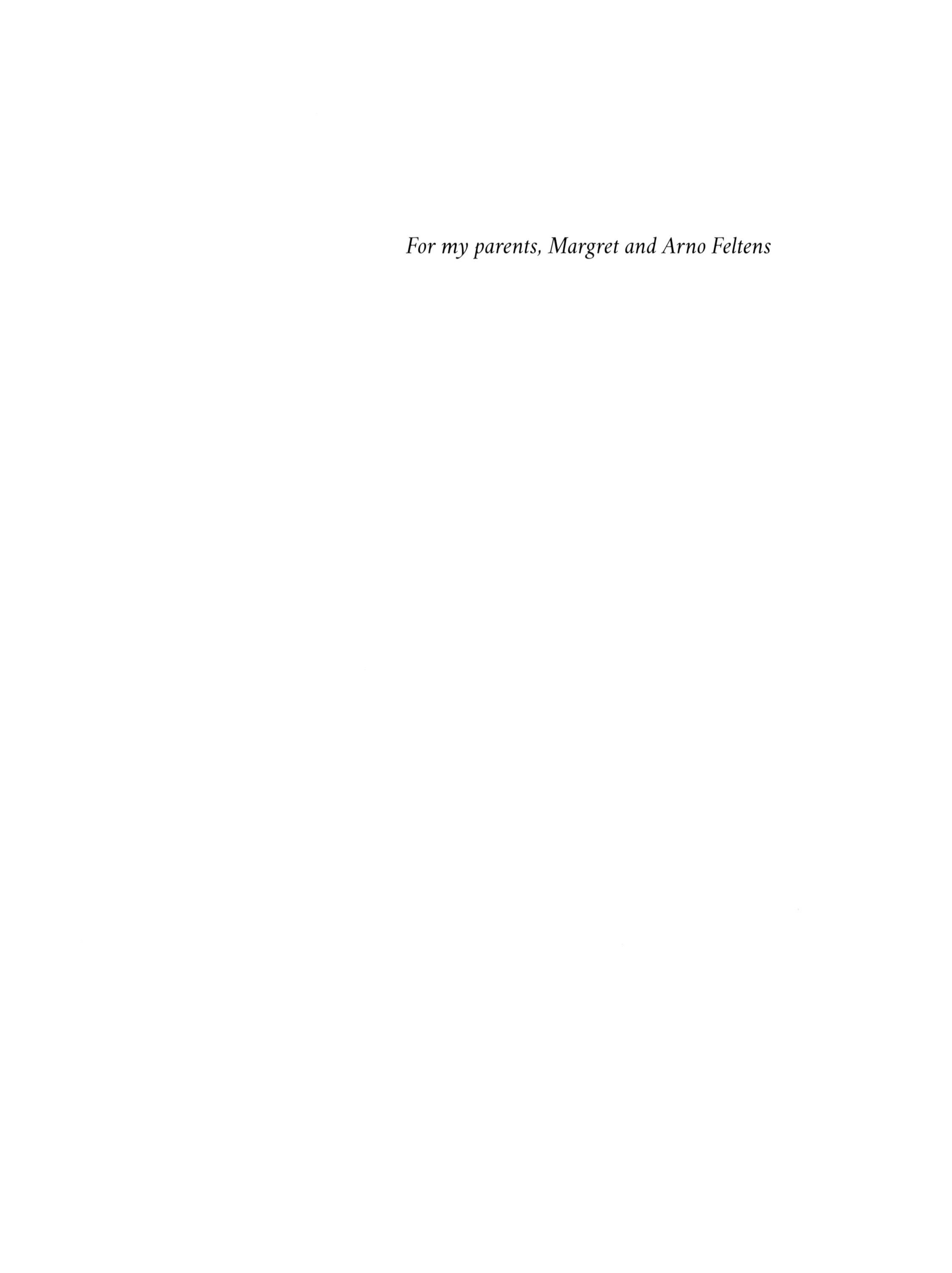

For my parents, Margret and Arno Feltens

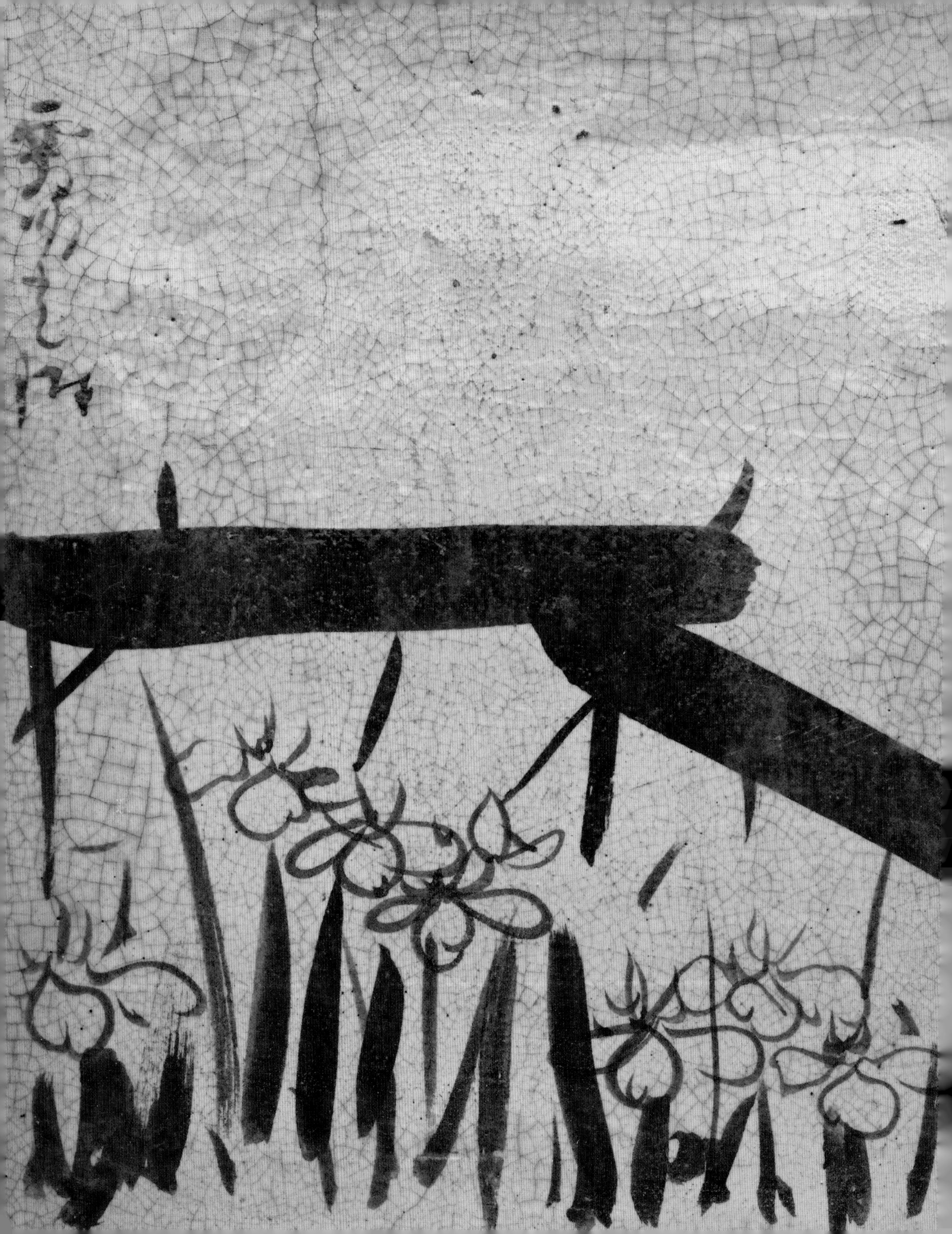

CONTENTS

ACKNOWLEDGMENTS

The joy of writing a book like this one lies in the opportunity to work with colleagues and friends throughout the field and beyond. This study has benefited from the knowledge and generosity of many individuals, and I am humbled by their presence along my path of pursuing the history of Japanese art. The groundwork for this book was made during doctoral studies at Columbia University, and I am grateful to my adviser, Matthew McKelway, for his unwavering support and guidance to this day. The manuscript was prepared during a residency at the Smithsonian Institution's Freer Gallery of Art and Arthur M. Sackler Gallery as an Anne van Biema Fellow. Afterward, as curatorial staff at the Freer and Sackler, many colleagues at the museum have been instrumental in shaping my thinking, and they have left a lasting imprint on my work and conduct as a scholar. Above all, I owe innumerable gratitude to James Ulak, whose restless intellect, sharp eye, and incomparable wit made learning from him and working at the Freer and Sackler a truly formative experience. His exacting feedback on early versions of the manuscript much enhanced the final product. Louise Cort shared a vast expertise on ceramics, and Ann Yonemura offered counsel on lacquer. The following current and former colleagues have in countless conversations in hallways, offices, and during afterhours made work at the museum all the more profound and enjoyable: Kit Brooks, Andrew Hare, Takako Sarai, Sonia Coman, Jirō Ueda, Akiko Niwa, Reiko Yoshimura, Jennifer Berry, Nancy Micklewright, Kathryn Phillips, Shu Yue, Mike Smith, and Alessandro Bianchi. Nancy Eickel's skills as an editor forever changed my outlook on writing.

During my four years as a visiting researcher at Gakushūin University, Tokyo, my adviser Sano Midori shared her wisdom and instructed me in the art of looking and critical thinking. She opened many doors that otherwise would have remained shut. I also thank Arakawa Masaaki, whose understanding of Kenzan is unparalleled, and Shimao Arata, who altered my view of ink painting. I will always remember the kindness of everyone who made the years at Gakushūin some of the most meaningful of my life.

A summer as a visiting researcher at the Tokyo National Research Institute for Cultural Properties provided the ideal environment for thinking about Kōrin, and ever since Emura Tomoko has been a guiding light as I have been venturing through the maze of studying Kōrin. Kobayashi Tadashi, Kobayashi Yūko, Satō Arisa, and Shioya Naoko of the Okada Museum of Art, Hakone, deserve special mention for their generosity in time, friendship, and collegiality. An internship at the Nezu Museum brought unparalleled exposure to some of Kōrin's greatest works—so close as to make out a tiny hair of his brush stuck on one of the *Irises* screens. For this and much more, I thank Nezu Kōichi, Matsubara Shigeru, Noguchi Takeshi, Nishida Hiroko, Shirahara Yukiko, and Arakawa Mamiko. Klaus and Yoshie Naumann were a steadfast fixture throughout my years in Tokyo and beyond. Klaus, in ways large and small, shaped the way I see and understand Japanese art, and I will never forget the many hours during which he generously shared his knowledge and experience.

In Japan, I also thank Kōno Motoaki, Robert Campbell, Wil Lautenschlager, Tamamushi Satoko, Nakamachi Keiko, the late Nakabe Yoshitaka, Hasegawa Yōko, Tanaka Atsushi, Furuta Ryō, Miyamoto Keizō, Itakura Masaaki, Tsukamoto Maromitsu, Takagishi Akira, Okudaira Shunroku, Hayashi Susumu, Tanaka Jun, Suzuki Ken'ichi, Watada Minoru, Higuchi Kazutaka, Tsuchiya Maki, Shiino Akifumi, Oyama Yuzuruha, Ishikawa Atsuko, Tanaka Jun'ichirō, Fujimoto Yūki, Imanishi Junko, Honda Yasuko, Yanagizawa Eriko, Melissa Rinne, Matsushima Jin, Tanabe Kōji, Ōkubo Kenshi, and Paul Berry.

Curators and staff at the following institutions have been generous in providing access to their collections for research: Tokyo National Museum, Kyoto National Museum, Museum of the Imperial Collections Sannomaru Shōzōkan, Idemitsu Museum of Arts, Nezu Museum, Suntory Museum of Art, Sensōji, Seikadō Bunko Art Museum, Hatakeyama Memorial Museum of Fine Art, National Diet Library, National Institute of Japanese Literature, MOA Museum of Art, Kenninji, Fukuda Art Museum, Hosomi Museum, Yamato Bunkakan, Osaka City Museum of Art, Itsuō Museum, British Museum, Museum für Asiatische Kunst Berlin, Metropolitan Museum of Art, Brooklyn Museum, Yale University Art Gallery, Cleveland Museum of Art, Art Institute of Chicago, Kimbell Art Museum, Asian Art Museum San Francisco, and Seattle Art Museum. I am also indebted to the private collectors whose artworks I was allowed to study and include in this book.

Faculty at Columbia and other universities were a beacon of inspiration that left an everlasting imprint on my life and work. Among them, I want to thank Robert Harrist Jr., Jonathan Reynolds, Miyeko Murase, Haruo Shirane,

Yukio Lippit, Andrew Watsky, Julie Nelson Davis, Melissa McCormick, Jamie Newhard, and the late Donald Keene. A number of friends and peers have been instrumental in ways large and small in shaping this project and my outlook on Japanese art history as a discipline. Above all, I am grateful to Aaron Rio, Talia Andrei, Joseph Scheier-Dolberg, Mimi Chusid, Sara Sumpter, Chun Wa Chan, Wai Yee Chiong, Kent Cao, Kristopher Kersey, Amy Riggs, Jens Bartel, Gloria Yu Yang, and Or Porath.

Many mentors, colleagues, and friends in the United States contributed to the completion of this volume. I am deeply indebted to Dawn Delbanco for her close reading and insightful feedback on the manuscript. Much gratitude for counsel, guidance, and graciously sharing expertise is deserved by John Carpenter, Kōichi Yanagi, Monika Bincsik, Rachel Saunders, Joan Cummins, Xiaojin Wu, Sinéad Vilbar, Michiyo Morioka, Midori Oka, Ying-chen Peng, and Amy Poster. The exhaustive comments by the two anonymous peer reviewers helped turn the text into publishable form.

My journey in the history of Japanese art began in my home country of Germany, where a number of teachers and colleagues—many of them now dear friends—paved the way that ultimately made this book a reality. Thank you to Alexander Hofmann, Melanie Trede, Nora von Achenbach, Katharina Rode, Wibke Schrape, Eugenia Bogdanova-Kummer, Sabine Bradel, Mio Wakita, Ching-Ling Wang, and Khanh Trinh. I am also grateful for the many conversations about Japanese art with Timothy Clark, Timon Screech, Estelle Bauer, and Koto Sadamura. Charlotte Horlyck kindly shared her understanding of Korean pottery that much benefited the chapter on *sabi-e*.

At Yale University Press, the manuscript could not have been in better hands. Katherine Boller, senior editor for art and architecture, believed in the project from the beginning and was exemplary in shepherding it to completion. Raychel Rapazza, editorial assistant, offered much help and guidance. Copyediting by Laura Jones Dooley and Heidi Downey ensured a polished final version. Many thanks also to Mary Mayer and the production team, who brought the project to completion and helped create a beautiful layout.

My very special gratitude is reserved for Daisuke Yajima and my parents, Margret and Arno Feltens. They were there—from thousands of miles away or right by my side—from the first days of exploring Kōrin down to the completion of this volume. Without their encouragement, inspiration, conversations, and simply offering a shoulder, none of this would have been possible.

NOTE TO THE READER

Japanese names of historic personages and Japanese scholars throughout the publication are written in the traditional order, surname first, such as Ogata Kōrin, except where a person's primary activity is or was outside of Japan.

Dates follow the lunar calendar and are given as, for example, first day of the first month in 1658. Era names are included in translations as they appear in the original.

All translations, unless otherwise noted, are my own.

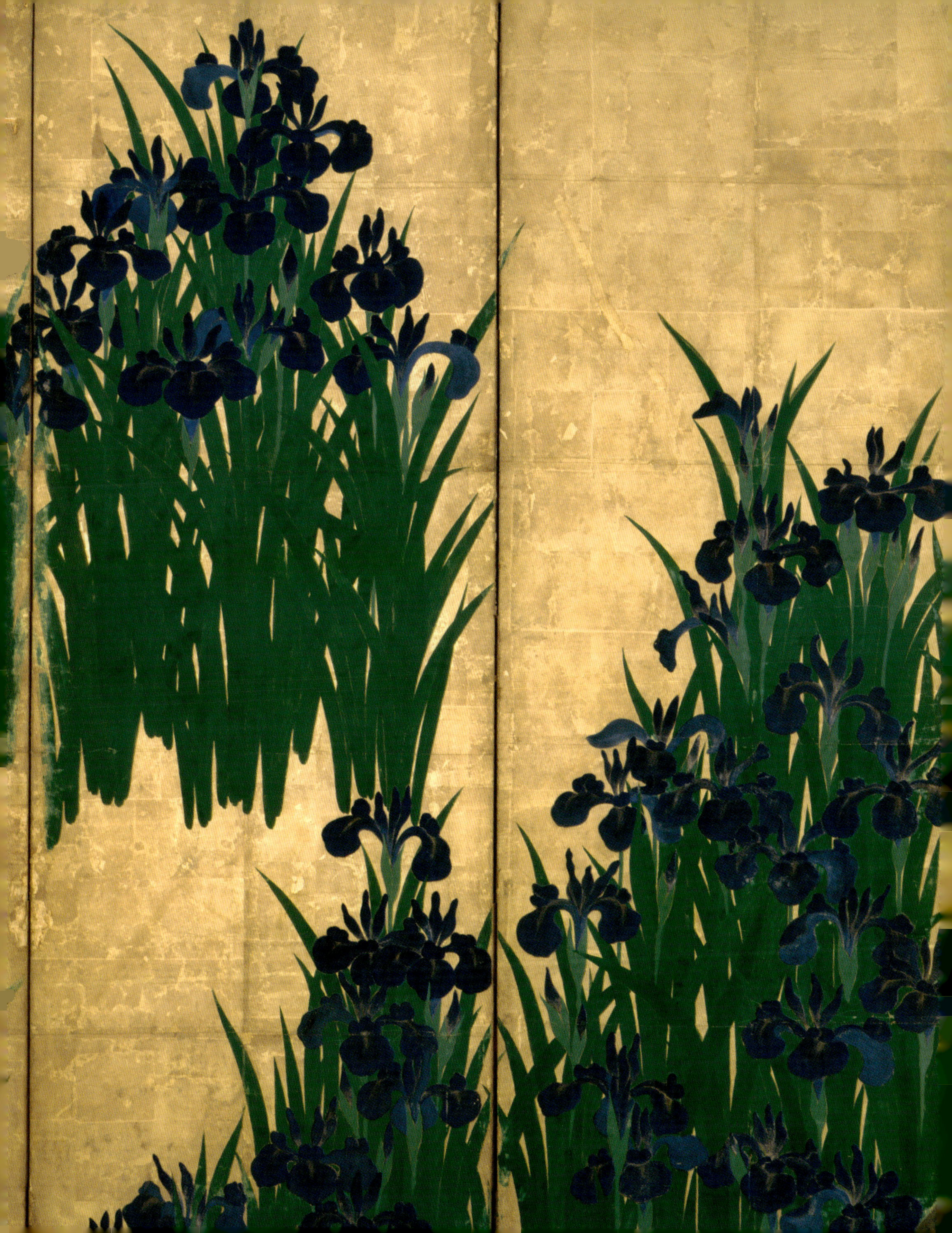

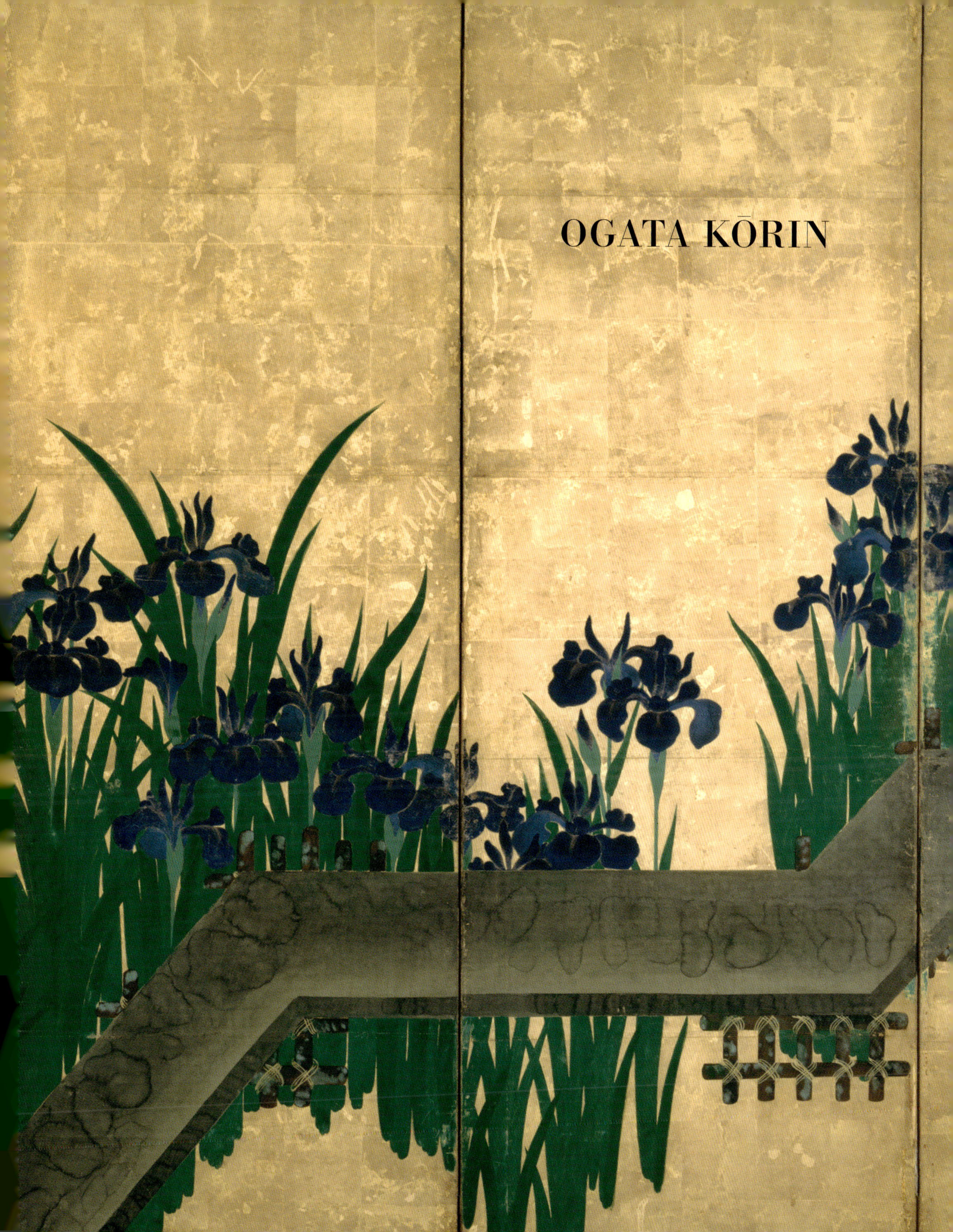

OGATA KŌRIN

Introduction

Ogata Kōrin (1658–1716) is a fixture in Japan's cultural landscape. Few other Japanese artists draw similar crowds of museumgoers and have spawned comparable numbers of publications. Hundreds of articles and books on Kōrin's work and countless artistic homages have been brought forth. Although he belongs to a distant past, Kōrin is part of the nation's self-image in a way achieved by few other artists. His range of impact is wide and diverse: the current five-thousand-yen bill features a detail of Kōrin's *Irises* screens on its verso, and the decorative motif of the carpet in the prime minister's residence takes the same painting as its model. A replica of Kōrin's pair of screens *Irises at Yatsuhashi* formed the backdrop of discussions by world leaders at the G7 summit at Ise Shima in 2014, reinforcing Kōrin's identity as a global artist and the poster child for Japan's national consciousness.

Already throughout the second half of the Edo period (1615–1868), Kōrin's name resonated among a public audience. His style circulated by way of popular kimono catalogues, and a number of artists mimicked his works. Kōrin's bold forms and watery ink techniques became hallmarks of modern Japanese-style painting. As such, knowledge of Kōrin is vital for understanding Japanese painting from the seventeenth century to the present.

Kōrin was born in 1658 as Ogata Ichinojō, the second son of Ogata Sōken (d. 1687), head of the Kariganeya, a prominent Kyoto textile business. Kōrin entered this earth during the waning years of his family's monetary privilege and social leverage. The Kariganeya had been the exclusive garment supplier to the retired empress Tōfukumon'in (1607–1678) and her household.[1] The contract and the substantial income expired with her death. Remaining, however, was the societal clout tied to the Kariganeya's name, a web of influence that would serve Kōrin well as he tried his hand at different career paths and, eventually, art.

Another vestige of the family's better past was a privileged education. Sōken's three sons received a thorough training in literature, theater, and painting, an education suited to members of Kyoto's upper-tier bourgeoisie. Sōken also made sure to insert Kōrin into his social circles, which encompassed high-ranking aristocrats, merchants, and theater professionals. Convinced of the longevity of the family's fortunes and sure of the exalted Ogata pedigree, Sōken, it seems, educated his son in beauty rather than business matters. Time would prove him wrong; Kōrin was unable to live the carefree life of a wealthy son. Instead, a remarkable talent for painting and a lack of money motivated him to become a painter. In its totality, Kōrin's life manifests the changing fortunes of early modern Kyoto's great families and makes clear how Japan owes one of its most remarkable artists to the fleeting nature of wealth.

A BRUSH OF FREE SPIRIT

When Kōrin arrived at the decision to make the arts his vocation in the 1690s, he showed a restless creativity from the start. In the words of the poet and literati painter Tachibana Chikage (1735–1808), Kōrin's brushwork was full of "free spirit" (*susabi*)—a pioneering style that shed itself of orthodox influences and introduced a fresh approach to painting (fig. 1).[2] Like many of his contemporaries, Kōrin initially trained with a Kano-school artist, a part of his vita that is discussed more fully in chapter 4. The Kano established the most sprawling painting atelier in Japanese history, with painters regularly serving the highest ranks of the country's leadership. Countless studios throughout the realm provided amateurs and aspiring professionals a vast infrastructure for

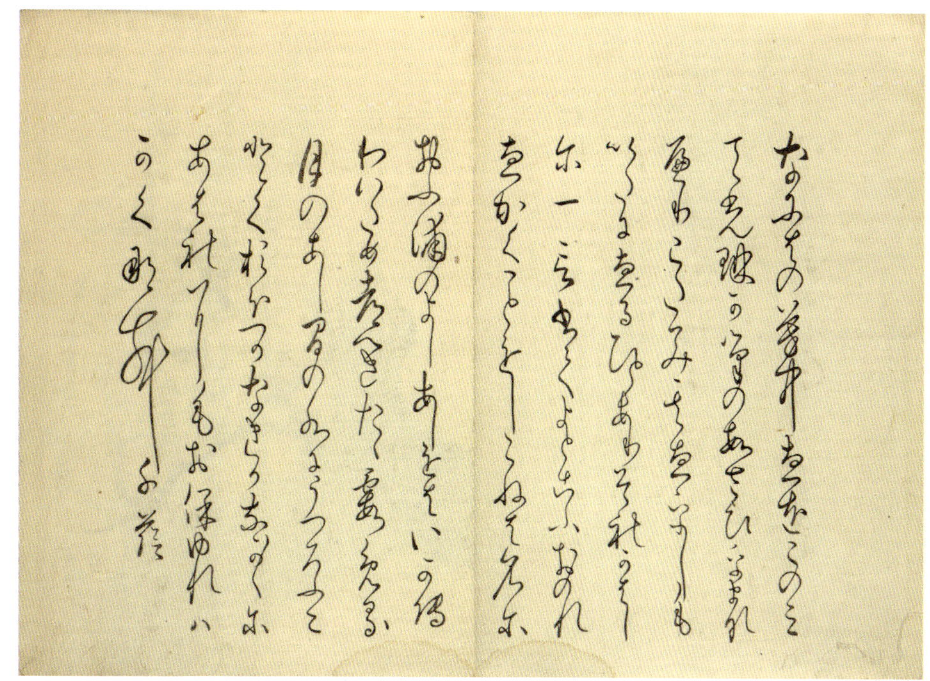

FIGURE 1

Tachibana Chikage, preface to Nakamura Hōchū, *Genealogy of Kōrin's Paintings* (*Kōrin gafu*), 1802. Woodblock-printed book; ink and color on paper. Freer Gallery of Art, Smithsonian Institution, Washington, D.C.: Purchase, The Gerhard Pulverer Collection—Charles Lang Freer Endowment, Friends of the Freer and Sackler Galleries and the Harold P. Stern Memorial fund in appreciation of Jeffrey P. Cunard and his exemplary service to the Galleries as chair of the Board of Trustees (2003–2007), FSC-GR-780.436.1–2.

apprenticeship in painting. However, Kōrin soon departed from the idiosyncrasies of scholastic painting. By embracing an extensive variety of techniques, genres, and media, Kōrin perfected a style that captivates by way of its fusion of simplicity and sumptuousness. Kōrin's sophisticated synergy of cultural acumen and artistic capacity resulted in paintings that reconfigure traditional subjects, such as the court classic the *Tales of Ise.*

Many of Kōrin's artworks employ a startling reduction of form paired with suggestive allure, traits that have enthralled and perplexed audiences for centuries. Contemporary scholars have invested considerable energy to unveil hidden meanings believed to be embedded in Kōrin's works, many of which offer intriguing avenues for understanding certain aspects of his work.[3] For example, Kōrin's engagement with theater, classical literature, and poetry has been the subject of some discussion. Similarly, psychological interpretations of Kōrin's work have been raised, inspired by the appeal of modern psychoanalysis and a quest for locating the subconscious in his art.[4] Yet, although Kōrin is one of the most frequently discussed painters in Japanese art history, the manifold studies of his life and work have focused on isolated, often disparate aspects of his biography and oeuvre, without considering Kōrin as part of a larger cultural and aesthetic framework.

Kōrin's life, paintings, lacquer works, and ceramics are a coherent whole of interlinked parts that perpetually reference and challenge one another. Yet previous scholarship has not embraced the reality that the core of Kōrin's story is formed by the symbiotic relationship between different, often unconnected artistic media and their links to his vita, a synthesis that can only be understood in its entirety and against the backdrop of his time. Kōrin's recognition in his age and since is the result of an alloy of factors, both internal and external. Kōrin was born into privilege and, through the widespread dissemination of his artworks and layered social connections, helped commodify the coveted culture of Kyoto's aristocracy. Most important, he did so by working across genres and media, uniting the efficacies of painting, lacquer, ceramics, and textiles, an accomplishment in eclecticism that few other early modern Japanese artists could claim. At the heart of this conglomeration was Kōrin's uncanny capacity of translating oft-painted subjects with deep roots in Japanese culture into novel visual experiences. In so doing, Kōrin manifested an acute awareness of the demands of his diverse clientele, a cognizance that led him constantly to evolve his manner by adding stylistic components that appealed to him and his patrons. The result was hybridized forms of expression that combined the known with the new. Moreover, Kōrin's upbringing among Kyoto's urban upper class instilled in him an awareness of personal status and the exalted education that came with it. His upbringing in the arts of painting, theater, and literature converted easily into works of art whose apparent simplicity seems to conceal deep-seated cultural meaning.

As such, understanding Kōrin and his art calls for a holistic approach, one that combines the study of his life and personal web of connections, the technical and material aspects of his artworks, the cross-mediality of much of his oeuvre, and efforts to unveil some of the ulterior cultural references that lie beneath the surface of his greatest pieces of art. This book assembles these elements into a coherent picture that traces Kōrin's trajectory from the beginnings to the end. Only by coalescing the various parts of Kōrin's layered existence and output can we grasp the full mastery and lasting impact of his artistry.

TASTE AND REFINEMENT

In early modern Japan, painting was commonly evaluated by the level at which an artist had managed to comprehend the past, instill it into his works, and rechannel it into something new. Early modern commentaries of art share a recurring focus on style and representation. Indeed, writings about painting during Kōrin's time established loosely defined benchmarks for evaluating skill. Major painting treatises of the seventeenth century, such as Kano Einō's *History of Painting of the Realm* (*Honchō gashi*) of 1693, explain the practice of painting in broad strokes. Summing up the essence of *yamato-e,* the Japanese-style painting that Kōrin and others engaged in, Einō (1631–1697) simply notes: "Japanese painting has many works by artists whose names are unknown. Works are handed down that display glimpses of the country's landscapes (*sansui shōkei*) and color is applied very thickly and there is much use of gold leaf."[5] Yet transcending tradition was always a core criterium of excellence. About the manner of the medieval monk-painter Sesson Shūkei (circa 1492–circa 1577), Einō says: "He strove to avoid ostentatiousness. Generally speaking, he largely brought forth new ideas [in his paintings]. He wielded his brush unconventionally and without restraint."[6]

Kōrin was appraised in a similar manner. In *Rustic Words on Painting Matters* (*Kaiji higen*), the influential literati theorist Kuwayama Gyokushū (1746–1799), wrote about Kōrin and his source of inspiration, Tawaraya Sōtatsu (d. circa 1643), that "in recent times, Sōtatsu and Kōrin followed another kind of painting. Even though Sōtatsu specialized in applying color in his flower and grass paintings, his works possess antique spirit (*ko'i*) in abundance. Also, in his boneless spirit resonance (*kiin*), Kōrin aimed at antique simplicity (*kosetsu*) in all his figure and flower paintings, and he often avoided the usual way of painters."[7] Gyokushū posits that Kōrin's works draw from images of the past but also surpass conventional expressions in painting. To early modern commentators,

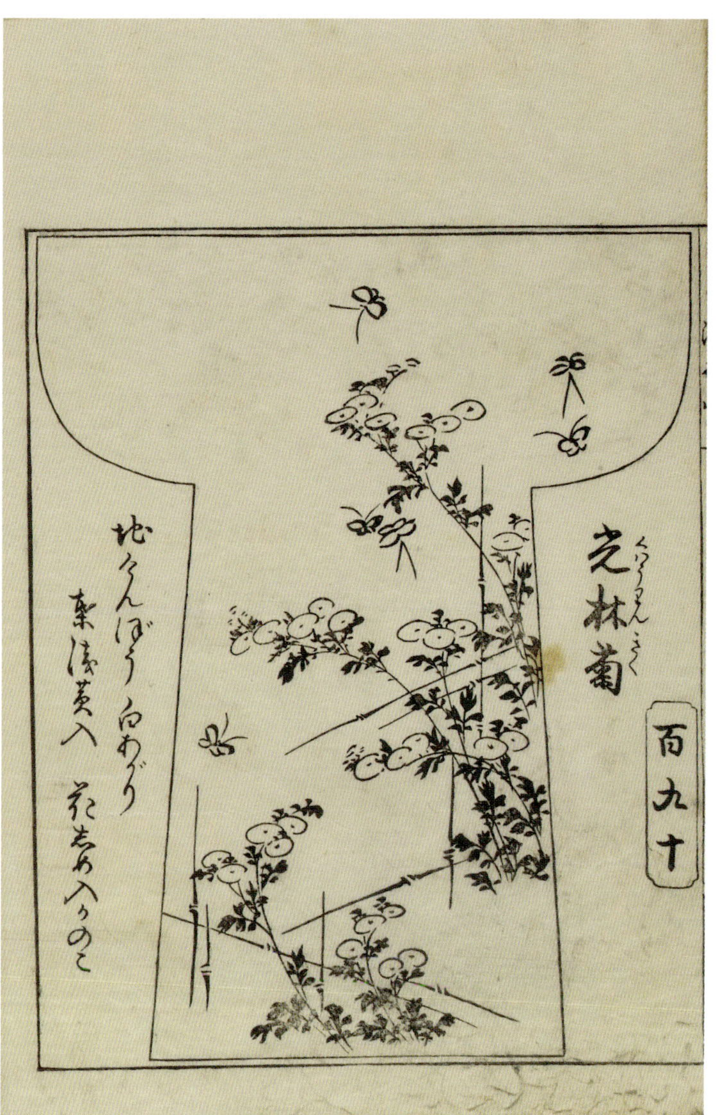

FIGURE 2

Mountain of Dye-Colored Patterns (*Hinagata someiro no yama*), (detail, "Kōrin chrysanthemums"), 1732. Woodblock-printed book; ink on paper. British Museum, London.

Kōrin's style reflected the much-called-for mastery of older modes while ultimately creating something new.

By devising a style that was affecting and catchy, Kōrin's pictures entered the memory of his clients and, later, the public consciousness. Kōrin's popularity in textile culture is evidence for the potency of his visual vocabulary. Key features of Kōrin's distinctive visuality—such as the shapes of his characteristic abbreviated flowers—appeared in popular books for kimono patterns throughout the eighteenth century (fig. 2).[8] Beyond the textile industry, Kōrin's name and style resonated far and wide. Although Kōrin's artworks were made for a limited circle of aristocrats, upper-tier samurai, and affluent townsmen, his persona and oeuvre appealed to a broad spectrum of contemporaries. The painter Ōoka Shunboku (1680–1763) included Kōrin in his model book *Picture Book Mirror* (*Ehon tekagami,* 1720) and aligned him with such prominent painters as Kano Tan'yū (1602–1674) in his personal manual *True Record of the Way of Painting* (*Gadō jitsuroku,* compiled 1735–51). Later, Sakai Hōitsu (1761–1829) and his espousal of Kōrin's style laid the foundation for the artist's popularity in the modern age. These diverse appropriations of Kōrin's art share one thing: devotees of Kōrin turned to him for his peculiar style and the arresting visuality of his art.

COMPETING STYLES

Kōrin himself laid the foundations for his absorption into the vernacular mainstream of the Edo period by way of creating an indelible brand. The early modern art market in Japan was replete with the work of painters of every imaginable variety. The pacifying of the country under the Tokugawa shogunate in the early 1600s after nearly a century of warfare initiated an unseen surge in creativity and competition among artists. The literature and art of the court, which in previous centuries had been held in secret and was passed on by hereditary transmission among select nobles, entered the broader aesthetics of Kyoto and Japan as a whole.[9] With the appearance of the first print editions of works of classical literature, such as the *Tales of Ise* and *Tale of Genji,* whose manuscripts were safeguarded by aristocrats over centuries, the culture of the court became a coveted commodity. The aristocracy provided an abundant source of inspiration for themes and styles as an increasingly affluent, assertive public sought access to beauty and cultural capital. During the seventeenth century, the urban classes of Kyoto and other cities gained power and wealth; this development was accompanied by a growing desire to outfit urban residences with art. Japanese art was made to be lived with, and traditional architecture required such furnishings as folding screens and wall paintings (*fusuma-e*). Fans and hanging scrolls were desired goods that enabled their owners to brandish wealth and taste. Kyoto-based seventeenth-century studios like that of Tawaraya Sōtatsu began to cater to an urban clientele with a desire to ingest aristocratic traditions into their own identities.[10] Often, these ateliers simultaneously catered to the court and commoners, reflecting the complex societal fabric and layered artistic production in early modern Kyoto.

The city was home to a sprawling number of ateliers that vied for customers. The traditional Kano and Tosa schools, which had their origins in centuries before the Edo period, controlled the market by the sheer numbers of followers and affiliates. Other ateliers, in their quest to distinguish themselves from orthodoxy, strove above all to find inventive ways to paint. Their route to success was to transcend convention and catch customers' attention through pioneering styles. Patrons throughout the Edo period hungered for works that were unorthodox and new to show their personal refinement or simply out of boredom with the mainstream. From the seventeenth century onward, style more than anything became the basis for making a personal mark—for artists and patrons alike.

In this way, Kōrin's work is symptomatic for much of early modern artistic practice. His emphasis on the efficacy of classical subjects, gorgeous colors, innovative brushwork, and the transposition of techniques from painting to such other media as lacquer and pottery highlights much of the core values of art-making at the time. Kōrin was inventive, and that sold well.

KONISHI FAMILY ARCHIVE

The study of Kōrin presents a special case among early modern painters in that his life and work are embellished by a large trove of documents that enable us to reconstruct a considerable portion of his life: the so-called Konishi Family Archive (*Konishi-ke monjo*). In 1700, San, a domestic employee in the Ogata household, gave birth to a boy. This illegitimate son of Kōrin would play an important role in preserving the artist's memory. Offspring born out of wedlock were unexceptional during Kōrin's time. Their frequency in Kōrin's case suggests that his wife, Tayo, seems to have been unable to bear children and to have sanctioned such affairs. In 1708, the son was adopted into the Konishi family of silver mint (*ginza*) officials, who soon after installed him as their heir. Then known as Konishi Juichirō, he maintained a close connection to his biological father, Kōrin, and, in spite of carrying a different surname, Juichirō regarded himself as the guardian of the Ogata legacy.[11] It was Juichirō on whom Kōrin bestowed the collection of documents on his own life and on the Ogata family that now make up the Konishi Family Archive. By taking in the written records of the Ogata family, Juichirō transformed the Konishi family into the custodians of the Ogata heritage; by the early twentieth century, before the Konishi Family Archive entered the ownership of the Japanese government and various private collections, the documents were still in the hands of Juichirō's descendants.[12]

The Konishi Family Archive has been a source for research into Kōrin and his life since at least the early nineteenth century. In 1807, Sakai Hōitsu contacted Konishi Hikoemon, a descendant of Juichirō, to receive information on Kōrin's family lineage.[13] Hikoemon drafted an undated biography of the Ogata family that is still part of the archive. The document has an addendum recording the restoration of Kōrin's grave in 1822.[14] In modern times, the art historians Fukui Rikichirō (1886–1972) and Aimi Kōu (1874–1970) introduced some contents of the archive—such as the will of Kōrin's father, Sōken—in separate articles in 1915.[15] In 1934, the archive left the ownership of the Konishi and was split among the Osaka City Museum of Art and a private collector. The Agency for Cultural Affairs later acquired the private collection portion, and in 2001, it was entrusted to the Kyoto National Museum, where it remains today.[16] Aimi's and Fukui's publications were followed in 1936 by Tanaka Kisaku (1885–1945) who introduced sketches from the archive, before Yamane Yūzō (1919–2001) provided the first comprehensive publication of its contents in 1962.[17] More recently, Kano Hiroyuki has published the archive's sketches, stencils, and painting studies in an annotated edition.[18]

The Konishi Family Archive reveals the complex mechanisms behind artistic practice and the personal motivations of an early modern painter. Sketches of medieval handscrolls and screens illustrate how Kōrin delved into his country's past to formulate his style. At the same time, he studied the oeuvre of more recent artists, such as Tawaraya Sōtatsu and Hon'ami Kōetsu (1558–1637).[19] In addition, Kōrin resorted to yamato-e, Buddhist works, and Kano-style paintings to draft his distinctive, eclectic expressions. The archive also preserves a large number of lacquer designs, textile patterns, and possible sketches for ceramics—a number of which I analyze at various points in this book.

One of the most revealing parts of the archive is a large number of private letters, some with incriminating content. Messages to and from a woman named Suma, one of Kōrin's romantic relations, disclose a coldhearted side of the artist's personality as he tried to evade responsibility for a child born out of wedlock. Other documents unveil more intimate details of the artist. We learn how Kōrin seems to have long suffered from colic pains, an ailment that becomes important when thinking about his late work, as I discuss in chapter 6.

The archive also contains numerous official pieces of correspondence on artistic and financial matters, making them a crucial source of reference for anyone seeking to understand Kōrin and, more broadly, the internal and external factors that determined artistic production in early modern Japan. Yet, in spite of their accessibility in published form, research has often been confined to a select number of documents, a practice that ignores the breadth and profundity of the archive's content and the complexity of Kōrin's existence. I attempt to overcome such limitations in this book by relying on the archive whenever possible in the hope of drawing a more comprehensive picture of this extraordinary painter and personality.

STRUCTURE

This book traces Kōrin's life and career as an artist, beginning in his late twenties, when he began to explore potential career options, and ending in the years leading up to his death. In chapter 1, we will retrace the road from Kōrin's substantial inheritance in the late 1680s toward his resolve to become a painter in the 1690s. Documentary evidence in the Konishi Family Archive and aristocratic diaries, such as the *Daily Records of the Nijō Family* (*Nijō-ke nainai gobansho hinamiki*) allow for a highly tactile picture of Kōrin's personal struggles and missteps as he lost his father's guidance and tried to find his own way in the world. This struggle was amplified by a pattern that recurs at multiple junctures of Kōrin's life: his penchant for engaging in amorous liaisons with uncertain (and sometimes unfortunate) outcomes. I identify several such episodes and reconstruct their impact on Kōrin's life and career. We will also look at the societal benefit of Kōrin's taste for performance, in particular Noh and an art of performative storytelling called *otogi*. Kōrin's considerable skill at performance paved avenues for cultivating lofty patrons, such as members of the imperial family.

Chapter 2 deals with Kōrin's early endeavors to establish a particular style, that of perhaps his most famous work: *Irises*. Kōrin progressed rapidly as a painter from his relatively conservative first works made in the 1690s to the sudden explosion of creative force found in *Irises* and other works made after 1700. In that context, we will explore how *Irises* functions as an archetype for iris-focused examples in early modern and modern Japanese painting. *Irises* formed the threshold and visual template for a significant tradition of artworks in all formats and genres—folding screens, hanging scrolls, fans, lacquer, and ceramics—that render irises, the poetic signifier of the fifth month and the ninth chapter of the *Tales of Ise*.

Chapter 3 considers how Kōrin branched out from painting to making lacquer works at an early time of his artistic enterprise. In his labors to transfer the aesthetics of his paintings to lacquer, he turned to the legacy and renown of his well-regarded great-granduncle Hon'ami Kōetsu. We will also see how Kōetsu additionally functioned as a model for outsourcing the actual production of lacquer pieces to specialized artisans. Painters like Kōrin simply lacked the proficiency necessary to perform the complicated techniques of lacquer-making. I propose that Kōrin used the sales techniques of textile businesses to create and market his lacquer works. For example, he compiled catalogues with spreads of designs from which clients could choose their desired motifs. This strategy draws from the role of pattern books in kimono production. In the process, we will see how Kōrin's art-making took on an increasingly streamlined quality, where the perpetuation of repetitive shapes helped reinforce Kōrin's trademark style among a growing and increasingly enthusiastic clientele.

Chapter 4 follows Kōrin's activities in Edo between 1704 and 1709. Until that time, Kōrin had never left his native Kansai region. But an appetite for exploring new patronage in Edo, in addition to encouragement from benefactors, prompted Kōrin to carry his trademark style to the bustling eastern power center. Edo offered intriguing opportunities for forging new connections and sell his work among its population of warrior elites—daimyo—and wealthy merchants. In preparation for his trip, Kōrin turned increasingly to the mode of Tawaraya Sōtatsu, a collaborator of Hon'ami Kōetsu, and an important source for Kōrin's artistic identity. Kōrin relied more than anything on an invention by Sōtatsu called *tarashikomi,* literally "dripping in," where ink or water were applied onto still-wet ink to generate appealing visual effects. Kōrin hoped to gain success in Edo by bringing with him a painting style of Kyoto, the capital. In Edo, however, Kōrin's ambitions met a reality that was distinctively different from Kyoto. Suddenly Kōrin, a man who mingled with aristocrats and was part of Kyoto's high society, found himself to be a painter among many others. He was forced to cater to the tastes of demanding clients, who encouraged him to turn to the great master of medieval ink painting, Sesshū Tōyō (1420–circa 1506). Altogether, Kōrin's time in Edo was a sobering and powerful experience that left lasting traces on Kōrin's life and art.

Chapter 5 returns to Kōrin's relationship with his family by exploring the ways in which he collaborated with his brother, the potter and painter Ogata Kenzan (1663–1743). After Kōrin's return from Edo to Kyoto in 1709, Kōrin and Kenzan began to produce ceramics that emulate the aesthetic of ink paintings—a move that effectively fused the aesthetics of two inherently different media. Their quest for transferring the features of ink painting to ceramic dishes was informed by Kōrin's experiences in Edo, where he was exposed to ink paintings by medieval master Sesson Shūkei.

Chapter 6 considers the twilight of Kōrin's life through the example of one of his most famous paintings, a pair of two-panel screens called *Red and White Plum Blossoms.* Produced during his final years, the screens are a case in point for the probability of growing involvement of studio assistants during the last years of Kōrin's artistic practice, a time when his works were experiencing their highest demand and he struggled with increasingly severe health problems—a dramatic zenith to a captivating life. The Epilogue rounds up the discussion by highlighting Kōrin's impact on later artists like Watanabe Shikō (1683–1755) and Sakai Hōitsu, whose embrace of Kōrin's style shaped his posthumous reception to this day.

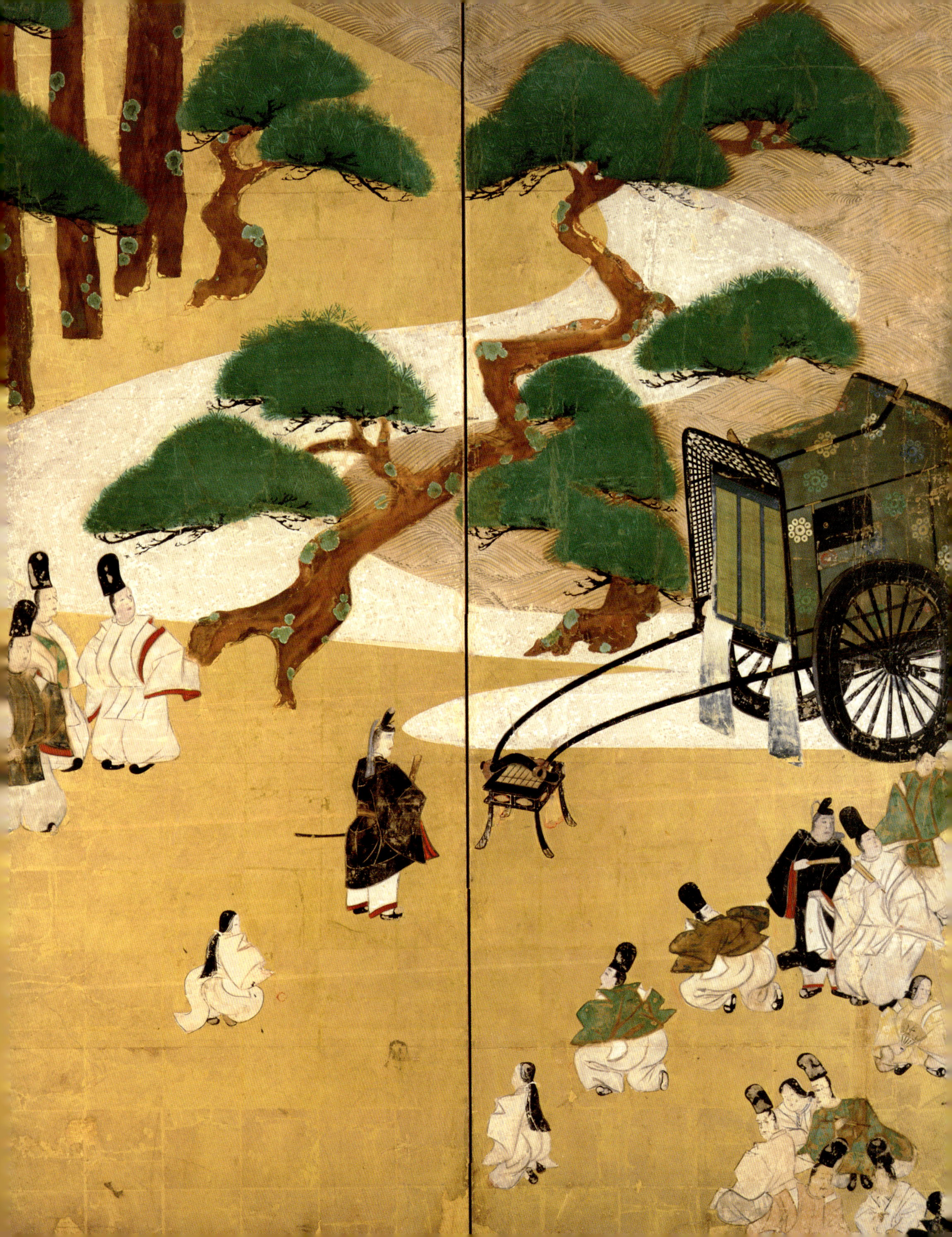

1 Before Painting

Ogata Kōrin and His Turn to Art

> Kōrin is shocking; he is movement and excess. He is a spuming wave above an elegantly curved, swaying stream.
>
> —Friedrich Perzynski, *Kōrin und Seine Zeit,* 1907

The beginnings of Ogata Kōrin's career as a painter are complex in that his resolve to become a professional artist seems to have been more fortuity than a well-planned move. Instead of choosing painting early in life, Kōrin was pushed to become an artist when a series of unlucky circumstances and poor decisions strained his finances.[1] Kōrin's case is exemplary of how the realm of the arts and artists diversified in early modern Japan, when painters came from all imaginable backgrounds and broke free of the hereditary system that defined such orthodox painting schools as the Kano and Tosa.

To understand the painter, we must first look at the man. A late starter, Kōrin began to make the visual arts his main vocation only when he was well into his thirties, an age far older than the starting age of painters who were born or adopted into professional ateliers. Those aspiring artists began training as children and often received their first commissions in their teens. Kōrin's road to becoming a painter in adulthood, by contrast, made him explore the arts as a means to ensure a steady source of income, not as a premeditated calling. In this way, Kōrin provides a lens onto the life, psychology, and motivations of a dilettante turned artist in early modern Japan.

PERSONAL SETBACKS

In late summer, on the seventeenth day of the eighth month in 1687, Kōrin took up a brush and composed a letter. Its matter-of-fact language conceals the sad nature of his missive. In the letter Kōrin laid claim to the inheritance left to him by his father, Sōken. Each of the three Ogata brothers—Kōrin (referred to as Ichinojō), Kenzan (referred to as Gonpei), and their elder brother Tōzaburō

Detail of fig. 5

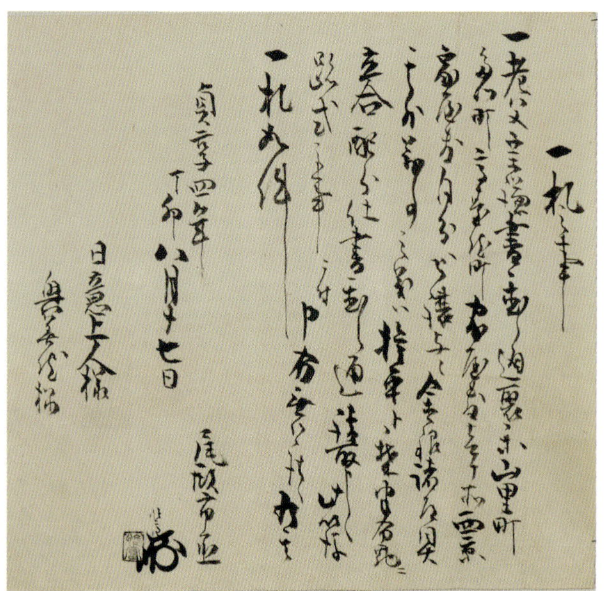

FIGURE 3
Ogata Kōrin, *Letter Accepting His Father's Bequest,* 1687. Ink on paper. Konishi Family Archive, Kyoto National Museum.

(also read Fujisaburō)—dispatched a similar document to Nichi'i, the abbot of Kōzen'in, the Kyoto temple that managed Sōken's estate (fig. 3). Kōrin wrote:

> In accordance with the will issued by my father, Sōken, I shall receive the mansion at Juraku Yamazatochō, Tamonchō, and Kōdaichō, as well as the mansion at Saikyō. [Part of] his fortune, miscellaneous furnishings, and all other remaining things shall be split evenly between Gonpei [Kenzan] and myself. I ask you to follow [my father's will]. I shall not claim any more beyond [the above].
> Jōkyō 4 [1687],
> eighth month, seventeenth day.
> Ogata Ichinojō [Kōrin]
> Koretomi [cypher]
> [seal:] Koretomi
>
> To Nichi'i Shōnin
> Kōzen'in[2]

His father's passing determined Kōrin's future and, with it, the future of painting in Japan. The death and the inheritance were the first in a series of events that eventually motivated Kōrin to explore new ways to distinguish himself and to make money. In the will, Sōken carefully explained his reasoning to Kōrin and attempted to assuage any uncertainty about his son's future, an anxiety that subtly seeps between the lines.

> [I am leaving to my son:]
> The family mansion at Yamazato[chō], however, excluding Tamonchō and Kōdaichō.

The mansion at Saikyō, and all [my] implements for the Noh theater.
Half of the remaining various implements.
Half of my entire collection of scrolls.
Invoices issued to daimyo, of which [you] shall share half with Gonpei [Kenzan].
This is your inheritance. Claim your share after consulting well about everything with Gonpei. I know you do not agree with my intentions [to pass on the leadership of the Kariganeya] to Tōzaburō. It pains me to exclude the two of you from inheriting [the business], but I am giving him the two mansions on Nakatachiuri[dōri] together with furnishings, money, and business contracts. I leave it [to you and Gonpei] to find a settlement [for splitting your parts of the inheritance]. So no one will challenge [the inheritance of] Ichinojō and Gonpei, I also entrust Tōzaburō with a copy [of the will] that each of you received. May the Buddha and deities watch over our ancestors, and may our children and grandchildren hold them dear.

Such is my will.

Jōkyō 1 [1684], fifth month, thirteenth day. Sōken, of the same name
[cypher] [seal]

To Ogata Ichinojō[3]

Sōken seems to have sought Kōrin's forgiveness for bequeathing the family business to his eldest son, Tōzaburō—an addition that does not appear in the will for Kenzan. The system of hierarchy of kin in traditional Japan by default favored firstborn sons. That Sōken went out of his way to explain his decision to Kōrin, his second son, implies that Kōrin might have hoped for a role in the Kariganeya, the family's dry goods business. Kōrin may have expressed a penchant for the textile industry.

Throughout his life Kōrin displayed an affinity for textile patterns and the intricacies of contemporary fashion. In some of his earliest works, Kōrin employed techniques used in textile designs, such as using repetitive patterns to render similar-looking clusters of irises within the same work, as seen in the *Irises* screens produced around 1701.[4] He also became directly associated with textile patterns early in his career as a painter, showing a penchant for the aesthetics and methods of the garment industry. For example, the 1699 novella *Story of a Love Letter* (*Kōshoku fumi denju*) contains a fictional episode in which the protagonist of the book commissioned Kōrin to paint an image of pines onto a garment of white satin.[5] It is not too far-fetched to imagine that Kōrin's inability to succeed his father as head of the Kariganeya might have motivated him to seek other ways to express his artistic interests, namely, painting.

Whatever Kōrin may have envisioned for himself, the will also exposes a deeper problem that affected Kōrin and his younger brother, Kenzan. In keeping with the traditional line of succession, Sōken bequeathed the lion's share of the family's assets to Tōzaburō. The decision left Kōrin and Kenzan with much less, a reality that becomes evident from Sōken's qualifier in the will, which reads as his reaction to Kōrin's and Kenzan's opposition of his intentions. Instead of large sums of money, Sōken hoped that the credits that the Ogata had given to daimyo—a common obligation for wealthy commoners—would one day be repaid and would sustain Kōrin and his brother. Yet most of these debts were never recognized. In fact, Kōrin himself passed them on to his wife, Tayo, in his own will of 1713.[6] Even after thirty years these credits had not been fulfilled. In short, Sōken's death thrust Kōrin from the comfortable lifestyle of a second-born son into the harsh reality of having to fend for himself.

BEGINNINGS OF A PAINTER

When did Kōrin begin to paint? Evidence points to the 1690s, when Kōrin was in his late thirties, as the time when he decided to make the pictorial arts the center of his life. Most of his earliest surviving artworks cluster around that time. It is no coincidence that Kōrin's first commissions occurred around the last decade of the seventeenth century; his choice to become an artist was in large part necessary for his survival.

Between 1687 and 1696, Kōrin fathered at least four illegitimate sons with four women, striking a considerable blow to his fortune. The first recorded affair occurred as early as 1686, a year before Kōrin received his inheritance. The artist immediately sought to broker a deal with a Kyoto merchant family named Matsuya for them to adopt the infant. Such arrangements were common practice in early modern Japan, but they often came at considerable expense.

> This year, my son by the name of Jirōsaburō was born.
> Although he is not your biological child, I would be immensely grateful if you could permanently adopt Jirōsaburō as your own [son]. I renounce any and all claims at all from my side in the future. Should you make him your child and declare him your family's heir, I shall humbly advance
> Two *kan* silver[7]
> as part of this agreement.
> I am also handing over five hundred *monme* silver [to cover] food expenses for Jirōsaburō. This document shall act as future proof [of my request].
> Jōkyō 4 [1687] Ogata Ichinojō [Kōrin]
> [Year of the] Rabbit, ninth month, nineteenth day
> To Matsuya Kanzaemon
> [and] wife[8]

The agreement, drafted one year after the affair, provides insights into the flourishing adoption industry in early modern Japan. Kōrin agreed to pay the substantial sum of two kan silver in order to entice Matsuya Kanzaemon to adopt the child. Food expenses were another familiar element of such fosterage agreements. The wording also includes a common proviso that prevented biological parents from laying claims to their children's future inheritance. Considering Kōrin's pecuniary malaise, the clause assumes an additional meaning: the family may have sought to keep him from meddling in their affairs, a wise decision since Kōrin's finances were particularly battered at the time.

In 1689, two years after claiming his inheritance, Kōrin borrowed twenty kan—an extraordinary sum, given that the permanent adoption of his son Jirōsaburō had cost a fraction of this amount—from a certain Nara Koshirō. Immediately following the exchange, Kōrin lent the even greater sum of some twenty-six kan to Sakakibara Toranosuke (1675–1726), a high-ranking samurai.[9]

> Receipt of a loan of silver.
> [The loan] amounts to a total of 26 kan and 600 monme.
> Sakakibara Toranosuke, lord of Murakami [Domain], names [Kōrin] *kuramoto* for the tributary rice shipped to [and stored] in Osaka.[10] [This document] acts as invoice for the loan and is proof [of the agreement between Kōrin and Toranosuke]. This contract establishes that the interest of the above amount shall be repaid with the revenue from the sale of next summer's rice [harvest].
> Genroku 2 [1689], sixth month
> Aizawa Kahei
> Harada Tarōbei
> Arayama Ichiemon
> Awata Kakuzaemon
> Kawauchi Sukebei
> Kageyama Jihei
> Ogata Ichinojō [Kōrin][11]

The loan was to be repaid through the annual cash revenue from selling the domain's rice harvest. As security for the loan, Kōrin was made *kuramoto,* or overseer, and thereby was put in charge of managing Sakakibara Toranosuke's rice sales in Osaka—a peculiar honor given the artist's cavalier attitude toward money. The timing was no less curious.

Just a year before, in 1688, Kōrin had caused a scandal that roiled Kyoto's upper bourgeoisie. Here, too, the cause was an illicit love affair that ended in a pregnancy. That year, a woman named Hosoi Tsune launched a lawsuit against Kōrin with the district elders, who wielded judiciary authority in early modern

Japan. The artist tried to evade responsibility for mother and child, but Tsune sought compensation. As the daughter of an urban merchant family that was likely of similar rank to the Ogata, she was able to demand a financially devastating fine. Kōrin was forced to hand over one of his recently inherited houses and make significant payments of money to cover the cost of raising the child. He was also ordered to supply furnishings for the property. The event decimated the inheritance that Kōrin had received just a year earlier.

> Announcement of the Verdict
> Last year [1688], on the ninth day of the twelfth month, and again on the fourth day of the second month of this year [1689], a woman by the name of Tsune saw me, Iseya Ryōsen of Shinmeichō, in order to press charges against Kariganeya Ichi[no]jō [Ogata Kōrin]. In accordance with the verdict decided by the district, [Kōrin] must hand over one mansion; several implements [to outfit the household]; tatami mats; twenty pieces (*mai*) of silver; and five hundred monme silver for last year's food expenses. The custody of [Kōrin's] son [with Tsune], Motonosuke, will be entrusted to the Hosoi family. Ichi[no]jō loses the guardianship of Motonosuke and [Motonosuke] shall forever renounce the right as heir to Ichinojō. This ruling shall not be disputed, and this document acts as proof of the decision made jointly by both districts' elders.[12]
> Genroku 2 [1689] Year of the Earth-Snake
> Second month, eighteenth day.
>
> Iseya Ryōsen of Shinmeichō,[13]
> Announcer [of the verdict] [seal]
> Tsune [seal]
> Younger Brother [of Tsune], Shichirōbei [seal]
> District Elder (*toshiyori*) of Shinmeichō, Jōjun [seal]
> Chiekōindōri Yamazatochō,[14] Ichi[no]jō [seal]
> District Elder of Chiekōindōri Yamazatochō, Jūemon [seal]
>
> [For the reference of] the Honorable Magistrate (*obugyō-sama*)
> [Envelope]
> One Sheet [recording the dispute with] Tsune. Genroku 2 [1689]
> Copy of the verdict, settled in the [Year of the Earth-]Snake [1689], second month, eighteenth day.[15]

This document is remarkable in many ways. Not only was Kōrin publicly humiliated, but his inheritance was curtailed only two years after he had obtained it. The punitive fine and the very fact that the pregnancy was brought to court speak to the scandalous nature of the liaison. Whereas Kōrin had managed to arrange the adoption of one illegitimate son after his affair in 1686, the events of 1687 and 1688 ended in a financial and personal fiasco.

An undated third romance soon followed, this time with a tragically romantic overtone.[16] The dalliance, which happened in the early 1690s, involved a woman called Suma, with whom Kōrin fathered a son named Bunzaburō. Suma evidently was of a lower social class than Kōrin and Hosoi Tsune, which may have prevented her from seeking judicial support. Instead, she was forced to resort to writing letters and pleading for Kōrin's compassion. "I am very grateful we could meet when I visited you two days ago. We would be delighted to welcome you for a meal every now and then. Also, I would like for Bunzaburō to go [and see you] again. I would like to go visit you today to thank you [as a courtesy for the recent meal]. Kōrin, although this is causing you a lot of trouble, I would like [for Bunzaburō] to stay with you for even [just] a day or two."[17] Kōrin seems to have evaded responsibility for Bunzaburō. Suma implored him to acknowledge their son, a request he apparently ignored. Although only three letters by Suma and none of Kōrin's responses survive, the complexity of the issue suggests a rigorous exchange, much of which is hidden to us today.

> Thank you for your letter. I have waited so long and would so like to come and see you, even just for a little bit. But I have fallen a little ill and have not been eating, so I cannot go to meet you. Given the position I find myself in now, both of my parents have been angered by your change of heart regarding our being together. I really would like you to acknowledge me as your partner. But given your recent change of heart, I cannot force you to do so. I do not ask for your financial support, but that does not mean I will return [to my parents?] for good. I am trying to struggle through this for now and wish that one day all this will be resolved. Thank you for looking after me. Do not worry about Bunzaburō, he can spend time with you whenever is convenient. Given the current circumstances [we find ourselves in], I cannot agree to meet with you. Please understand this. All my best to you.[18]

Suma's letter is preceded by two others—one by her and another by Oken, a woman who may have been her guardian—that convey a similar message. Whereas Hosoi Tsune's brother sued Kōrin, Suma was left to seek his goodwill. A second letter from Suma reads like her final note to Kōrin. Suffused with a sense of finality, it remains a moving example of human interaction despite the passage of centuries (fig. 4).

> I read your letter. You say you are suffering from abdominal pain. It seems you are feeling quite distressed, so I would like to call on you and see how you are. But, to tell you the truth, I am also suffering, so when we last met I got very angry that we can't be together.[19] Also, throughout the winter you withdrew and avoided seeing me. For that reason, I listened to what Oken had to say. I do not need your money and I will surely not ask for it. I will return [to my parents]. You must think

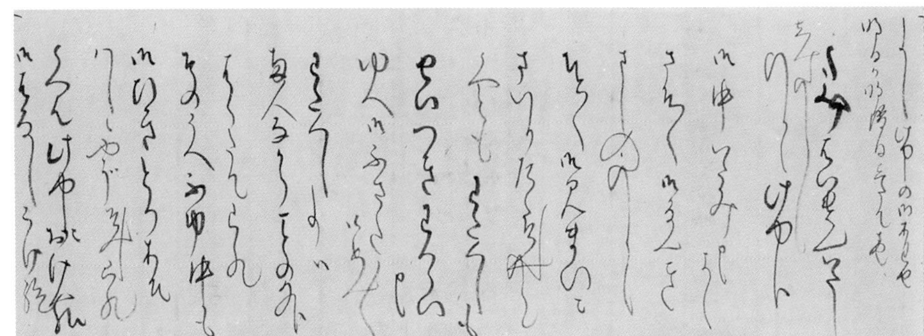

FIGURE 4
Letter by Suma to Kōrin, probably late 1690s. Ink on paper. Konishi Family Archive, Kyoto National Museum.

> I caused you a lot of trouble, but I think neither of us acted in a despicable way. Although we did succeed in building some common ground, we never felt as one. You don't seem to entertain the thought of us getting together, so please leave me be.
>
> I wish you all my best, [Suma][20]
>
> [Sentence written between the first two lines of the text above:]
> [P.S.] I think the kimono (*on'awase*) you ordered will be ready by tomorrow, or the day after.[21]

The letter's postscript, added after the bulk of the letter had been written, marks a stunning break from the rest of the document. It provides a hint about Suma's relationship to the Ogata family. Despite the emotional gravitas of the letter, Suma's informing Kōrin of the completion of his order suggests that she may have belonged to a family of weavers or dyers who worked in the orbit of the Kariganeya, the Ogata family's dry goods business. Suma's letters, however, seem to have had little effect in persuading Kōrin to acknowledge their relationship and their child. Although Kōrin's answers are no longer extant, Suma's pleas reveal a chilly side to the artist's personality and lay bare frictions between social classes. Kōrin did little to arrange an adoption with another family, as he had done with his first son. No letters remain after Suma's last note. The noticeable absence of Suma and Bunzaburō from other documents related to Kōrin suggests that his strategy was successful; he never assumed custody of the child.

Suma's dilemma is one of the most candid episodes preserved in Kōrin's surviving correspondence. Although Kōrin engaged in several other salacious encounters, Suma's letters are the only written evidence of a woman's affection for him. Such exposure of their intimate relationship was likely never intended for the public eye. These letters illustrate the unedited condition of the Konishi Family Archive and the candid nature of its content.

Other documents detail Kōrin's struggles during the late 1680s and the early 1690s. In 1691, his financial troubles grew to the extent that he was forced to sell one of his two remaining residences. Kōrin was also obliged to pay interest to various creditors, such as Kōzen'in, the Ogata family temple and manager of his father's estate. From a range of receipts issued either by or to Kōzen'in we learn that the artist repeatedly borrowed money from the temple and often scrambled to pay back just its interest.[22]

The payments that Kōrin had to shoulder within a short time span during these decades quickly diminished his inheritance. Around this time of arduous financial hardship, Kōrin began to appear in the circle of the influential courtier Nijō Tsunahira (1672–1732), who would become one of his most important benefactors. The timing hardly seems arbitrary. The series of personal mishaps apparently encouraged Kōrin to forge social connections and cultivate potential sources of patronage. The groundwork for Kōrin's successful inclusion in Tsunahira's circle, however, had been laid in prior decades. As early as the mid-1670s, Kōrin began to use the performing arts as his way to enter the top strata of Kyoto's court society.

FROM PERFORMANCE TO PAINTING

Kōrin made his debut in the upper tiers of society in Kyoto not through painting but by way of performance. As the master of one of the capital's leading dry goods businesses, Kōrin's father, Sōken, had the financial means and social clout to give his son a thorough training in literature, theater, and painting. Befitting the elevated status of the Ogata, Sōken injected Kōrin into his personal circle of high-ranking aristocrats, upper-class townsmen, and theater professionals.

In 1675, at the age of eighteen, Kōrin performed Noh at Sanbōin, a subtemple of the Daigoji monastery in Kyoto. Together with his elder brother, Tōzaburō, Kōrin was brought before Kōken (1639–1707), the aristocratic abbot of Sanbōin.[23] An entry in the priestly journal of the temple, *Daily Records of the Sanbōin* (*Sanbōin hinamiki*), records the event.

> Ogata Tōzaburō and Ichinojō [Kōrin] of the same surname were summoned to perform divine Noh (*shinrai nō*) together with Shibuya Shichizaemon. Ichinojō was asked by His Excellency [abbot Kōken] himself to perform before him one time [and then] another. Both performers [Tōzaburō and Kōrin] were brought before His Excellency and given a drink. Tōzaburō presented a violet *fukusa* [a cloth used to purify tea utensils] and a *chakin* [a small fabric also used for purification]. Ichinojō presented three fans.[24]

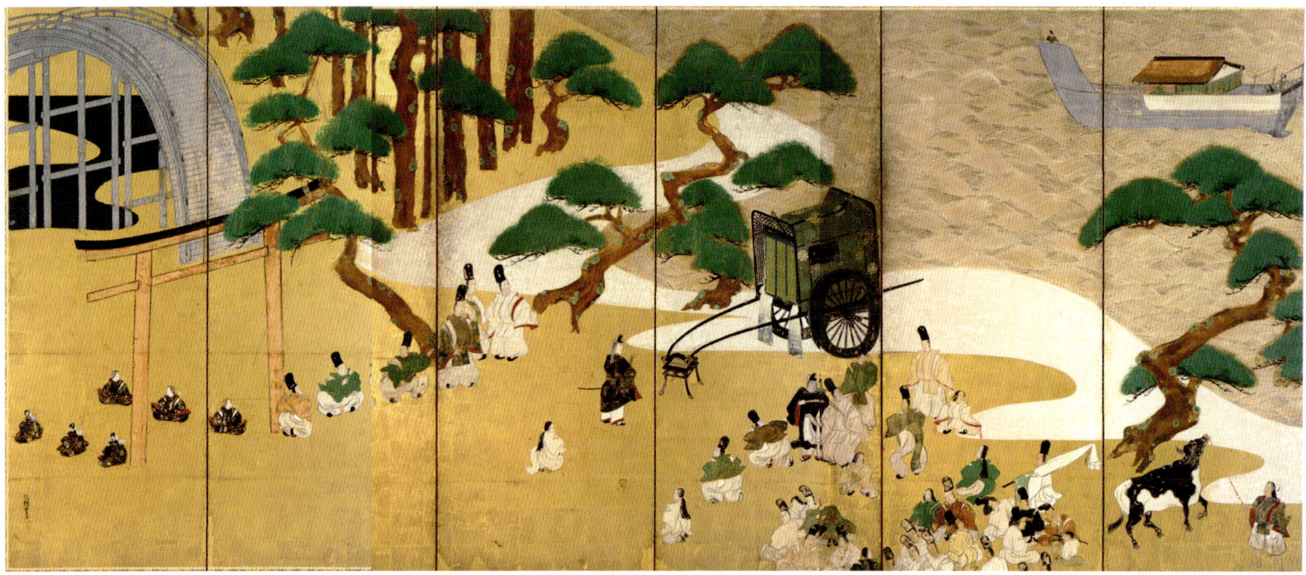

FIGURE 5
Tawaraya Sōtatsu, *Gate House (Sekiya) and Channel Buoys (Miotsukushi) from the Tale of Genji*, circa 1631. Pair of six-panel folding screens; ink and color on gold leaf. Seikadō Bunko Art Museum Image Archives / DNPartcom.

This passage marks the first in a string of events in which Kōrin either performed or watched Noh at the temple. Other performances in which his brothers, Tōzaburō and Kenzan, took turns followed Kōrin's debut at Sanbōin in 1675.[25] At these performances, the revered Noh actor Shibuya Shichizaemon presented the Ogata brothers one by one. Exactly a month later, the brothers appeared in a series of performances, also led by Shichizaemon.[26] The event celebrating the annual chrysanthemum festival lasted more than four days. Kōrin and Kenzan arrived on the seventh day and were immediately brought before Kōken, who seems to have taken a liking to the teenage Ogata brothers. On the final day, Tōzaburō and Kōrin were invited to join the abbot at an outing. There followed a small reception of sweets and liquor, at which Kenzan was also present.

The performances apparently impressed Kōken. In the next month the brothers were summoned on three more occasions and performed numerous pieces of Noh-chanting (*utai*) and dances (*shimai*). They also spent the night at the temple. Though it is not specifically recorded in the Sanbōin records, the brothers must also have stayed at the temple during the chrysanthemum festivities earlier that year, since most activities lasted late into the night. The *Daily Records of the Sanbōin* state that Kōken returned to the temple the next day, the day after the festivities, an indication that he spent the night with the Ogata brothers at the temple quarters, not at his own residence.[27]

The path to such privileged attention was long, and Kōrin had prepared for that moment at least since 1672, when he jotted down notes pertaining to a set of Noh plays—*Tadanori, Atsumori,* and *Shōki.* He rehearsed core passages

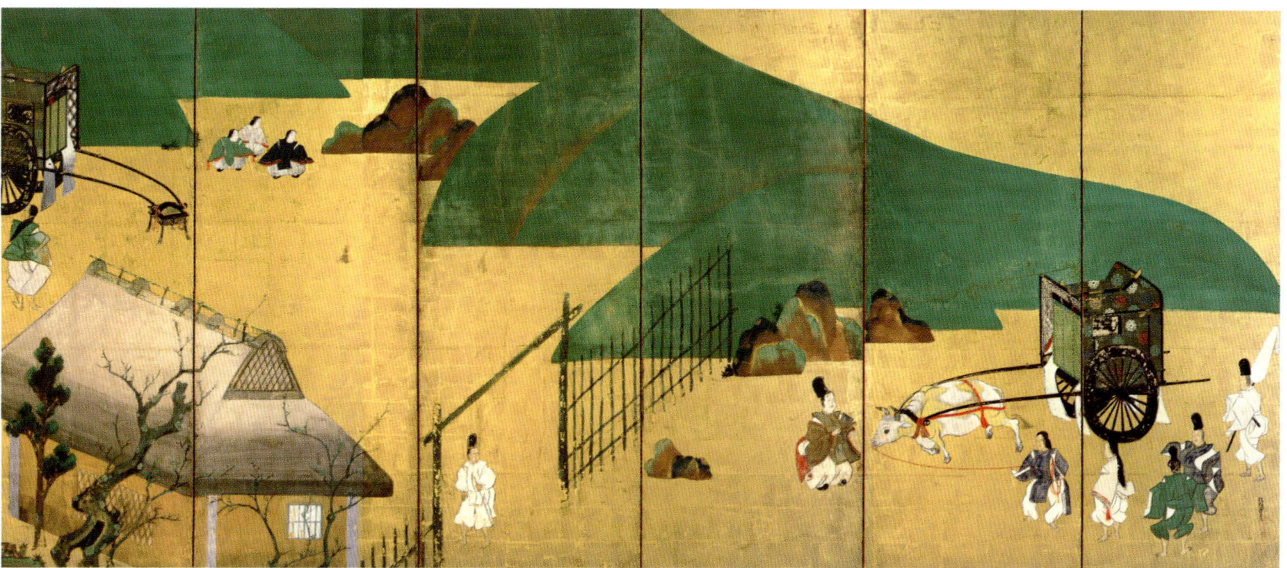

of these plays with Shibuya Shichizaemon, who instructed him in Noh and escorted him to such high-ranking patrons as Kōken of Sanbōin. This process of Noh instruction continued after 1676, when the Noh master Kobatake Ryōtatsu (d. 1710), Kōrin's second Noh teacher, presented him with a manual on conveying emotions in different plays.[28] By contrast, the first evidence of a painting by Kōrin dates to some twenty years later, in the early 1690s. Kōrin obviously indulged in performance much earlier than in painting.

Kōrin's early association with the theater is reinforced by Sōken's will. Echoing his son's predilection for the arts of the stage, Sōken bestowed his collection of accoutrements for Noh to Kōrin. In light of his inheritance and Kōrin's extensive training in theater, Sōken may have envisioned his son becoming a Noh performer—a profession not all that unusual among the wealthy commoner class. For example, the Noh actor Kobatake Ryōtatsu, with whom Kōrin studied in the mid-1670s, belonged to a dyeing business similar to the Kariganeya.[29] Sōken, who took up the brush on occasion, may have regarded Kōrin's initial training in painting as merely one part of the educational fabric of a cultured Kyoto townsman like himself.

Still, Kōrin's devotion to Noh performance and his early appearances at Sanbōin shaped his future as a painter. The temple was home to some of the greatest paintings by Tawaraya Sōtatsu. By the time Kōrin performed Noh for abbot Kōken, the temple owned a famous pair of screens depicting the chapters "Gate House" and "Channel Buoys" from the eleventh-century court classic the *Tale of Genji* (fig. 5). The work appears in Daigoji's records as early as 1631, when Sōtatsu made them for the temple.[30] Although similar documentary evidence remains to be found, other paintings by Sōtatsu existed in abundance at Daigoji—and probably during the time of Kōrin's visits. One such work is a pair of screens with fans scattered across the surface. With its array of subjects painted in different manners, the work encapsulates Sōtatsu's artistry.

The sheer number and stylistic breadth of Sōtatsu's works at Daigoji may have impressed young Kōrin, but he did not immediately turn to Sōtatsu and the Tawaraya for inspiration. Not until the turn of the eighteenth century did Kōrin begin to incorporate the stylized forms and flat compositions of Sōtatsu's paintings into his works. Until then, performance served as an important catalyst for Kōrin's development as a painter.

Following the string of Sanbōin recitals, Kōrin's penchant for performance continued to be his main conduit for attaching himself to the aristocracy and for cultivating potential clients for paintings. When Kōrin and Kenzan first began to frequent the home of the aristocrat and future patron Nijō Tsunahira, they were often asked to perform otogi, a form of performative storytelling that dates back to the Muromachi period (1336–1568). The adopted son of the regent (*kanpaku*) Nijō Mitsuhira (1625–1682) and a son-in-law of emperor GoMizuno'o (1596–1680), Tsunahira belonged to the highest stratum of the aristocracy, making him an ideal person to know. Whereas otogi was initially performed mainly as a diversion for the sick (or with the hope of healing through the power of spoken words and tales), by the Edo period it had become an admired art form that required sophisticated, conversant performers.[31]

Such a skill, honed by his early Noh study, helped Kōrin cultivate a relationship with Tsunahira, who made him a fixture among his aristocratic salon. Kōrin is first mentioned in the Nijō family journal, *Daily Records of the Nijō Family* (hereafter Nijō records), in 1689. Around that time, his visits occurred only sporadically, but after he performed otogi in the tenth month of 1693, his presence in the Nijō household increased dramatically.[32] Kōrin must have displayed a special talent for otogi. Tsunahira, who demanded this form of entertainment from many visitors to his residence, repeatedly called on Kōrin to display his skill. Between 1694 and 1700 Tsunahira summoned Kōrin to his mansion to perform otogi on almost three dozen occasions.[33] Concurrently, the total number of his visits to Tsunahira's residence for other social gatherings rose sharply, illustrating how otogi was a segue to the aristocrat's favor and, eventually, to painting commissions.

Tsunahira also asked other artists, such as Kōrin's alleged teacher, the Kano-school painter Yamamoto Soken (d. 1706), to perform otogi before asking them to paint for him, revealing a pattern of sponsorship that started with performances and culminated in orders for artworks.[34] This was also true for Kōrin. The steep increase in otogi performances coincided with his first painting commissions. The fourteenth day of the second month in 1695 marks the first recorded mention of a painting by Kōrin. "As requested by the Second Princess [Tsunahira's wife], Ogata Kōrin handed over five fans [mounted on] hanging scrolls with paintings by him intended for Her Majesty [Retired Empress Shinjōsaimon'in]."[35] Aspiring painters often used fans as a means to introduce their skills to prospective clients.[36] Their small format and practicality made them ideal presents within the complex gift culture of the Edo period, and Tsunahira frequently ordered them for this purpose. In 1695, the aristocrat acted as an intermediary between his wife, the Second Princess, and her mother, the retired empress Shinjōsaimon'in (1653–1712). The princess used Kōrin's fans as gifts to her mother—a high honor that reflects his personal status among Kyoto's court society and the value his paintings had garnered by the mid-1690s. Kōrin's skills in otogi likely expedited such commissions from aristocrats. For example, as a New Year's present in 1697, Kōrin gave Tsunahira a set of six small-format pictures (*shikishi*).[37] Just four days later, Tsunahira again summoned Kōrin to display his skills in otogi. Performance and painting evidently went hand in hand.

Tsunahira and the arts of performance also connected Kōrin with Nishi Honganji, a major Jōdo Shinshū temple in Kyoto and the possible patron of one of his most famous works, the pair of screens *Irises*. In the fall of 1694, Tsunahira took Kōrin to a Noh recital at Nishi Honganji. Jakunyo (1651–1725), the temple's head abbot, and Jūnyo (1673–1739), his acolyte and successor, attended the performance. Jūnyo was Tsunahira's brother.[38] In light of such family connections, Tsunahira and Kōrin were likely seated near Jakunyo and Jūnyo. Kōrin was no doubt introduced to both clerics on that occasion, if not earlier. His friendship with Jakunyo and Jūnyo evolved during the 1690s. For example, Kōrin performed otogi during a farewell banquet held for Jūnyo at Tsunahira's residence to send off the monk on a trip to Edo. Tsunahira probably also connected Kōrin to other early patrons.

EARLY PATRONAGE

Kōrin's earliest surviving painting, a hanging scroll depicting the medieval poet and literary commentator Sōgi (1421–1502), dates to around the time when he began to establish his early network of patrons. The work carries an unsigned inscription that is convincingly attributed to Shōren'innomiya Sonshō (1651–1694).[39] Kōrin must have made the portrait sometime before or in 1694, the year Sonshō died. As a son of emperor GoMizuno'o and the prince abbot of Shōren'in, Sonshō was part of Tsunahira's social sphere, and the commission was likely facilitated by Kōrin's ties to Tsunahira.

The aristocrat himself also made repeated use of Kōrin's skills as a painter. In 1698, following Kōrin's fan paintings for Shinjōsaimon'in of 1695 and the set of shikishi that he brought as a New Year's gift in 1697, Tsunahira ordered Kōrin to produce a picture at a banquetlike gathering. This event marks a rare documented in situ painting performance by Kōrin. Following this, the artist gave fans as courtesy presents for New Year's in 1699, a practice he continued in 1701, 1703, and 1704, when he gifted either fans or shikishi.[40] All these paintings, including the Sōgi portrait, dovetailed with the rise of Kōrin's visits to Tsunahira's residence and his otogi performances there.

In 1695, the year of his first painting commission from Tsunahira, Kōrin's financial malaise reached a new depth. He raised funds by pawning an heirloom dagger, attributed to the fourteenth-century sword smith Seki Naotsuna, together with a second sword, for a total of four hundred monme silver, a solid amount.

> One dagger (*wakizashi*) by Seki Naotsuna with one sheath, one Utsu dagger with one sheath. The two items are pawned at [a value of] four hundred monme silver. By the sixth month in the coming Year of the Rat [1696] the above amount shall be returned to the lender. This document acts as proof that the wakizashi have been received.
>
> Naka[partly illegible] Shōan [?] [seal:] Naka-shi Shōan
>
> Genroku 8 [1695], Year of the Pig, twelfth month, twenty-fourth day.
>
> To Ogata Kōrin[41]

Around the same time, his brother Kenzan issued two letters to Kōrin. Kenzan reveals his sober attitude toward money by advising his elder brother on how to handle his current monetary hardships. One letter reveals the depth of Kōrin's debt.

> For your reference
>
> I have looked at your accounts for three years, from 1693 to 1695.
>
> The balance until last winter [1695] amounts to seven kan, nine hundred eight monme, and three *bu*.[42] [Written in smaller script:] But by the New Year [1696] [the amount] was repaid.[43]
>
> This amount includes the one kan and one hundred monme that were repaid to you by Lord Nagato (*Nagato no kami*), Lord Tosa (*Tosa no kami*), and Chōkurōzaemon.[44] This is nothing more than the interest.
>
> With each of their [full] repayments, the original amount would decrease bit by bit. The same is true for Nagai Ichimasa's.[45] I also cannot say when he will repay [his debt]. The situation is a nightmare. Even if you had the total amount of [all outstanding loans] in your hands now and received most of the interest, it would by no means match the amount [that you owe].

> You have to pay off the amount somehow. But I know that it is difficult for you to raise any money on your own at this point. You should show me the invoices of all things you pawned. We could redeem these objects and sell them off. But you must use that money wisely. In your current situation, since the majority [of the money] in your hands was borrowed from Hinoya, it wouldn't be helpful if you had to pay any unnecessary interest.[46] [Any money you can save] will be practical for whatever may come at this point. Once your debt is repaid and, some day, the four or five credits [to daimyo and others] are redeemed, you may use that money for yourself. Also, if we leave the pawned objects as they are for now, their interest will gradually add up. This way, they won't be of much use to us at a later time. Don't you know a way to retrieve them?
>
> Your screen[s?] entrusted to Recluse Jihei are up for sale since last winter and we agreed that I receive the money once they are sold. When I go to see Jihei next time and if the screens are not sold yet, I will ask him to advance the sales price so we can use the money for you. What do you think about this? The screens will surely sell.[47]
>
> For four hundred monme, we would be able to retrieve the *tanzaku* album from Sagamiya. [Then] we could also sell it off.
>
> Recently I met with Tōzaburō to assess [your] lack of money. [He suggested] we should also redeem the pawned objects from Hiranoya. If you could give me your share [of selling those objects], I could pay back the amount in full.
>
> Other than that, you should see if Uzaemon or anyone else has any [advice] at all. I can't think of any more [at the moment]. Should you have any ideas on how to solve this problem, please let me know. I will leave it at that for now. I don't know what we can work out for you and I am at my wits' end.
>
> Third month, eleventh day Shinsei [Kenzan] [cypher]
>
> To Kōrin[48]

In his letter Kenzan provides a wealth of information and shows the extent of his struggle to solve Kōrin's crisis. He also mentions the credits lent to daimyo. Since most of the money was never repaid, the loans eventually burdened Kōrin's finances further. The Kariganeya was nearing bankruptcy at the time, a reality that amplified the need for new sources of revenue.

Tōzaburō, the eldest brother and head of the Kariganeya, exhibited little aptitude for business matters. When consulted, he recommended a common strategy: Kōrin should sell or pawn heirloom artworks. As the de facto head of the family, Tōzaburō's advice carried weight, and Kōrin and Kenzan followed it by pawning a colorful array of items, including in 1695 the dagger. Although Tōzaburō does not directly mention art, surviving documents show that Kōrin mainly pawned artworks and used their monetary value to his advantage. The

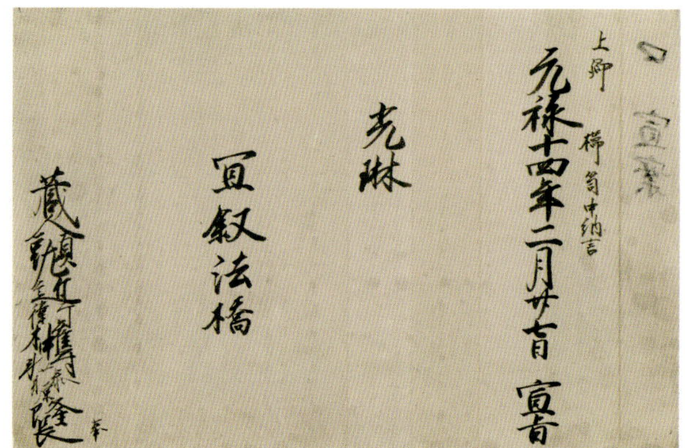

口宣案

上卿 中納言

元禄十四年二月 宣旨

光琳

宜叙法橋

FIGURE 6

Certificate Granting Kōrin the Hokkyō Title, 1701. Ink on paper. Konishi Family Archive, Kyoto National Museum.

substantial prices that some of those works brought may have provided an additional incentive for Kōrin to turn to painting. A receipt for items pawned in the 1690s almost exclusively lists artworks, among them a screen by Tawaraya Sōtatsu, whose work Kōrin may have encountered during Noh performances at Daigoji in the mid-1670s.[49]

In 1701, Kōrin was granted the *hokkyō* (literally "dharma bridge") title by the court. The title was awarded to artists as a certification of accomplishment (fig. 6). Originally a priestly sobriquet of Buddhist origins, it was given to painters by the court to highlight advanced artistic achievement and the solicitation of aristocratic patronage. Hokkyō was part of a ladder of honorary epithets, each marking a higher level of distinction, that painters could achieve. Although hokkyō was the most basic tier, it commanded respect and marked official recognition as an artist. With this honor Kōrin effectively transitioned from an amateur painter to a professional artist. Many painters never gained the title; others, such as Sōtatsu, received it only late in life. The privilege was often as much the result of political savvy as it was of artistic skill, and Kōrin's recognition likely relied in part on his talent in otogi and Tsunahira's sponsorship. This combination inserted the artist into a social circle whose members would play life-changing roles. On several occasions from 1697 to 1699, a courtier named Washino'o Takanaga (1672–1736) was present at Tsunahira's soirées. Takanaga was the signatory of the certificate that bestowed the hokkyō title on Kōrin. The seal of approval from the trend-setting court often initiated a desirable increase in commissions. After almost a decade of trying to gain his footing as a painter, with the hokkyō title Kōrin achieved professional validation. Kōrin, a painter who began late in life and was unconnected to the clout of major ateliers, needed the sobriquet as a rite of passage as he made a name for himself.

While hokkyō meant prestige and marked accomplishment for most painters, the machinations necessary to receive the title were often complex and involved supporters in high ranks. Washino'o Takanaga's presence at gatherings at Nijō Tsunahira's home that included Kōrin hints that an elaborate web of associations with the court elite, rather than artistic merit alone, prompted Kōrin's receipt of the designation.[50] It is easy to imagine that a combination of Kōrin's close ties with Tsunahira, skill at otogi, and increasingly frequent patronage from people in Tsunahira's orbit influenced the honor. After all, as we have seen, Kōrin concurrently presented numerous small-format paintings and fans to Tsunahira and other members of his class, showing how his skill in art, otogi, and social clout propelled his early career.

✤ ✤ ✤

Kōrin's road to becoming an artist was anything but straightforward. The decision to make the visual arts his profession seems to have been more happenstance than planned. Filled with both astonishing and charming episodes, Kōrin's path to becoming one of Japan's great masters involved a string of fateful events and encounters. While his paintings emanate from an artist with remarkable skill, the many documents by or about him describe a man who struggled with himself and the world around him. In this way, Kōrin embodies the diversified world of artistic production in early modern Japan, where people with different social backgrounds and personal stories chose the arts of the brush as their trade. Each of these stories commences with its own beginning. Kōrin's tale lies in the performing arts, love affairs, money problems, and a decades-long effort to find a career that suited his carefree character.

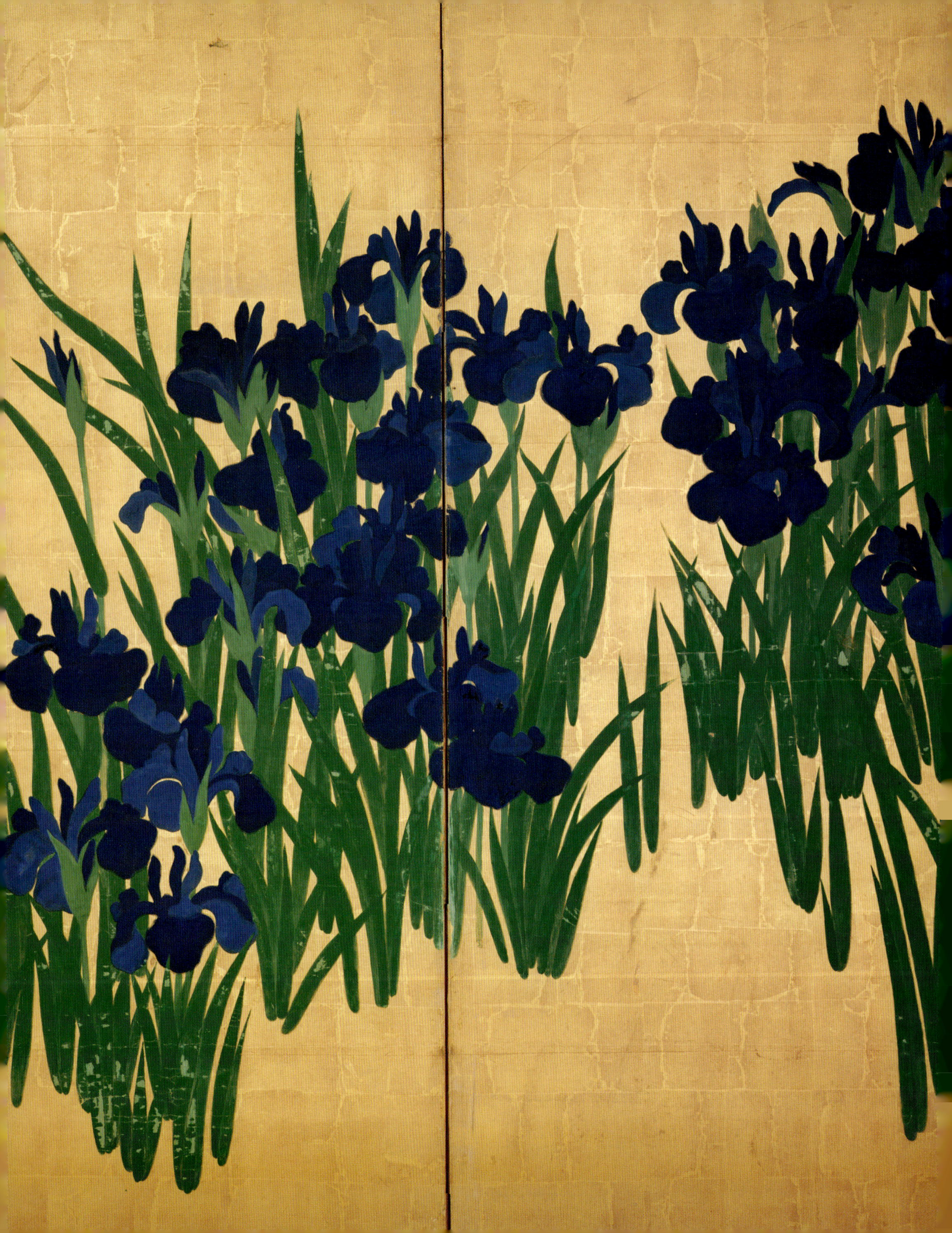

2 Of Poets and Flowers

Kōrin's Early Paintings

> Kōrin's art reflects the final stages of the aristocratic tradition, and at the same time it is full of the fresh vitality of a new era. This paradoxical spirit in his art marks his individuality. An artist encounters himself in his work seeking to reconcile his own inner contradictions and transcend himself. Kōrin encountered the point of his essence in his paradoxical nature and transcended himself in the creation of his unique and unprecedented style.
>
> —Okamoto Tarō, "Ogata Kōrin," 1971

Faced with a series of personal and financial setbacks, Kōrin apparently took up the brush and decided to make the arts his main vocation in the first years of the 1690s. His initial paintings tell the story of a careful but confident artist, one who engaged with the styles of luminaries of bygone times in order to promulgate his name in the art world of his day. An abundance of sketches and a handful of early paintings by Kōrin illustrate his insatiable appetite for a wide range of motifs and styles. Kōrin was a painter whose works refuse to fit into a comfortable mold. Instead of adhering to a single, signature style, he turned his gaze to whatever painterly fashions he deemed beneficial to hone his skills and cultivate an audience.

The early years of Kōrin's career reveal the eclecticism that would leave a distinctive imprint on early modern art-making. They also showcase Kōrin's careful consideration of the art market of his time, illustrating the external and internal factors that prompted him to turn to a variety of styles to shape his art. In their totality, Kōrin's early works exemplify the artist's close ties to the highest echelons of the court aristocracy, whose aesthetic consciousness he absorbed into his own. At the same time, his work is reflective of the larger implications of a shifting economy during his time, where artists' modes of production and sale diversified from custom fabrications made for small groups of elite clients to readymade goods catering to socially and economically varied

Detail of fig. 17

consumers. A member of the urban commoner class, Kōrin was the offspring of a high-end business selling bespoke garments to the aristocracy. By this pedigree alone Kōrin learned how to negotiate culturally sensitive groups of clients and challenging modes of artistic production.

His life and work are also summations of the increasingly porous social hierarchies and the commodification of upscale culture of the Edo period. From his youth onward, Kōrin mingled with aristocrats and members of his own class, the wealthy elite of Kyoto. This cultural conditioning, pride, and awareness of status informed the heart of his artistic practice and personal thinking. Throughout his life, Kōrin drew from the subjects, styles, and aesthetics of the aristocracy and upper urban milieu of the capital. Yet, although Kōrin came of age within a culture of privilege, his work as an artist was decidedly heterogenous in terms of patronage, production, and distribution. The sophisticated infrastructure of his own time facilitated the diversification of Kōrin's clients and modes of making art.

ARTISTIC INFRASTRUCTURE

Kōrin availed himself of systems of indirect art production by using outsourced craftsmen, as is evident in his lacquer pieces, which he had made by specialized lacquer artists after his designs (see chapter 3). He also used networks of long-distance distribution and commissions of artworks through so-called *karamonoya,* dealers of new and antique arts who functioned as intermediaries between artist and client.[1] During the first half of the Edo period, Kyoto art dealers commuted between the capital and Edo to sell goods to high-ranking daimyo clients. The business culminated in the establishment of branch offices in Edo and other places, which increased the flux of art objects between different locales, especially in Kōrin's own time, the late seventeenth and early eighteenth centuries. Dealers ensured the movement of objects between Kyoto, Edo, and other cities by sea or land. The role of art dealers illustrates the growing mercantile side of art-making in Kōrin's time, a beneficial development that enabled access to new markets and a smoother solicitation of orders—especially for budding artists. For example, a letter by Kōrin about the long-distance sale of a piece of ceramic by his brother Kenzan discusses the proper way of wrapping so that it would not break during transport by ship (fig. 7). The addressee, Nishimura Seiiku, was probably a merchant dealing in antiques and mediating orders for newly made works. He collaborated with Kōrin and Kenzan in the sale of various art pieces. Among Kōrin's correspondence, three letters are addressed directly to him.

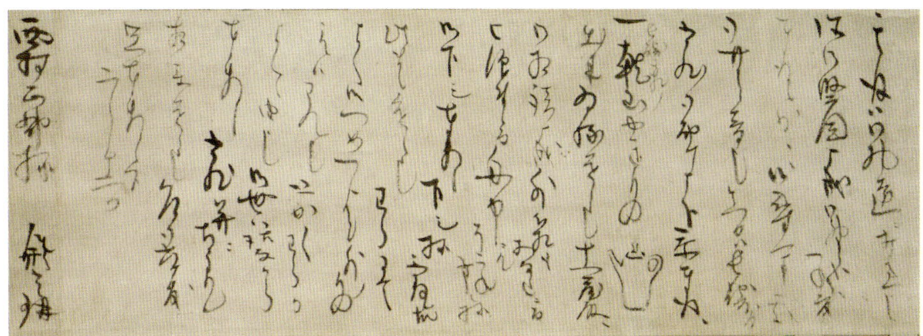

FIGURE 7
Ogata Kōrin, *Letter to Nishimura Seiiku* (*or Masakuni*), late 17th century. Ink on paper. Private collection.

> It has been a while and I hope you are well. Please allow me a quick question since I have not heard from you [recently]. The other day, I received this letter from Nagasaki.
>
> [Enclosed] the letter from Nagasaki.
>
> Concerning the ceramic piece by Kenzan [includes sketch of an ewer],
> it is ready now and [I will] send it. I have asked Master Jūichiya for advice on this. He advised me on the accompanying box (*sotobako*) and the place where we should send it. Send it by ship, but make sure it won't break. I am not sure about the best way to wrap the piece [so it won't break during transport], so I am sending it to you. Please wrap it well in straw and keep it separate from others. Straw is the best material for wrapping. Thank you for kindly assisting with this. With this letter, I am also including the order for your reference.
> Second month, twelfth day.   Ogata Kōrin
> To Nishimura Seiiku[2]

The Ogata brothers collaborated in selling Kenzan's ceramics shortly after he established his first kiln at Narutaki in 1699. Dated to around that year or shortly after, the letter discusses business with an unnamed client residing far away from Kyoto. Kōrin and Kenzan evidently endeavored to cultivate an early client base in different locations. Through the letter, the brothers also unveil their lack of experience in packing ceramics and arranging long-distance shipments. Such questions reveal their relative absence of routine as they took their first steps into unknown territory. Art dealers were there to help fledgling artists and more seasoned veterans alike as intermediaries to tap into markets near and far.

It has been argued that Nagasaki in the letter may indicate the neighborhood of Nagasakichō, an area of Reiganjima in Edo, rather than the port city in Kyūshū.[3] But considering that Kōrin had a habit of referring to Edo in his letters by name and never abbreviated neighborhoods—such as Kyōbashi Itchōme or Yabunouchichō—it would seem atypical to do so here. Whatever the true identity of the described locale may be, early on, Kōrin used karamonoya for selling to clients in Kyoto and locations farther afield, such as Edo and other places.[4] Relying on external services enabled Kōrin to work in media and reach patrons who otherwise would have been outside his reach, reflecting the complex modes and services populating the art market in early modern Japan.

In his paintings, lacquer works, and ceramics Kōrin was one among a growing number of artists whose works and systems of selling channeled a culture of privilege into the broader public sphere. The Kyoto that Kōrin knew was filled with painters of every imaginable creed. Numerous schools, including the Kano, Unkoku, Tosa, Sumiyoshi, Kaihō, and Yamamoto, maintained ateliers in the city, making for fierce rivalry in a colorful market consisting of aristocrats, merchants, and urban townspeople of varying financial means and social clout.[5] When Kōrin began to shape his career as a painter, he entered an established infrastructure of artistic services that demanded a personal niche. Kōrin did so by devising a bold new style whose genesis was rooted in a reshuffling of tradition. In his first paintings, made in the 1690s, Kōrin trod carefully and referred to an established visual language with which his patrons were familiar. Almost immediately after this, however, in the early 1700s, Kōrin created some of his most striking and innovative works.

In both situations, for inspiration Kōrin turned to his homeland's bountiful aesthetic traditions, a well-established mechanism with a long history in Japanese art. For centuries, painters mined the past as a source of creativity in the present. As painting instruction was increasingly codified in the early modern period, familiarity with older traditions became the quintessential measure of an artist's acumen. Painters in the present were appraised through their command of the past. Kōrin's older contemporary Kano Yasunobu (1613–1685) voiced this notion in the beginning of his *Cornerstones of the Way of Painting* (*Gadō yōketsu,* 1680): "When [a painter] fails to be exhaustive in [his study] of the styles of the ancients, his method will hardly be inspired. For that reason, the rule of painting is to consider the excellent ways of old [painting]."[6] Commentators such as the lacquer artist and textile designer Nonomura Chūbei detected and praised this quality in Kōrin's paintings. In his *Illustrated Guide to Kōrin* (*Kōrin ehon michi shirube*) of 1735, Chūbei writes: "With light brushwork, the painter Kōrin turned the many flowers and plants in this world into paintings possessing taste and refinement. He appreciated talented paintings [of the past] and gained sublimity by [studying] them."[7]

The road to such praise, however, was long and arduous. It involved a discriminating process of trial and error, one in which Kōrin embraced and

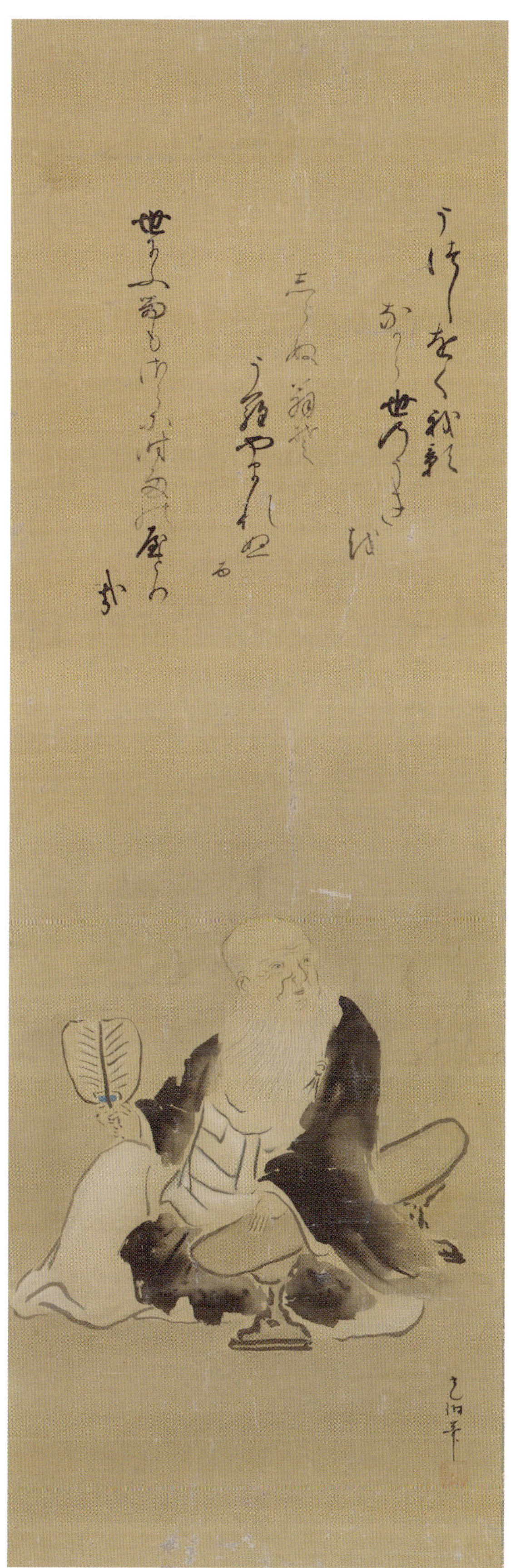

discarded a considerable variety of inspirations in order to find a suitable language in painting. His earliest artworks, in addition to numerous surviving sketches and painting studies, provide a pageant of Kōrin's artistic practice. They draw a tactile picture of a skilled painter on a ceaseless quest for tradition, but also ingenuity and experimentation to find styles that would appeal to his patrons.

THE ARCHETYPE

Kōrin launched his career as a painter carefully, by turning to sources close at hand. Mindful of the competition from the professional ateliers in his native Kyoto, he tapped into his aristocratic network and gradually began to establish himself as a painter of both figures and flowers. For inspiration in those genres, which gained him long-lasting fame, he turned to the early seventeenth century, albeit with vastly differing results.

The archetype of his figure paintings is a portrait of the late medieval poet and literary commentator Sōgi (fig. 8). The painting can be dated by way of an inscription of two verses by Sōgi commonly inscribed on portraits of him.

> My reflection is floating
> in this world like clouds,
> and it stirs an unknown feeling.
>
> This world I long for,
> is touched by the rain that is falling on my abode.

Although the inscription is unsigned, Kohitsu Ryōetsu (dates unknown), a nineteenth-century connoisseur of calligraphy, ascribed the writing to Sonshō, the abbot of Shōren'in, thus establishing 1694, the year of the abbot's death, as the latest time for producing the portrait.[8] Kōrin's early signature and seal used in the work support that date. The portrait of Sōgi is Kōrin's earliest surviving painting. It is a manifesto of his first

FIGURE 8

Ogata Kōrin, *Sōgi*, late 17th century. Hanging scroll; ink and color on silk. Idemitsu Museum of Arts, Tokyo.

commissions and the processes of study and patronage that were at the heart of his artistic practice in the 1690s.

The corpus of figure paintings that Kōrin produced in the 1690s had ink as their primary visual trope. The material is rarely associated with Kōrin, since his vibrantly polychromatic works have come to overshadow his substantial oeuvre in that genre. Like the majority of his earliest works, the portrait is done mainly in ink, with light touches of white for the inner robe, beard, and stubble of the monk's unshaven head—a representation of the poet's aloofness to worldly conventions. Sōgi's pose is typical of portraits of venerable poets, harking back to early medieval renderings of such ancient poets as Kakinomoto Hitomaro (660–724), who was often shown casually leaning on an armrest and gazing into some imaginary distance. From his sketch of a Hitomaro portrait, we realize that Kōrin was well aware of this iconographic link (fig. 9). In his portrait of Sōgi, Kōrin composed a symphony of expressive ink washes and heavily modulated lines that give the poet an unkempt appearance.

Like most portraits of Sōgi, Kōrin's work was intended to be hung at poetry gatherings or memorial services for the poet. Considering Kōrin's close association with Nijō Tsunahira and his patronage of fans and other small-format works in the mid-1690s, the Sōgi portrait fits that pattern and could have been made for someone in Tsunahira's circle.

To paint *Sōgi,* Kōrin turned to a stylistic source popular among the aristocracy during the seventeenth century, the monk painter Shōkadō Shōjō (1582–1639).[9] The early Edo period painter studied ancient paintings in the collections of temples and aristocrats and became a fixture among court circles during the early seventeenth century. By relying on a similar mix of aristocratic clients as Kōrin would later, Shōkadō became renowned for his expressive portraits—an established model that Kōrin turned to for shaping his own position as a budding painter. The relaxed posture and characteristic furrows of Sōgi's face are echoed in portraits by Shōkadō; he used similar brushwork in a self-portrait and in a depiction of Anrakuan Sakuden (1554–1642), one of Shōkadō's close acquaintances (fig. 10). Shōkadō himself is supposed to have painted several portraits of Sōgi, but none survives.[10] Shōkadō created the bulk of his works for his aristocratic and upper-class friends. In a letter written in 1626, for example, Kuwayama Sōsen (d. 1632), the lord of Gose Domain and a tea aficionado, requested a painting of Hotei from Shōkadō.[11] Many clients of similar caliber received or inscribed the monk painter's works, installing them as a part of the paraphernalia of the seventeenth-century intelligentsia.

The combination of a portrait of Sōgi in the style of Shōkadō was powerful. Early modern tea diaries reveal how the late verses and calligraphy by the medieval poet were a popular item to display at tea gatherings. One of several

FIGURE 9

Ogata Kōrin, *Sketch of a Portrait of Kakinomoto Hitomaro,* late 17th or early 18th century. Ink on paper. Konishi Family Archive, Osaka City Museum of Art.

FIGURE 10

Shōkadō Shōjō (painting) and Anrakuan Sakuden (inscription), *Portrait of Anrakuan Sakuden,* early 17th century. Hanging scroll; ink on paper. Hankyu Culture Foundation, Itsuo Art Museum, Ikeda.

occasions is recorded in the *Matsuya Tea Records* (*Matsuya kaiki*), where a painting by Shōkadō was viewed during tea in 1625.[12] Shōkadō's paintings were equally well received, and their quantity mentioned in tea diaries is surpassed only by the number of works of such painter-luminaries as Kano Tan'yū or Sesshū Tōyō.[13] The significant number of forgeries of Shōkadō's paintings also attests to their early modern esteem. Kōrin's emulation of Shōkadō's style taps into the monk painter's popularity and seeks to claim it for setting foot into the art world.

Kōrin's embrace of Shōkadō as his artistic model was not an arbitrary choice. The early seventeenth-century painter linked Kōrin to previous decades and the vestiges of the medieval age among elite aesthetics of his own time. The era of Shōkadō was an age of aesthetic flourishing that laid the groundwork for a substantial part of seventeenth-century culture. Shōkadō and his contemporaries searched for references in the medieval past by studying ink paintings by Japanese and Chinese masters.[14] Few of these paintings may have been genuine—the painter Hasegawa Tōhaku (1539–1610) wrote in his *Tōhaku's Explanation of Painting* (*Tōhaku gasetsu*) that only a small number of authentic works by Mokuan (d. 1345) were around—but Shōkadō certainly managed to see some masterpieces.[15] The protective box for a painting of Kanzan and Jittoku by the Southern Song artist Liang Kai (active late 12th and early 13th centuries), for example, that was in the collection of the daimyo and tea master Kobori Enshū (1579–1647) carries an inscription by Shōkadō.[16] Genuine paintings and those of questionable pedigree alike provided Shōkadō with references to an accepted metaframework of these artists' styles. Shōkadō's retrospective turn to the sixteenth century and to Song dynasty painters famous in Japan supplied Kōrin with a digested version of medieval aesthetics. Further, Shōkadō helped build the rudiments of upper-tier culture in the late seventeenth and early eighteenth centuries, a culture of which Kōrin would become a major representative. With this artistic authority in mind, Kōrin may have drawn to varying degrees from Shōkadō's artistic legacy. In other words, Shōkadō's paintings provided Kōrin with a combination of easy access to medieval paintings and to the popular style of Shōkadō himself, a potent combination for a budding artist.

On a personal level, Kōrin's esteemed ancestor Hon'ami Kōetsu may have provided an additional incentive for him to appropriate Shōkadō's style. Shōkadō frequented the same circles as Kōetsu. A passage in *Activities of the Hon'ami Clan* (*Hon'ami gyōjōki*), the records of Kōetsu's family, indicates that Shōkadō visited his home at Takagamine and painted for him.[17] Later Edo period writings closely associate the two artists. For example, *Annals of Early Modern Eccentrics* (*Kinsei kijin den*) by Ban Kōkei (1733–1806) links them and lays out how they may have influenced each other.[18] Kōkei writes that Kōetsu was close to Shōkadō Shōjō and that they frequented court circles together. Like Shōkadō, Kōetsu was an integral part of the culture of the court and the aesthetic environment of urban intellectual circles.

Even more, the men were posthumously linked as two of the so-called Three Brushes of the Kan'ei Era, an honor that illustrates their cultural connection.[19] Kōrin revered Kōetsu, his great-granduncle, and made repeated references to his persona and aesthetic, especially in his early steps as an artist. In sum, Kōrin's turn to Shōkadō in *Sōgi* and other early paintings may have been motivated by a blend of personal connections, artistic veneration, and a desire to cater to his patrons' tastes.

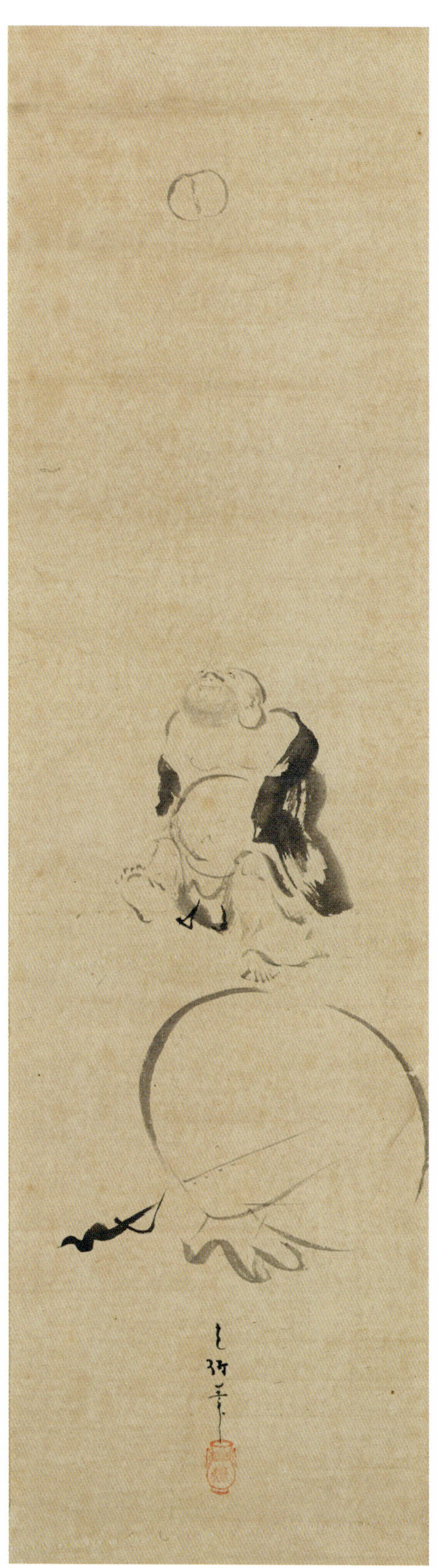

A STYLE TEMPLATE

The most important thing about *Sōgi* is perhaps the destiny it set for Kōrin as a painter and his reception for generations to come. It established a formula for an entire subsection of his figure paintings. The first such example followed almost immediately after Kōrin painted the Sōgi portrait. A monochrome ink painting of Hotei kicking a ball into the sky, for example, was produced only a few years after the portrait (fig. 11). Kōrin used a similar strategy by creating an emphatically vertical space, but the narrower and longer painting of Hotei tests the potency of the vertical format. Kōrin painted *Hotei Playing Kemari* on a narrow sheet of paper. Hotei kicks a ball high above his head, providing a dynamism that contrasts with the serenity of the Sōgi portrait. The ball resembles the moon, thus alluding to a Zen parable of monkeys pointing at the reflection of the celestial body in water—a symbol for the illusory nature of reality.

Kōrin's composition of Hotei echoes the Sōgi portrait in many ways. Made only a few years apart, the swift and assertive brushwork in the Hotei painting results from a more seasoned painter than that of the Sōgi portrait. The slightly later work—made around the late 1690s—reveals how Kōrin had honed his skill and quickly advanced to the high level of proficiency that characterizes much of his work. Kōrin even felt comfortable to embed a pun on the Kano school within the Hotei painting. His cauldron-shaped seal, placed along an invisible vertical line extending through the center of the painting, evokes the seals of maestros, such as the iconic painter Kano Motonobu (1476–1559), whose name was synonymous with the apex of painterly aptitude in Kōrin's time. Such less-than-subtle references speak to the artist's increasing self-esteem.

The portrait of Sōgi was a stylistic beacon for Kōrin. Followed by *Hotei Playing Kemari,* it established an early template for virtually all his figure paintings in ink throughout his career. As an example, a hanging scroll in monochrome ink of the early medieval writer Yoshida Kenkō (circa 1283–circa 1352) uses the same blend of broad, curved strokes to depict Kenkō's jacket (fig. 12). The figure gazes to the left in the same way as Sōgi; the left arm of each casually rests on an object before

FIGURE 11

Ogata Kōrin, *Hotei Playing Kemari,* late 17th century. Hanging scroll; ink on paper. Idemitsu Museum of Arts, Tokyo.

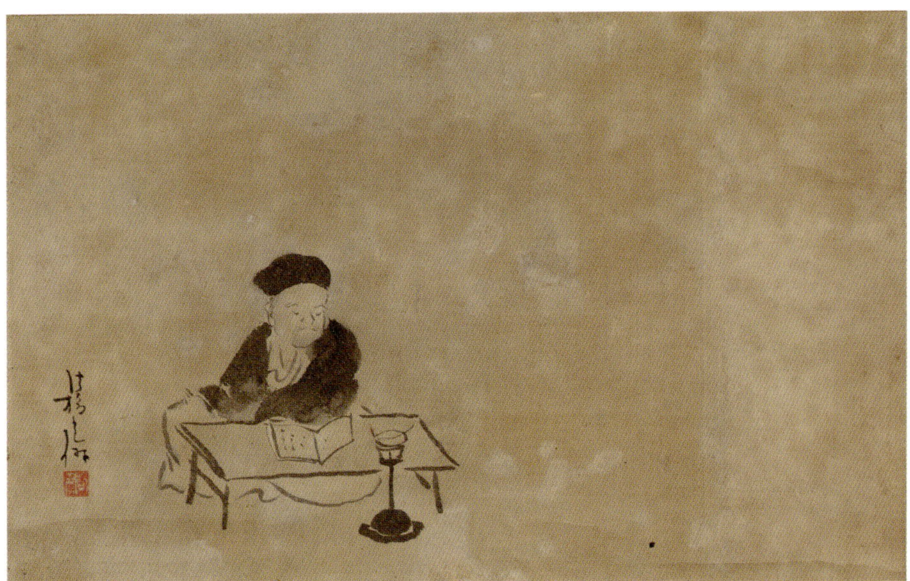

FIGURE 12
Ogata Kōrin, *Yoshida Kenkō*, early 18th century. Hanging scroll; ink on paper. MOA Museum of Art, Atami.

him. Kenkō is depicted at night. A small paper lamp at his desk suggests that he is immersed in writing part of his famous *Essays in Idleness* (*Tsurezuregusa*).

Kenkō's portrait bears the signature Hokkyō Kōrin, along with the painter's Kansei seal, a pseudonym he seems to have used during the first four or so years after receiving the hokkyō title in 1701.[20] In the signature, Kōrin abbreviated the first character of his name in a manner that is close to his signatures in earlier paintings, suggesting that he painted the portrait sometime within a span of less than five years after 1701.[21] The portrait of Kenkō elucidates how Kōrin transposed the visual language first employed in *Sōgi* to paintings in monochrome ink. By relying on this set stylistic palette, Kōrin shows his awareness of the efficacy of repeated tropes. This succession of paintings also provides evidence of how Kōrin disseminated the aesthetics of Kyoto's elite culture among an increasingly heterogenous clientele. We do not know the patrons for paintings like *Yoshida Kenkō*, but from the early 1700s onward Kōrin painted for an array of townspeople, daimyo, and merchants in Kyoto, Edo, and elsewhere. Many paintings like *Yoshida Kenkō* entered the ownership of these diverse patrons. The number of Kōrin's figure paintings that follow Shōkadō's model—a significant quantity of images of Hotei, along with literary figures and other popular early modern subjects—illustrates how he assimilated Shōkadō's visual language into a central element of his artistic identity.

As his visual repertoire developed, Kōrin strove for increasingly innovative forms of expression. Yet he did so by augmenting existing features with original ones, not by completely reinventing his basic style. He kept absorbing new inspirations and thereby created a fusion of his early artistic training with his exposure to other artworks. This strategy is evident in a late work, possibly painted within the last five years of his life (fig. 13). The portrait depicts the Chinese statesman and calligrapher Huang Tingjian (1045–1105), a subject Kōrin painted several times. It represents Kōrin's final advancement of his early studies of Shōkadō, and it epitomizes the way in which Kōrin continued to refer to the early foundations of his training even decades after.

Once he found an effective template, he rarely abandoned it. The facial features, with a furrowed forehead, modulating strokes for nose and ears, and the arched line and dot for the eyes in *Huang Tingjian* resemble those in *Sōgi* and echo Shōkadō's style in portraits, such as that of Anrakuan Sakuden. The expressive strokes Kōrin used in the poet's clothing reveal his early artistic training, yet the work is infused with features that Kōrin added by way of his direct study of Kano Tan'yū and medieval painting while in Edo from 1704 to 1709. We learn from paintings like *Huang Tingjian* how Kōrin merged his early education in ink techniques with his study of the style of the Edo-based Kano school and one of its most venerated representatives, Tan'yū. Although textual evidence about Kōrin's exposure to Tan'yū's mode is scarce, the Kano artist's virtuosic command of ink washes and abbreviated expressions clearly made their way into Kōrin's artistic language. He juxtaposed the conspicuous black strokes used for the sash and some of the outlines of the figure of Huang Tingjian with the gray, emphatically liquid washes in the rocks to evoke the brushwork and chromatic pairings in many of Tan'yū's works (fig. 14). He seamlessly blended his own manner with that of the Kano master (see chapter 4). Although Kōrin used Shōkadō during the 1690s as a filter for the medieval past, he turned directly to medieval artists in the 1710s, eventually fusing these two sources of inspiration into his figure paintings. In collocating these two artistic influences, Kōrin constructed a personal vocabulary.

Kōrin transformed his study of the early seventeenth century into an eighteenth-century reincarnation. The sequence of the paintings *Sōgi, Yoshida Kenkō,* and *Huang Tingjian* traces the evolution of Kōrin's early artistic education and his development of a distinctive visual language based on Shōkadō's paintings. Several of Kōrin's figure paintings follow the manner he adopted from Shōkadō Shōjō and perpetuated his style within the broader mainstream of early modern painting. Ultimately, this trademark manner became associated with Kōrin. Not only did he appropriate Shōkadō's style, but he also expropriated it. Artists in the following decades recognized Kōrin's late paintings, such as *Huang Tingjian,* as exemplars of his artistry. Throughout the eighteenth and nineteenth centuries, artists like Watanabe Shikō and Sakai Hōitsu absorbed Kōrin's habits of figure paintings into their own. Two paintings of Jurōjin, one of the seven deities of fortune, by Shikō and Hōitsu are strikingly close to Kōrin's

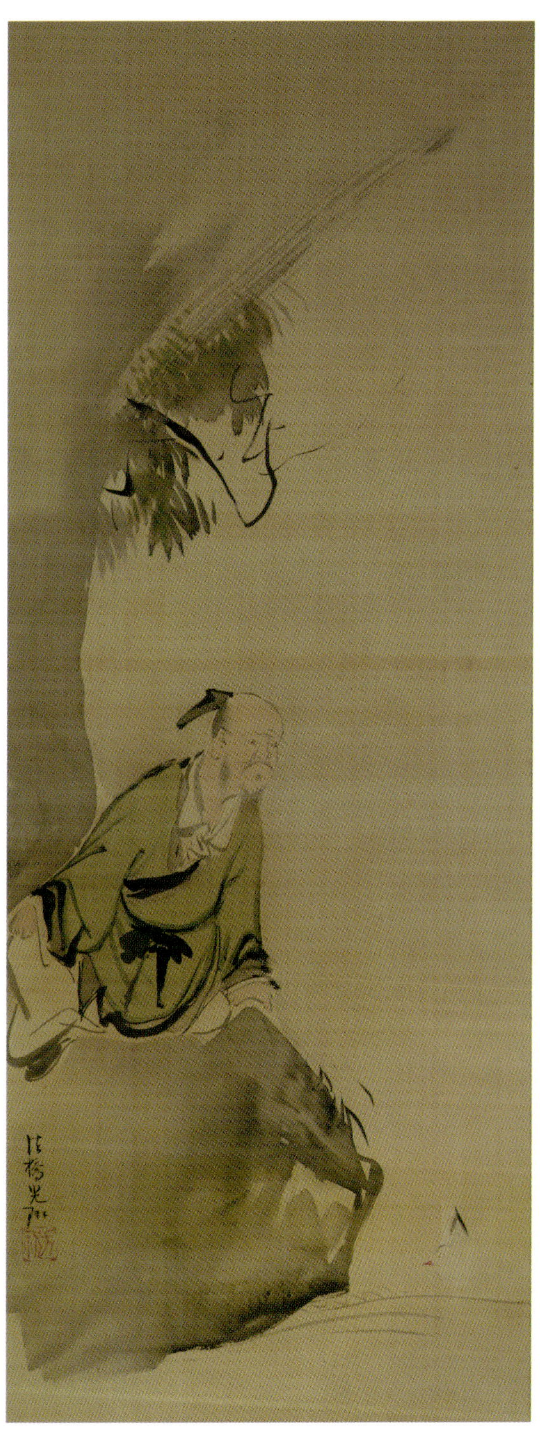

FIGURE 13

Ogata Kōrin, *Huang Tingjian,* early 18th century. Hanging scroll; ink and color on silk. Former Fujita Museum Collection, now private collection.

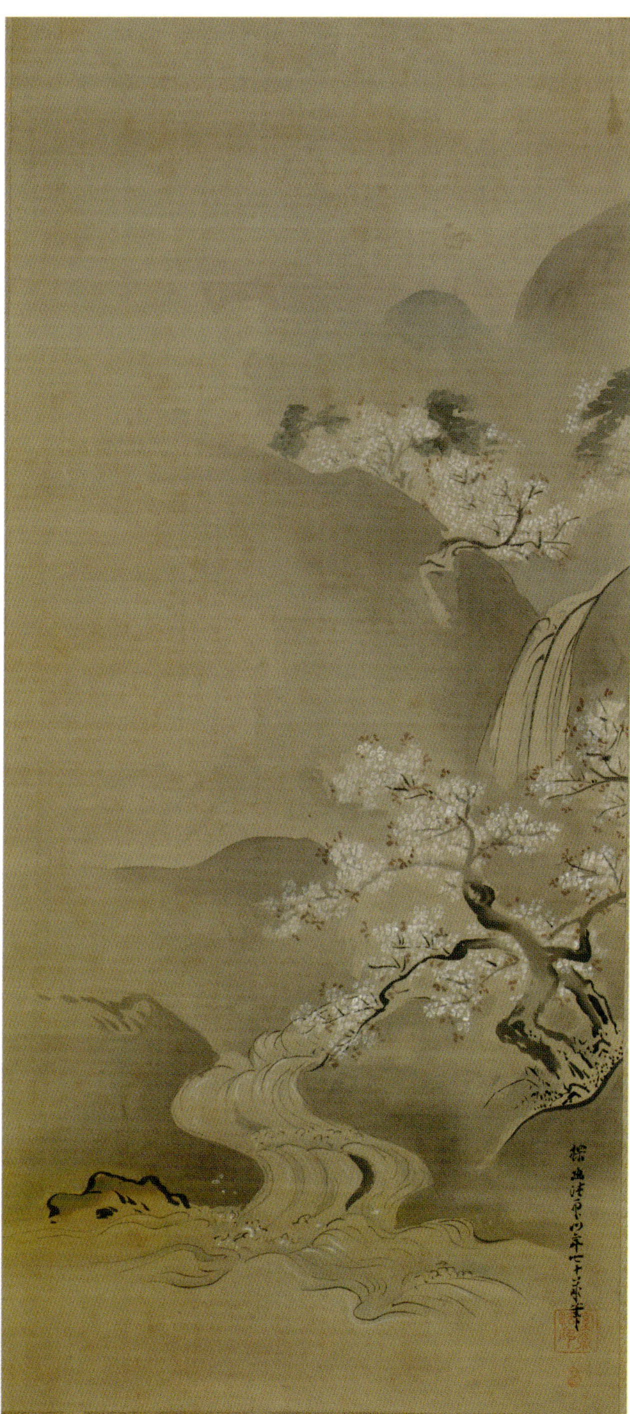

FIGURE 14

Kano Tan'yū, *Spring Landscape,* 1672. Hanging scroll; ink and color on silk. Freer Gallery of Art, Smithsonian Institution, Washington, D.C.: Gift of Charles Lang Freer, F1892.28a–c.

Huang Tingjian (figs. 15, 16). Drawn to Kōrin's style, both painters played a central role in perpetuating his visual language in the artistic industry of the early modern period. In both works the face of the deity—the recognizable frown, downcast, weary eyes, upturned eyebrows, furrowed forehead, and a similar way of rendering the cheeks and ears—echoes Kōrin's original design. In this way, the model established by Kōrin outlived him by more than a hundred years.

Shōkadō occupied an overarching presence in the circles that Kōrin frequented during his first years as a painter, a fact that no doubt furnished him with ample motivation to incorporate his predecessor's style into his own. It is unclear if later commentators of Kōrin's work noticed a stylistic resemblance or whether they simply decided to pair these painters who tested the boundaries of convention. In his eighteenth-century writings, Kuwayama Gyokushū linked Shōkadō, Sōtatsu, and Kōrin. The fact that later commentators uttered Kōrin's name in the same breath as Shōkadō indicates that posterity at least connected them on a conceptual level—as two artists who

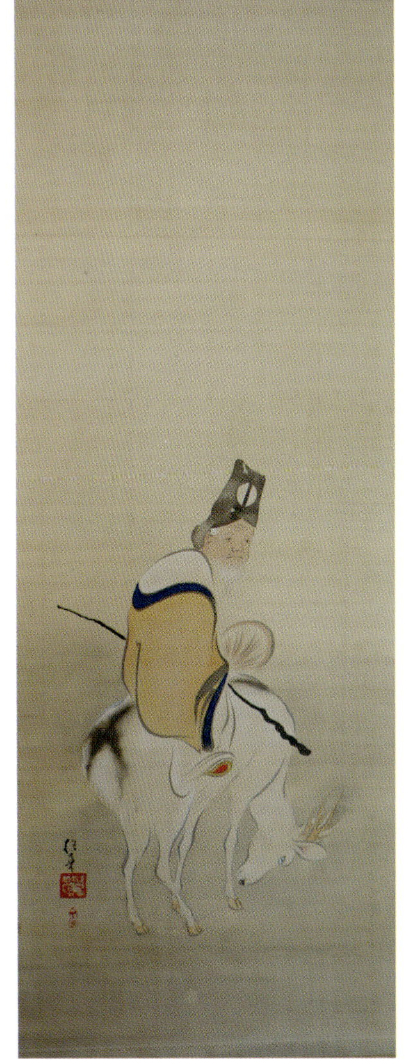

FIGURE 15
Watanabe Shikō, *Jurōjin,* 18th century. Hanging scroll; ink and color on silk. Hosomi Museum, Kyoto.

FIGURE 16
Sakai Hōitsu, *Jurōjin,* first half of 19th century. Hanging scroll (part of a triptych); ink and color on silk. Private collection.

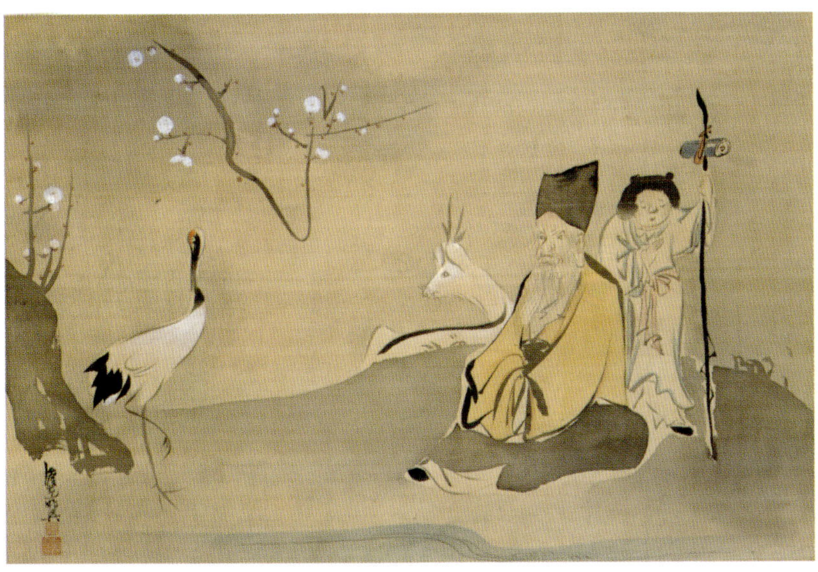

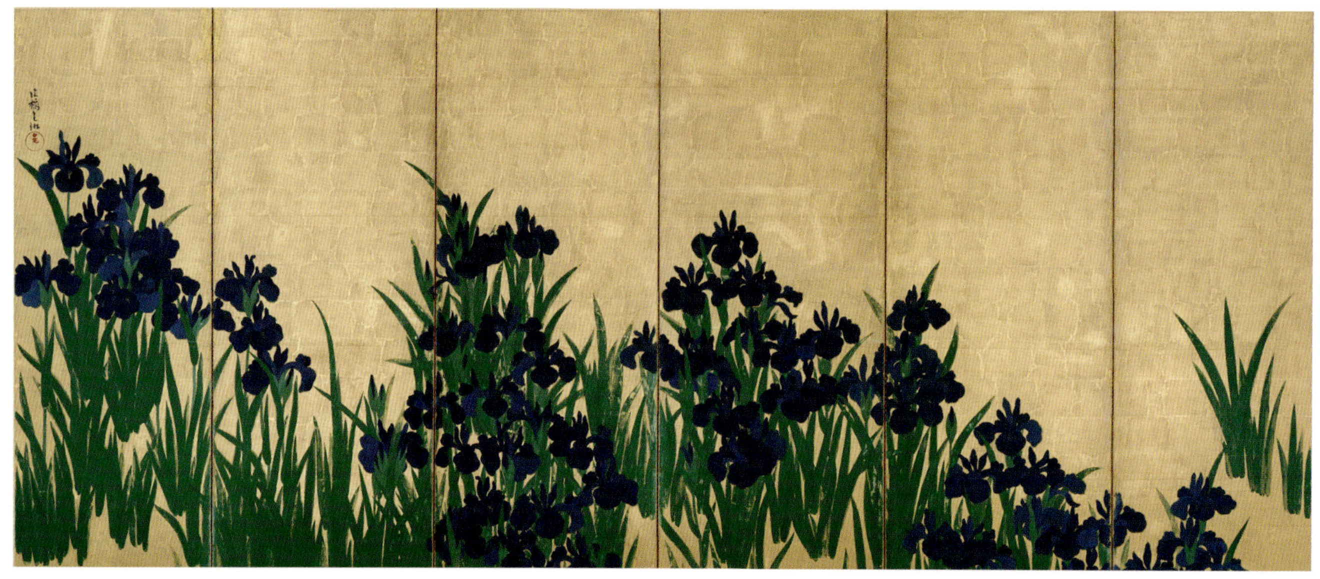

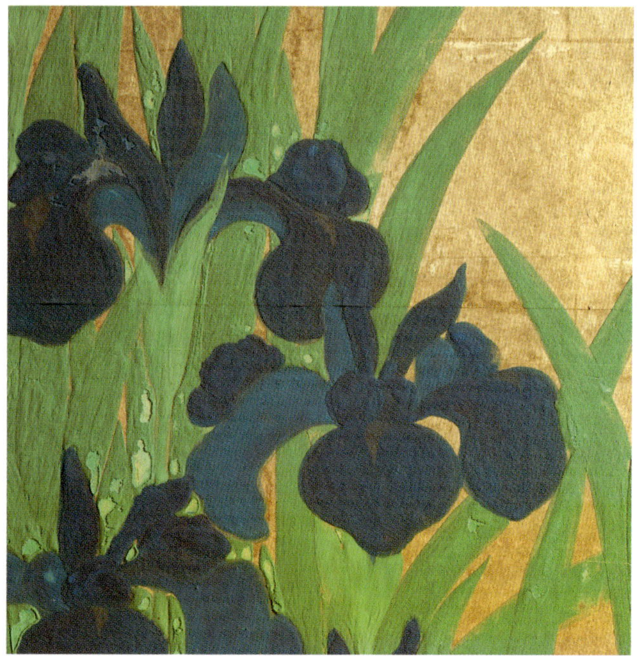

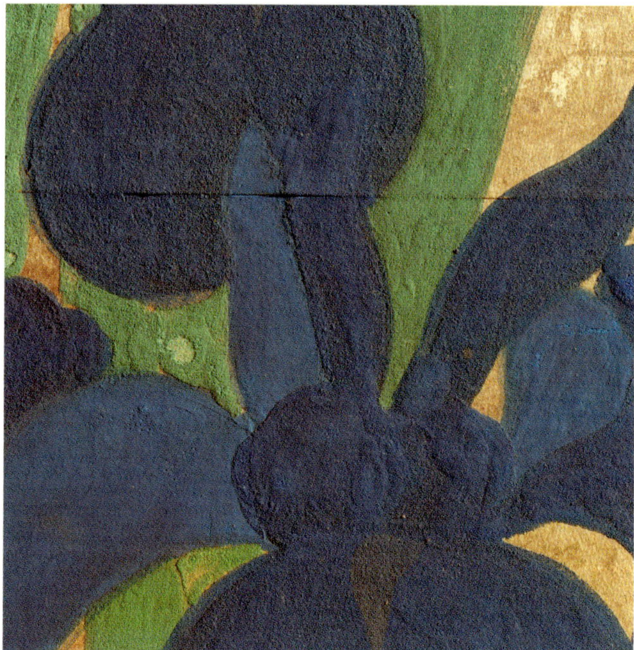

FIGURE 17

Ogata Kōrin, *Irises,* early 1700s. Pair of six-panel folding screens, plus details; ink, color, and gold leaf on paper. Nezu Museum, Tokyo.

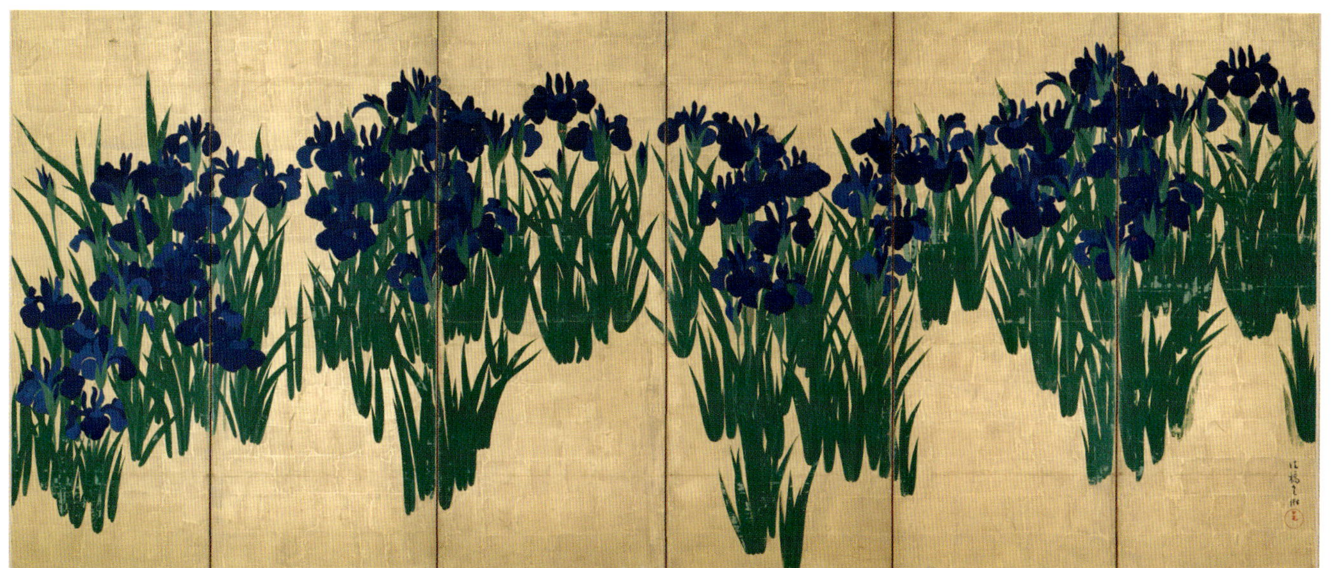

departed from convention and expanded the paradigms of Japanese painting. Yet the stylistic overlap between Kōrin and Shōkadō, by contrast, seems to have gone unnoticed, since many biographies of painters are strangely silent on Kōrin's early veneration of Shōkadō.

Indeed, Shikō's and Hōitsu's takes on Kōrin's figure paintings make clear that painters came to associate that particular style above all with Kōrin, not with Shōkadō. The manner that Kōrin created in the process helped embed his style among a number of important early modern painters. His strategy of repeating a specific visual language over extensive periods of time is also found in numerous other works and set the direction for much of his artistic output.

After his early steps in figure paintings, Kōrin soon moved to painting flowers, a genre that continues to determine his reception as an artist to this day. One such work shaped his artistic persona more than any other painting: his pair of screens *Irises.* The sophistication and expense necessary to paint the screens offer a case in point for the impressive speed at which Kōrin had progressed in his skill and in developing influential patronage from the 1690s and after. *Irises* formed the threshold for taking Kōrin's art and renown into a new level.

PAINTING FLOWERS

Painted around the beginning of the eighteenth century, *Irises* is one of Kōrin's best-known works (fig. 17). The pair of six-fold screens presents a vista of gorgeous irises arranged against surrounding gold leaf. Creating a symphony of gold and color, each flower forms part of a well-balanced synergy of shape and composition. In Kōrin's time, irises could stand for a range of possible allusions, a fact that embodies the multivalence and ambiguity of many of Kōrin's paintings. The irises could simply be flowers and harbingers of early summer, given their role as a floral symbol of the fifth month.[22] They could also be a reference to more complex cultural frameworks. Given how often the flower was associated with the ninth chapter of the *Tales of Ise,* Kōrin was likely referring to the ninth-century collection of stories in his screens. The court narrative had been popularized among a broad readership since the time of its first printed edition, in 1608 (fig. 18).[23] The *Tales of Ise,* and particularly the irises celebrated in its ninth chapter, were repeated often in early modern art and were the subject of Noh theater plays, which popularized the tale among an educated early modern audience that enthusiastically viewed and practiced the arts of the stage. Here, however, Kōrin rendered the flower not as part of a narrative scene, as was the common convention. Instead, he presents a simplified, suggestive panorama of sumptuous irises—a radical move away from orthodox painting traditions that imbues the work with complexity through simplicity.

The ninth chapter of the *Tales of Ise* is one in a series of episodes in which the protagonist of the tales, commonly identified as Ariwara Narihira (825–880), travels eastward to the Kantō region.[24] The journey is set in motion in the seventh chapter of the tales, when Narihira flees the capital after a scandalous love affair.[25] The notion effectively renders *azuma kudari*—literally "descending eastward"—as an emblem of transience and escape, which in turn embodies the fascination with travel in premodern times.[26] Within the succession of the eastward travel chapters of the *Tales of Ise,* the irises stand synonymous with Narihira's peripatetic fate and the distant, poetic site associated with it. Along the way eastward, he and his companions arrive at the delta of the Azuma River. An eight-plank bridge, with irises blooming in the marsh, crosses the water. The colorful scenery inspired the protagonist to compose a lyrical response expressing his gloom at being far from home. In Japanese art and literature, the ninth chapter embodied the melancholy of journeys and the sorrow of being away from loved ones. Especially among the increasingly mobile society of Kōrin's time, the chapter became a popular subject in the arts.

Kōrin reconfigured the iris flower into one of his most baffling paintings. With a height of about 1.5 meters, each screen is more or less the dimension of a standing early modern person. When seated in front of the works—as would have been the case in a traditional Japanese setting—the viewer would have felt immersed in a sea of towering irises. Kōrin chose expensive mineral pigments—azurite and malachite—to paint his larger-than-life irises, endowing them with a rich crystalline luster that creates a sensation not unlike the velvety surface of real iris flowers. Azurite and malachite had been mined in

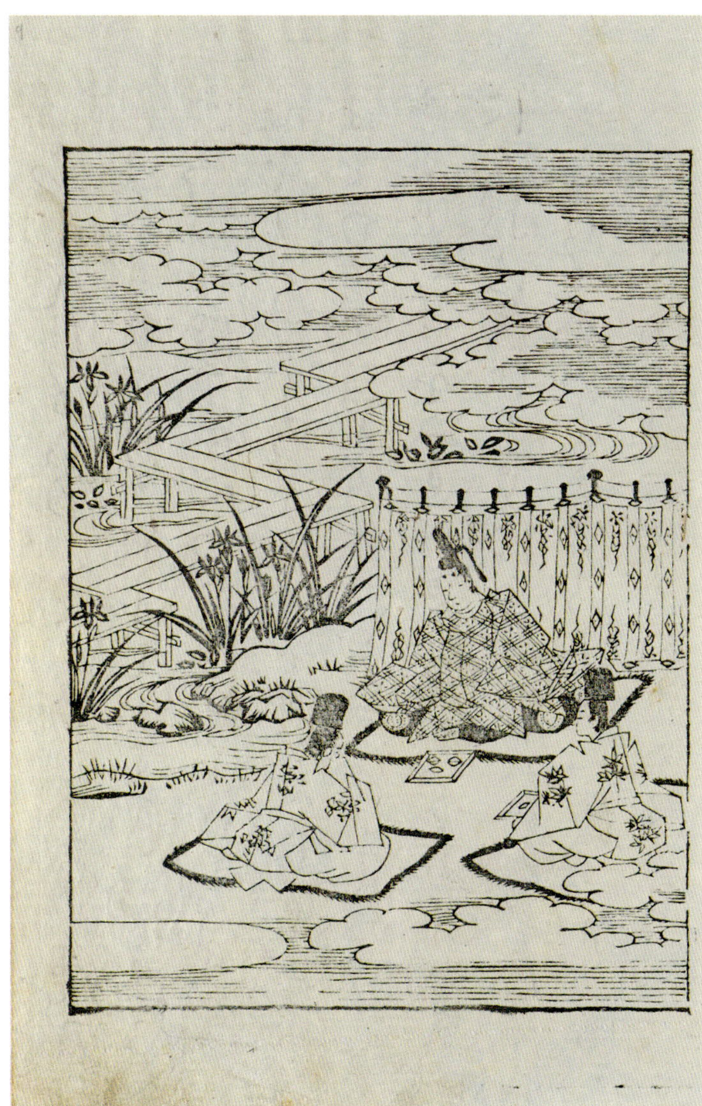

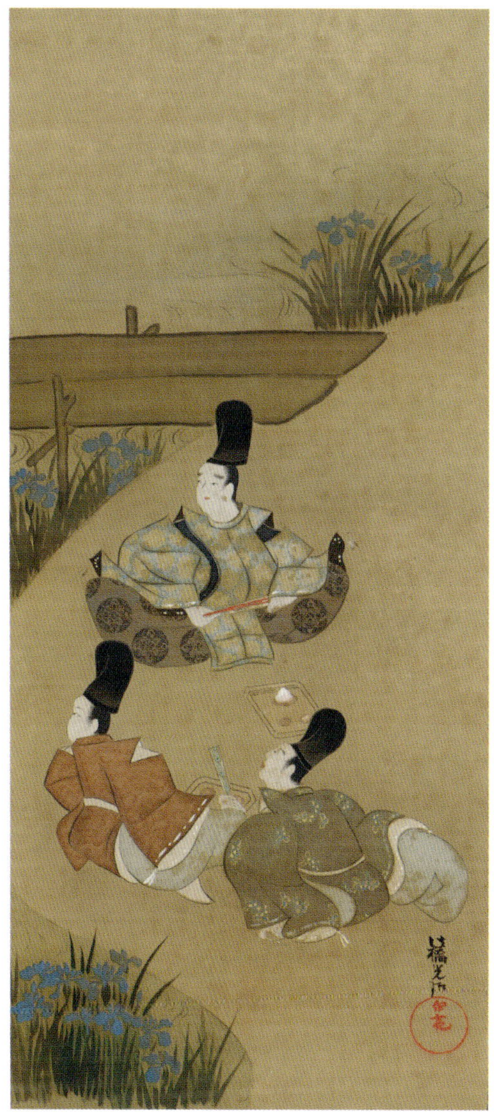

FIGURE 18
Tales of Ise (*Saga-bon*), vol. 1, 1608. Woodblock-printed book; ink on paper. British Museum, London.

FIGURE 19
Ogata Kōrin, *The Tales of Ise: Yatsuhashi,* early 18th century. Hanging scroll; ink and color on silk. Tokyo National Museum, Image: TNM Image Archives.

Japan since at least the Heian period (794–1185). Domestic production, however, was not perfected until the early eighteenth century.[27] As a result, the pigments often had to be imported from China, which made them extremely expensive. Kōrin's choice of dark azurite was achieved through adding layers of large-size particles of the pigment. Kōrin organized the composition carefully, with clusters of irises meandering along the line that is created by the inward and outward folds of the six-panel screens. In this way, the seemingly flat composition gains striking three-dimensionality when the panels are angled.

Irises differed from contemporaneous works depicting the subject, even those by Kōrin himself (fig. 19). In a hanging scroll that dates to roughly the same time as the screens, Kōrin chose to depict the ninth chapter as it is found

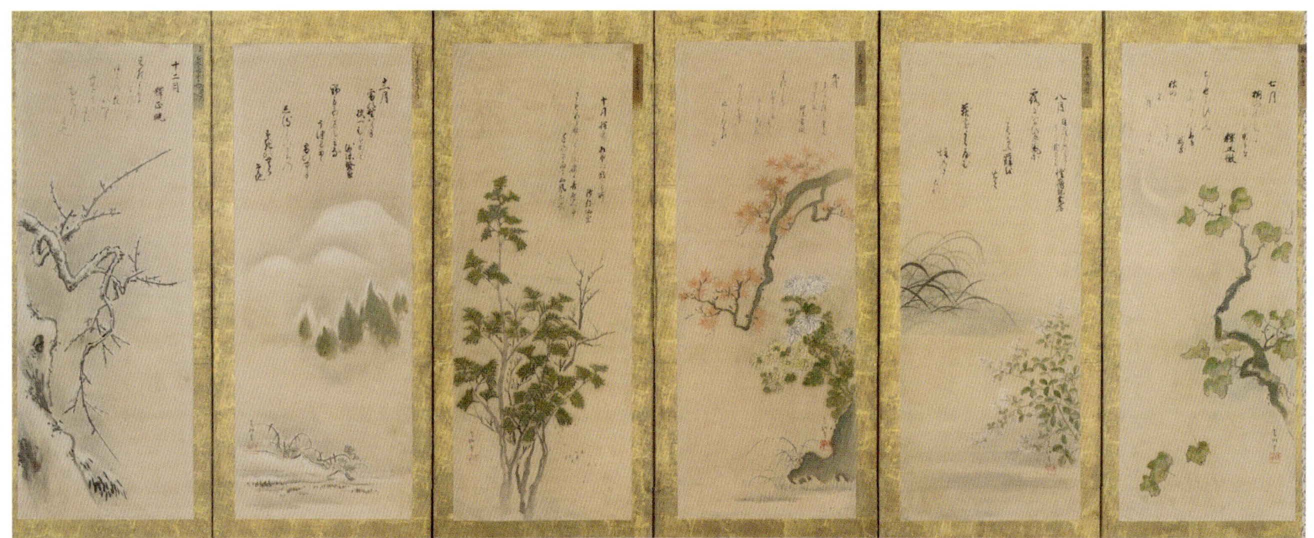

FIGURE 20
Ogata Kōrin (paintings) and Takatsukasa Kanehiro and other courtiers (calligraphy), *Poetic Meanings of the Twelve Months,* late 17th century. Pair of six-panel folding screens; ink and color on paper. Fukuda Art Museum, Kyoto.

in printed books such as the edition of 1608—with human protagonists present and the flowers as props arranged around them. In *Irises,* however, the blossoms become the dramatis personae themselves. *Irises* was created only a few years after Kōrin produced *Sōgi* and his first screen painting, *Poetic Meanings of the Twelve Months* (fig. 20). Visually, the two pairs of screens could hardly be more different. *Twelve Months,* made around the last years of the 1690s, is parsimoniously painted mainly in ink with light colors on paper. It reflects a style that relies in part on the Kano atelier. Bearing inscriptions by Takatsukasa Kanehiro (1660–1725), minister of the left (*sadaijin*) at the time, and other courtiers, the screens were no doubt an aristocratic commission. Like *Irises,* in spite of their aesthetic differences, and other works produced around this time, the screens embody the complex web of Kōrin's patronage by the nobility in the orbit of Tsunahira and others. For example, Kanehiro's uncle Kōken, the abbot of Sanbōin, was well acquainted with Kōrin and Kenzan since the brothers performed Noh for him in 1675, a connection that could have facilitated the production of *Twelve Months.* The frugal use of pigment and paper made the painting a relatively simple work that keeps in line with other screens of the same subject ordered by the court. On the other hand, *Irises,* painted around 1701, offers a radical vista of imposing flowers created from exceedingly expensive, thickly applied mineral pigments with gold leaf added around them. In just a few years, Kōrin apparently underwent a fundamental shift in his aesthetic and in his general approach to art.

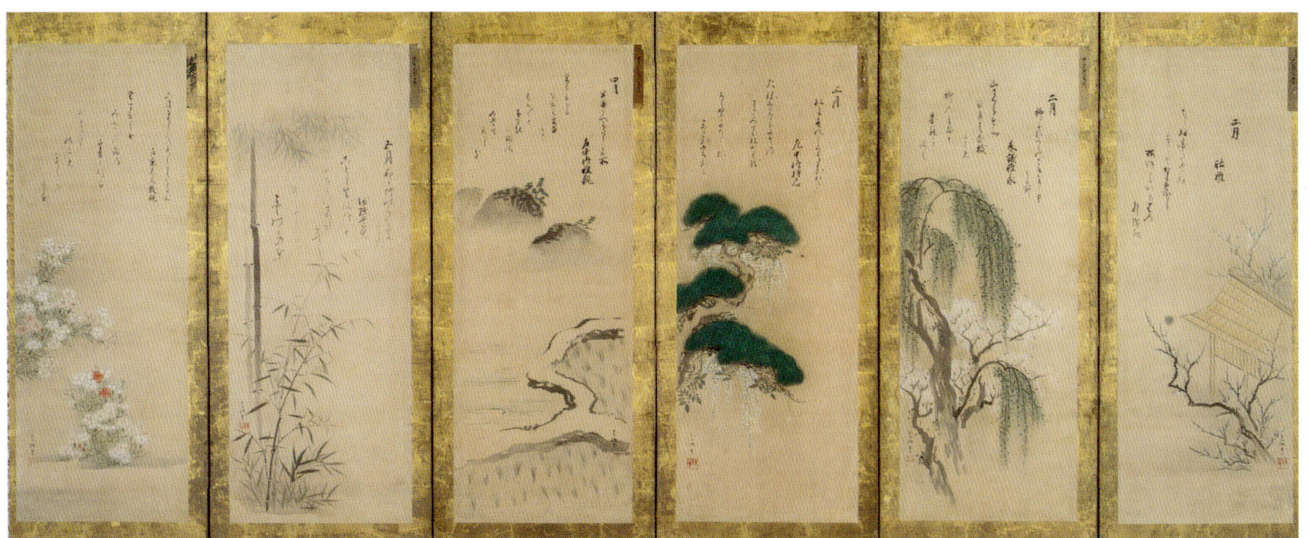

MODULARITY

In his screens, Kōrin played with vision and perception by repeating several clusters of flowers. This is perhaps the most significant feature in *Irises,* but it is also the least recognizable—it was not described until 1960.[28] Kōrin engaged the viewer in a game of visual hide and seek. Repeated arrangements of flowers are embedded into the overall composition, a strategy that shrouds them from immediate detection. For example, the configuration of flowers in the first and second panels of the right screen is replicated in the fourth and fifth panels. Likewise, the same iris cluster in the first panel of the left screen is mirrored in its third panel. Such repetition is subtle enough to be inconspicuous, yet it fosters an unconscious, cognitive identification. When examined closely, the blossoms reveal the individual recipe that Kōrin used for each one. No part was painted with the same kind of stroke, just as in nature no flower is an exact copy of another. By combining the carefully calculated repetition of the iris clusters with a naturalistic rendering, Kōrin endowed the work with a visual tension that encourages us to respond to its peculiar structure.

Such strategy helped to enhance the recognizability of Kōrin's style and created optical stimuli, two effects he employed throughout his career thereafter. Kōrin's reliance on repetition as a visual tool may also be a vestige of his family's dry goods business, the Kariganeya.[29] Textile patterns regularly use repetition and rely on recognition as a means to foster a distinctive trademark image. Several design books from the Kariganeya provide a glimpse of how prevalent repeated patterns—also of irises—were in the fashion world around

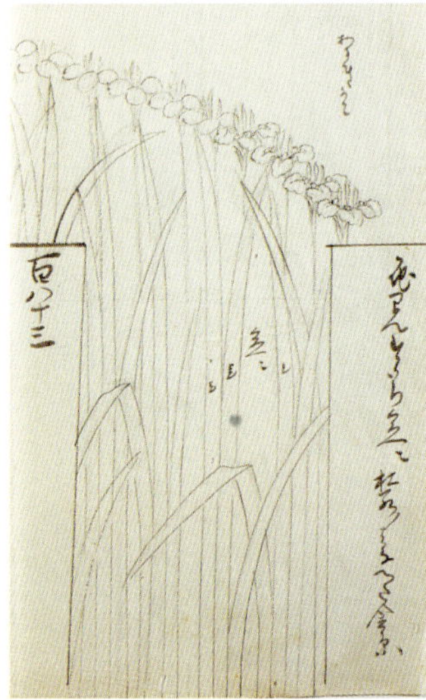

FIGURE 21
Kariganeya Design Catalogue (*On'e chō*) (detail), 1661 and 1663. Bound book; ink on paper. Osaka City Museum of Art.

Kōrin (fig. 21). Such works exemplify the subject's popularity among the early modern audience, a fact that might have motivated Kōrin to revisit his family's heritage when creating one of his first screen paintings.

Much less conspicuous than in garment designs, however, was his modular use of flowers. In Japanese textiles, the same motif was often repeated over and over, with the same recurring design filling the entire kimono. In *Irises,* on the other hand, the reiteration of the modules of flowers and the way they are embedded within the screen make the repetition difficult to notice. Furthermore, scholars have suggested that Kōrin used stencils in *Irises,* a customary technique for creating repetitive textile designs.[30] This may be true. When examined closely, however, the repeated clusters of irises show enough differences to suggest that they were painted freehand, perhaps using a preliminary drawing as reference. If Kōrin indeed employed stencils, he sought to conceal their use by subtly alternating the flower arrangements—a clever technique that likely camouflaged the repetition in *Irises* for centuries.

The painting tradition established by Tawaraya Sōtatsu made extensive use of modules, where the same shapes of figures were reused in a variety of contexts. Such works may have been an additional inspiration for Kōrin. Sōtatsu established his name in the late sixteenth and early seventeenth centuries as an important player in the artistic landscape of Kyoto. At a time when the city had just begun to emerge from the ruins of the civil war that raged throughout much of the sixteenth century, the Tawaraya studio began as a so-called picture shop (*eya*) that offered a variety of paintings in storelike settings to urban customers. Under Sōtatsu's leadership, the business transformed into a supplier of paintings to the upper ranks of the nobility, and the emperor himself ordered works from Sōtatsu.[31]

Sōtatsu's work was of paramount importance for Kōrin. Against the backdrop of Kōrin's family trade in textiles, the artist could have adopted the approach found in *Irises* through his study of Sōtatsu and his atelier's style, whose planar compositions and penchant for repeating forms had a conceptual connection to textile designs. The timing also supports a link to Sōtatsu; Kōrin seems to have turned to his art around the late 1690s, shortly before he made *Irises.* A string of financial misfortunes preceded this decision, supplying a sequence of events that may have led to Kōrin's artistic embrace of Sōtatsu.

In the wake of his money problems, Kōrin pawned several artworks to raise money. The selection of items he entrusted to the pawnbroker Kamenokōya Kishichi included quotidian objects, such as a rag, a kettle for heating sake, and different ceramic pieces. Among this haphazard array of daily-use artworks, Kōrin offered a two-panel screen by Tawaraya Sōtatsu. Kamenokōya

Kishichi held two sales for Kōrin in the eleventh and twelfth months of an unspecified year.

Record of Sales and Purchases

Sold items at the gathering on the eleventh day of the twelfth month.[32]

First	One hundred eighty monme	Sōtatsu two-panel screen
Second	Eleven monme, six bu[33]	Shigaraki [ware] vase
Third	Twenty-three monme, five bu	Tray for sweets
Fourth	Seventy-seven monme	*Chaire* [tea caddy]
Fifth	Sixteen monme, five bu	Eight colored [ceramic] plates
Sixth	Ten monme	Colored brazier
Seventh	Twenty-seven monme	Five Seto [ware] sake cups
Eighth	Six bu	Water pitcher
Ninth	Ten monme	Tray with [décor of] deer in mother-of-pearl

Total sum of three hundred fifty-six monme and two bu

Including seventeen monme eight bu

Net amount of three hundred thirty-eight monme and four bu

Purchases

First	Seventeen monme, two bu	[Lacquer] *maki-e* tobacco tray
Second	One hundred monme	Small brazier [used for lighting tobacco] with red picture [ceramic piece with a picture in iron oxide]
Third	Sixty-five monme	Amida altar
Fourth	One monme, five bu	Price for foods

Total of one hundred eighty-three monme, seven bu

Minus a total of one hundred fifty-four monme, seven bu paid

Twelfth month, nineteenth day. From Kamenokōya

Ki[shichi]

To Kōrin[34]

Although Kōrin also bought items at the same occasion, the revenue from his sales greatly exceeded his purchases, an indication that he was keen to raise money for covering the interest payments of his loans late in the year. These payments occurred around the end of each year, and here they coincided with the time when Kōrin sold the Sōtatsu screen. Although the year of the sale is not recorded, the urgency with which Kōrin divested himself of artworks suggests that it occurred sometime around the height of his money troubles, the late 1690s.

With a substantial price of 180 monme, the Sōtatsu screen—its subject is not identified—was by far the most expensive item Kōrin sold. The screen's sum alone illustrates the market value of Sōtatsu's works more than a half-century after his death. Although Kōrin might have encountered works by Sōtatsu during his Noh performances at Sanbōin in 1675, this sales record is the only written evidence that he even knew Sōtatsu's name. Aside from the aesthetic appeal of Sōtatsu's works of art, the high monetary value of paintings by Sōtatsu on the early modern art market may have provided Kōrin with an additional incentive to adopt his style. Kōrin's finances continued to be hard-pressed, and Sōtatsu's legacy provided propitious associations. A famed Kyoto artist who had risen from a townspainter (*machi eshi*) to serving emperor GoMizuno'o, Sōtatsu was the embodiment of a model artist, and by Kōrin's time his aesthetic had grown deep roots within the culture of the court.[35]

We have seen that Kōrin had turned to the popular Shōkadō Shōjō a little earlier, illustrating how the art associated with the aristocracy formed an early bedrock in Kōrin's oeuvre. During his first years as a professional artist, Kōrin displayed an omnivorous appetite for a range of artistic inspirations and formats. He produced everything from fans, shikishi, hanging scrolls, and folding screens to writing boxes and *inrō* in lacquer. The lack of a fixed repertoire reflects Kōrin's attempt to cover a wide range of patronage, and it accommodated the inclusion of a versatile assortment of artistic inspirations. Conspicuously, many of these works were informed by the late medieval aesthetic, the vestiges of which survived in the work of Sōtatsu and Shōkadō.

While a sense of nostalgia for a bygone era unites Kōrin's body of work, the aesthetic shift between his earliest paintings of the 1690s and *Irises* is remarkable. It marks the most significant rift within his oeuvre. The basis for his awareness of the efficacy of patterns surely was laid through his family's textile business, but Kōrin may have arrived at the idea of isolating and

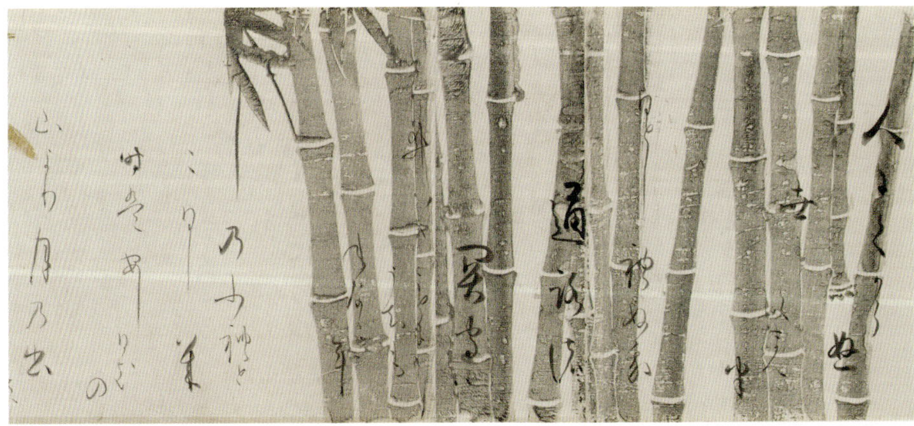

FIGURE 22
Tawaraya Sōtatsu (paper décor) and Hon'ami Kōetsu (calligraphy), *Collection of Old and New Poems (Kokin wakashū)*, early 17th century. Handscroll; ink, gold, silver, and mica on paper, Freer Gallery of Art, Smithsonian Institution, Washington, D.C.: Gift of Charles Lang Freer, F1903.309.

enlarging a single floral motif through Sōtatsu-related paper décors. These he could have accessed through his Hon'ami ancestors, who held a perpetual presence among Kōrin's life.[36] Hon'ami Kōetsu, Kōrin's great-granduncle, inscribed his sought-after calligraphy on a range of paper designs attributed to Sōtatsu and his Tawaraya studio. Among those, the artists who supplied Kōetsu with decorated paper perpetually employed repeating modular forms. This repetition is sometimes overt and at other times inconspicuous, as in *Irises*. A scroll with poems from the early tenth-century *Collection of Old and New Poems* (*Kokin wakashū*) displays this visual strategy by way of stamped paper design in silver and gold (fig. 22). The middle section has a stretch of bamboo printed by repeatedly impressing the exact same configuration of bamboo stalks. Yet, the arrangement conceals its repetition by altering angles and overlapping impressions of the woodblocks. This approach disguises the use of modular forms in a similar way to *Irises*.

Family connections to the Hon'ami and their residence at Takagamine in the northwestern outskirts of Kyoto no doubt made works like the *Collection of Old and New Poems* scroll readily available to Kōrin, access that is reflected in the studies he made of elements used in their paper décor, including cranes and bamboo (figs. 23, 24). Throughout his early years as a painter, Kōrin was drawn

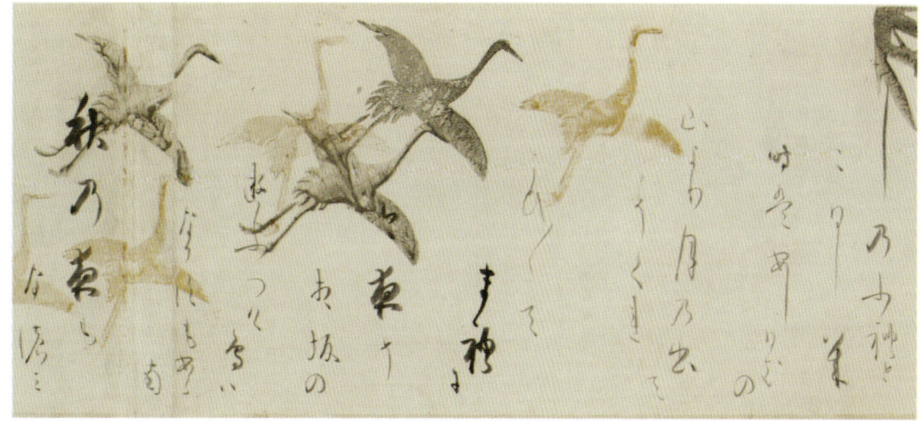

FIGURE 23
Tawaraya Sōtatsu (paper décor) and Hon'ami Kōetsu (calligraphy), *Collection of Old and New Poems* (*Kokin wakashū*), early 17th century. Handscroll; ink, gold, silver, and mica on paper. Freer Gallery of Art, Smithsonian Institution, Washington, D.C.: Gift of Charles Lang Freer, F1903.309.

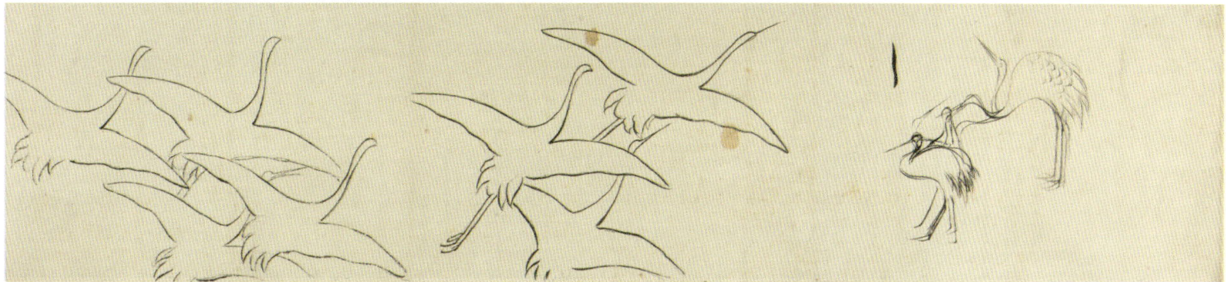

FIGURE 24
Ogata Kōrin, *Sketches of Cranes*, late 17th or early 18th century. Ink on paper, Konishi Family Archive, Osaka City Museum of Art.

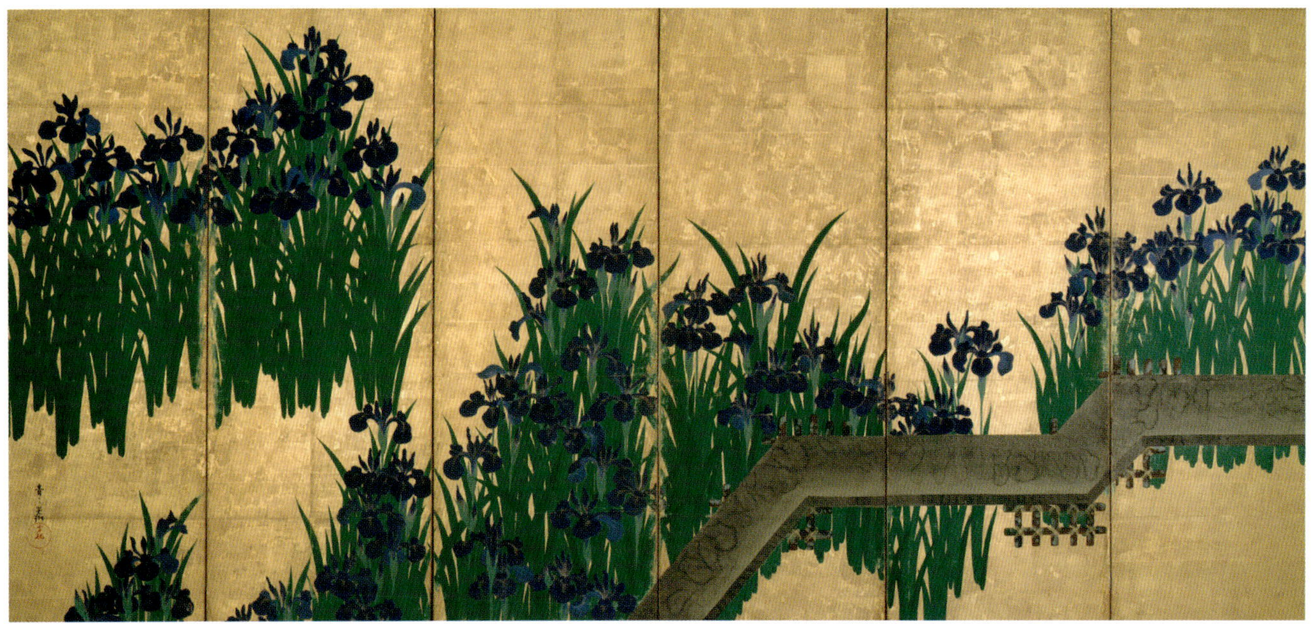

FIGURE 25
Ogata Kōrin, *Irises at Yatsuhashi (Eight-Plank Bridge), from the Tales of Ise,* after 1709. Pair of six-panel folding screens; ink and color on gold leaf on paper. The Metropolitan Museum of Art, New York, Purchase, Louisa Eldridge McBurney Gift, 1953, 53.7.1, .2.

to Hon'ami Kōetsu as a model. The famous calligrapher, lacquer designer, and potter became a source of constant reference for Kōrin as he forged his early artistic identity. The larger Hon'ami clan also played a part here. In an early letter relating to Kōrin's financial hardships during the 1690s, his brother Kenzan promises to solicit counsel from the Hon'ami: "Tomorrow, I will head for Takagamine to ask for more advice."[37] Founded by Kōetsu, the artistic-religious community in the northwest of Kyoto functioned as the base of the Hon'ami family. That Kenzan hurried to Takagamine for advice on personal debt and similar matters is testimony to the close relationship between the Ogata and the Hon'ami.

In this way, Kōrin's awareness of the pecuniary value of Sōtatsu's style and his access to examples of it through the Hon'ami may have formed the aesthetic foundations for *Irises,* a work that established an entire genre within Kōrin's artistry. His enthusiasm for Sōtatsu and his legacy left a lasting imprint on his artistic practice and added the key ingredient for formulating the visual vocabulary for which he became best known.

UNIDENTICAL TWINS

In its use of repetitive patterns, *Irises* represents a radical turn away from the more restrained, conservative works Kōrin had begun his career with in the 1690s.[38] *Irises* carries a Hokkyō Kōrin signature on both screens, together with

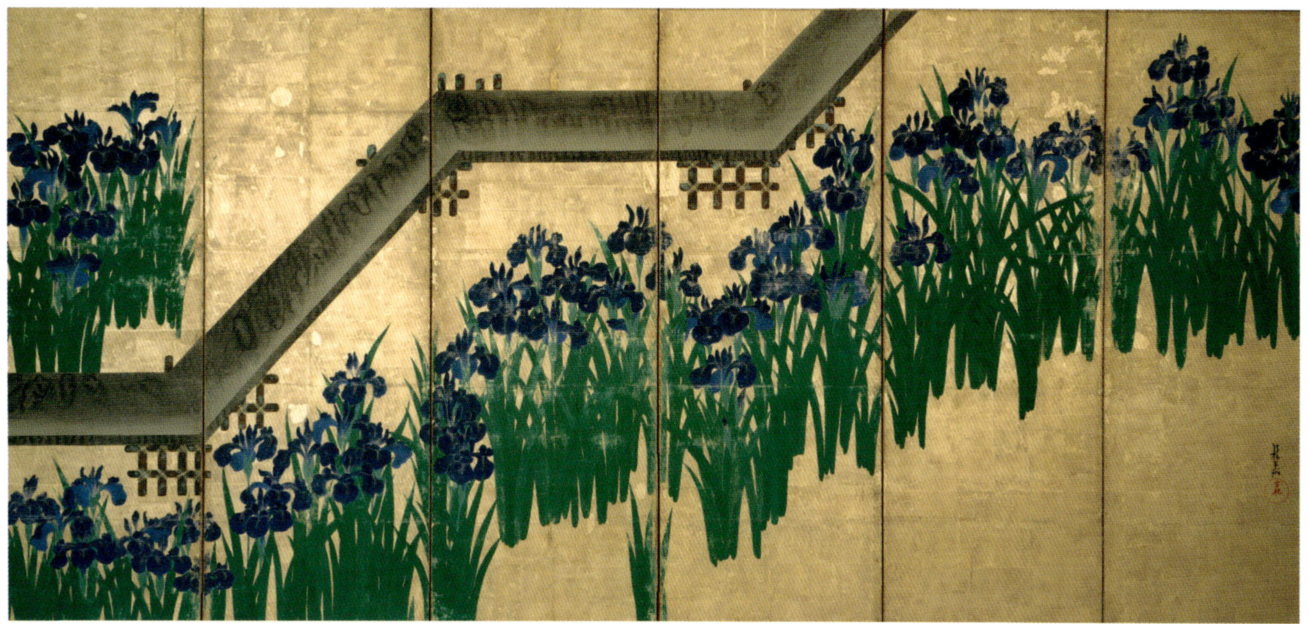

the artist's early, round Iryō seal, a reference to Sōtatsu's Inen seals. The work was painted shortly after Kōrin received the hokkyō title in 1701, yet the screens present a visual sophistication unseen in prior works. The work illustrates the high degree of artistic versatility Kōrin had achieved within a few short years.

Kōrin's choice of irises for one of his earliest screen paintings was also the overture to a lifelong devotion to the *Tales of Ise.* Beginning with *Irises,* Kōrin produced a staggering number of works related to the tales in all genres and formats of the early modern arts. Among these, the iris flower became a dominant trope and trademark for Kōrin that traversed his entire career. The most outstanding sister work—and farthest apart in time of production—of *Irises* is a pair of six-panel screens called *Irises at Yatsuhashi* (fig. 25). Separated from *Irises* by almost a decade, the *Irises at Yatsuhashi* screens depict an array of flowers with delicate blossoms in azurite blue on slender stalks in malachite green. An emphatically flat bridge in ink and faint touches of malachite crosses the vista of upright irises.

These screens bear the signatures Hokkyō Kōrin on the right one and Seisei Kōrin on the left. The latter signature, in addition to the round Masatoki (also read Hōshuku) seal impressed on both screens, suggests that Kōrin painted the work during the last five years or so of his life, after he returned to his native Kyoto from Edo around 1709.[39] The size of the early and late works creates a different first impression. The arrangement of the flowers amplifies this contrast in visual effect. In *Irises,* Kōrin concocted the floral vista to correspond with the screens' angles, a compositional feature that reveals his keen awareness of the physicality of the work. In the right screen of *Irises,* for example, the first two panels along with the fourth and sixth panels bear groups of irises that form an elongated oval shape which, by way of the screen's respective inward and outward folds, generates the appearance of gigantic, three-dimensional flowers meandering up and down. The sculptural quality thus created stands in delicate contrast to the flat nature of the flowers' overall painterly rendering. In *Irises at Yatsuhashi,* Kōrin employed the ink and malachite bridge—an equally flat object that gains three-dimensionality through the screens' folds—to generate an illusion of depth. The shadows generated by light falling onto the folds of the standing screens clad the bridge's zigzagging pattern in areas of dark and light that make the composition appear to twist backward and forward in space.

Another feature that distinguishes each work is the flowers' proportions. In keeping with the narrow rectangular panels of *Irises at Yatsuhashi,* Kōrin rendered most of the flowers in roughly the same height. In *Irises,* he distributed plants of varying sizes, allowing the viewer to experience the irises amid the marshes and from different vantage points. *Irises at Yatsuhashi,* by contrast, feels more like a panorama of flowers seen at a slight distance.

Kōrin also altered his approach to painting the flowers in *Irises at Yatsuhashi.* He replaced the plump, stylized blossoms in *Irises* with slender, wavy petals in a seeming attempt to endow the flowers with an even stronger sense of naturalism. His extant sketches of irises are closer to the flowers in *Irises at Yatsuhashi* than in *Irises,* suggesting that, after he painted the earlier screens, Kōrin may have sought to enhance the level of lifelikeness in his signature motif by studying irises in nature (fig. 26).

Although Kōrin painted *Irises* and *Irises at Yatsuhashi* roughly a decade apart, he made sure to connect the pair through compositional choices. He reemployed some of the clusters of flowers he used in the *Irises* screens in *Irises at Yatsuhashi.*[40] The areas that correspond in both screens are not exact copies; instead, they are linked through parallel shapes and arrangements. The correlation not only discloses a remarkable consistency between Kōrin's large-format iris paintings but also connects two works that are separated by a significant stretch of time.

In terms of color and materials, *Irises at Yatsuhashi* relies on *Irises* as its precedent, but its most conspicuous difference is the prominently placed abstract bridge. The bridge traverses the screens' composition and connects both works, reaching from the upper right screen to just beyond the center of the left screen. Also, in *Irises at Yatsuhashi* Kōrin painted his composition of flowers in mineral pigment onto a shell-white ground. In contrast, the azurite and malachite of *Irises* was applied directly onto the paper ground.[41] Adding

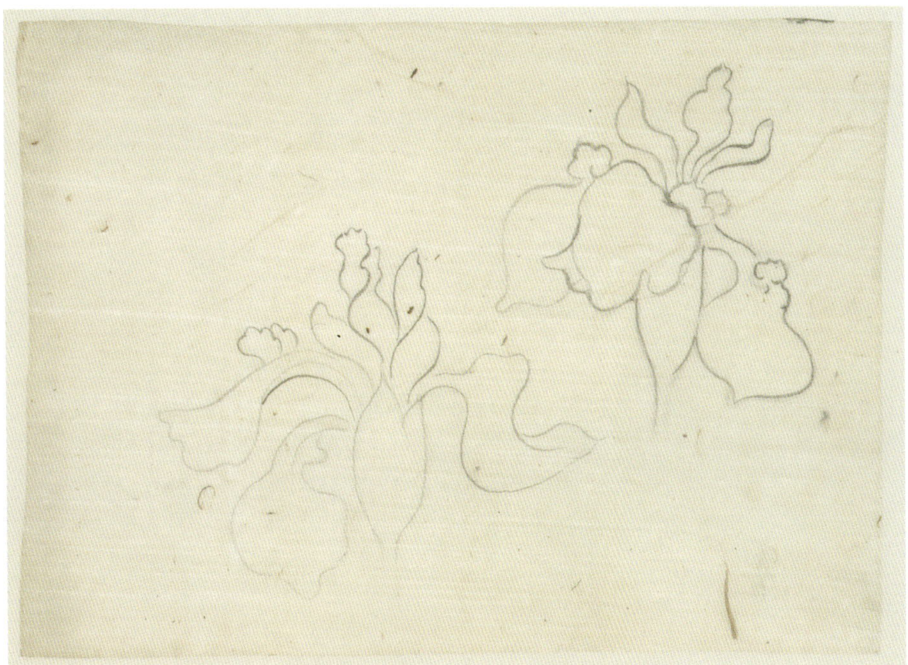

FIGURE 26
Ogata Kōrin, *Sketches of Irises,* late 17th or early 18th century. Ink on paper, Konishi Family Archive, Kyoto National Museum.

white as a base layer for mineral pigments was an accepted practice in early modern Japanese painting. For example, the painter Tosa Mitsuoki (1617–1691) writes in his *Great Account of Painting Methods in the Realm* (*Honchō gahō taiden*) that blending shell-white with azurite blue is adequate for creating a lighter hue.[42] The stalks in malachite green, however, lack a shell-white foundation. Kōrin seems to have used the same technique for the bridge, where shell-white may have formed a base for the ink. Also, this ground layer for the flowers probably provided traction for the azurite blue. Kōrin applied the blue in visibly thinner—hence, more economical—layers than in *Irises,* even though it resulted in a similarly dark hue. The corresponding colors exemplify how *Irises* served as a chromatic and conceptual template for *Irises at Yatsuhashi*.

The painting process in both works differs in other ways as well. Kōrin drew the composition of *Irises* onto the paper surface of the screens, applying gold leaf around the main composition of the flowers. In *Irises at Yatsuhashi* he painted directly onto the ground of gilded paper. Here, the gold covers the entire surface of the pair of screens. The approach used to paint *Irises* is singular among Kōrin's works and makes the screens an anomaly within his oeuvre. This special feature could also have resulted from the fact that the screens were Kōrin's first expensive commission. In initially sketching the composition on an inexpensive ground, he might have wished to leave room for errors. Patrons could have been reluctant to supply him with a fully gilded screen, a challenge

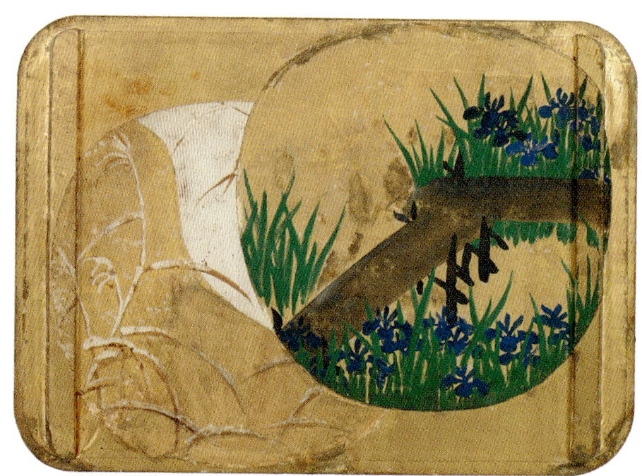

FIGURE 27
Ogata Kōrin, *Fans with Designs of Irises at Yatsuhashi and Reeds in Winter* (detail, box with pasted fans), late 17th or early 18th century. Gilded wooden box with fans; ink and color on gold. Yamato Bunkakan, Nara.

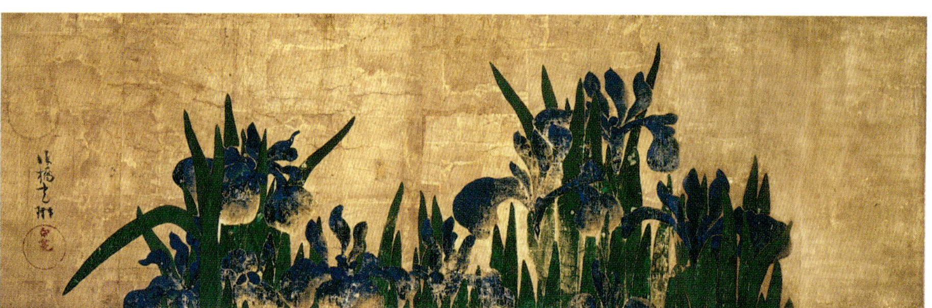

FIGURE 28
Ogata Kōrin, *Irises,* early 18th century. Hanging scroll; ink and color on gilded paper. Osaka City Museum of Art.

he did not face with later commissions, such as *Irises at Yatsuhashi,* when he was more established. Both of Kōrin's earliest screen paintings—*Twelve Months* and a pair of six-panel screens with autumnal plants—were executed on a paper ground.[43] Thus, the technique used in *Irises* is reminiscent of this early trait. Scientific analysis has revealed that a second late work, the screens *Red and White Plum Blossoms,* which are thought to postdate *Irises at Yatsuhashi* by a few years, were also painted directly onto the gilded ground. Kōrin apparently discarded the technique used in *Irises* in his late oeuvre.[44]

Irises represented a new stage in Kōrin's artistic career, and the painted screens formed the threshold to an entire category among the artist's work. They also established the iris as one of Kōrin's most frequently painted subjects (figs. 27, 28). The screens formed the foundation for later paintings such as *Irises at Yatsuhashi,* produced when Kōrin was a prominent painter with an atelier. The evolution from *Irises* to *Irises at Yatsuhashi* reflects more than Kōrin's development as a painter. The screens also embody traces of Kōrin's early education and the cultural formation that came along with it.

PAINTING THE STAGE

In their reduction of form and cultural suggestiveness, *Irises* and *Irises at Yatsuhashi* are groundbreaking works. For those reasons alone, they merit an attempt at tying them into Kōrin's biography. Kōrin likely arrived at the two pairs of screens not in an ad hoc decision but through a discerning process in which he drew from a combination of artistic precedents, such as Sōtatsu, and cultural contexts that shaped his thinking.

Kōrin had a penchant for performance, which is manifest in his skill in otogi and his fervent study of the Noh theater during his teens and after. Between 1675 and 1701, Kōrin watched or partook in twenty-four recorded Noh performances.[45] Continuing his perennial engagement with theater, from 1701 to 1704, Kōrin painted a number of works with immediate connections to Noh, attesting to his artistic engagement with drama at the time that he made *Irises.* For example, connections to Noh have been identified for works like *Cormorant Fisher* and *Hakurakuten,* which both refer directly to specific plays (figs. 29, 30).[46] During his late teens, Kōrin received extensive training in Noh, as evidenced by his many notes on specific plays, costumes, and evocative moods. Knowledge of such intricate aspects showcases Kōrin's deep appreciation and advanced level in this medieval form of Japanese theater. During the first half of his life, Kōrin was so focused on learning and engaging in the arts of performance that it is easy to imagine how Noh and otogi left traces within his approach to painting. We cannot know for sure if Noh was the source for Kōrin's iris paintings, but his devotion to the theater adds an intriguing layer that connects this substantial portion of his artistic output with his education and interests. Thereby, Kōrin's works provide a window onto the cultural conditioning that affected members of his class, an education that he may have channeled into serving the wider art market of his day.

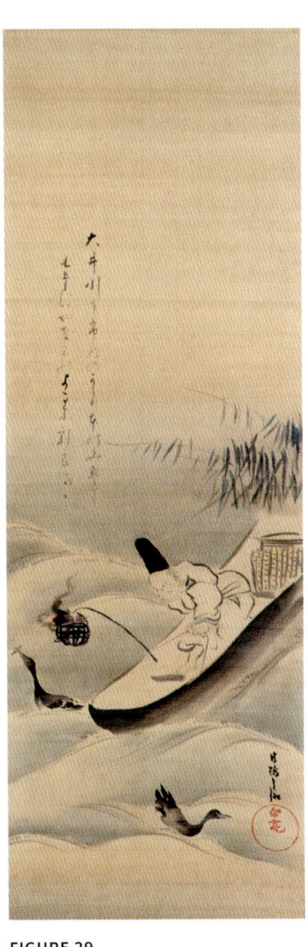

FIGURE 29
Ogata Kōrin, *Cormorant Fisher,* early 18th century. Hanging scroll; ink, color and gold on paper. Seikadō Bunko Art Museum Image Archives / DNPartcom.

Highly educated from a young age, erudite painters like Kōrin produced their works within a shared framework of personal knowledge and cultural expectations, whose levels of accessibility varied with each audience. As a result, works of art like *Irises* and *Irises at Yatsuhashi* might consist of different strata of conspicuous and concealed meaning. One of the most overt associations of the pairs of screens lies in their depiction of a specific literary site (*meisho*): the irises along the eight-plank bridge in the eastern province of Mikawa. The *Tales of Ise* and other classical narratives established poetic locales that existed largely in the mind and acted as fictional stimuli for imagination. Already by the early eleventh century, a young lady known only as Sarashina wrote of her dismay at seeing neither the eight-plank bridge nor the irises praised in the *Tales of Ise* when she passed by the site in Musashino: "Only the place-name Yatsuhashi (eight-plank bridge) remains; there is not the merest

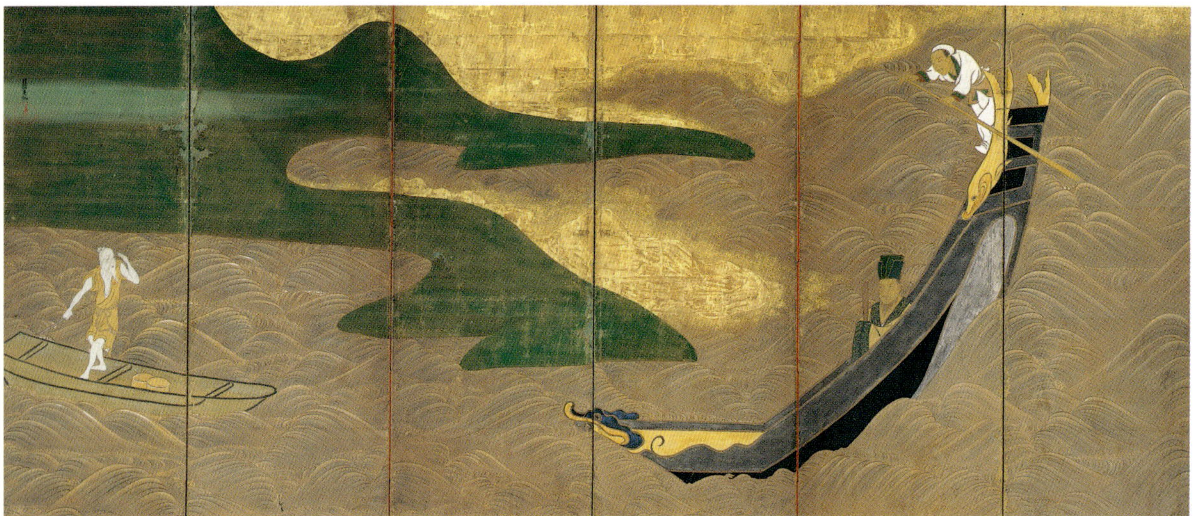

FIGURE 30
Ogata Kōrin, *Hakurakuten,* early 18th century. Six-panel folding screen; ink, color, and gold on paper. Nezu Museum, Tokyo.

remnant of any bridges, and nothing else to see, either."[47] Sarashina's diary is arguably the first recorded instance of the evanescence of famous sites in classical tales. By medieval times, and especially during the early modern period, the *Tales of Ise* came to represent a narrative frozen in time whose famous sites existed only in the poetic fancy of literature, painting, and theater. Pictorial renderings, including Kōrin's extensive corpus of *Tales of Ise*–related works, are visual interpretations of literary sites whose cultural currency was built on artistic invention. Pictures like *Irises* and *Irises at Yatsuhashi* acted as substitutes for the actual locales; for a viewer, they gave shape to places that did not exist and enacted events that likely had never taken place in that way. These places lived in the realm of imagination and became manifest only through literary and pictorial creative power. The Noh theater, which drew heavily from classical literature, served an extended similar role of giving shape to fictional places and events. The same is true for Noh plays focusing on the *Tales of Ise.*

One such play is *Kakitsubata,* literally "irises," which takes Ariwara Narihira's encounter with the eight-plank bridge and irises as its theme. Probably written by the late medieval playwright Konparu Zenchiku (1405–before 1471), the play tells of a priest encountering a young woman who identifies herself as the spirit of the irises, tied to this earth by her deep longing for a long-lost love, Narihira. Ultimately, by divine intervention, the spirit sheds herself of this passion and achieves enlightenment.[48] The narrative is a complex weave of literary and religious references. At the immediate center, however, stands the imagined vista of the iris flowers that the play tirelessly emphasizes throughout the plot and which form the subject of Kōrin's *Irises* and *Irises at Yatsuhashi.*

A similar thematic overlap between picture and Noh play occurs in other works by Kōrin, such as the *Hakurakuten* screens, a subject he also rendered as a fan painting. The play recounts the fictional visit of the famous Chinese poet Bai Juyi (772–846) to Japan in order to test the poetic ability of the Japanese. Setting out by boat from China and vowing to challenge the first Japanese he encounters in a match of poetry, Bai Juyi unwittingly confronts the Sumiyoshi Deity (*Sumiyoshi Myōjin*), the god of poetry, who hurries to the rescue of the Japanese and defeats the Chinese poet. Kōrin's two screens, which have identical compositions, depict the Sumiyoshi Deity floating on a raft offshore with Bai Juyi heading toward him, one of the key moments in the play.

Rather than focusing the plot on a human protagonist, *Kakitsubata,* with which Kōrin was no doubt familiar, speaks of the singularity of the iris blossoms whose uncanny color sets them apart from other plants.

> Naturally, the flowers that make this place famous
> are dyed purple one shade deeper
> than ordinary flowers, to which
> they must not be compared;
> these *kakitsubata* alone deserve
> your special attention,
> as you would know if you were a
> traveler of any sensitivity![49]

In spite of the religiosity that permeates *Kakitsubata* and is common in many other Noh plays, *Kakitsubata*'s plot zeroes in on the iris flower and effectively makes its rich hue the dramatis persona. In the same way, *Irises* and *Irises at Yatsuhashi* take as their core theme the iris flower, even though it is actually a small detail within the narrative of the ninth chapter of the *Tales of Ise.* The play *Kakitsubata*'s emphasis on the same part of the narrative suggests at least a tentative connection. What is more, a set of dishes by Kenzan weave a more direct thread between the play *Kakitsubata* and the paintings *Irises* and *Irises at Yatsuhashi* (fig. 31).

Each dish in the early eighteenth-century set depicts Noh theater plays on the front with a key quotation from each libretto on the verso. The image echoes the compositional and stylistic choices of *Irises* and, even more, of *Irises at Yatsuhashi.* The protagonist of the *Tales of Ise* is deleted and the focus is on the irises and eight-plank bridge alone. The quotation from *Kakitsubata* on the back makes clear how Kenzan, who collaborated with Kōrin during different stages of their careers, associated the iconography of the painting with the Noh play. The dish records a key passage from the libretto that speaks of the bond between two people—*yukari*—symbolized by the dark purple color of the fragrant iris flower.[50] "Here, the famous eight-plank bridge and the fragrant iris along the marsh edge, associating their deep purple with his love (*yukari*), 'How is she?'

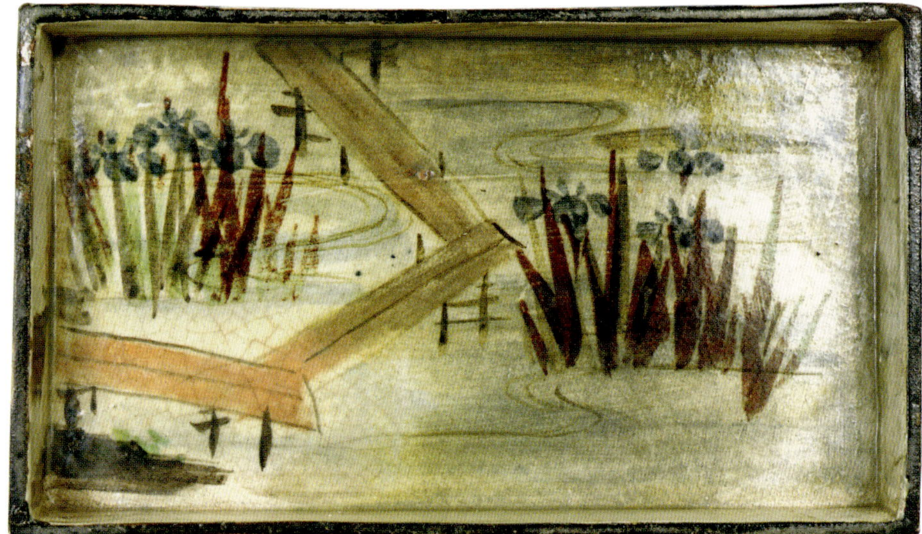

FIGURE 31
Ogata Kenzan, *Rectangular Dish with Design of the Noh Play "Kakitsubata"* (from a set of ten), early 18th century. Buff clay with pigment under transparent lead glaze. Idemitsu Museum of Arts, Tokyo.

wondered the man from the capital."[51] The piece is the only example in Kenzan's set of ten Noh dishes that mentions a specific color. No other quotations from Noh plays on the remaining dishes contain a similar chromatic specificity. This aspect highlights the *Kakitsubata* dish's special connection between the deep color of the irises sung in the Noh play and their depiction in the painting on the front and, by extension, in Kōrin's *Irises* and *Irises at Yatsuhashi,* whose unusually rich use of azurite creates an emphatically dark hue. Indeed, the picture on the dish is similar in that the potter sought to create a dark blue tone in an approximation of the flowers' purple discussed in the play.

The correlations among Kenzan's dish, the play *Kakitsubata,* and Kōrin's screens lead to tempting speculations about a potential connection between painting and performance. Although such a link can find definitive proof only in documentary evidence, Kōrin's penchant for Noh and his profound exposure to performance during his formative years suggest at least some impact on his painting practice. Kōrin's reinvention of the eight-plank bridge and irises overlaps with Kenzan's illustration of the play *Kakitsubata* and puts the two in relation with each other.

In this way, the screen paintings give shape to the complex web of cultural associations that formed the backdrop of Kōrin's art-making. In addition to Kōrin's personal interests and cultural conditioning, the screens provide further evidence of his expanding network of patrons and his move away from the aristocratic sponsorship of his early years to a new clientele in Edo.

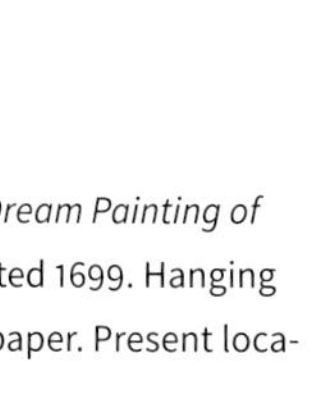

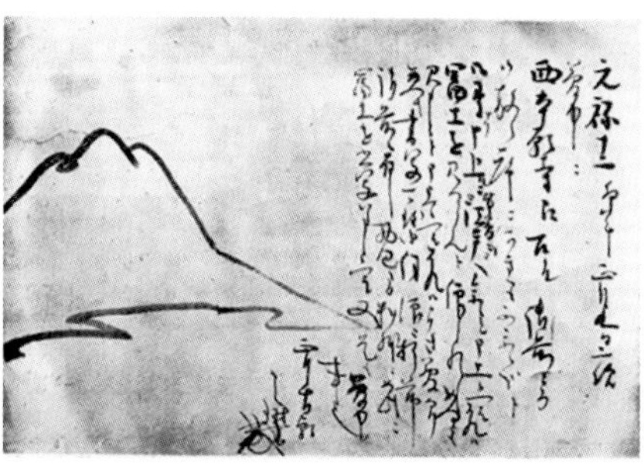

FIGURE 32
Ogata Kōrin, *Dream Painting of Mount Fuji,* dated 1699. Hanging scroll; ink on paper. Present location unknown.

PROVENANCE

Reconstructing the provenance of *Irises* and *Irises at Yatsuhashi* offers a glimpse at the human dimension of artistic patronage during Kōrin's time and the afterlife of his paintings. Auction records indicate the *Irises* screens were at the Kyoto temple Nishi Honganji, a centuries-old patron of the arts and a center for Noh performances, during the early twentieth century.[52] The American art historian Ernest Fenollosa (1853–1908) mentions that the temple owned *Irises* as early as 1882.[53] Although the early modern art market was free-flowing and ownership of works oscillated among patrons, temples often guarded their possessions closely. Due to the general prosperity of Nishi Honganji throughout the early modern period and the temple's close ties to Kōrin, scholars now speculate that *Irises* was commissioned by the institution's abbacy.[54]

Kōrin was friends with Jakunyo, the aristocratic head of the temple, and Jūnyo, his pupil, prime acolyte, future successor, and the younger brother of Tsunahira. He had met the two priests through the Noh theater a few years before he painted *Irises.* The Nijō family journal records that in 1694, "Ogata Kōrin came to express his gratitude [to Nijō Tsunahira] for taking him to view Noh together yesterday at Nishi Honganji."[55] From 1695 to 1700, Kōrin associated frequently with Tsunahira, the period immediately before he painted *Irises.* Their close relationship is evident in their visit to Nishi Honganji, a considerable honor for the commoner Kōrin, who was in debilitating financial trouble at the time.

Kōrin's friendship with Jakunyo and Jūnyo blossomed. Their relationship is best illustrated by a strange, now lost painting done in 1699, in which Kōrin recorded a dream of Mount Fuji (fig. 32). Struck with the notion that this vision was an omen for the journey to Edo that his friend Jūnyo planned to undertake a month later, Kōrin hastened to the temple to report the dream to Jakunyo. Also in the dream, the abbot advised Kōrin to paint the mountain, which he did. In the morning, the artist, now awake, grabbed brush and paper and recorded his dream.[56] The painting is a personal manifesto to the friendship among

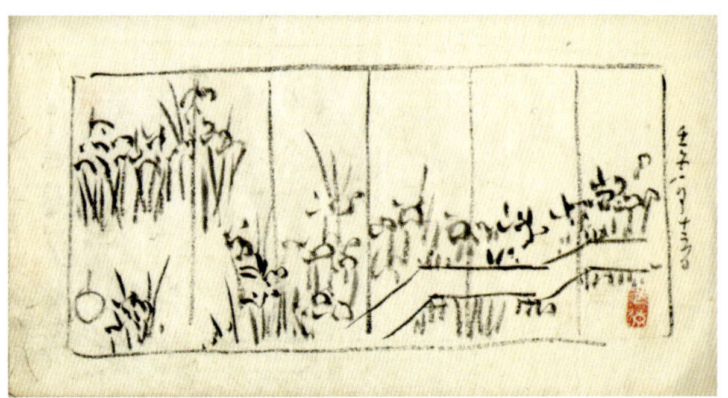
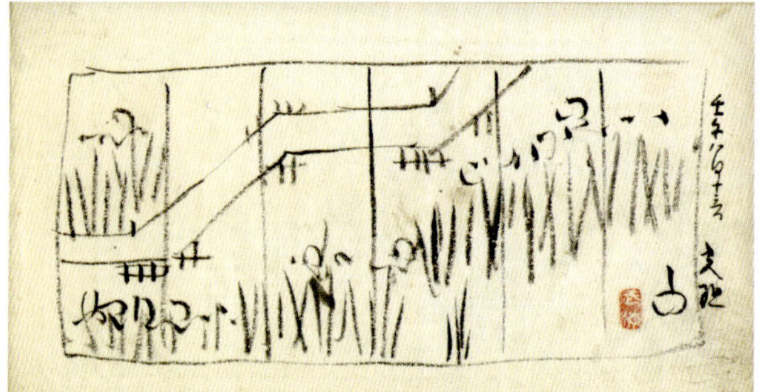

FIGURE 33
Kita Busei, *Sketch of a Version of Irises at Yatsuhashi,* early 19th century. Paper-bound book; ink on paper. Tokyo National Research Institute for Cultural Properties.

Kōrin, Jakunyo, and Jūnyo, and in light of the timing of Jūnyo's journey to Edo, *Irises* may well have symbolized travel to the eastern regions—the site of the irises and the eight-plank bridge from the *Tales of Ise.*

Irises likely exemplifies the aristocratic sponsorship and court circles that shaped Kōrin's early years as a painter. It is not too far-fetched to assume that *Irises* could have resulted from Kōrin's close association with Nijō Tsunahira and his brother Jūnyo at Nishi Honganji. Temples were grand sponsors of the arts, and large complexes like Nishi Honganji required numerous paintings to decorate their many buildings and subsidiary temples. *Irises* was not the only painting of that subject at the temple. An auction catalogue from 1913 records a single six-panel screen of irises growing along a stylized stream as one part of a pair of paintings with birds and flowers of the four seasons.[57] At different auctions held in 1917, the temple sold several other paintings and lacquer works attributed to Kōrin, including a painting of geese and one of Jurōjin.[58] The number of works linked to Kōrin's name attests both to the presence of his works at Nishi Honganji and the enthusiasm for his art among modern collectors.

Whereas *Irises* was likely made under aristocratic auspices during the first half of Kōrin's career, *Irises at Yatsuhashi* embodies features of his late patronage. Though the exact provenance of the screens is obscure, they may be linked to the Fuyuki family, a dynasty of wealthy lumber merchants based in Edo. The clan is the only known premodern private owner of an iris painting by Kōrin. In 1822 the painter Kita Busei (1776–1857) sketched two pairs of screens by Kōrin in his study book: one couples Mount Fuji with a vista of pine islands, and the other shows irises and a zigzagging bridge that closely resembles *Irises at Yatsuhashi* (fig. 33). Busei's notes record that he sketched both works on the same day, an indication that they were owned by the same collector in Edo. Two pairs of screens with Mount Fuji and pine islands and irises and a bridge were

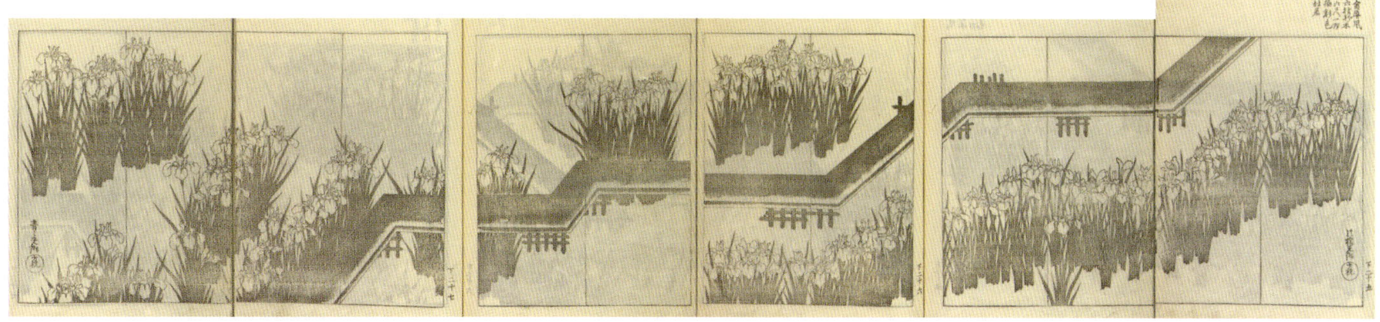

FIGURE 34
Sakai Hōitsu, *One Hundred Pictures by Kōrin* (*Kōrin hyakuzu*), 2nd ed., vol. 2, 1826. Woodblock-printed book; ink on paper. Freer Gallery of Art, Smithsonian Institution, Washington, D.C.: Purchase, The Gerhard Pulverer Collection—Charles Lang Freer Endowment, Friends of the Freer and Sackler Galleries and the Harold P. Stern Memorial fund in appreciation of Jeffrey P. Cunard and his exemplary service to the Galleries as chair of the Board of Trustees (2003–2007), FSC-GR-780.476.1–2.

also reproduced in Sakai Hōitsu's second edition of *One Hundred Pictures by Kōrin* (*Kōrin hyakuzu*), published in 1826 (fig. 34). As Hōitsu's homage to Kōrin's legacy, the publication relied on thorough research into the painter's life and work.[59] While researching *One Hundred Pictures by Kōrin,* Hōitsu's pupil Suzuki Kiitsu (1796–1858) mentions in an undated letter seeing a pair of screens, depicting Mount Fuji and islands, that were owned by the Fuyuki.[60] Since the pairs appear together in both painters' reproductions, it seems that the Fuyuki also owned the iris screens seen by Busei and Hōitsu.

Busei's sketches bear strong similarities with the composition of Kōrin's *Irises at Yatsuhashi,* insinuating that both Busei and Hōitsu probably had access to those screens and not some different, now lost example.[61] What is more, the early nineteenth-century *Record of Glancing at the Past* (*Kaganroku*), written by Kitamura Nobuyo (1784–1856), includes sketches of three iris flowers alongside copies of Kōrin's signatures "Hokkyō Kōrin" and "Seisei Kōrin," both of which appear in a similar way in *Irises at Yatsuhashi* (figs. 35, 36).[62] Nobuyo labels them as "signatures of the Yatsuhashi screens owned by the Fuyuki." In light of these Edo connections, Kōrin's *Irises at Yatsuhashi* was apparently owned by the Fuyuki family at least by the early nineteenth century. Later, however, the screens changed ownership. An 1880 exhibition catalogue records the screens as being in the possession of Matsudaira Naritami (1814–1891), formerly the lord of Tsuyama Domain. They seem to have remained with the erstwhile daimyo until 1919.[63]

Among all this evidence of the pair's nineteenth-century provenance, the question remains whether Kōrin painted the screens for the Fuyuki family in the first place. Though his surviving correspondence does not mention any patrons among Edo's bourgeoisie, it has been suggested that Kōrin received early training in the tea ceremony together with a certain Fuyuki Goroemon, who may have been Fuyuki Masachika (d. 1703), the clan's head at the time.[64] Although definite proof of their connection has yet to be found, the tea classes,

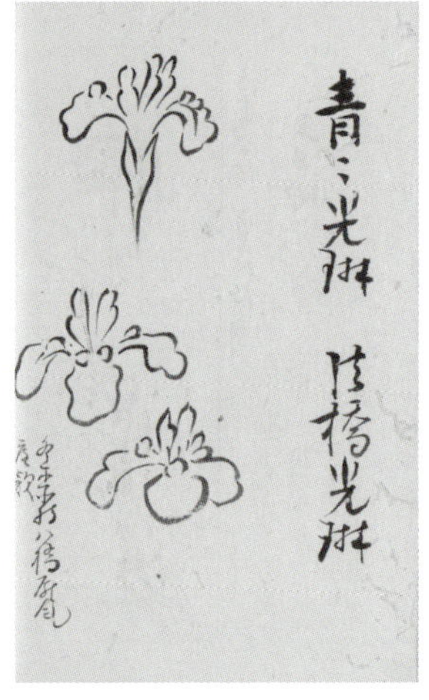

FIGURE 35
Kitamura Nobuyo, *Record of Glancing at the Past* (*Kaganroku*), vol. 3 (detail), early 19th century. Paper-bound book; ink on paper. National Diet Library Digital Collections, Tokyo.

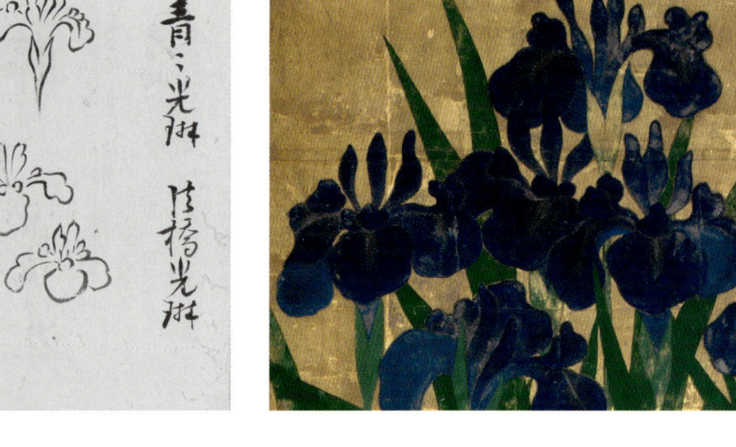

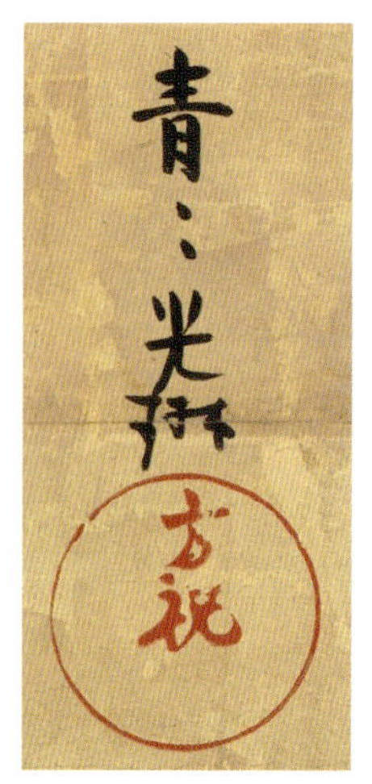

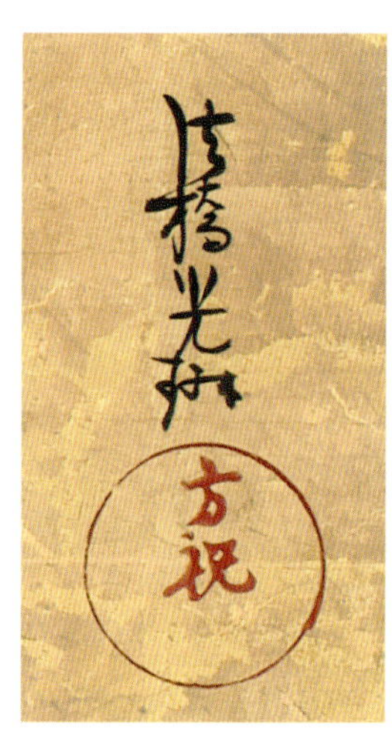

FIGURE 36 Three details, fig. 25.

supposedly conducted by the fifth head of the Omotesenke lineage, Zuiryūsai Sōsa (1650–1691), could have established an early connection between the painter and the Fuyuki. The chronicle *Activities of the Hon'ami Clan* contains a detailed passage on the Fuyuki with special emphasis on their collecting activities.[65] Perhaps the Hon'ami and the Fuyuki knew each other quite early, even before Kōrin's time.

Hon'ami Kōetsu's grandson Kōho (1602–1682) was acquainted with Kōshin Sōsa (1613–1671), the fourth-generation head of the Omotesenke. Kōho attended a gathering specially held for him by Kōshin in 1640.[66] As we have seen earlier, the Ogata also owned a house at Takagamine, the colony founded by Kōetsu and where Kōho and his descendants lived until the early 1700s. Through this real estate connection alone, there remains little doubt that up to their teenage years the Ogata sons could have been in frequent contact with Kōho, who was the head of the Hon'ami clan. The Hon'ami might have helped facilitate an early connection between Kōrin and the Fuyuki through their shared appreciation for the tea ceremony. During and after his activities in Edo, Kōrin could have taken advantage of this relationship to gain the Fuyuki's patronage.

Although Kōrin's works entered the collection of the Edo-based Fuyuki, the clan initially resided in Kyoto. During the Genroku era (1688–1704), Masachika frequently stayed in Kyoto for extended periods of time, and he later remained there until his death. In fact, he was the last Fuyuki family member to be buried in Kyoto. After his death, the family fully relocated to Edo, the site of the core of their business.[67] Masachika's presence in Kyoto at the time of Kōrin's early activities as a painter there could have led to connections with the Fuyuki family before the artist's work in Edo. Since Kōrin made *Irises at Yatsuhashi* after he had returned to Kyoto around 1709, he could have sent the painting via sea or land to Edo, something he did with a number of commissions during his final years. Such connections between Kōrin and the Fuyuki make their patronage of works like *Irises at Yatsuhashi* at least not unlikely.

❖ ❖ ❖

Kōrin's numerous iris paintings and their characteristic appearance, as seen in the screens *Irises* and *Irises at Yatsuhashi,* are illustrative of his education, web of personal connections, and artistic inspirations. The layered provenance of the screens also highlights the complex afterlives of paintings and how they shaped the reception of an artist. *Sōgi, Irises,* and eventually *Irises at Yatsuhashi* formed the foundations for Kōrin's enduring fame, and they established the templates by which later artists absorbed Kōrin's style. He created *Sōgi* and *Irises* in his early forties, less than a decade after he decided to become an artist. The paintings and their reincarnations during Kōrin's career and in the oeuvre of later admirers shaped the destiny of his career and reception. Aside from his mastery of composition and brushwork, the repetition he employed in his artistry helped to install his approach to painting among a growing circle of wealthy patrons and into posterity, creating a trademark that outlived Kōrin for centuries.

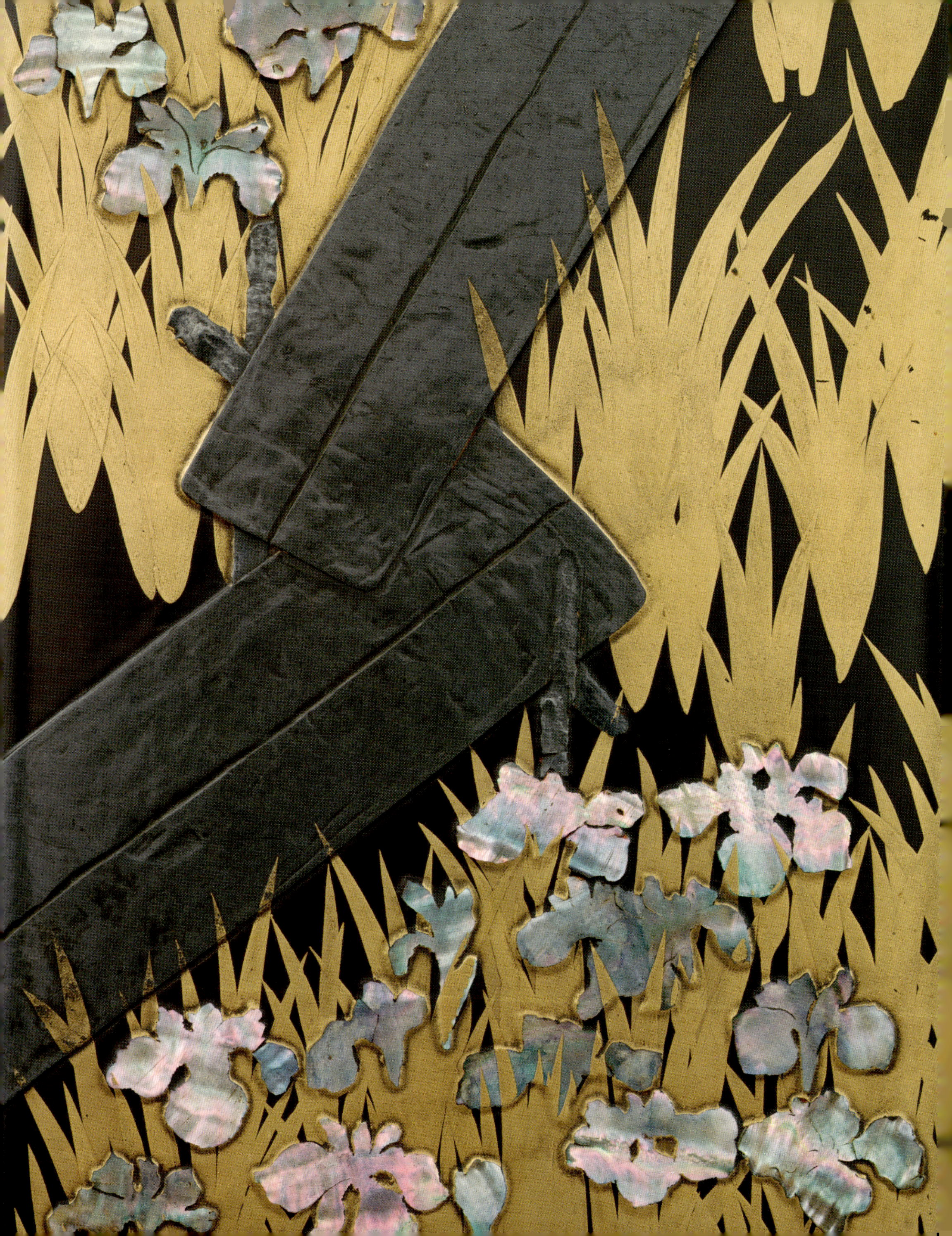

3 Art and Family

Kōrin's Lacquer Works and Hon'ami Kōetsu

> From far and wide one hears that Kōrin painted with an admirably upright brush. He reflects the inner spirit of the people in his time; both old and young cherished him. When contemplating the painted flowers by him, they seem just as if one gazed at a real flower arrangement. One can say, [his paintings capture] the chromatic vibrancy of flowers. Through his swift, precise brush they seem as if sprinkled with rainfall.
>
> —Ōoka Shunboku, *Hand Mirror of Painting* (*Ehon tekagami*), 1720

Kōrin began creating lacquer works when he took his first steps as an artist in the 1690s. From the beginning, Kōrin intended to cater to diverse tastes and needs. Within this ambition, lacquer remained an important part of his artistic identity. His pieces reached such iconic status and were copied so frequently that Kōrin's initial reception in the West was above all through lacquer.[1] Kōrin's designs in that medium come in a variety of shapes and subjects, but as in his paintings, the most recognizable theme is flowers. Kōrin's *suzuribako*—a box used to store implements for writing—with a design of hollyhocks against a stylized stream encapsulates his approach to lacquer (fig. 37). Large flowers, variously done in shining mother-of-pearl and dark lead, dominate the upper surface of the lid and imbue the work with a sense of visual weight. The feeling of heaviness, however, is lightened by a gently flowing creek rendered in gilded lacquer. Produced by mixing gold dust with lacquer sap, the lines were applied directly onto the smooth, expertly polished black surface of the box. Such a combination of sumptuousness and elegance is characteristic of many such pieces by Kōrin.

Handling the toxic juice of lacquer trees, mixing pigment into that fluid, applying the lacquer layer upon layer, and polishing the work to a lustrous sheen—all these techniques required extensive skills that Kōrin did not possess.[2] Thus, even though lacquer represents a core aspect of Kōrin's artistry, a distinguishing factor of these works is that he likely did not make them

Detail of fig. 57

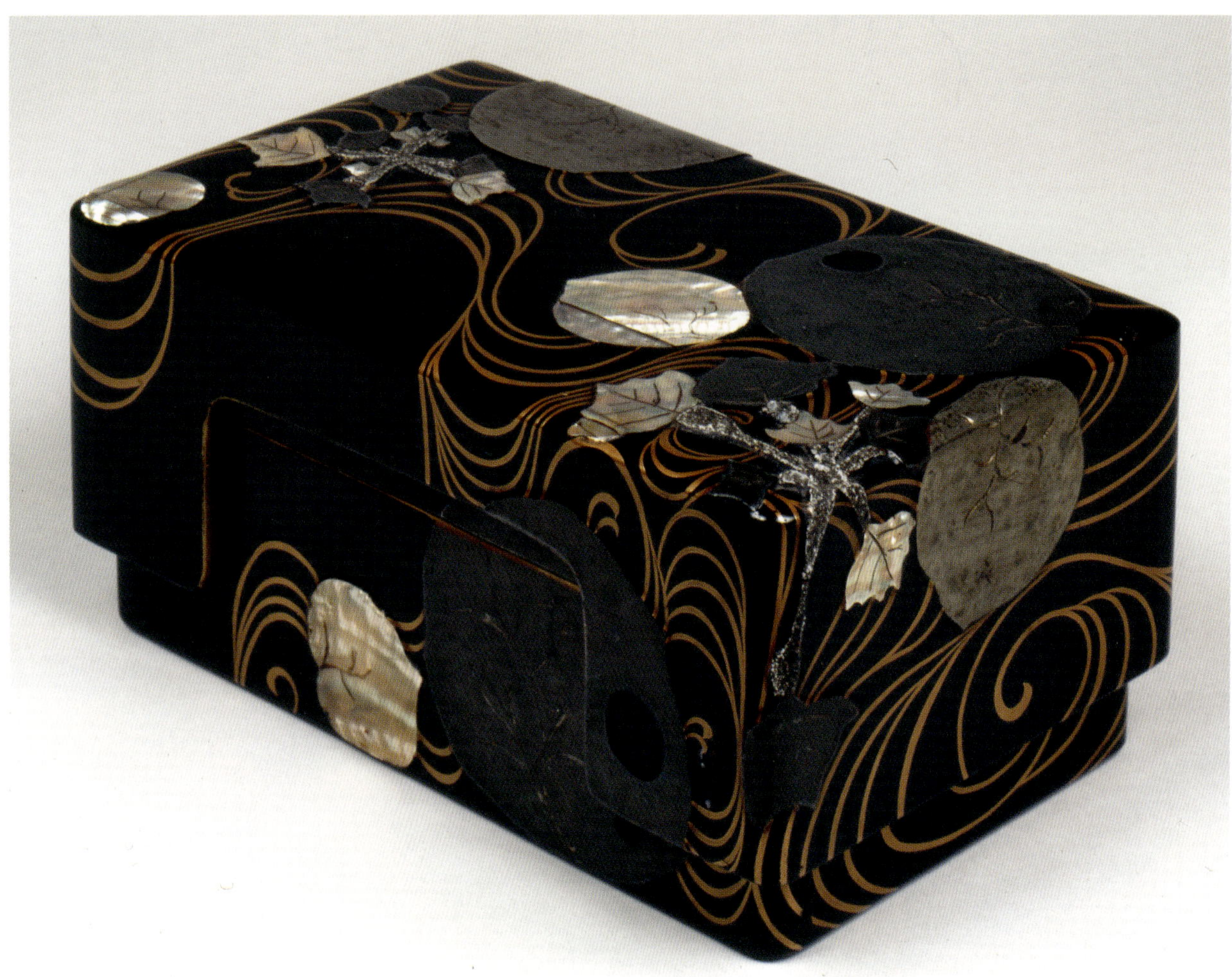

FIGURE 37
Ogata Kōrin, *Suzuribako with Design of Hollyhocks,* early 18th century. Lacquer on wood with gold, lead, and mother-of-pearl. MOA Museum of Art, Atami.

himself. Instead, he solicited the help of specialized craftsmen who followed his painted designs and specifications conveyed in person, through sketches, and in writing. As such, Kōrin's lacquer works embody the complex levels of labor division in art production during the early modern period.

Kōrin's artistic practice was not unique, and it shows how an artist's direct agency was not necessarily required to produce an original work of art. As Kōrin forayed into lacquer and perfected his artistic identity, nobody offered a more important source of inspiration than his great-granduncle Hon'ami Kōetsu. Kōrin's turn to Kōetsu as an artistic and cultural reference is a case in point for the manner in which Kōrin hand-picked elements of his own environment and digested them into his art. To understand Kōrin's self-image as an artist, it is crucial to consider his bond to Kōetsu: the early seventeenth-century ancestor provided a posthumous role model for Kōrin to fashion his identity and for outsourcing the production of lacquer objects, two key components of Kōrin's practice. Kōetsu's example taught Kōrin that recognizable stylistic features in his artworks and signature, along with his close involvement in planning and designing the pieces, were sufficient to tie them to his name. Through a combination of written documents, artworks, and the broader context of lacquer production in Kōrin's time, this chapter draws a picture of his motivations, modes of making, and avenues of inspiration that led him to pursue lacquer production, concoct an expedient identity, and create works that relied on his ideas rather than his direct touch.

BONDS OF KINSHIP

During the early 1690s Kōrin changed his given name, Ichinojō, and adopted the name by which he is known today. In doing so, he embarked on the path of reconfiguring his identity into that of a full-fledged artist. In premodern Japan, a change of name often accompanied a personal or professional juncture, and it is possible that his restyling marks the threshold when Kōrin resolved to make the arts his main vocation. He initially adopted the first character for *Kō*rin around 1689 in veneration of his father, who had died two years earlier and had used the pseudonym *Kō*sai. In 1692, however, at a time of increasing financial hardships and the ensuing pressure to earn a living, Kōrin shunned his earlier homage to his father and adopted a new set of Chinese characters for his nom de plume. This step illustrates Kōrin's growing ambition to form a distinctive self-image that was removed from the pedigree of his father and the family business. It shifted his identity from an upper-class gentleman-amateur like his father to that of an independent artist.

In his new selection of idioms, Kōrin cast an eye on his great-granduncle Hon'ami Kōetsu. Kōetsu was born in 1558 into a family of sword polishers, a much-venerated profession, particularly in the mid-sixteenth century when civil war required arms and different factions of the military elite vied for dominance over the realm. Swords, seen as both weapons of choice and symbols of status, required elaborate techniques to make and maintain them. Kōetsu carried on the family trade in peacetime, but his artistic prowess and extensive personal network led him to branch out into areas as diverse as calligraphy, publishing, lacquer, and pottery.[3] Kōrin took the *kō* character, meaning "radiant," from Kōetsu's name and combined it with the character *rin* for "jewel," the name by which he is known to this day. The idiom *kō* alluded not only to Kōetsu but also to the entire male lineage of the Hon'ami. Kōetsu used it first in his name, as did his son and grandsons and later male descendants of the family. This practice was common also among lineages of professional painters. For example, a number of students of the seventeenth-century Kano Tan'yū, whose personal name was Morinobu, adopted the first character, *mori,* for their own names, such as in the case of the painter Kusumi Morikage (circa 1620–circa 1690). This practice was intended to highlight one's affiliation to a distinguished artistic ancestry, a practice that was both filial and self-serving in that it promoted the talents of the bearer of such a name. Kōrin's decision followed the same intention. As a result, Kōrin's homage to Kōetsu positioned him as a de facto continuation of his great-granduncle's artistic legacy and family lineage.

The change of characters to write the name Kōrin marked a crucial development in his self-fashioning and self-perception: Kōrin was no longer a dilettante but sought to portray himself as a professional artist. In light of a pseudonym's power as a defining feature of an artist's identity, careful rumination preceded Kōrin's new choice of characters for writing his name. One undated piece of paper records the divination of a variety of idioms for "Kōrin," perhaps in an attempt to find a suitable pseudonym.[4] Still, Kōrin never used any of those alternate spellings, a decision reinforced by a favorable divination of the "radiant jewel" characters. In 1692 Kōrin asked the astrologer Nakane Genkei (1662–1733) to prognosticate the fortunes of his new name.[5] The artist sought celestial blessing at other turning points in his life, underlining the importance of the early 1690s in the formation of Kōrin's self-image. Genkei's positive prognostication helped establish one of the most recognizable names in Japan's early modern art world, a name with an unmistakable link to Kōetsu. Kōrin had definitively tied himself to Kōetsu's exalted heritage, and this surely boosted Kōrin's résumé.

As Kōrin attempted to gain a footing in the art world, Kōetsu provided him with something that his Ogata ancestors—merchants who only occasionally forayed into the arts—could not: an artistic pedigree. Kōetsu was a leading cultural figure of early seventeenth-century Japan, and his name resonated among the upper classes of Kōrin's time and beyond. Aware of Kōetsu's prominent standing, Kōrin sought to appropriate it when he was busy crafting his persona as an artist. In addition to providing cultural leverage, Kōetsu was family—a fact that mattered in the kinship-oriented society of early modern Japan. Kōetsu's elder sister had married Kōrin's great-grandfather, thus making the early seventeenth-century master a part of Kōrin's family tree. This genealogical connection gave Kōrin an indisputable justification for adopting a part of Kōetsu's name.

Kōrin was not part of a professional atelier, such as the Kano, which created allegiance and aesthetic lineage by bestowing a character of the teacher's name on its pupils. Yet Kōrin's reference to Kōetsu's name signified the same claim to artistic successorship. By virtue of his name alone, Kōrin asserted fealty to a man he had never met but who was a part of his ancestral pedigree and the source of his aesthetic inspiration. In this way, the change of Kōrin's pseudonym illustrates a conscious move to seize on Kōetsu's sway more than half a century after his death.

CALLIGRAPHIC CONNECTIONS

The Hon'ami remained a presence in the lives of the Ogata family for decades after the death of Kōetsu in 1637. During Kōrin's financial troubles of the 1690s—when he changed his name—his brother Kenzan solicited advice from Takagamine. The Ogata had a residence at this religious-artistic colony, which Kōetsu founded on land the Tokugawa shogunate gave him in 1615. The Ogata property at Takagamine was located directly opposite the main residence. This had been Kōetsu's home, and it served as the base of successive Hon'ami patriarchs. The prime location of the Ogata residence, which passed to Kenzan after Sōken's death in 1687, confirms the strong bonds between the Ogata and the Hon'ami. The close relationship between the two families seems to have given Kōrin convenient access to Kōetsu's artistic legacy through the treasures and counsel of his descendants. Such connections through ancestry, real estate, and direct interaction amplified the presence of the Hon'ami clan in Kōrin's life. Kōetsu's afterlife and, with it, his artistic reputation no doubt felt within easy reach to Kōrin.

Another reason for Kōrin to turn to Kōetsu's legacy might have been financial. Kōetsu's lacquer pieces were highly prized, and they commanded staggering prices. Records of wealthy officials of the silver mint, such as Fukae Shōzaemon (dates unknown) and Nakamura Kuranosuke (1668–1730), show that some suzuribako designed by Kōetsu sold for as much as four kan, an astronomical sum.[6] For comparison, when Kōrin's widow, Tayo, sold their mansion in Kyoto in 1717, the asking price for the entire property was little more than five kan. By Kōrin's time, lacquer works by Kōetsu had become collectible items among the moneyed elite. Kōrin began to associate with Nakamura Kuranosuke in the late 1690s—when he first made lacquer objects. The collecting habits of Kuranosuke and other rich men, in addition to the high prices garnered by Kōetsu's lacquer works, may have encouraged Kōrin to venture into lacquer. Kōrin's lacquer pieces, too, became sought-after objects that gained considerable renown. Though they were anything but cheap, with the most expensive works selling in the realm of five hundred monme in 1714, they nevertheless commanded between a quarter and an eighth of the price of Kōetsu's examples.

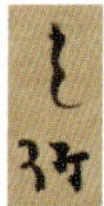
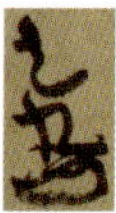

FIGURE 38
Left: Detail, left screen, fig. 11; Right: Hon'ami Kōetsu, *Letter* (detail), early 17th century. Hanging scroll; ink on paper. Gift of Tsutsui Kuniko, Tokyo National Museum, Source: ColBase (https://colbase.nich.go.jp/).

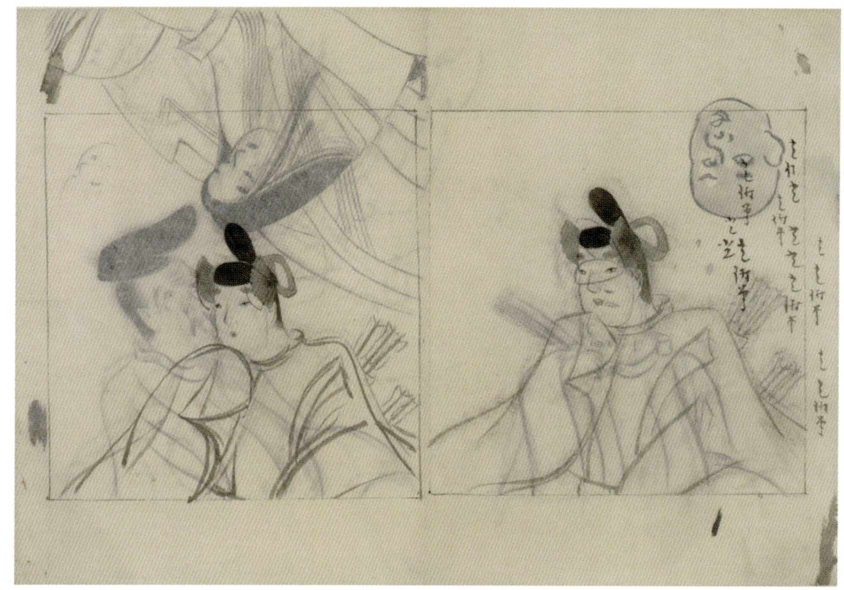

FIGURE 39
Ogata Kōrin, *Signature Practice*, late 17th century. Ink on paper. Konishi Family Archive, Kyoto National Museum.

In an attempt to align his artistic identity with that of his famous ancestor, in his earliest works Kōrin began to brush the first character of his name in the same way as Kōetsu (fig. 38). Contemporaries who wrote in a fashion similar to Kōetsu—a style of calligraphy that was highly popular during the early seventeenth century—rendered the character differently, showing how Kōetsu developed a personalized way to sign his works and letters.[7] Throughout the 1690s and early 1700s, Kōrin abbreviated his new signature to a single line ending in a pronounced right hook, an inflection that matches Kōetsu's signature and thus represents a nod to his great-granduncle's cultural presence. Kōrin's embrace of this distinctive style and the reference to Kōetsu's name bolsters his decision to craft multilayered links to his famous ancestor.

A curious example survives in which Kōrin practiced writing out the *kō* in Kōetsu's characteristic fashion on the back of sketches for a set of playing cards illustrated with poets from the anthology *One Hundred Poets, One Poem Each* (*Hyakunin isshu;* fig. 39).[8] The leaf hints at his strenuous efforts to model his persona after Kōetsu by appropriating the deceased ancestor's legacy. In fact, the style Kōrin used when writing his new name on the *One Hundred Poets, One Poem Each* sketch corresponds closely with his signatures on such early works as *Sōgi* and *Hotei Playing Kemari.* This overlap establishes a direct link between Kōetsu's cultural clout and Kōrin's earliest activities as a painter sowing the seeds of his artistic reception.

Kōetsu's calligraphy and signature were widely known in part through his avid correspondence and publishing efforts. This was especially true among Kōrin's target clientele, the upper classes of Kyoto. Kōrin's ancestor was instrumental in disseminating the courtly classics during the early seventeenth century through printed editions, the so-called *Saga-bon,* made in collaboration with wealthy townsmen and aristocrats. For example, in 1609, together with the courtier Nakanoin Michikatsu (1556–1610), Kōetsu published a printed edition of *Commentaries on the Tales of Ise Heard by Shōhaku* (*Ise monogatari shōmonshō*), the collection of the poet Sōgi's teachings on the *Tales of Ise.*[9] Michikatsu provided the text, which his family had preserved as handwritten manuscripts, and Kōetsu supplied his calligraphy as the basis for the printed book. Through this prestigious project and others like it, Kōetsu's reputation and aesthetic became tied to the guardians of Japan's literary legacy, such as the aristocratic Nakanoin family. Kōetsu's efforts also included publishing other books that were related to classical literature, for which he either lent his distinctive style of writing for printed works or used his hand-brushed calligraphy in manuscripts. The books often feature paper décor inspired by Heian period examples. By disseminating the classics, Kōetsu and his circle breathed life into a centuries-old tradition whose survival was threatened during the warfare of the sixteenth century. Kōetsu's role in this revival made him a familiar name in the literary and visual arts of early modern Japan.

Kōrin's self-conscious move toward his new professional career and his attempt to shape an artistic personality are evident in his earliest artworks. Given the prominence of works by Kōetsu in elite circles during the seventeenth century and beyond, it is not surprising that Kōrin selected his great-granduncle as a key source of artistic inspiration when he sought to build a name for himself as an artist. Kōetsu's stature and artistry were synonymous with the aesthetics of the early seventeenth century, a time that in many ways bridged the late medieval period of Kōetsu and the early modern age of Kōrin. In this way, Kōetsu offered Kōrin a colorful combination of the past and the present that he eventually wove into the fabric of his own artistic creativity.

MANAGING LACQUER

More than anything, Kōetsu inspired Kōrin to work in lacquer, influencing both his style and his processes for creating such objects. Kōetsu rarely engaged physically in the production of lacquer pieces and pottery attributed to his name. In the same way that he provided his distinctive calligraphy as the aesthetic model for such printed editions as *Commentaries on the Tales of Ise Heard by Shōhaku,* endeavors in other media also relied on Kōetsu's creative mind rather than on his direct physical agency. Instead of creating the objects himself, Kōetsu often instructed specially trained lacquerers, potters, and other craftsmen via letters and verbal directions in the production of his artworks.

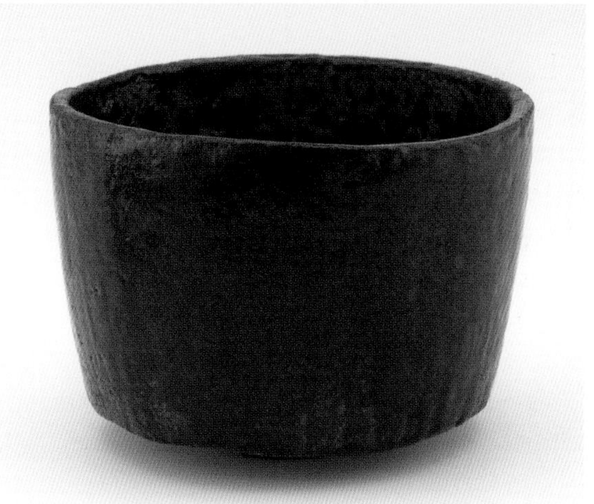

FIGURE 40
Hon'ami Kōetsu, *Tea Bowl named "Minogame,"* early 17th century. Earthenware with black Raku glaze. Freer Gallery of Art, Smithsonian Institution, Washington, D.C.: Gift of Charles Lang Freer, F1899.34a–c.

Fortunately, some of these letters survive. They draw a vivid picture of the parameters of art production in early seventeenth-century Japan—guidelines that Kōrin himself eventually adopted.

For example, Kōetsu's name is linked to numerous tea bowls (fig. 40). In fact, he is known to have been the first artist to sign the accompanying wooden boxes of his tea bowls, asserting authorship in a way that no potter before him ever did.[10] Kōetsu, however, frequently did not make these objects all by himself. In one letter, he orders a potter named Taemon to apply the glaze only thinly and to leave an area of the vessel unglazed. Kōetsu also advises the artisan to leave the door of the kiln open during the firing process, perhaps as an experiment or as a way to attain a certain result. In the same letter, he announces his visit to the kiln. It is possible that he preferred to give instructions on the finish of the tea bowl in person.

> Regarding the three tea bowls in white clay,
> and concerning their glazes:
> I ask you to [apply] the upper glaze very faintly so that it stops in one place.
>
> Regarding the black tea bowl and two incense containers:
> This time, after the glaze is applied, I ask you to
> fire them while the kiln's door is left open.
> I will inquire again on the second day next month.
>
> Fourth month, twenty-fifth day. [From] Kōetsu
> To Taemon[11]

Although Kōetsu probably sculpted the tea bowls himself, the letter also makes it clear that he was only tangentially involved in the physical act of glazing and firing the objects, complex affairs that required technical training and skill.

Rather, expert craftsmen followed his instructions and did the job for him. Yet in the end it was Kōetsu alone who signed the bowls' boxes. This modus operandi conveys the stratified nature of artistic hierarchy during Kōetsu's time and exemplifies the obvious gap between gentlemen-artists like Kōetsu and artisans of humbler status and prominence. The letter's language is curt and straight to the point, using simple syntax and an emphasis on the easily readable syllabic *hiragana* script rather than more complicated Chinese characters. In another letter to the potter Raku Kichizaemon, written in a similar fashion, Kōetsu also asked the potter to send white clay and red clay, which Kōetsu might have used to mold tea bowls before sending them off for glazing and firing.

> I ask you to deliver white and red clay
> for about four tea bowls, and be quick about it.
>
> Sincerely
> First month, sixteenth [day]. Kōetsu
>
> To tea bowl maker
> Kichiza[emon] [From] Kōetsu[12]

The language, style, and content of these letters provide semantic evidence for the chasm in position and education between an upscale man of letters like Kōetsu vis-à-vis professional potters like Taemon and Raku Kichizaemon. The orders also demonstrate Kōetsu's creative process and how he enlisted professionals to execute his unconventional ideas while retaining some sense of involvement in the making.

Kōetsu issued similar missives to lacquer craftsmen, although, for these works, even more so than for his pottery, virtually the entire production was left to professional artisans. After extensive scrutiny of Kōetsu's correspondence and artworks, the art historian Uchida Tokugo outlined a possible pattern of production for Kōetsu's lacquer pieces.[13] First, Kōetsu prepared a sketch of the work in consultation with his patron—much in the same way as an artist sketched a painting for approval before starting to work and adding costly pigments. As the second step, Kōetsu instructed and supervised a lacquer master in the object's production, frequently updating the patron and adjusting the work as needed. In an undated letter to a man named Shinbei, Kōetsu offers a glimpse of this process.[14] After he informs Shinbei that the metal décor (*kanagai*) is largely complete, he invites his patron to examine the piece. Then, Kōetsu lists several points that require the patron's approval. For example, he deems a few of the floral leaves in the design to be unsatisfactory and offers a remedy: "Some of the leaves in cut metal are too long, but we can cover the unsightly parts (*minikuki tokoro*) in ink."[15] Earlier in the letter he asks if the overall number of leaves should be increased. For all of these questions, Kōetsu specifically requests written feedback, an indication that he sent his letter along with the unfinished object to the patron for immediate inspection. Finally, Kōetsu mentions that he will report back to a certain Yashi, presumably the professional lacquer master in charge of making the work.

Kōetsu retained the role of artist-intermediary between the patron and the artisans who executed his designs, situating himself as the planner and mastermind behind the piece. In another letter, Kōetsu informs an unknown patron that the order for a suzuribako is complete and that he will soon visit the lacquer master to examine the writing box.[16] He continues that he will later dispatch the artwork to the patron, which is the same sequence described in his letter to Shinbei. Kōetsu maintained close connections with the Igarashi, a family of lacquer masters employed by the Maeda clan of present-day Kanazawa. It has been suggested that the Igarashi, among other artisans, provided Kōetsu with their services in executing his designs.[17] Several letters survive between Kōetsu and different members of the Igarashi clan. Only in one letter, addressed to an unknown person, does Kōetsu refer to a "stacked box" (*jūbako*), which may or may not designate a lacquer piece. Most of Kōetsu's correspondence with the Igarashi deals with tea and the Noh theater, highlighting his customary pattern of using these two arts as a way to connect with people. In one letter, Kōetsu mentions receiving shark meat from Igarashi Tahei, illustrating the gratitude he received for their collaboration and the bond he had formed with his lacquer artisans.

Kōetsu drew from an extensive network of professional artisans, from potters to lacquerers, who supplied him with their specialized skills. His letters reveal that he relied on at least two potters to make his tea bowls. His matrix of lacquer masters likely involved more than one go-to source. A contemporaneous map of Kōetsu's Takagamine colony lists the residences of two lacquer artisans named Tōjūrō and Tsuchida Sōtaku, a presence that established an onsite infrastructure for lacquer production. In every case, Kōetsu likely acted as the designer and intermediary between his patron and the artisan. Kōrin adopted this trifold process of direct and indirect communication among artist, patron, and specialized craftsman as well.

KŌRIN AND LACQUER

Although Kōrin began as a painter, he quickly expanded his talents into other areas. Only a few years after the earliest evidence of his small-format paintings in the mid-1690s, he commenced making lacquer pieces. In a letter, tentatively dated to around the same time, Kōrin writes:

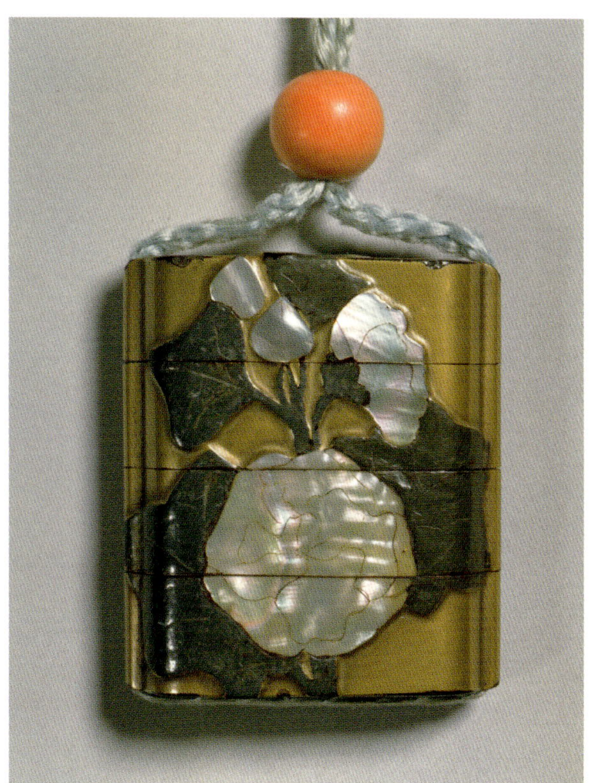

FIGURE 41
Ogata Kōrin, *Inrō with Design of Hollyhocks,* early 18th century. Lacquer on wood with gold, gold leaf, lead, and mother-of-pearl. MOA Museum of Art, Atami.

> Thank you for your help the other day. I received the money from my neighbor.[18] This is entirely thanks to you and I cannot express enough how grateful I am. I would like to show you the rectangular stacked suzuribako today. If it suits you, could you please come and pick it up? If you could also hand over the payment, I would be most grateful. This is all for now. Yours sincerely, [Kōrin].
> Second month, twenty-third day.
> [P.S.] I have completed the *inrō* with butterfly motifs according to your wishes. It is precious [to me] and I keep it safely tucked away in my kimono. I would like you to send it to Nagasaki. I am also waiting to hear from Nagasaki about the motif of the screen[s] [they ordered]. My neighbor is waiting [to hear from you], so could you please meet him? This is all for now.[19]

This document—one of the earliest, if not the earliest, surviving letters in Kōrin's hand—was composed around 1697, at the cusp of his career as an artist. The missive shows that lacquer works in different formats were a pillar of Kōrin's artistry from the beginning of his career. Kōrin asks his correspondent to inspect the suzuribako that he had made, a request that echoes Kōetsu's language in his letters about lacquer works and his role as artistic director. Kōrin also created *inrō,* small decorative containers worn at the sash (fig. 41). Like fans, inrō were a staple of early modern attire and were produced in large quantities.

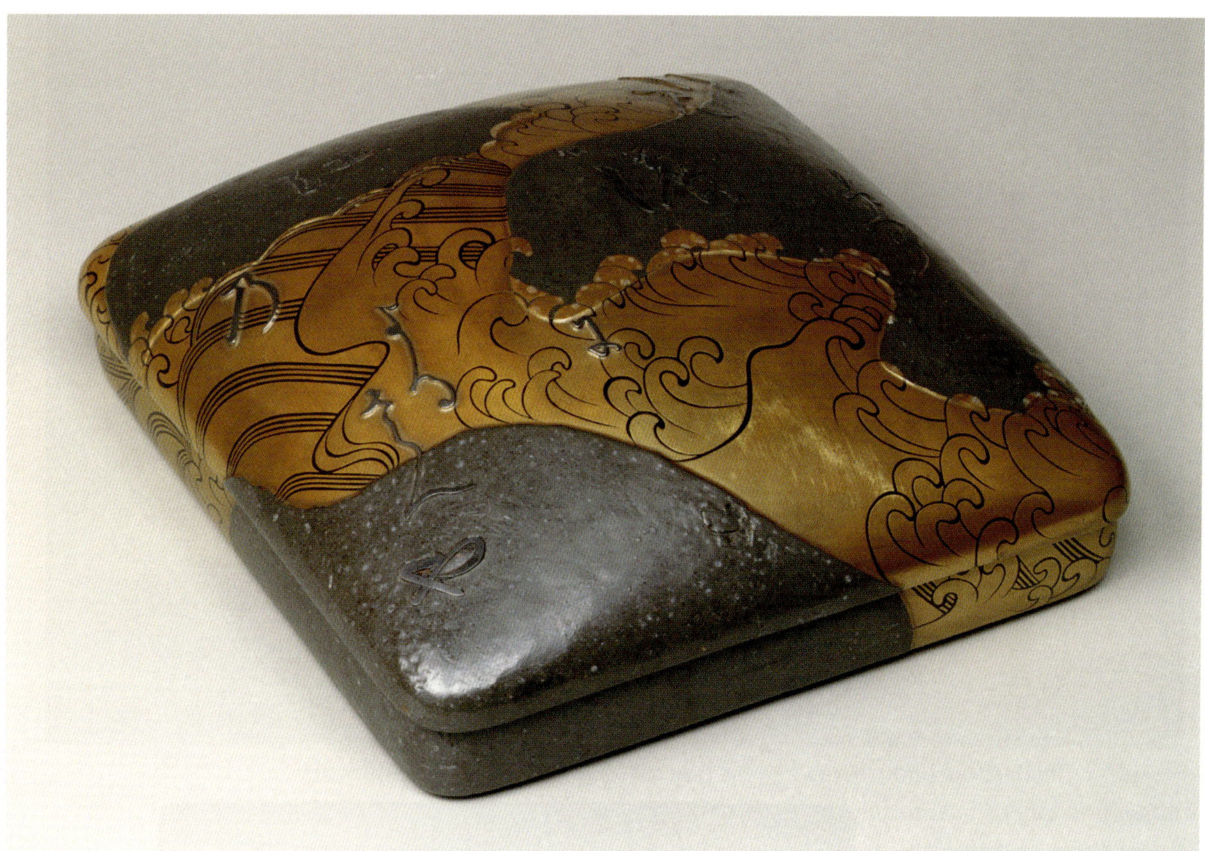

FIGURE 45
Ogata Kōrin, *Suzuribako with Design of the Shore of Suminoe*, late 17th or early 18th century. Lacquer on wood with gold, lead, and silver. Seikadō Bunko Art Museum Image Archives / DNPartcom.

Kōrin accepted his great-granduncle's style fully. Kōrin's suzuribako of the shore at Suminoe, a literary site near Osaka, prominently displays his connection to Kōetsu (fig. 45). As with Kōetsu's *Pontoon Bridge,* Kōrin juxtaposed large areas of lead with eye-catching gold lacquer. In fact, his use of lead to depict stones along the shore at Suminoe is even more extensive than in Kōetsu's work. Apparently, he wanted to expand on his great-granduncle's visuality. Although Kōrin pushed certain pictorial and material aspects of Kōetsu's work, he also injected ideas of his own—an idiosyncrasy encapsulated in the praise by Inaba Tsūryū's quoted earlier. Kōrin chose to accentuate the stylized waves in his work with thin calligraphic lines of black lacquer, a feature absent in Kōetsu's suzuribako. He carved through the gilded coating to reveal the underlying layer of black lacquer; none of Kōetsu's pieces uses this technique. The visual and material allusions to Kōetsu, however, remain clear. To amplify that connection, Kōrin recorded the following on the accompanying wooden box of the *Suminoe* suzuribako: "Made after Kōetsu, a resident of the Daikyoan at Takagamine. Hokkyō Kōrin."[28]

Even without Kōrin's declaration, the reference to Kōetsu must have been readily visible to anyone familiar with the aesthetic style of the early seventeenth-century master. The *ashide* in Kōrin's box, calligraphy scattered in silver around the depicted seascape, is rendered in Kōetsu's writing style. It quotes a poem by Fujiwara Toshiyuki (d. circa 901), drawing a link between Kōetsu's distinctive hand and classical literature that was a trope in Kōetsu's own works. On the lid of his *Pontoon Bridge* is inscribed a poem from the tenth-century anthology *Later Anthology of Japanese Poems* (*Gosen wakashū*) written in his own style of calligraphy.[29] In replicating the aesthetic of Kōetsu's works and thereby aligning himself with his great-granduncle's legacy, Kōrin made sure to cover every possibility. It is not known to which Kōetsu work Kōrin referred when he made the *Suminoe* box, but it surely must have resembled *Pontoon Bridge.*

Kōrin's embrace of the deeply poetic nature of Kōetsu's lacquer works and the way he incorporated classical verses in Kōetsu's handwriting stand at odds with Kōrin's own poetic acumen. Whereas Kōetsu was at the forefront of promoting broad public engagement with Japan's classical poetry, Kōrin could not boast such achievements. All told, the only poem that survives by him reflects at best a mediocre talent for balladry.

> In the sorrow of our parting, the sleeves of my sunlit robe
> are drenched with many layers of blossom scent,
> alas, this means farewell.[30]

The verse, composed as a parting gift to a friend, uses common poetic tropes and communicates little of the literary creativity and poetic learning that Kōrin expressed in his paintings and lacquer works. Nevertheless, Kōrin created many lacquer pieces with literary connections. Though he imbued his works with allusive poetic meanings, the literary nature of Kōrin's *Suminoe* box draws a link to Kōetsu and the venerated aesthetics of the early seventeenth century. By relying on Kōetsu's materials, style, and calligraphy, the work takes advantage of an aesthetic that was formulated at a time when the foundations for early modern Kyoto culture were laid. Kōetsu remained popular well beyond his lifetime, and family ties made Kōrin's embrace of Kōetsu all the more reasonable. Kōrin, the first person to draw a direct artistic connection to Kōetsu, benefited from his ancestor's popularity. In fact, his turn to Kōetsu may have met a demand for Kōetsu-style lacquer works among an increasingly wealthy urban clientele. The prices his suzuribako eventually commanded confirm this story.

In light of the stellar amounts that lacquer works by Kōetsu and Kōrin fetched on the eighteenth-century art market, it is surprising that more lacquer artists did not follow this master's style. Around the time that Kōrin embraced Kōetsu's model, the discipline of making lacquer underwent dramatic changes. At the forefront of these aesthetic shifts was Ogawa Haritsu (1663–1747). In a fundamental difference from the sweeping, opaque designs of Kōrin and

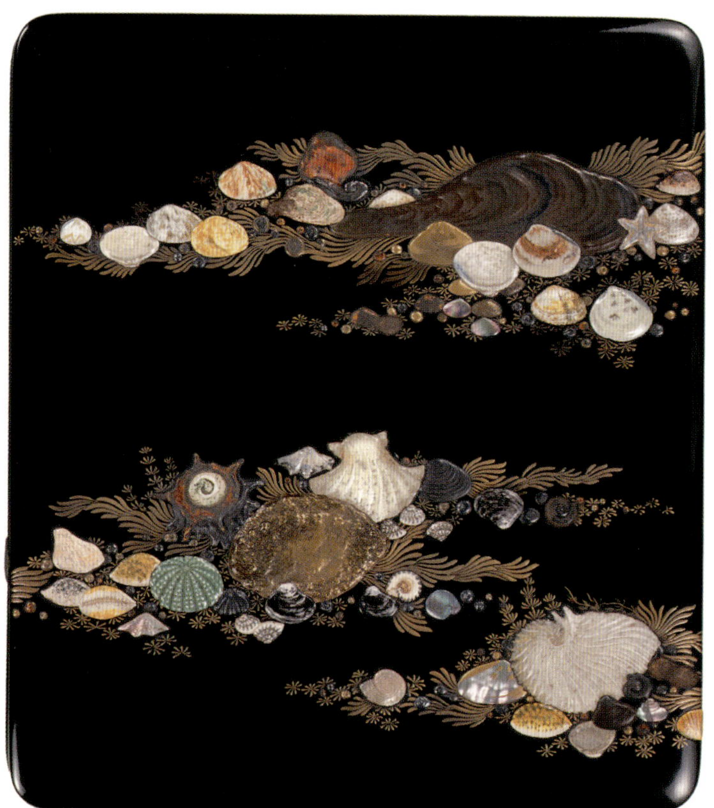

FIGURE 46
Ogawa Haritsu, *Suzuribako with Design of Shells,* 18th century. Lacquer on wood with gold, mother-of-pearl, lead, tin, and clay. Suntory Museum of Art, Tokyo.

FIGURE 47
Nagata Yūji, *Portable Set of Drawers with Design of Plovers and Waves,* early 18th century. Lacquer on wood with gold and lead. Gift of Nishiwaki Kenji, Tokyo National Museum, Image: TNM Image Archives.

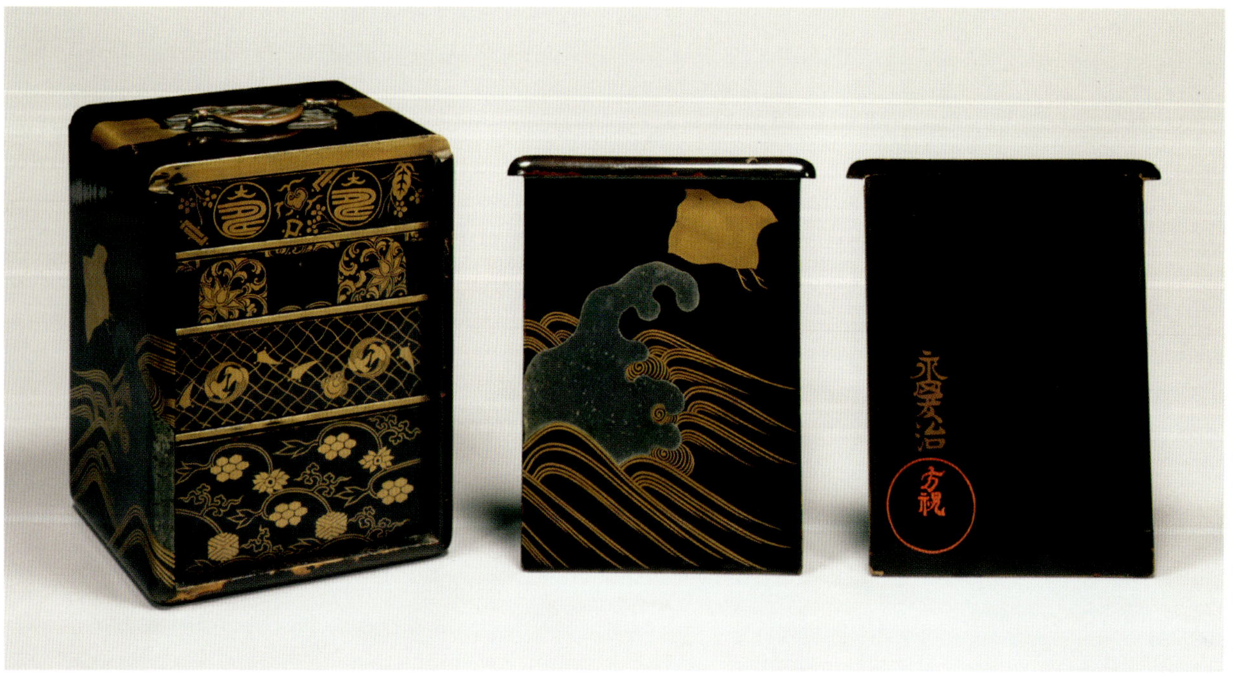

Kōetsu, Haritsu's complex lacquer works employ new materials and the effect of the wood grain (fig. 46).[31] In comparison to Kōrin, Haritsu was a radical innovator in lacquer. Geography played a likely role in this: Haritsu is said to have worked mainly in Edo, whereas Kōrin sought to convey a decidedly Kyoto-inspired feel in his lacquer pieces.

In his early paintings, as in his lacquer pieces, Kōrin assumed a retrospective approach and aligned himself with the early seventeenth century, an epoch associated with an almost classical feeling by Kōrin's time. Kōetsu and his eclectic clique of aristocrats and wealthy commoners helped shape the highbrow aesthetics of Kyoto. Kōrin repeatedly referred to that culture throughout his artistic career. In doing so, he laid the groundwork for a new tradition. In the eighteenth century, Nagata Yūji, a lacquer artist active in Kyoto, followed in Kōrin's footsteps (fig. 47). By way of indirect transmission—Kōrin never studied with Kōetsu, and Nagata Yūji never met Kōrin—the tradition established by Kōetsu continued well into the eighteenth century.

MODES OF MAKING

In a move that departed from Kōetsu's gentlemanly model, Kōrin added a decidedly commercial dimension to his lacquer works. He apparently allowed customers to choose their desired design by looking at readymade sketches.

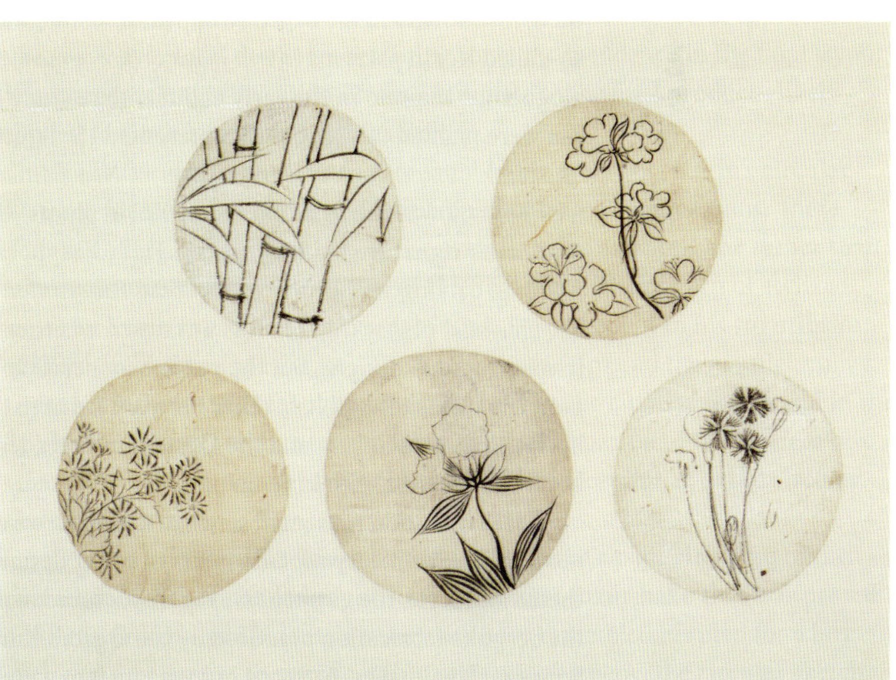

FIGURE 48

Ogata Kōrin, *Circular Sketches for Lacquer Designs,* late 17th or early 18th century. Ink on paper. Konishi Family Archive, Kyoto National Museum.

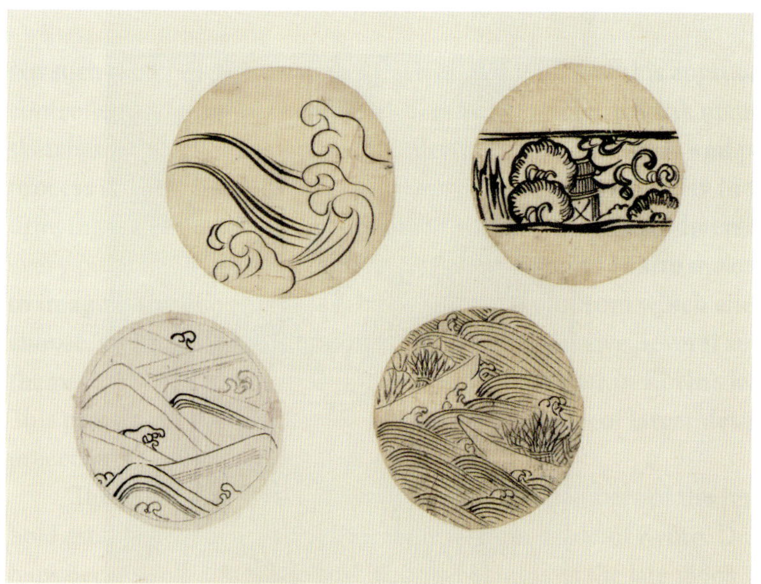

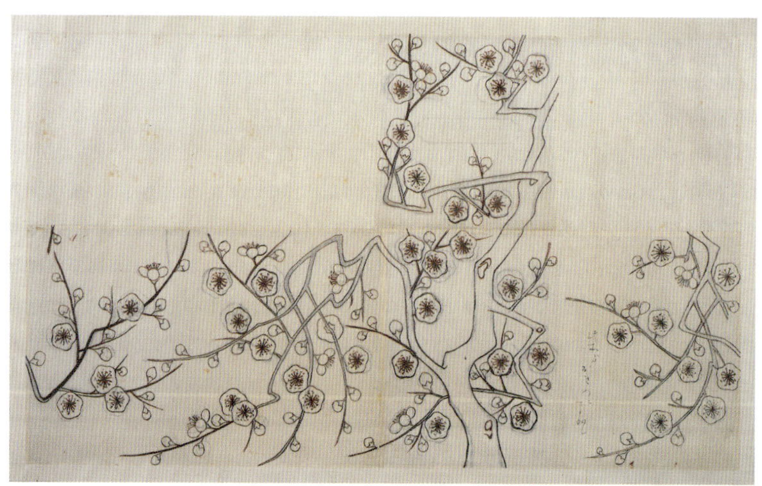

FIGURE 50
Ogata Kōrin, *Circular Sketches for Lacquer Design,* late 17th or early 18th century. Ink on paper. Konishi Family Archive, Osaka City Museum of Art.

FIGURE 51
Ogata Kōrin, *Sketch for Suzuribako with Design of Plum Blossoms,* late 17th or early 18th century. Ink and red pigment on paper. Konishi Family Archive, Osaka City Museum of Art.

represents the layout concisely. It enabled the patron to imagine the work's final appearance. For example, if someone chose a plum or wave design, the scale model approximated the finished piece. When folded along the edges, the plan for the plum blossom box forms a three-dimensional mockup the same size as the final suzuribako. At the same time, the drawing worked as a template for the lacquer artist, who would trace each line of the image and, while still wet, impress it onto the object to silhouette the décor's composition.[34] Kōrin's paper template is painted in ink, but the sketch contains visible remnants of red pigment drawn on top of the ink outlines. These red markings show that a professional artisan received the dummy from Kōrin and imprinted the plum blossom design in red pigment onto the lacquer work in order to execute the artist's

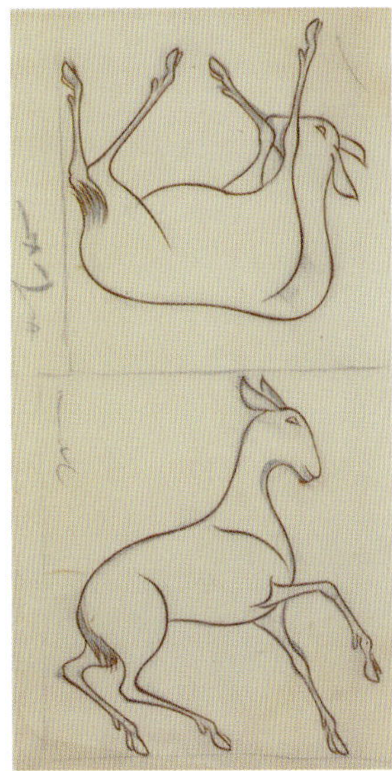

FIGURE 52
Ogata Kōrin, *Sketch for Inrō with Design of Deer,* late 17th or early 18th century. Ink and red pigment on paper. Konishi Family Archive, Kyoto National Museum.

conception as faithfully as possible.[35] A number of extant designs by Kōrin show similar remains of tracing in red. Kōrin's handwritten instructions on the model—on a deer design for inrō Kōrin clearly labeled the appropriate pictures as "front" (*mae nari*) and "back" (*ushiro*)—provided further guidance to lacquer artisans (fig. 52).

The sequence of production insinuates a carefully curated manufacture process. A set repertoire of designs guided and streamlined the process for meeting the considerable demand for Kōrin's lacquer pieces while helping to ensure thematic and stylistic consistency within his output. The Konishi Family Archive contains substantial numbers of preparatory studies and templates for lacquer designs, attesting to their popularity among Kōrin's clients. These sketches include plans for entire pieces and parts of them. Kōrin's hand-drawn models show the extent of his involvement in masterminding and managing the production of his lacquer works.

Kōrin also retained thematic model books, such as his collection of sketches titled *Book of Deer Designs for Inrō* (*Inrō shika no hon*) (fig. 53). Almost all of the deer designs for inrō in the Konishi Family Archive appear to be by Kōrin's own hand. The book contains nine pictures of deer that each are roughly the size of an average inrō. The deer designs are strikingly similar to the paper décor by Sōtatsu onto which Kōetsu inscribed his calligraphy, drawing an aesthetic link to Kōrin's ancestor (fig. 54).[36] In addition, one of Kōrin's deer designs corresponds to a picture in *Assortment of Designs for Lacquer* (*Maki-e tamei warabegusa*), a 1705 compendium of motifs for creating lacquer objects.[37] Its overlap with the early eighteenth-century publication suggests that Kōrin either referred to this book or similar ones or, more likely, elements of Kōrin's midcareer lacquer practice were inserted into the compendium—a phenomenon akin to Kōrin's inclusion in hinagata bon. If the latter was the case, Kōrin's prolific output of lacquer works must have quickly garnered a public following. Other preparatory drawings by him abound, and Kōrin probably used them as go-to references for his sprawling lacquer-making. In fact, he made lacquer works throughout his career, from the 1690s until his death in 1716, further attesting to their ceaseless demand and Kōrin's interest in the medium.

In a late letter to his son Juichirō, Kōrin writes, "Concerning one of the three inrō [we discussed] the other day, the frontal design of camellia and young pines should reach around to the backside. The other two were sent back and I will make new ones instead."[38] The letter dates to sometime around 1715 or 1716, the final years of Kōrin's life. In the same document the artist refers to a screen that he asks to be returned so that he can sketch it for future reference. Clearly, his desire to produce model books was not confined to lacquer. The subject of the inrō he mentions in the letter—pines and camellia, a seasonal

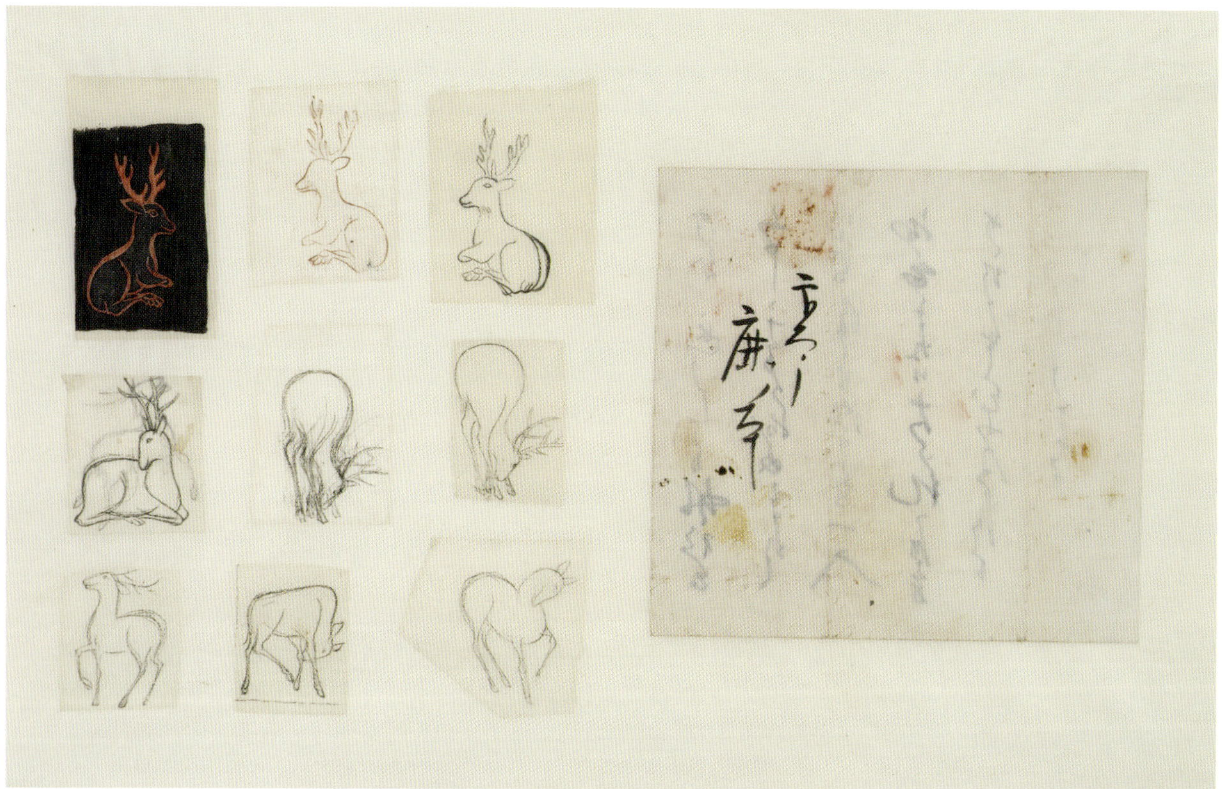

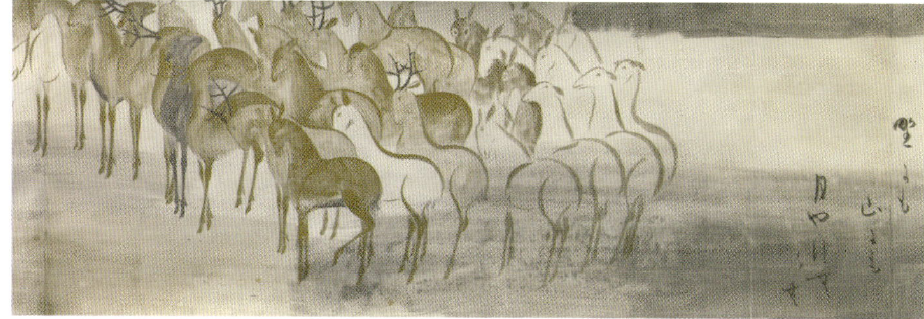

FIGURE 53
Ogata Kōrin, *Book of Deer Designs for Inrō* (*Inrō shika no hon*), late 17th or early 18th century. Ink and red pigment on paper. Konishi Family Archive, Kyoto National Museum.

FIGURE 54
Tawaraya Sōtatsu (painting) and Hon'ami Kōetsu (calligraphy), *Poem Scroll with Deer,* 1610s. Handscroll; ink, gold, and silver on paper. Seattle Art Museum, Gift of Mrs. Donald E. Frederick, 51.127.

theme befitting the beginning of a new year—is the same one in a suzuribako that Kōrin sold to silver mint officials for the high sum of five hundred monme around the same time. Evidently, Kōrin offered his clients a fixed repertoire, one that he laid out by way of preparatory drawings, circular sketches, and portfolios like his deer book.

This repetition of subjects in a particular style enhanced the recognizability of his practice. Kōrin's workshop activities in lacquer and his secondhand presence in textile culture created a high level of public visibility for his name and style. In fact, Kōrin's position in textile culture and his output in lacquer were so noticeable that some commentators conflated the two genres. In 1734, two decades after Kōrin's death, Kikuoka Tenryō (1680–1747) in his *Stories of This World's Affairs* (*Honchō seiji danki*) wrote, "Ogata Kōrin of the capital [belonged to the house of] official dry goods merchants to the court. He established an artistic lineage and in the not-so-distant past he drew on clothing and lacquer vessels. His fancy was to draw [pictures] after their shadows cast on paper sliding doors."[39] Other eighteenth-century works also reflect Kōrin's proclivity in lacquer production, and fakes soon appeared in circulation. *Encyclopedia of Lacquer Designs* (*Maki-e taizen*), written by Ōoka Shunboku and published in 1759, includes inrō designs of "Kōrin chrysanthemums" (*Kōrin giku*) as well as "Kōrin pine, bamboo, and plum" (*Kōrin shōchikubai*). Both terms are taken directly from Kōrin patterns in hinagata bon used as references for textile production.[40]

The desire for Kōrin-style lacquer in the eighteenth century was set in motion by the artist himself. His industriousness in dispatching his lacquer works to Edo and other far-flung places, along with his efficient system for selecting designs from a set repertoire, led to a substantial output that reached a diverse clientele and disseminated his trademark style across the country.

A PERSONAL TOUCH

Kōrin quoted frequently from Kōetsu and used a largely fixed repertoire of designs. But he was also keen to inject his works with traces of his own hand and creativity. One of those was the practice of producing lacquer works that seem to be painted by Kōrin himself. Despite the orchestrated process of creating his lacquer wares, Kōrin attempted to give some of his works the semblance of having been made by his own hand. The best example of this is one of his earliest and most famous surviving pieces, a suzuribako depicting his signature theme of irises alongside an eight-plank bridge (fig. 55). Probably made in the first years of the eighteenth century and shortly after his *Irises* screens, the suzuribako embodies the persistence with which Kōrin repeated subjects throughout his career.

The *Eight-Plank Bridge* writing box exemplifies his creativity in lacquer. It not only demonstrates Kōrin's indebtedness to Kōetsu, but it also transcends his ancestor's example and emerges as one of the great achievements of Japanese lacquer. Onto a pitch-black lacquer ground, we find a bridge in thick pieces of uneven lead that resemble the surface of well-worn wood. Glistening mother-of-pearl, which retains its mesmerizing sheen more than three hundred years later, represents the blossoms of the irises. The striking combination of mother-of-pearl, gold lacquer, and broad swaths of lead on a shining black lacquer ground echoes other works by Kōrin, such as his suzuribako with hollyhock designs. A circular drawing that depicts the same subject might have served as the basis

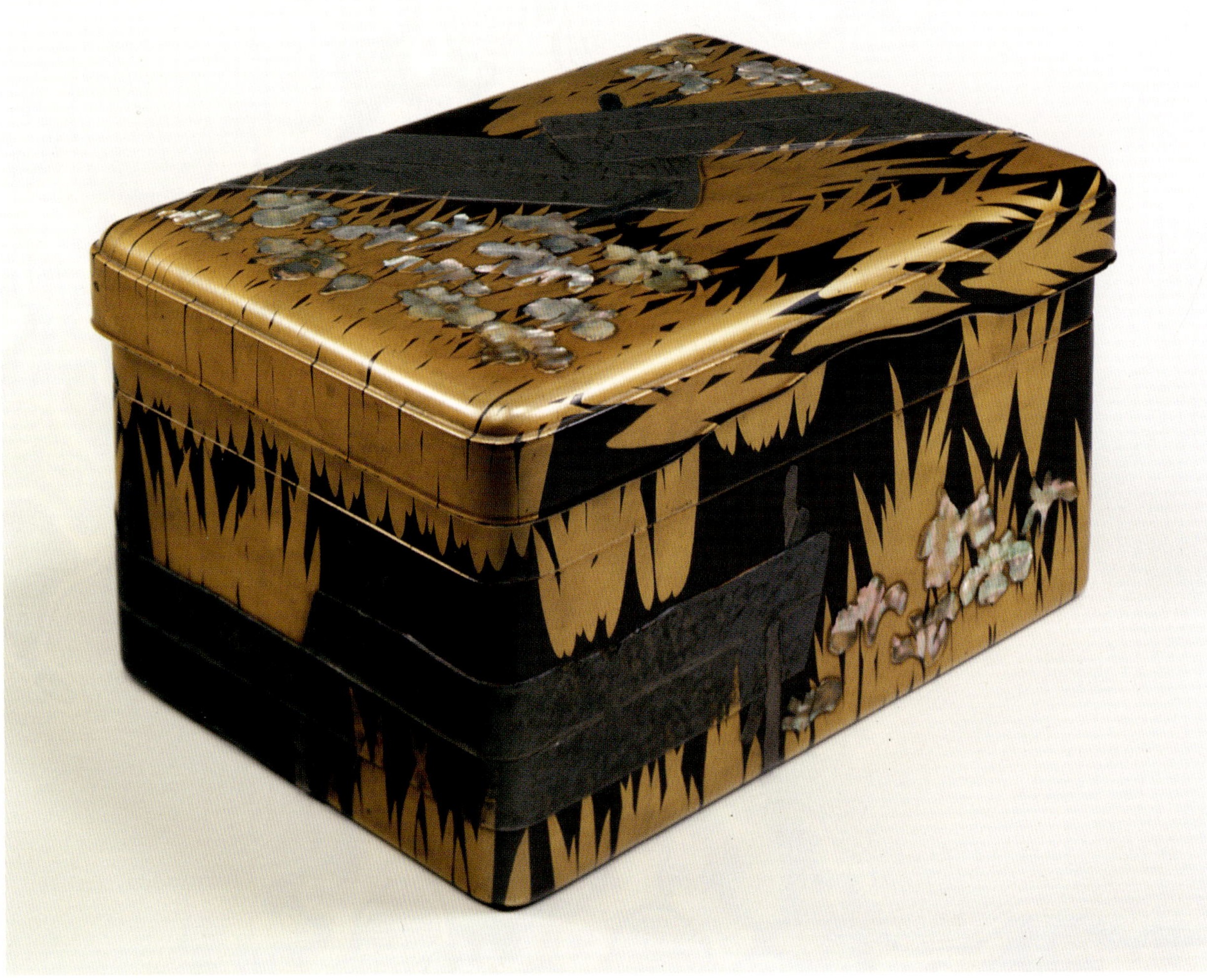

FIGURE 55
Ogata Kōrin, *Suzuribako with Design of Eight-Plank Bridge, from the Tales of Ise,* early 18th century. Lacquer on wood with gold, lead, and mother-of-pearl. Tokyo National Museum, Image: TNM Image Archives.

for the work's design. The shape of the iris flowers and stalks, in addition to the two-plank composition of the bridge and the construction of its legs, correspond directly with the finished suzuribako (fig. 56).

Although Kōrin was probably involved only in drafting the initial design and in managing the production process, the *Eight-Plank Bridge* writing box illustrates how he was keen to retain the appearance of personally made, artistic immediacy (fig. 57). On the box, the iris leaves were added after the mother-of-pearl flowers and lead bridge were attached to the black lacquer ground. The rendering of the leaves in the suzuribako resembles the sharp strokes with tapering upper edges and round lower ends found in Kōrin's screens *Irises* and *Irises at Yatsuhashi.* Because the suzuribako was likely produced shortly after *Irises* but years before *Irises at Yatsuhashi,* it represents a critical juncture between the two screen paintings. It alters the reductionist beauty of *Irises* by

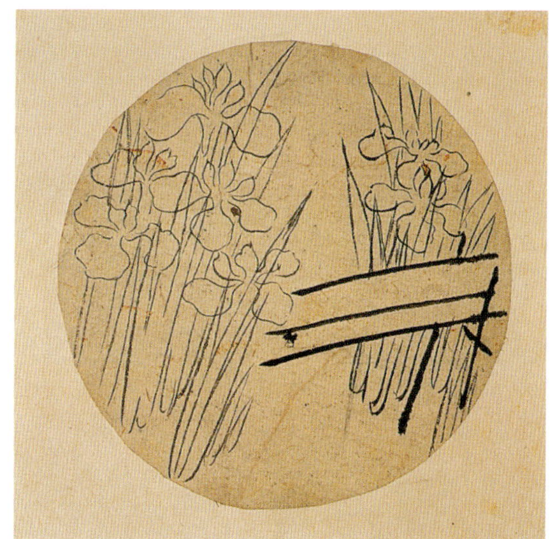

FIGURE 56
Ogata Kōrin, *Circular Sketches for Lacquer Designs,* late 17th or early 18th century. Ink on paper. Konishi Family Archive, Osaka City Museum of Art.

introducing the eight-plank bridge described in the ninth chapter of the *Tales of Ise.* In *Irises at Yatsuhashi,* Kōrin refers to the aesthetic of his suzuribako by transforming its lead bridge into a bridge in ink—two hues that resemble each other closely. As much as Kōrin adhered to the theme of irises from the *Tales of Ise,* he played with the infinite creative possibilities of his subject, repeatedly adjusting the blooming stalks to the medium at hand.

In the case of the *Eight-Plank Bridge* box, the most conspicuous connecting link between the paintings *Irises* and *Irises at Yatsuhashi* is how the plants are rendered. In the screen paintings, Kōrin himself drew each leaf in long strokes of malachite green, layering stroke after stroke to deepen the pigment's hue. The suzuribako replicates the appearance of this direct, freehand application, albeit by employing a process that required division of labor. On close inspection, the box reveals a typical technique of *maki-e* lacquer décor. Each leaf is built up of thin, carefully calibrated lines of gold pigment that were painstakingly added with a thin brush. This process of applying the viscid gilded lacquer required patience and careful measure. The labor-intensive procedure needed to apply the toxic lacquer sap onto the surface of the wooden core and to achieve the correct hue of gold demanded years of training. Even if Kōrin tried his hand at making lacquer pieces himself, it was unlikely that he acquired the expert-level skill needed for making the *Eight-Plank Bridge* box, a complex masterpiece.

Even so, the piece is nothing but a work by Kōrin, though his hand may have never touched it during its production. The gold pigment partially overlaps other parts of the composition, namely, the flowers and bridge, in an attempt to increase the illusion of quickly executed virtuoso brushwork. Such details bring to mind the artist's hand moving across the surface and adding the final touches—a feature that conjures up the appearance of his paintings. All of this,

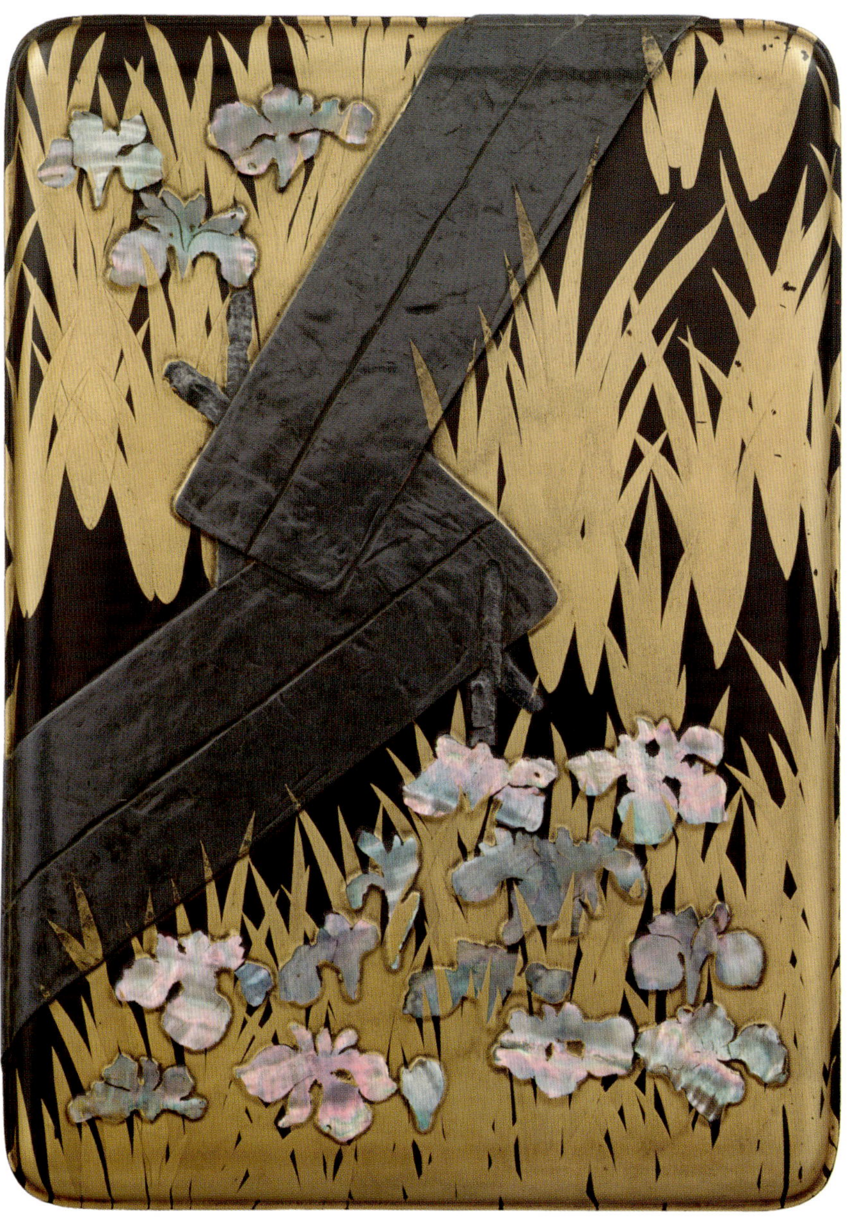

FIGURE 57 Top view, fig. 55.

however, was probably the result of Kōrin's written or spoken instructions to a professional lacquer craftsman. In lacquer, the *Eight-Plank Bridge* box seems to say, an artist's verbal mandate functions as an extension of and substitute for his hand. In other words, generating the conceptual idea behind a lacquer piece sufficed to make it an original, in spite of the absence of the artist's touch in the making of it.

As a result, the notion of originality in Kōrin's time was more nebulous than simple rules of individual authorship. The case of Kōrin's lacquer works presents a glimpse at the stratified macrocosm of lacquer artists, potters, and textile makers that lent their technical skills to artists who may have lacked them. Such divisions of labor are emblematic of the complex environment of art-making in early modern Japan. Instead of representing a system of intentional deception, this environment was mutually beneficial. It enabled artists to diversify their portfolio and produce works that would otherwise be impossible to accomplish.

The carefully calibrated aesthetic of Kōrin's lacquer works beguiled the eighteenth-century public. In 1786, for example, the artist directory *New Selection of Japanese and Chinese-Style Painting and Calligraphy* (*Shinsen wakan shoga ichiran*) identifies Kōrin as a painter proficient at "lacquer vessels (*shikki*) and images drawn in gilded lacquer (*byakukin*)"—indicating that contemporaries considered Kōrin's works as hand-painted by himself.[41] Similarly, other designs by Kōrin struck viewers with their reduced efficiency and painterly quality. The 1732 guide to making inrō, titled *A Wealth of Occupations in a Nutshell* (*Bankin sugiwai bukuro*), lays out how to make Kōrin's idiosyncratic chrysanthemums economically and quickly. The book emphasizes that the design can be "finished in one single brushstroke" (*fude ippon nite sumu*), a practice that seems to depart from conventional lacquer designs, which required longer and more complex processes of making.[42] Kōrin was successful in imbuing his lacquer works with the carefree semblance of painterly immediacy—an effect made possible only by their multitiered method of making.

❖ ❖ ❖

Kōrin's work in lacquer operated on two fronts: designs with a streamlined production process and an efficient system of manufacture, as well as highly complex designs that evoked the artist's apparent direct involvement. All told, on the basis of his great-granduncle Hon'ami Kōetsu's model, Kōrin invigorated eighteenth-century Japanese lacquer by rethinking personal creativity and the manufacture process. He did so in other media—such as ceramics—as well, thereby expanding the paradigm of making art during his lifetime and in the decades beyond. As a result, Kōrin collapsed the boundaries between painting and other early modern art forms, a pioneering feat that helped form part of his artistic identity.

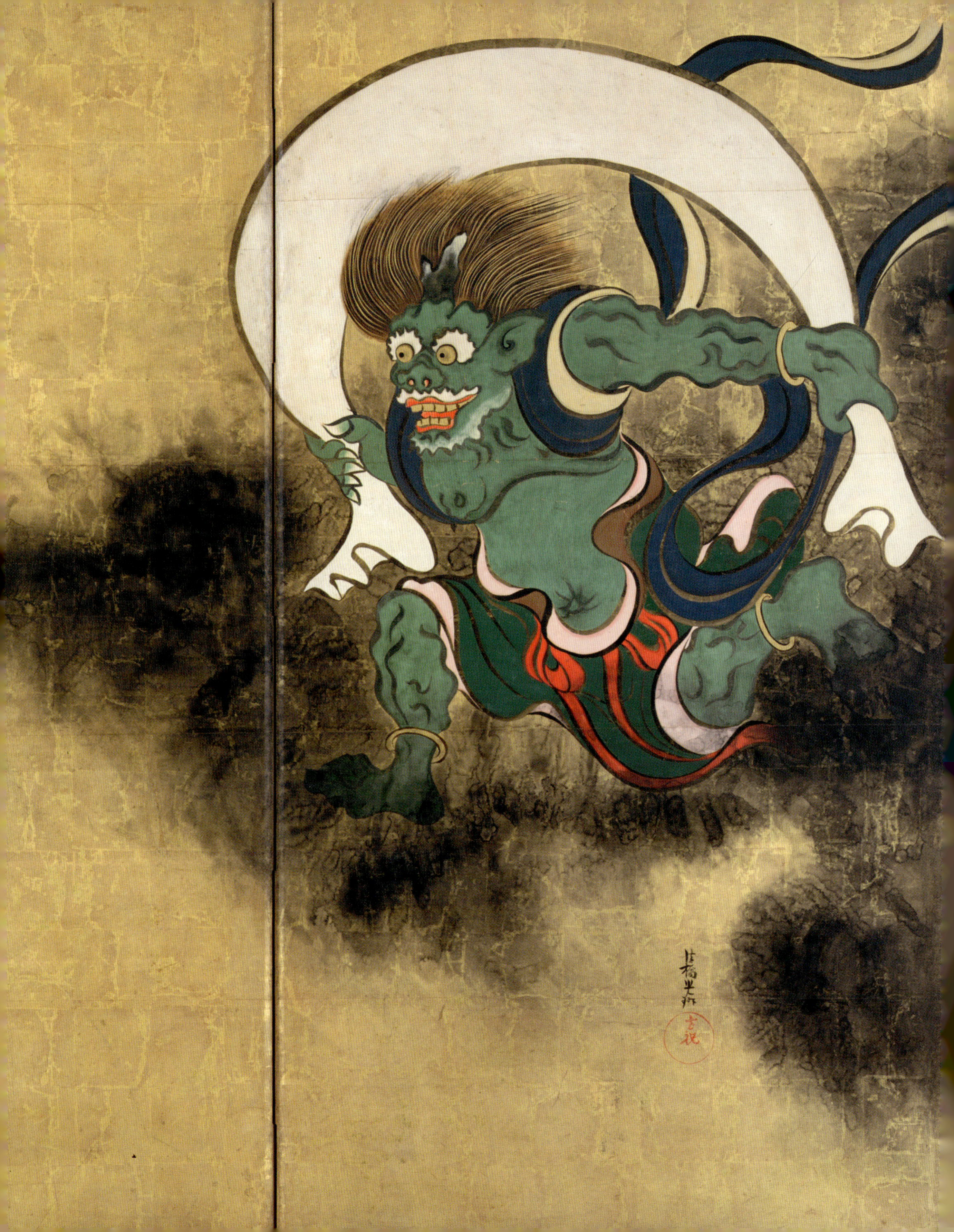

4 Heading East

Kōrin in Edo

> After [my dream that night], I rushed to Nishi Honganji to see His Excellency [abbot Jakunyo]. He would not let me leave before I told him [of my dream]. I explained that in my dream I traveled to Edo and saw Mount Fuji. Once he heard this, Jakunyo exclaimed, "This is a good dream," and he told me to quickly put it to paper. I did so immediately.
>
> —Ogata Kōrin's inscription on his *Dream Painting of Mount Fuji,* dated 1699

In 1704 Kōrin packed his bags and left his native Kyoto for the eastern power center of Edo. In doing so, he aligned himself with generations of people from the capital who ventured eastward. Kōrin did not completely relocate but instead commuted back and forth between Kyoto and Edo for five years, from 1704 to 1709. As described by poets and adventurers like Matsuo Bashō (1654–1694), traveling in early modern Japan was common.[1] Yet it was anything but safe and convenient, even on such heavily traveled corridors as the Tōkaidō, the road connecting Kyoto and Edo.

Kōrin was not an avid traveler, and this journey marked his first known trip outside the Kansai region. Few other events following Kōrin's earliest steps as a painter had such a profound impact on his career as did his activities in the seat of the shogunal government. Ostensibly in anticipation of his departure for Edo, Kōrin spent the first years of the eighteenth century preparing himself. As a part of this readying, he absorbed the style associated with the tradition of Tawaraya Sōtatsu. In the following years, Kōrin's desire to adopt Sōtatsu's aesthetic and make it his own grew increasingly stronger.

The timing of Kōrin's turn to Sōtatsu is conspicuous and hints at the multifaceted process of artistic inspiration that preceded his departure for Edo. Kōrin apparently intended to transport the Kyoto-based visual language of Sōtatsu and his atelier to the eastern city, hoping that it would appeal to clients there. But by the time he relocated in 1704, Edo had developed its own aesthetic consciousness, and it appears that clients were not fully receptive to

Detail of fig. 81

Kōrin's form of capital chic. This dissonance between personal expectation and objective reality encouraged him to match his approach to painting with the local tastes of Edo, a fusion that influenced Kōrin's art for the rest of his life. His strategy of merging preferences resulted in hybrid artworks that combine Kyoto-related features taken from Sōtatsu's style with those of unconnected painterly traditions, such as the Edo-based Kano school. His five years in Edo made Kōrin acutely aware of early modern tastes, creating a desire to accommodate them through his ability to reshape conventions.

Among his patrons in Edo—many of whom hailed from the warrior elite—Kōrin encountered the omnipresence of the Kano atelier and the referential legacy of Kano Tan'yū.[2] Through the filter of that atelier, which claimed stylistic ancestry in medieval ink painting, Kōrin was exposed to the style and interpretations of one of the luminaries of ink painting in the Muromachi period, Sesshū Tōyō. His experiences in Edo exemplify the seemingly disparate aesthetics of Kyoto and Edo, and they show how early modern Japanese painters struggled with negotiating the conventions imposed by the Kano atelier and refocusing them to nurture creativity.

In addition to a desire to cater to local clients, Kōrin's turn to Sesshū via the Kano hints at an attempt to add orthodoxy to his otherwise comparatively unconventional approach to painting—a requirement he encountered in Edo. An amateur turned professional painter, Kōrin was unaffiliated with any of the large ateliers. This autonomy imposed both the burden of expectations and the opportunity to carve his own niche. By mastering and reformulating the art of Sesshū, Kōrin gained the ultimate seal of approval as a painter. After all, he slid into his role as an artist not through professional determination but through personal desire and necessity. In this way, the demands and resources of Edo imposed a struggle that provides insight into the artistic and personal mechanisms that defined Kōrin's work as a painter.

WORLDLY AND DIVINE PREPARATIONS

Kōrin seems to have made three separate trips eastward from his home of Kyoto to the capital city of Edo.[3] His first journey extended from the eleventh month of 1704 to the third month of 1705. He returned to Edo in the fifth or sixth month of 1705, before going back to Kyoto briefly in the fourth month of 1707. He left for Edo again roughly a year later. Kōrin's final trip home to Kyoto occurred around the third month of 1709, after which he remained in his native city for good. On the fourth day of the sixth month in 1709, his lifelong acquaintance the aristocrat Nijō Tsunahira held a welcome-back banquet for the artist.[4] His circle of friends in Kyoto was apparently glad to have him back.

The painter's initial reluctance to leave the comfort of Kyoto is felt in a farewell letter that he dispatched to a friend before his second trip to Edo.

> Please let me come again in a little while.
> Thank you for your letter from yesterday. Please also accept my gratitude for your parting gift of five bundles of small paper (*kogami*).
> *In the sorrow of our parting, the sleeves of my sunlit robe*
> *are drenched with many layers of blossom scent,*
> *alas, this means farewell.*
> I will visit you in time to express my gratitude.
> Yours sincerely.
> Fourth month, thirteenth day. Kōrin [cypher]
>
> To Ueshima Gennojō (or Gen'in) [From] Ogata Kōrin[5]

To understand Kōrin's resolve to move to Edo, it is necessary to look back at his early days as an artist. Kōrin's dealings with Edo clients began years before he actually traveled there in 1704. Several years earlier, Kōrin sold a lacquer suzuribako to an Edo patron, an indication that his artworks had acquired distant admirers. Already during the late 1690s, when Kōrin initiated his first steps as an artist, Edo appears to have been a destination for his works. His early connections to art dealers may have formed a strategic position for his relocation to the city a few years later. As we have seen, the commodification of art from the seventeenth century onward, and the increase of collecting activities throughout the realm, provided Kōrin with a substantial infrastructure of middlemen that enabled established and emerging artists alike to cultivate their clientele far beyond their local environment.

The establishment of the Tokugawa shogunate and the pacification of the realm that followed gave rise to an increasingly mobile society where, in spite of roadside perils, travel for business and leisure became commonplace. In addition, the system of alternate attendance that required regional daimyo to spend specific amounts of time in Edo and leave their families there created a huge demand for paintings to outfit their residences. That vast market attracted many fortune-seeking artists, Kōrin among them. But before he left Kyoto, Kōrin wanted to ensure that heaven was on his side.

Kōrin heeded the implications of celestial will on worldly existence, and this belief played its part preceding his departure for Edo. Kōrin kept company with the prominent mathematician and astrologer Nakane Genkei. Their relationship is documented through several divinations that Genkei conducted for Kōrin in the 1690s. Kōrin's unusually frequent changes of pseudonyms and choice of characters for his first and last names reflect his superstition. He called on Genkei four times at important junctures during his life when he felt that seraphic testing was necessary.[6] For example, a divination took place in 1702. That year Kōrin desired a good omen for his nom de plume Kansei. Two years later, Genkei performed another divination for a new pseudonym, Dōsū. In this case, Kōrin clearly searched for favorable portents in the months before his departure for Edo. During his back-and-forth travels between Kyoto and Edo, the artist impressed his works with Dōsū seals, demonstrating the significance of Genkei's favorable divination for his activities in the east. Such prognostications were so important to Kōrin that during a brief return from Edo to Kyoto in 1705, he asked Genkei to test the fortunes of yet another set of characters for his last name, Ogata.

In addition to celestial preparations, financial considerations played a part in readying Kōrin for his work in Edo. Around the time of the divinations, the perpetually penniless Kōrin attempted to sell his property at Nakamachi Yabunouchichō, a bustling and affluent neighborhood north of the imperial palace in Kyoto. He had inherited the large mansion from his father. On being unable to sell the house, he agreed to an exorbitant mortgage payment of seventy-nine *ryō* in gold from a townsman named Kawai Heiemon.[7] Finalized roughly two months before Kōrin departed for Edo in 1704, the transaction repaid some of his accumulated debts. The urgency with which Kōrin sought to clear his name in Kyoto suggests that he aimed for a smooth departure and perhaps wished to avoid looking like a runaway—a notion supported by the fact that his wife, Tayo, remained in Kyoto during his first trip to Edo. Kōrin's extensive predeparture arrangements, artistically and personally, indicate that he envisioned a lengthy stay in Edo, with brief return visits home.

In another part of his departure arrangements, Kōrin gradually changed the style of his signature around 1703. He initially wrote the first character of Kōrin in the way of his famous great-granduncle Hon'ami Kōetsu. Around 1703, however, Kōrin began to articulate each stroke of the first character clearly (fig. 58). Works bearing the Kansei seal, produced in the years leading up to his departure for Edo, carry both writing styles for his signature. Around 1704, the year he went to Edo, he settled on this distinctly personalized imprimatur, writing it prominently on his paintings, ceramics, and some lacquer pieces. Kōrin's decision to find an individualized way of writing his name may indicate an effort to emancipate himself from the cultural leverage of his well-known ancestor before setting off for Edo, where Kōetsu's name resonated less than in Kyoto.

In these years Kōrin also renewed his connection with Nijō Tsunahira—probably recalling the social clout that such court connections could bring him in Edo. Kōrin visited Tsunahira only once in 1701, but in 1703 alone he had held seven audiences with the influential courtier.[8] His move to Edo also coincided

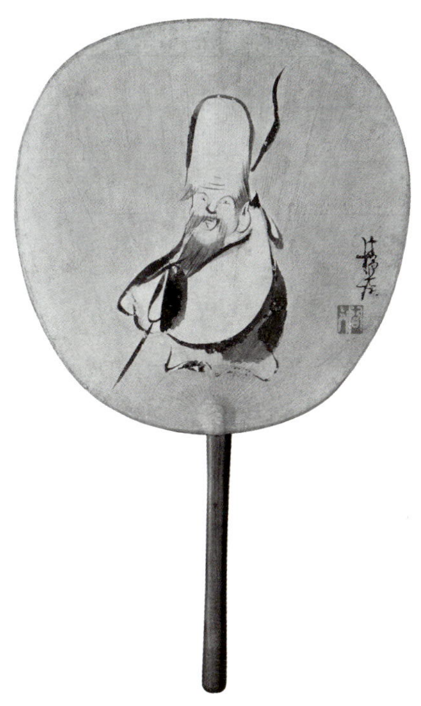

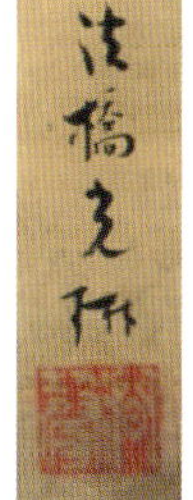

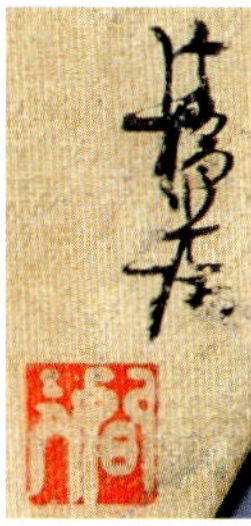

FIGURE 58
Near right: Detail, fig. 59; Middle and far right: Ogata Kōrin, *Jurōjin* (detail with entire work), early 18th century. Oval fan; ink and gold on paper. MOA Museum of Art, Atami.

with the relocation of the temple of the Fuyuki family from Kyoto to Edo following the death of Fuyuki Masachika in 1703.[9] In addition to being one of Kōrin's main patrons in Edo, the Fuyuki family at one time owned his *Irises at Yatsuhashi* screens (see chapter 2). Members of the clan also spent extensive amounts of time in the capital. After 1703, however, their focus shifted to Edo and to clients there.

All in all, the years preceding Kōrin's departure were eventful, and so was 1704, the year he left Kyoto. It marked the end of the Genroku era and the beginning of Hōei. Such astrological circumstance likely gave added impetus to Kōrin's decision to venture eastward. In the same year, Tsunahira was appointed minister of the center (*naidaijin*), a prestigious post.[10] The connection with Tsunahira, along with Kōrin's illustrious ancestry, no doubt carried considerable cultural weight and eased the painter's entry into circles of upper-tier merchants and daimyo—his most important patrons in Edo.

EDO INFRASTRUCTURE

The divine and mundane preparations that preceded Kōrin's departure coincided with his increasing association with the silver mint official Nakamura Kuranosuke, a man of paramount importance for Kōrin during the last two decades of his life. Their friendship began around 1700 and lasted until Kōrin's death in 1716. The earliest evidence of their relationship is Kōrin's appointment as an official to the Osaka copper mint in 1701.[11] Even though Kōrin's duties remain unclear, the post was probably facilitated by Kuranosuke, who wielded considerable power over the currency system of early modern Japan. In 1702 both men drafted a contract in which Kōrin agreed to take in Kuranosuke's newborn daughter, Katsu, and educate her for five years.[12]

> Personal draft, One sheet
> I [Kōrin] shall take your [Nakamura Kuranosuke's] daughter Katsu, born this year, into my fosterage and raise her until she is five years old. For this, I shall be given a yearly [allowance] of one kan silver. I shall use this amount for various expenses incurred by Katsu's education. As instructed, I shall return her in the next Year of the Dog [1706]. [This document] shall act as future proof [of this agreement].
> Genroku 15 [1702], Year of the Horse, seventh month, first day.
> Ogata Kōrin [seal:] Koresuke
> Nakamura Kurōemon [Kuranosuke][13]

Katsu would later marry Kōrin's illegitimate son Juichirō, who was himself adopted by the silver mint official Konishi Hikokurō, an acquaintance and colleague of Kuranosuke. According to Kōrin's will, Kuranosuke brokered the adoption of Juichirō and soon assumed a protective role in Kōrin's life.[14] This comradeship with Kuranosuke coincided with a temporary decline in the number of times Kōrin visited the Nijō family after he received the hokkyō title in 1701 until about 1703.[15]

Kōrin and Kuranosuke probably met through the artist's high social status in Kyoto. The financially stricken Kōrin gratefully received Kuranosuke's support while offering him some aristocratic glamour. For example, in 1703 Kōrin took Kuranosuke for an audience with Nijō Tsunahira—a privilege that could have been intended as a reciprocation for the favors the artist had received from the silver mint official.[16] On that occasion, as a gift offered at the end of the year, Kuranosuke received a set of ten decorated poem leaves with a preface written by Kōrin. Evidently, Tsunahira had commissioned Kōrin to create a gift for Kuranosuke, a gesture that symbolized their triad of friendship. Visiting and receiving a gift from a relative of the emperor must have impressed a status-conscious man like Kuranosuke. At least the gesture was strong enough to pull Kōrin further into his circle of favorites and culminate in a commission for a portrait.

Among the many paintings that Kōrin created before he left for Edo, the portrait of Kuranosuke encapsulates best his approach to painting and patronage (fig. 59). The work depicts the silver mint official in full stature, as a man of wealth, fashion, and erudition. Such portraits were typically commissioned as objects of veneration on an ancestor's death. An inscription by the astrologer Nakane Genkei communicates as much by recording the name Kuranosuke would assume posthumously.

> This year, [Ogyū Sorai] bestowed upon Fuji[wara] Nobumitsu [Kuranosuke], aged thirty-six, the posthumous pseudonym of Recluse of the Bright Heart and the Ever-Radiant Changing Dusk (*Shinkōin jōshō iseki koji*). Thus, [Kuranosuke] ordered a picture to be made. I, then, inscribed that portrait in the northwestern [upper left] corner, as a memento of the passage of time. Genroku 17, [Year of the] Wood Monkey [1704], third month. Hiraaki Genshin [Nakane Genkei]

When the portrait was inscribed in 1704, presumably a short while after Kōrin had completed it, Kuranosuke was still very much alive. Indeed, he lived another twenty-six years. Rather than being part of his preparations for the afterlife, the painting was a statement for the present-day. By asking Ogyū Sorai (1666–1729), a Confucian scholar and one of the most prominent intellectuals of his day, to choose a lavish posthumous name, Kuranosuke made sure that his societal status and exalted self-perception would extend into the afterlife.

The painting assumes the dual function of displaying Kuranosuke's status as well as Kōrin's command of Tawaraya Sōtatsu's aesthetic. Kōrin turned the bureaucrat into a simulacrum of a Sōtatsu-style figure painting. When compared to Sōtatsu's early seventeenth-century poem leaves of the *Tales of Ise,* the similarities are evident (fig. 60). The pale white face and crimson lips are reminiscent of Sōtatsu's depictions of the courtier Ariwara Narihira, the protagonist of the *Tales of Ise.* In fact, the proximity of Kuranosuke's figure to paintings of courtly tales effectively turns the silver mint official into an avatar of an ancient courtier in Sōtatsu's style. A fan decorated by Kōrin illustrates how he had direct access to poem leaves by Sōtatsu and his studio around the time he painted Kuranosuke's portrait. Portrait and fan carry the same Kansei seal that Kōrin used in the years leading up to his activities in Edo (figs. 61, 62).

A portrait from this era need not reflect the actual likeness of the sitter as much as it should create a symbolic image of him. Role-defining attributes were more crucial than detailed resemblance. Following this tradition, Kōrin added signs of status and learning, a sword and a scroll, to depict the powerful silver mint official. Before Kuranosuke's seated figure, the artist placed a folding fan that is dwarfed by the towering bureaucrat. On inspection, the fan displays a plum tree done in a way that reflects a number of Sōtatsu-made fan paintings (figs. 63, 64). Rendering the fan and Kuranosuke in Sōtatsu's style employs that aesthetic as a vehicle for the silver mint official's own self-perception as a man of status and refinement. As such, Kōrin's painting is as much a portrait of

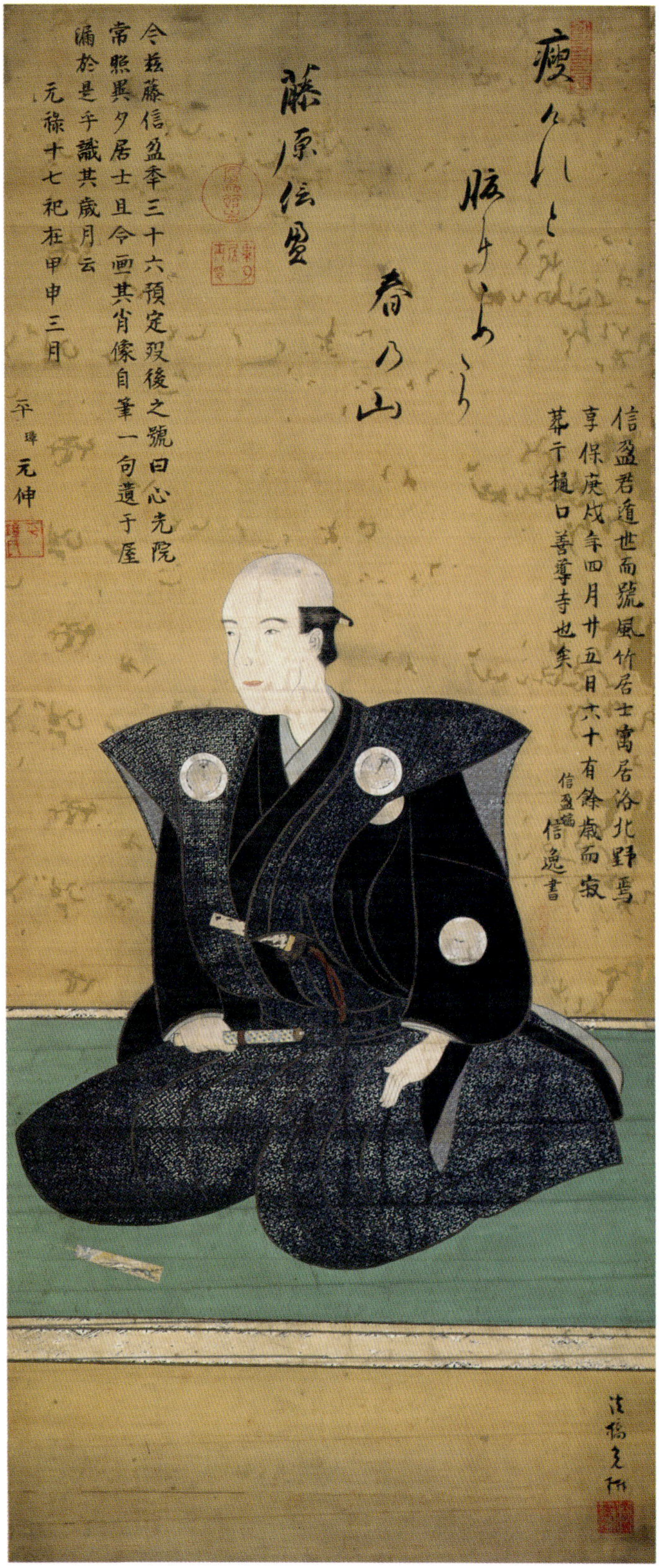

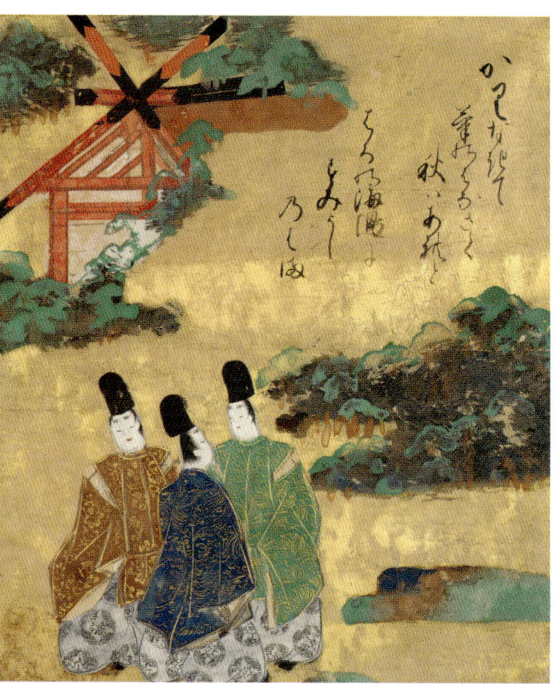

FIGURE 60

Tawaraya Sōtatsu, *The Beach at Sumiyoshi, from the Tales of Ise,* 1600–1640. Poetry sheet mounted as hanging scroll; ink, color, and gold on paper. Cleveland Museum of Art, John L. Severance Fund, 1951.398.

FIGURE 59

Ogata Kōrin, *Portrait of Nakamura Kuranosuke,* 1704. Hanging scroll; ink and color on silk. Yamato Bunkakan, Nara.

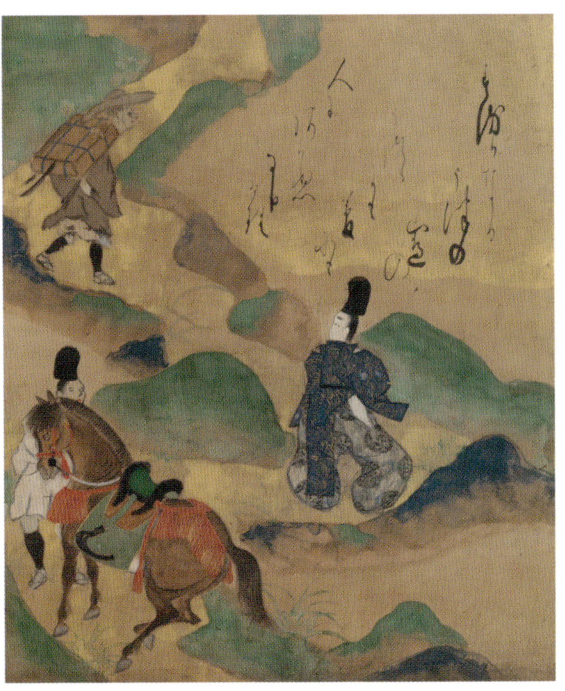

FIGURE 61
Tawaraya Sōtatsu, *Mt. Utsu, from the Tales of Ise,* early 17th century. Poetry sheet mounted as hanging scroll; ink and color on paper. The Metropolitan Museum of Art, New York, Mary Griggs Burke Collection, Gift of the Mary and Jackson Burke Foundation, 2015, 2015.300.88.

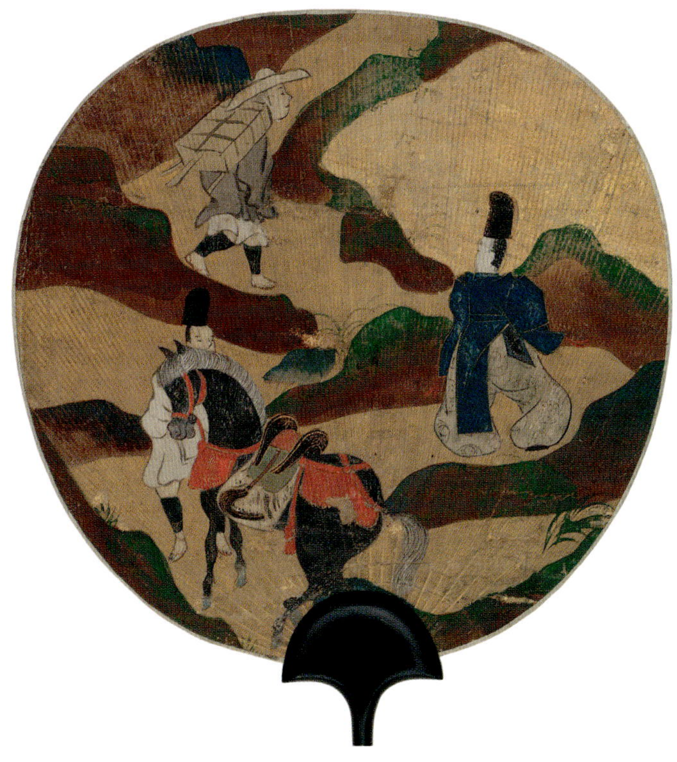

FIGURE 62
Ogata Kōrin, *Mt. Utsu, from the Tales of Ise,* early 18th century. Oval fan; ink, color, and gold on paper. Freer Gallery of Art, Smithsonian Institution, Washington, D.C.: Gift of Charles Lang Freer, F1903.1.

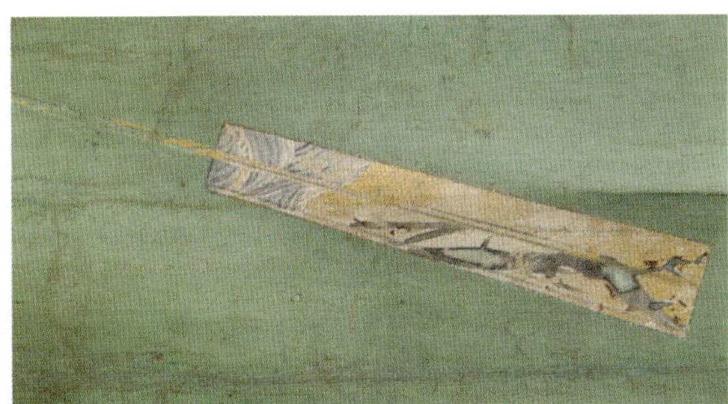

FIGURE 63 Detail, fig. 59.

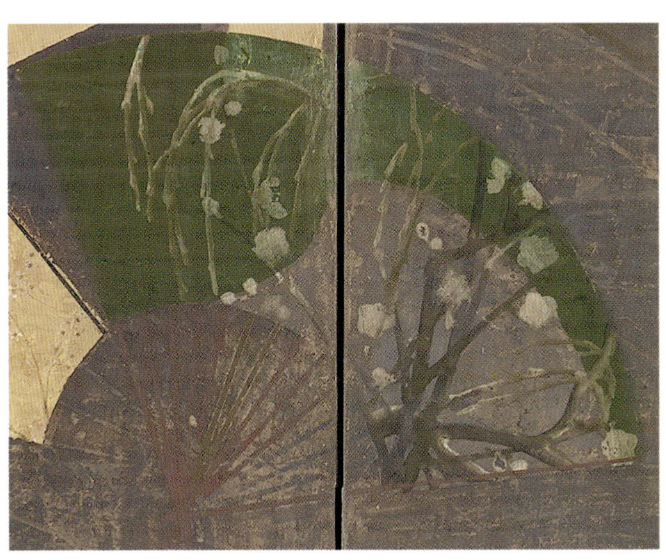

FIGURE 64
Tawaraya Sōtatsu, *Ivy Vines, Bridges, and Floating Fans* (detail), early 17th century. Pair of six-panel folding screens; ink, color, gold, and silver on paper. Freer Gallery of Art, Smithsonian Institution, Washington, D.C.: Gift of Charles Lang Freer, F1902.102–103.

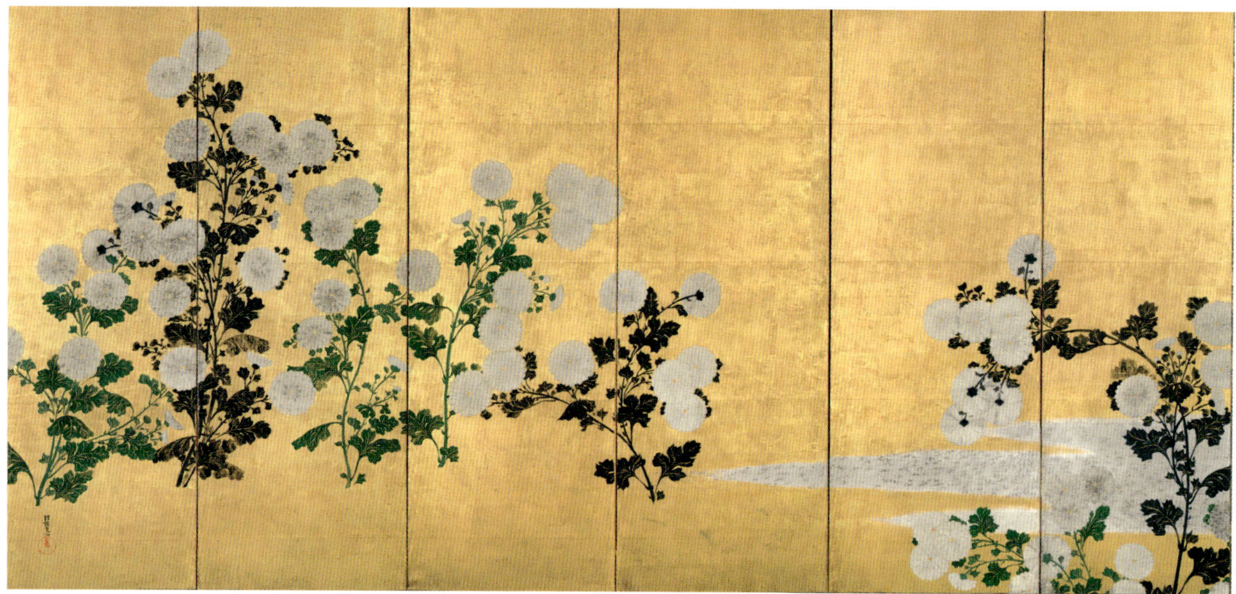

FIGURE 65
Ogata Kōrin, *Chrysanthemums,* early 18th century. Pair of six-panel folding screens; ink, color, and gold on gilded paper. Okada Museum of Art, Hakone.

Kuranosuke's position as it is an expression of the role that Sōtatsu's visual language played in the aesthetic identity of the upper-tier society in Kyoto.

Kuranosuke had gained considerable riches following the currency reform that the silver mint administered in 1695. Before this, silver mint officials led only modest existences, a fact that perhaps encouraged Kuranosuke to flaunt his newfound wealth.[17] Kōrin's portrait not only displays this consciousness of status but explains how the aesthetic of Sōtatsu helped Kuranosuke and similar men to fashion themselves after the court and the urban upper class of Kyoto. After all, Sōtatsu received commissions from the emperor GoMizuno'o and the imperially sponsored monastery Daigoji. In addition, members of the haute bourgeoisie in Kyoto, such as Kōrin's father, Ogata Sōken, had joined princes and high-ranking courtiers in inscribing leaves with pictures by Sōtatsu and his atelier.[18] The aesthetic was as much a part of Kyoto as the court itself. Further, the price commanded by Sōtatsu's screen, which Kōrin had sold a few years earlier, illustrates the popularity of that style in the mid-Edo period. In light of these circumstances, it seems obvious that a rising official like Kuranosuke would try to clad himself in the capital's elite aesthetic. Kōrin's espousal of Sōtatsu's style at that time precisely supplied this cultural gravitas. He likely had this connection in mind when he studied and appropriated paintings by Sōtatsu and the Tawaraya studio in the years leading up to his activities in Edo.

Eight months after painting Kuranosuke's portrait, Kōrin headed off to Edo under the protective umbrella of the silver mint official. His turn to Kuranosuke as his main sponsor played a defining part in encouraging the

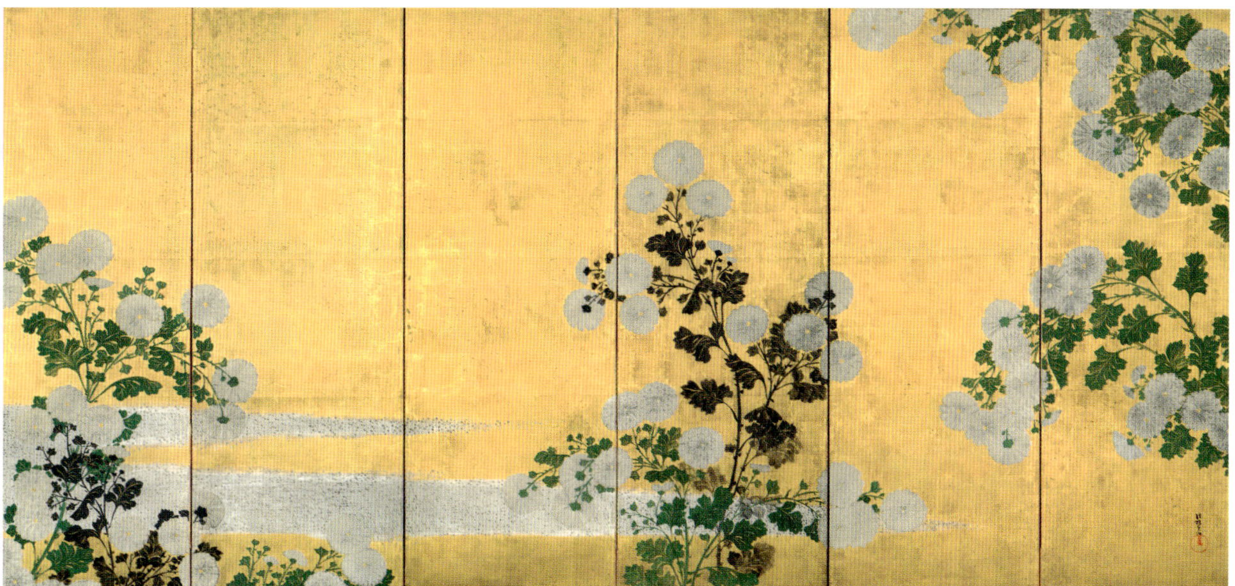

painter to tap into the thriving art market of Edo. In his official capacity, Kuranosuke was used to commuting back and forth between Kyoto and Edo. When Kōrin left for Edo, Kuranosuke resided there on silver mint business.[19] During his first weeks in the city of the shogun, Kōrin lodged at one of the silver mint's properties, usually reserved for high-ranking officials. Kuranosuke must have arranged this accommodation, and he apparently helped Kōrin establish his social footing. Shortly after arriving, the artist wrote to a friend in Kyoto:

> I received your letter from the eighteenth day of the last month, and I am delighted to hear that your family is well. On the second day of this month, I arrived safely in Edo (*chakufu*) and took up lodgings at the silver mint mansion at Kyōbashi Itchōme. Once the weather is suitable [for safe travel], my relations [his wife, Tayo?] will join me.[20] I was overjoyed to be granted an audience with Ogiwara Shigehide [1658–1713, a shogunal commissioner] so soon [after my arrival]. In the meantime, I have been receiving orders for paintings from various clients (*tokorodokoro*). I quickly finished a pair of chrysanthemums screens. Kō[ken?] is also well and I take him along to appointments [with clients] to paint.[21] I am pleased to receive praise from all sides and have even been invited for tea two times already. I am overjoyed. Please also tell [your brother] about [what I said in this letter].[22] He should let me know if he desires my services [for painting instruction].[23] Please also send my best wishes to your father.
> Sincerely,
> Ogata Kōrin [cypher]

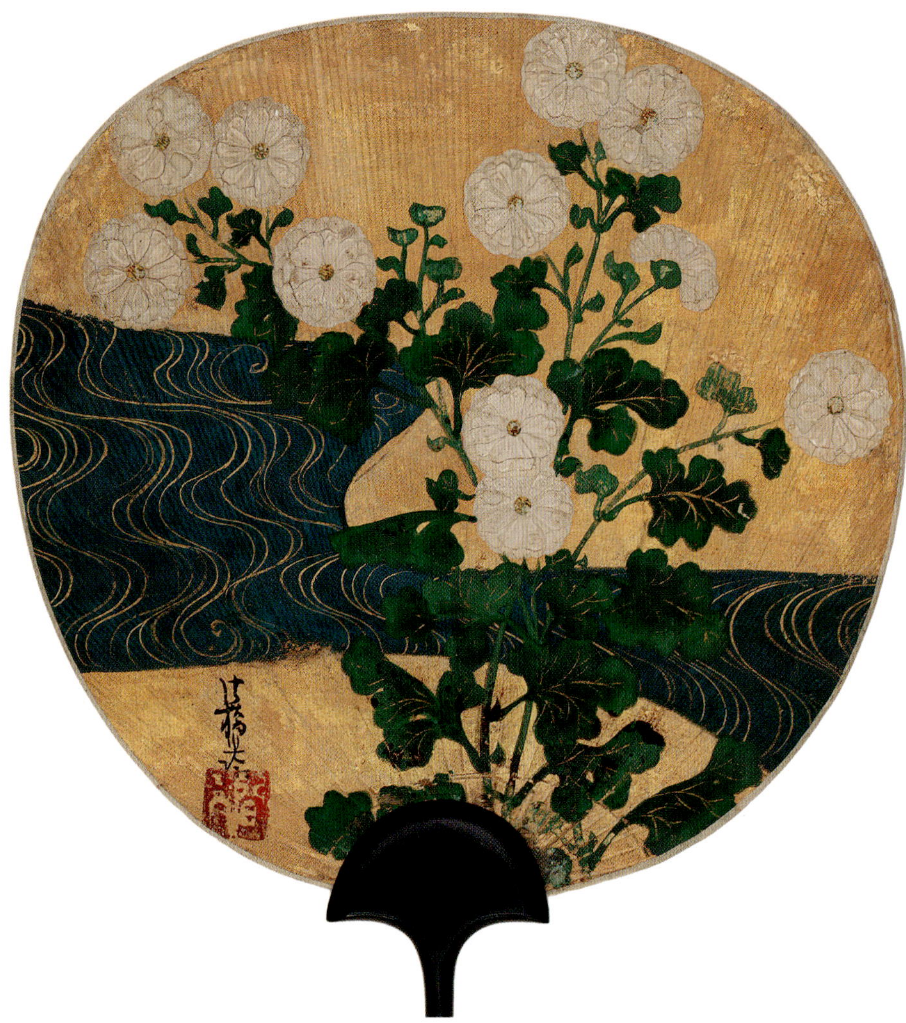

FIGURE 66
Ogata Kōrin, *Chrysanthemums* (verso of fig. 62), early 18th century. Oval fan; ink, color, and gold on paper. Freer Gallery of Art, Smithsonian Institution, Washington, D.C.: Gift of Charles Lang Freer, F1903.1.

> Eleventh month, fifteenth day [1704?].
>
> To Ueshima Gennojō [also read Kamijima Gen'in]
>
> P. S. The other day, [the Noh performer] Hōshō Tomoharu [1654–1728] was summoned by Nakamura Kuranosuke [here, Nakakurō] and he performed [the plays] *Seiganji* and *Hanagatami.* It was quite marvelous and I am at a loss for words.

Kōrin arrived in Edo in the winter of 1704 and immediately attended performances of the Noh theater, one of the prime venues for early modern socializing and one of his personal passions. Many doors opened at once for Kōrin, and he soon received commissions and audiences with powerful men. He specified that he painted a screen with chrysanthemums, perhaps showing pride in

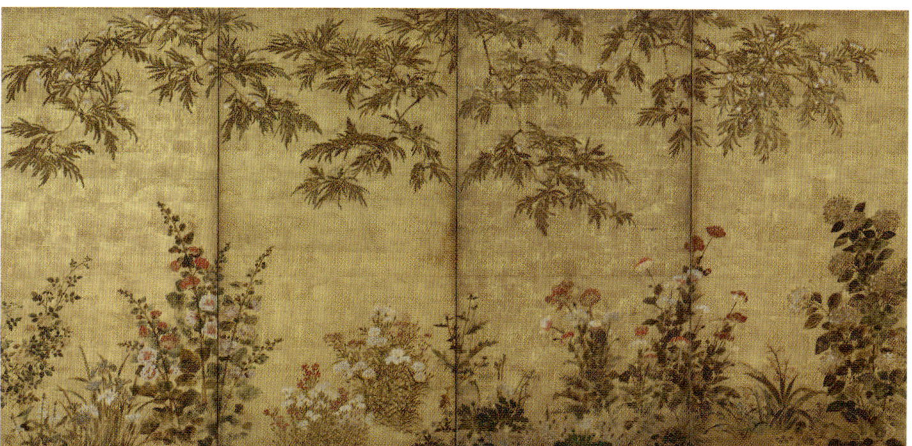

FIGURE 67
Tawaraya Sōsetsu, *Mimosa Tree, Poppies, and Other Summer Flowers,* 17th century. Four-panel folding screen; ink, color, and gold on paper. Freer Gallery of Art, Smithsonian Institution, Washington, D.C.: Gift of Charles Lang Freer, F1902.92.

having been asked to produce a large-format painting so early into his stay in Edo. This now-lost work likely resembled a pair of screens and fan that survive today (figs. 65, 66). The screens carry a signature style and Iryō seal, suggesting that they were painted sometime between 1701, when Kōrin received the *hokkyō* title from the court, and 1704, the year he left for Edo. The fan likewise was made when he used his Kansei seal before 1704. Both paintings employ a similar wheel-like shape of blossoms embossed in layers of shell-white.

The screens in particular showcase Kōrin's juxtaposition of leaves in ink and malachite green. Serving as his inspiration were works by followers of Sōtatsu's legacy, such as the painter Tawaraya Sōsetsu (active mid-seventeenth century), who took over the master's studio in Kyoto before moving to the Kaga Domain and serving the Maeda clan (fig. 67).[24] The screens and the fan demonstrate the way of painting that Kōrin must have carried with him to Edo. If he made a chrysanthemum painting in Edo around the year 1704, it likely looked something like these two examples—in other words, like a Tawaraya painting. Since chrysanthemums are one of the first subjects Kōrin painted in Edo, his comment in the letter also manifests how he carried traditional themes to a place where the predominant aesthetic was informed by other schools. It appears that Kōrin was determined to transport Kyoto to Edo.

Further into his time in Edo, Kōrin eventually confronted the more conservative demands of his clients. Their aesthetic preferences had been shaped by a centuries-old affection for Chinese-inspired ink paintings and their Kano adaptations. Eventually, Kōrin expressed his frustration with his demanding clients, many of whom belonged to the warrior families that resided in Edo part-time. Midway during his stay, Kōrin wrote to a friend in Kyoto that "I am not to be envied for being brought before daimyo." The euphoria of his early days in Edo gave way to exasperation. Some patrons seem to have failed to recognize him as the accomplished, original painter he was viewed as in Kyoto. Instead, they expected the same effort from him that they received from professional ateliers and the Kano industry. Kōrin, a man who mingled with the highest strata of aristocratic society in Kyoto, suddenly found himself not painting chrysanthemums but instead copying the works of the medieval master Sesshū, a core artistic reference of the Kano workshop.

THE KANO CONDUIT

Like many of his contemporaries, Kōrin had studied with a Kano master in his youth. Yet he only embraced the style fully during his time in Edo, when he was already in his late forties, reversing the common pattern of art education in early modern Japan. Being taught as a youth or young man by one of the countless Kano painters who operated across Japan was not only a prerequisite for any aspiring painter but also a customary practice among the upper-class bourgeoisie to which Kōrin belonged. His father, Ogata Sōken, had also learned painting in the Kano style, so it was only natural that his son did so as well. Other than his father, Kōrin's early Kano study left little traction in his work. However, his experiences in Edo did.

Early modern connoisseurs, relying on similarities of style between Kōrin and other masters, proposed a variety of names for his possible early Kano teacher, which only confused the question.[25] A definitive answer is absent to this day. *Overview of Paintings in Japanese and Chinese Styles* (*Wakan shoga ichiran*) of 1771, for example, suggests Kano Yasunobu, but this possibility is largely discredited. Yasunobu was based in Edo and resided in Kyoto only for short intervals. By the time of Kōrin's first trip to Edo in 1704, Yasunobu had long since died. The late Edo period anthology of painters *Compendium of New and Ancient Calligraphy and Painting of This Realm* (*Honchō kokin shoga binran*, 1813, 1818) opts for Kano Tsunenobu (1636–1713). The entry on Kōrin in the *Compendium* contains significant factual errors, such as mistaking his dates of life, which suggests that the author lacked sufficient insights into the artist's life.

Yamamoto Soken, one of Kano Tan'yū's Kyoto-based pupils, is frequently considered Kōrin's initial instructor in the Kano mode.[26] This conjecture is based on an obscure text by Asai Fukyū cited by Sakai Hōitsu, one of Kōrin's late Edo period admirers, in his *Concise Chronology of Seals of the Ogata School* (*Ogata-ryū ryaku inpu*), published in an expanded version in 1815. "After [Kōrin's father], Ogata Sōken, released him from his care, [Kōrin] was drawn to the style of Sōtatsu and became a pupil of Yamamoto Soken. Later, he received the hokkyō [title]. This [information] we can glean from Asai Fukyū's *Inpu*."[27] Hōitsu relied on an unidentified chronology of seals (*inpu*) by Asai Fukyū, which modern scholarship identifies as Fukyū's book *Chronology of Seals of Painters of This Realm* (*Honchō gaka inpu*), which does not survive.[28] Fukyū was a mid-Edo period connoisseur whose *Compendium of Famous Painters of Japan* (*Fusō meikō gafu*), written sometime during the Kyōhō era (1716–36), became an influential reference work for artist biographies. In his studies of Kōrin, Hōitsu evidently trusted Fukyū's scholarship. Yet it is unclear whether Fukyū formulated the idea of Soken as Kōrin's teacher or whether Hōitsu simply used Fukyū's name to validate his claim. After all, Fukyū's life overlapped with Kōrin's last years, and he appears to have been in Kyoto by 1710, around the time Kōrin returned to his native city from Edo.[29]

Hōitsu's theory resulted in the overarching presence of Yamamoto Soken in discussions of Kōrin's early Kano study. This wide acceptance left little room for other theories to take hold. No documentary evidence suggests that the two painters even knew each other before 1703, when both attended a soirée at Nijō Tsunahira's estate.[30] Kōrin's earliest surviving paintings reveal significant differences with works by Yamamoto Soken. Soken may have been responsible for Kōrin's study of Kano modes before the 1690s, but Kōrin seems to have quickly turned from such obvious reflections of the Kano style. In short, Soken could have laid the foundations for Kōrin's paintings, but the Kano painter's eventual impact on Kōrin's work was slim, even if he did actually teach him.

A significant number of sketches by Kōrin still survive, which intensifies the mystery of his exposure to the Kano atelier. However, the level of accuracy with which he embraced the Kano traits in most of the sketches remains at odds with many of his paintings before his time in Edo. In fact, the degree of immersion in the intricacies of Kano practice that is evident in almost all of his Kano-related studies is much more apparent in works produced later than the late seventeenth century when he purportedly studied with Yamamoto Soken, namely, around the time he resided in Edo and thereafter.

Take, for example, his sketch of the Tang dynasty poet Li Bai (701–762), a popular figure in Japanese painting (fig. 68). Kōrin's sketch is based on Kano model books. The tree is rendered much as it is in Kōrin's *Misogi,* a painting of a religious ceremony featured in the *Tales of Ise* (fig. 69). *Misogi* bears a Dōsū seal, the name Kōrin used while in Edo. The painting is a skillful hybridization of the Kano and Sōtatsu styles—a novelty that must have appealed to his Edo clientele. Heavy in ink washes with a lack of outlines, the style is associated with Tan'yū, one of the Kano school's most exalted representatives. By studying paintings by Chinese academy artists as well as by Sesshū and other Japanese painters, Tan'yū introduced into the Kano practice a soft palette of ink that generations of later artists embraced.

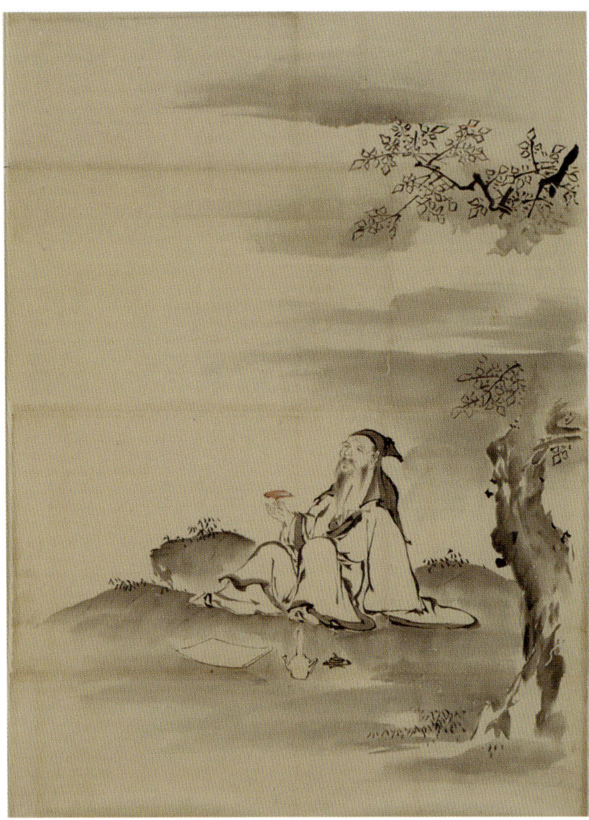

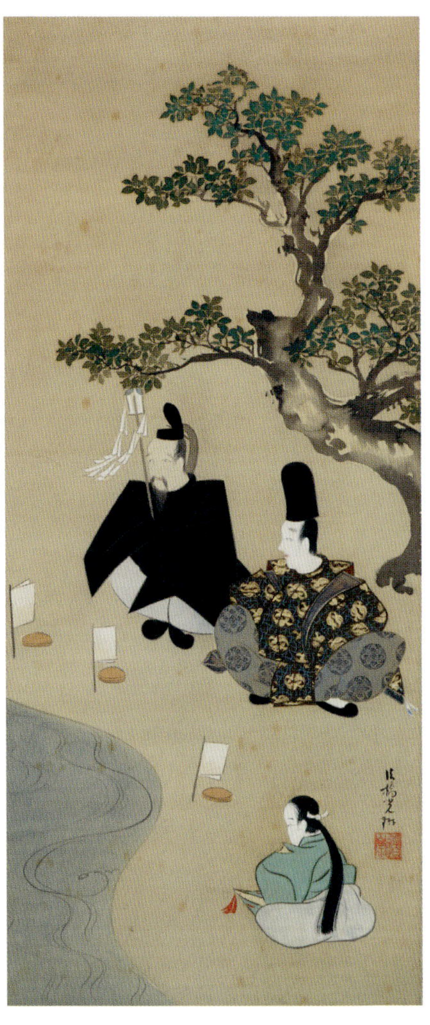

FIGURE 68 Ogata Kōrin, *Li Bai,* late 17th or early 18th century. Ink and light color on paper. Konishi Family Archive, Kyoto National Museum.

FIGURE 69 Ogata Kōrin, *Misogi,* early 18th century. Hanging scroll; ink and color on paper. Hatakeyama Memorial Museum of Fine Art, Tokyo.

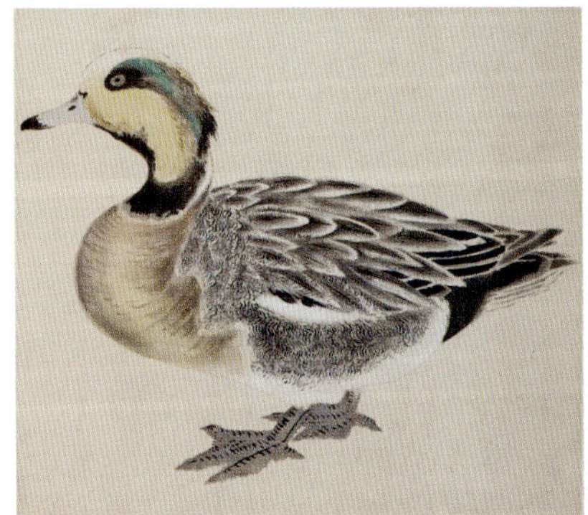

FIGURE 70
Ogata Kōrin, *Bird Studies* (detail), late 17th or early 18th century. Handscroll; ink and color on paper. Konishi Family Archive, Kyoto National Museum.

Other sketches by Kōrin reveal his study of Tan'yū's style. This choice made perfect sense in Edo, where Tan'yū's studio was based and his mode was most popular.[31] Different large-format sketches that may have been intended as studies for a screen painting combine elements found in various works by Tan'yū. The effect extended over a range of other subjects, including a scroll with an extensive selection of bird studies (fig. 70).[32] He meticulously painted the plumage for each of the sixty-six bird species and paid close attention to their talons and beaks. Kōrin learned much about verisimilitude from these studies, and he translated that knowledge into the stronger sense of representational veracity seen in his later works. The extensive exercise of copying the work aided Kōrin in his quest to capture the naturalistic features of his subjects. The bird studies also hark back to Tan'yū, who painted the ur-type of them. The source and timing for Kōrin's studies are not recorded, yet their close resemblance to Tan'yū's originals has clarified that Kōrin based them on Kano models circulating among the atelier, if not even those by Tan'yū himself.[33]

We know that Kōrin held Tan'yū in great esteem. In a letter addressed to Takabayashi Tokusai, an art dealer, Kōrin writes:

> The triptych by Tan'yū Hōgen, depicting Taigong Wang, Chinese pines (*karamatsu*), and monkeys, is outstanding. The signature, written in such large characters, is rare. Although the triptych was promised to me, Ikari has asked for the flanking picture of monkeys and Esa would like the Chinese pines. This is unfortunate, but I shall relent and let them take their desired paintings. The middle one, of Taigong Wang, will remain with me. Please instruct [Ikari and Esa] to take great care of the paintings. Yours sincerely.
> Tenth month, sixteenth day. Masatoki [cypher]
>
> To Takabayashi Tokusai Ogata Kōrin

The handwriting suggests a late date for this letter, possibly a few years before Kōrin's death.[34] This document is the only instance when Kōrin refers to a Kano painter by name, indicating that he probably had his greatest exposure to Tan'yū during and after his sojourns to Edo, the center of Tan'yū's activities. It is not surprising, then, that the bulk of Kōrin's painting studies bears a stylistic link to Tan'yū and his atelier. Most of Kōrin's Kano studies likely stem from his time in Edo or after—evidence corroborated by the conspicuous presence of such features in his late paintings. Further, the level of complexity and painterly accomplishment simply exceeds Kōrin's skills of the 1690s. Only later did he achieve the competency necessary to produce faithful renderings of figures and the plumage and physiognomy of his avian subjects. Kōrin apparently had access to model books of the Kano atelier while he lived in Edo. The very existence of his figure and bird studies correlates with the amount of energy he used to immerse himself into making the Kano style his own. By copying such core features of Kano painting education, Kōrin might have sought to improve and adjust his skill set.

Kōrin's goal to recalibrate his oeuvre to his local clientele is most evident in works such as *Seiōbō* (Chinese, Xiwangmu) (fig. 71). The painting carries his Dōsū seal alongside a type of signature that adorns his works produced in Edo. The image of the Queen Mother of the West, a mythical Chinese figure, was adapted from sketches that Kōrin made from works of the Kano school. A near mirror image of a reading female figure in one of Kōrin's Kano studies, the painting raises the possibility that it and the study were painted relatively close

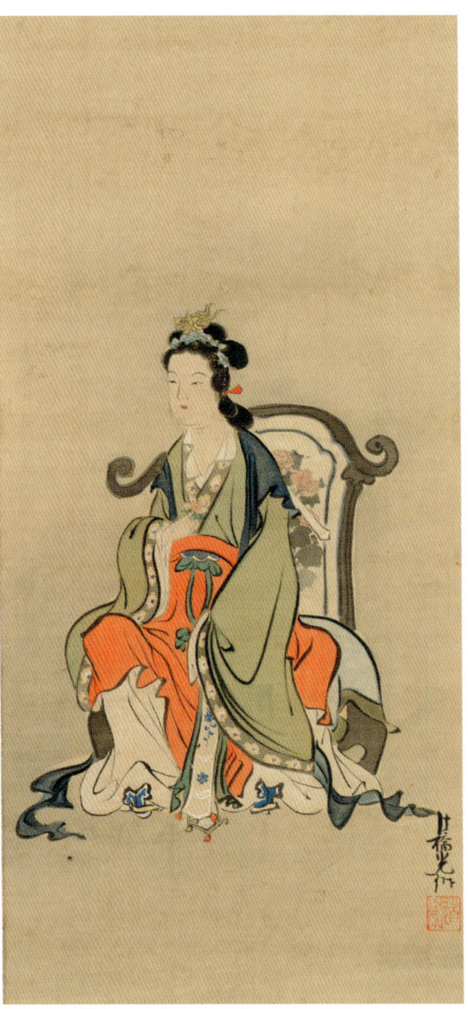

FIGURE 71

Ogata Kōrin, *Seiōbō* (*Queen Mother of the West*), early 18th century. Hanging scroll; ink and color on silk. Kimbell Art Museum, Fort Worth, Texas, AP 1967.08.

FIGURE 72

Ogata Kōrin, *The Four Accomplishments* (detail), late 17th or early 18th century. Ink and color on paper. Konishi Family Archive, Kyoto National Museum.

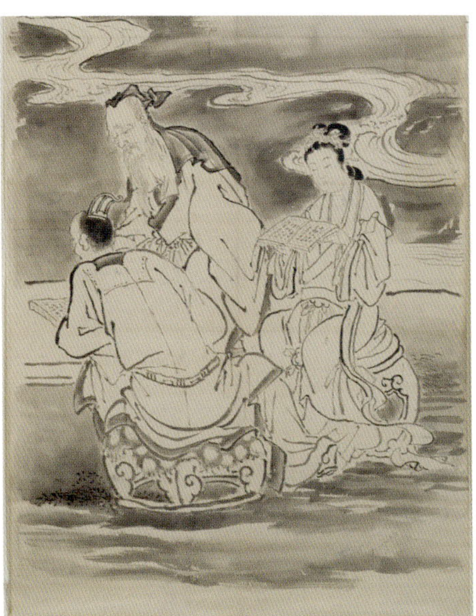

in time (fig. 72). This confluence between perfecting his command of the Kano mode and personal creativity solidifies the assumption that the bulk of Kōrin's Kano sketches cluster around the five years he was active in the shogunal seat of power and after.

Seiōbō and other works made there are also a case in point for the degree of flexibility to which Kōrin adjusted his style to local demands. He attempted to attract the attention of Edo's visual mainstream through necessity or by pushing his seemingly undiscerning clients—or both. His decision to absorb the methods of the Edo-based Kano studio confirms the atelier's far reach in art production of the early modern era. On a personal level, Kōrin's move had far-reaching implications for him as a painter, with the Kano channeling medieval styles into his own artistry.

INK MOUNTAINS

Over the years, Kōrin's trademark images of vibrantly colored flowers on sumptuous gilded grounds have obscured his considerable oeuvre in ink, a facet of his practice that was substantially inspired by the early modern clout of one of the most venerated masters of medieval ink painting, Sesshū Tōyō. The Kano atelier provided Kōrin with a conduit for accessing and absorbing that style. During the early modern period Sesshū achieved legendary status, and few other artists have exerted such a profound impact on art in Japan. Versions of his visual language permeated almost every aspect of Japan's artistic practice. The Kano, for example, claimed artistic ancestry from Sesshū: mastery of the Kano mode was a prerequisite in painters' training, but command of Sesshū's style symbolized the validation of artistic aptitude.

Sesshū laid the origins of his lasting fame himself. The mastery of Chinese paintings was a crucial criterion of artistic excellence in late medieval and early modern Japan. To tap directly into this source material, Sesshū traveled to China, where he perfected his painting and Zen studies (fig. 73). Through this exposure, he developed the ability to understand, interpret, and surpass the modes of Chinese painters respected in Japan, making him a paragon for other artists. It has been argued that the self-fashioned persona of Zen religiosity and artistic excellence that Sesshū cultivated around himself, and which numerous followers disseminated, established him as a fixture among Japanese ink painters even during his lifetime.[35] Sesshū's nomadic lifestyle furthered the spread of his paintings in the collections of daimyo beyond his main patrons, the Ōuchi clan in western Japan. Later, in the tea culture of *chanoyu* during the seventeenth century, Sesshū's works assumed the most desired category of Japanese-made Chinese-style paintings (*kanga*) to be hung during tea gatherings.[36] Within this context, regional daimyo brought works by Sesshū to Edo, where they became prized possessions and were shown to well-known connoisseurs for approbation.

Sesshū's role as a standard by which a painter's acumen was measured is reflected in the late seventeenth-century *History of Painting of the Realm*. In this widely read biography of artists, Kano Einō devotes one of the longest entries to Sesshū.[37] Einō praises Sesshū's command and transcendence of Chinese paintings from the Song and Yuan dynasties. Sesshū so thoroughly understood these models that he used them to build an original and praiseworthy visual language, a measure of perfection to Einō and his Kano peers.[38] Like other Kano painters, ateliers, and biographers before him, Einō sought to embed Sesshū into the genealogy of the Kano. So powerful was Sesshū's sway that numerous schools—the Unkoku, Kaihō, and Hasegawa, among others—professed stylistic and spiritual descendance from him.[39] Yet, by Kōrin's time,

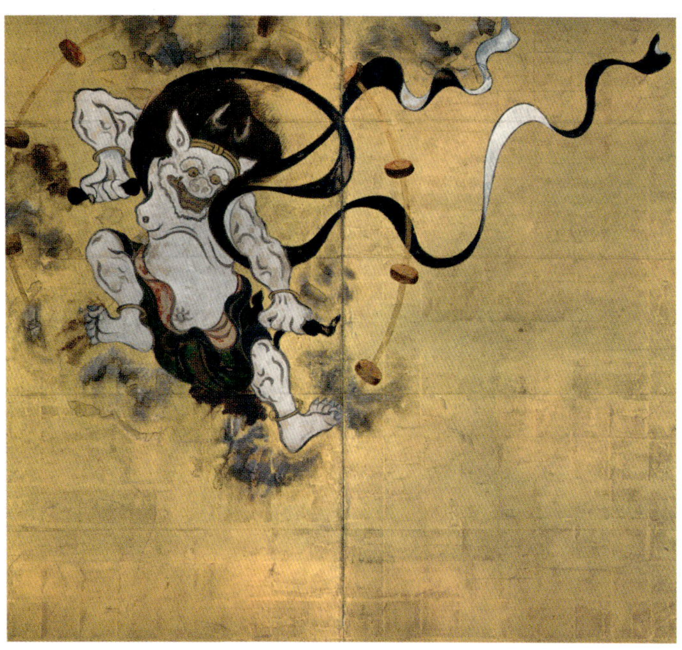
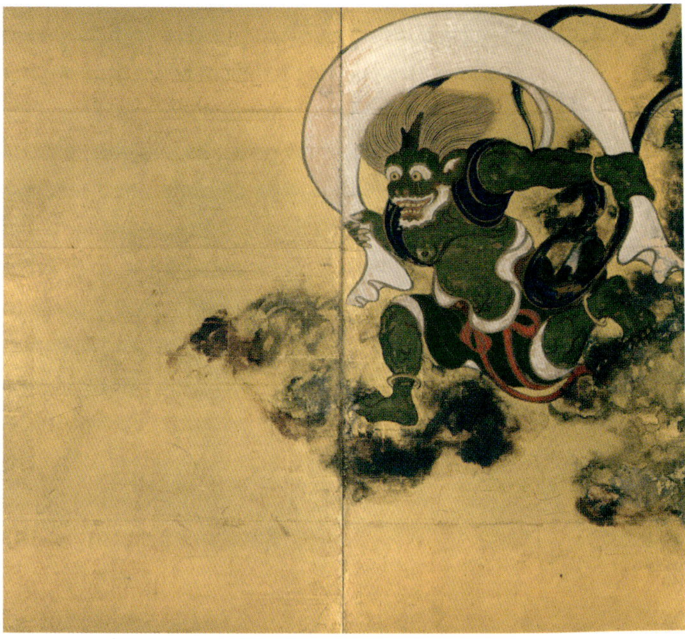
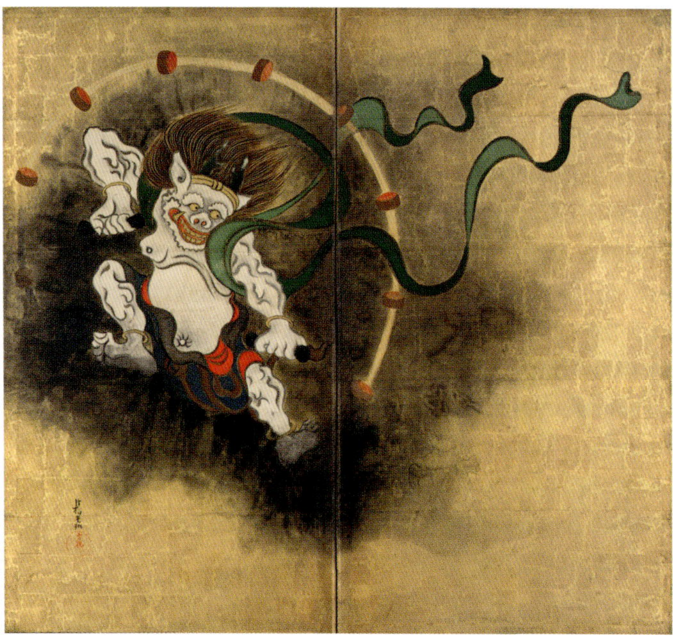
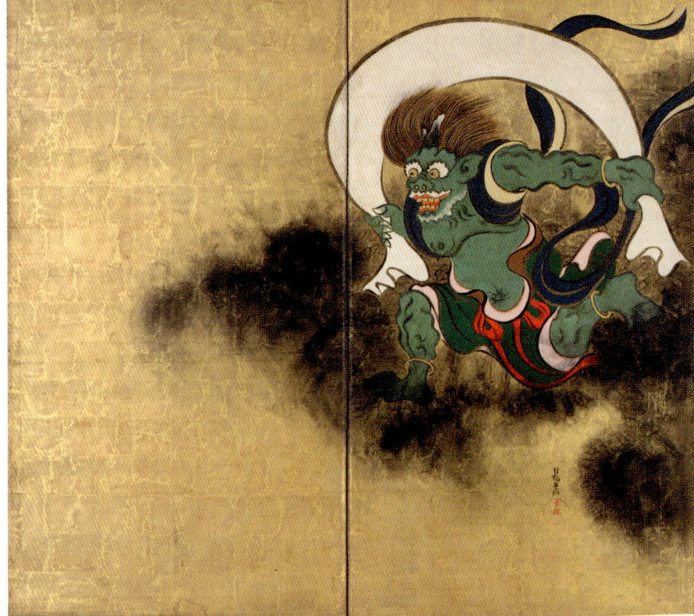

FIGURE 80

Tawaraya Sōtatsu, *Gods of Wind and Thunder,* early 17th century. Pair of two-panel folding screens; ink and color on gold. Kenninji, Kyoto.

FIGURE 81

Ogata Kōrin, *Gods of Wind and Thunder,* early 18th century. Pair of two-panel folding screens; ink and color on gold. Tokyo National Museum, Image: TNM Image Archives.

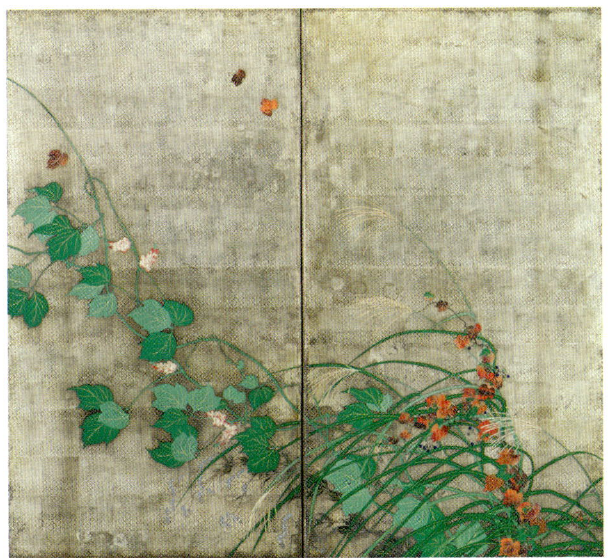
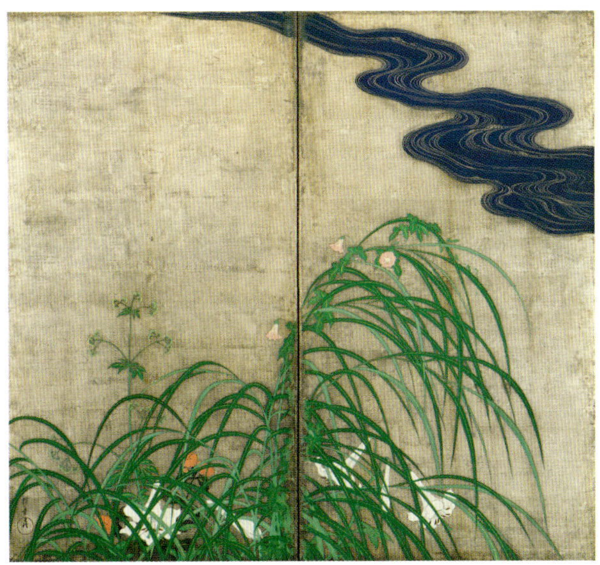

FIGURE 82
Sakai Hōitsu, *Plants of Spring and Autumn,* 1821. Pair of two-panel folding screens; ink and color on silver. Tokyo National Museum, Image: TNM Image Archives.

Many of Kōrin's large-format paintings made after he returned to Kyoto in 1709 bear a round Masatoki seal. The bulk of his works that have the provenance of a daimyo or other patrons with Edo residences carry that seal and date from 1709 to his death in 1716. Several of those works refer directly to paintings by Sōtatsu and his atelier. Most of these Sōtatsu works were in the collections of Kyoto temples, so Kōrin would have had to see them in situ if he wished to copy them. This is especially true of his *Gods of Wind and Thunder,* which rely so closely on Sōtatsu's original at Myōkōji. Located northwest of Kyoto, the temple was a short walk from the kiln of Kōrin's brother Kenzan at Narutaki, which he operated until 1712.[49] Almost immediately on his return from Edo, Kōrin and Kenzan began to collaborate in making ceramics, an activity that likely required frequent trips to the kiln outside the gates of the temple Ninnaji. Kōrin had ample opportunity to visit nearby Myōkōji and see Sōtatsu's *Gods of Wind and Thunder,* create his version of the work, and dispatch it to his customer in Edo.

Though Kōrin could have easily employed the network of art dealers that had expedited long-distance sales of his screens and lacquer works throughout his career, it is not known how his paintings entered the collections of their daimyo owners or even whether they were made for them in the first place. The Hitotsubashi branch of the Tokugawa was established only in 1735 by Tokugawa Munetada (1721–1765), a son of the shogun.[50] If the Tokugawa family did indeed commission *Gods of Wind and Thunder* from Kōrin, another member of the clan or a retainer might have been responsible. The uncertainty of original patronage arises with virtually all of Kōrin's paintings. Not a single provenance can be traced back seamlessly to Kōrin's time.

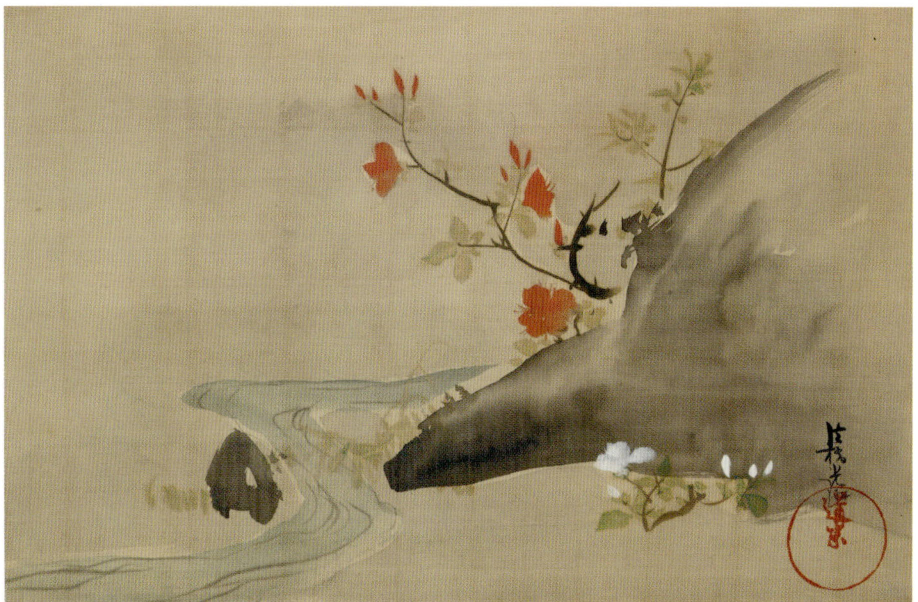

FIGURE 83
Ogata Kōrin, *Azaleas,* early 18th century. Hanging scroll; ink and color on silk. Hatakeyama Memorial Museum of Fine Art, Tokyo.

We do know, however, that after his return to Kyoto, Kōrin continued to dispatch his artworks to Edo and to the infrastructure of patronage that he had established there. In particular, the ruling house of the Tokugawa could have been patrons for Kōrin, since he mentions an audience with Ogiwara Shigehide, a shogunal commissioner (*kanjō bugyō*), in his early letter from Edo. The high-ranking official was involved in implementing the 1695 currency reform and had close ties to the silver mint and its bureaucrats, including Kōrin's friend Nakamura Kuranosuke. The important Confucian intellectual Ogyū Sorai, who had chosen Kuranosuke's posthumous pseudonym, served Yanagisawa Yoshiyasu (1658–1714), an adviser and paramour of shogun Tokugawa Tsunayoshi.[51] Kuranosuke's circle of acquaintances in Edo consisted of the highest ranks of the warrior class and probably gave Kōrin access to their sponsorship.

Soon after his return to Edo from a brief stay in Kyoto in the sixth month of 1705, Kōrin seems to have gained the support of a branch of the Sakai clan, who were the lords of Maebashi Domain in present-day Gunma Prefecture. His association with the Sakai began almost immediately after Kuranosuke left for Kyoto, which suggests that his involvement played a role in connecting the artist to the daimyo house.[52] According to the Sakai family records, *Gathering of Old Events* (*Tekiko saiyō*), from 1705 to 1707 Kōrin received notable favors, not unlike those granted to an official painter-in-waiting. The journal states that in 1707 Kōrin received ten retainers—a considerable number—from Sakai

Tadataka (1648–1720), head of the family. Tadataka's main consort belonged to the Kuroda clan from Kyūshū, who themselves owned a number of Kōrin's works. For example, a small painting in ink and colors on silk depicting azaleas along a stream, using the kind of wet brushwork that Kōrin adopted from studying Sesshū, was once in the possession of the Kuroda (fig. 83). The work carries a Dōsū seal, indicating that it was probably produced in Edo. Similar to Kōrin's ink landscape screen, the azalea painting is a hybrid between the tarashikomi method that Kōrin brought to Edo and the ink techniques of medieval painters like Sesshū that he studied there. The link between the Sakai and the Kuroda illustrates the web of mutual referral that could have enabled Kōrin to cater to a number of daimyo families with residences in Edo during his final years.

While in Edo, Kōrin also went back to Kyoto again in the fourth month of 1707 to fetch his wife, Tayo, who had remained in the capital. Tayo likely stayed behind to fulfill Kōrin's fosterage agreement to raise Kuranosuke's daughter Katsu; the contract ended in 1706. The journey followed just three months after receiving the gift of retainers, a time when Kōrin grew increasingly busy. Probably in light of the aftermath of the Hōei earthquake that wreaked havoc on Edo in the tenth month of 1707, Kōrin did not return to the city until 1708. On his arrival, the artist was immediately given twenty more retainers by Tadataka, who apparently was pleased to have a favorite painter back in town.

> Since His Lordship Seikyū [Sakai Tadataka] had an affection for [Kōrin's] paintings, on the sixth day of the first month of 1707, [Tadataka], in his kindness beyond compare, graced [Kōrin] with ten retainers (*fuchi*). [Kōrin] had left his wife in Kyoto, so he went there in the fourth month of the same year [1707] to bring her. Then, too, [His Lordship] bestowed Kōrin with one bottle of *awamori* [an alcoholic drink from the Ryūkyū islands], two dried salmon, and two rolls of silk. This is also recorded in [his lordship's] correspondence. In the next year [1708], Kōrin returned to Kantō and on the twelfth day of the fifth month was granted twenty retainers for as long as he remained in Edo. On the eighteenth day of the same month, as an expression of gratitude for the retainers, [Kōrin] extended a box of delicacies. This is also recorded in the [Sakai family's] official ledger of gifts. Such as it is, [Kōrin] did not remain in Edo and frequently went back and forth [between Kyoto and Edo]. Kōrin died on the second day of the sixth month in Kyōhō 1 [1716].[53]

It is unknown what role these retainers served in Kōrin's employ. It is likely that they were household servants or farmers, reflecting the artist's rising status and increasing financial means. The entry not only elucidates that Kōrin received extensive favors from the Sakai—the family of Sakai Hōitsu, one of his most ardent admirers in the late Edo period—but suggests that Kōrin established a flourishing enterprise and, presumably, a temporary atelier while in Edo. In fact, Kōrin's 1704 letter notes that he took an unidentified pupil with him. The extensive volume of extant commissions that bear the Dōsū seal alone indicates Kōrin must have had assistance from other painters.

Though *Gathering of Old Events* is widely quoted and generally accepted as reliable, it is worth remembering that the author, Matsushita Kōjo, lived during the late Edo period and compiled his record from a variety of sources. The first volume, for example, contains a preface dating to 1827. Still, Kōjo relied heavily on the diaries of various Sakai lords, which likely added to the validity of his chronicle.[54] Sakai Tadataka also collected works by other artists who employed an aesthetic similar to Kōrin's, such as the potter Nonomura Ninsei (active circa 1647–1678). With this general interest in the arts of the capital, his patronage of Kōrin seems plausible.[55] *Gathering of Old Events* omits mention of Kōrin's paintings, but according to two diaries kept by Sakai Tadazane (1756–1790), a head of the Himeji branch of the clan, the family owned works by Kōrin at least by the late 1780s. Tadazane's personal journal *Diary of the Black Tortoise* (*Genbu nikki*) records a painting of Ariwara Narihira's travel to the east, a signature subject of Kōrin. Tadazane's tea record, *Diary of Transcendent Taste* (*Yukō nikki*), mentions seeing a diptych of a dragon and a tiger by Kōrin at a tea gathering in 1781.[56] Although none of these documents refers to direct purchases from Kōrin, it is entirely possible that the artist completed commissions for the Sakai and other daimyo clients during his time in Edo from 1704 to 1709 and after.

❖ ❖ ❖

Kōrin's time in Edo was transformative—personally, artistically, and financially. He returned to Kyoto exhausted but inspired and monetarily stable. From a late document, we learn that Kōrin was able to repay an old mortgage on a property he had inherited from his father.

> One sheet
>
> Concerning the mortgage of forty-five ryō gold, [agreed upon] thirteen years ago, in the Year of the Rooster [1705].[57] In accordance with the conditions of the mortgage, [the current] repayment of ten kan silver, made on the thirteenth day of the seventh month in this Year of the Snake [1713], should fully erase the debt. I am asking you to send an official receipt to the two of us [Kenzan and Kōrin] quickly, and at the latest by the thirtieth day of the first month in the Year of the Horse [1714]. I hope [my request] will not cause you too much inconvenience. This letter acts as proof of my request.
>
> Ogata Shinsei [Kenzan]

Shōtoku 3, Year of the Snake [1713] Yoshida Chiseki, on behalf of Shichizaemon

Eleventh month, twentieth day
To [District Elder of] Nakamachi Yabunouchichō
Shichibei[58]

Though signed by Kenzan, the text appears to have been written by Kōrin himself. Kōrin probably copied the original for his records. Two years before, in 1711, Kōrin completed construction on a new residence, one built after his own designs in the Nijō Shinmachi area of Kyoto. From there, he no doubt continued to dispatch works to Edo and other locations. Kōrin had radically expanded his circle of patrons. Having begun with an initial group of aristocrats and townsmen, he now counted daimyo and wealthy merchants in Edo among his premier sponsors. On his homecoming to Kyoto, Kōrin entered the most prolific period of his life, creating a substantial number of large-format paintings that often entered the collections of faraway clients. Although questions of original provenance are difficult to solve, it is fair to assume that many of Kōrin's late works were made for members of the network he established in Edo. Kōrin's reconfiguration of Sōtatsu's mode with the ink techniques he encountered in Edo created an intriguing mélange of artistic precedents that ultimately offered a novel interpretation of a familiar paradigm. In spite of complaining about ill health and exhaustion, Kōrin remained productive and innovative. After returning to his native city, he also began his collaboration with Kenzan in creating iron-oxide paintings on ceramics. These images, brush-drawn in dark hues onto ceramic surfaces, created approximations of ink paintings, an expansion of the traditional ink-on-paper-or-silk medium. Clearly, Kōrin's encounter with ink modes in Edo sparked his creativity and culminated in an innovation that helped redefine the genre of ink paintings.

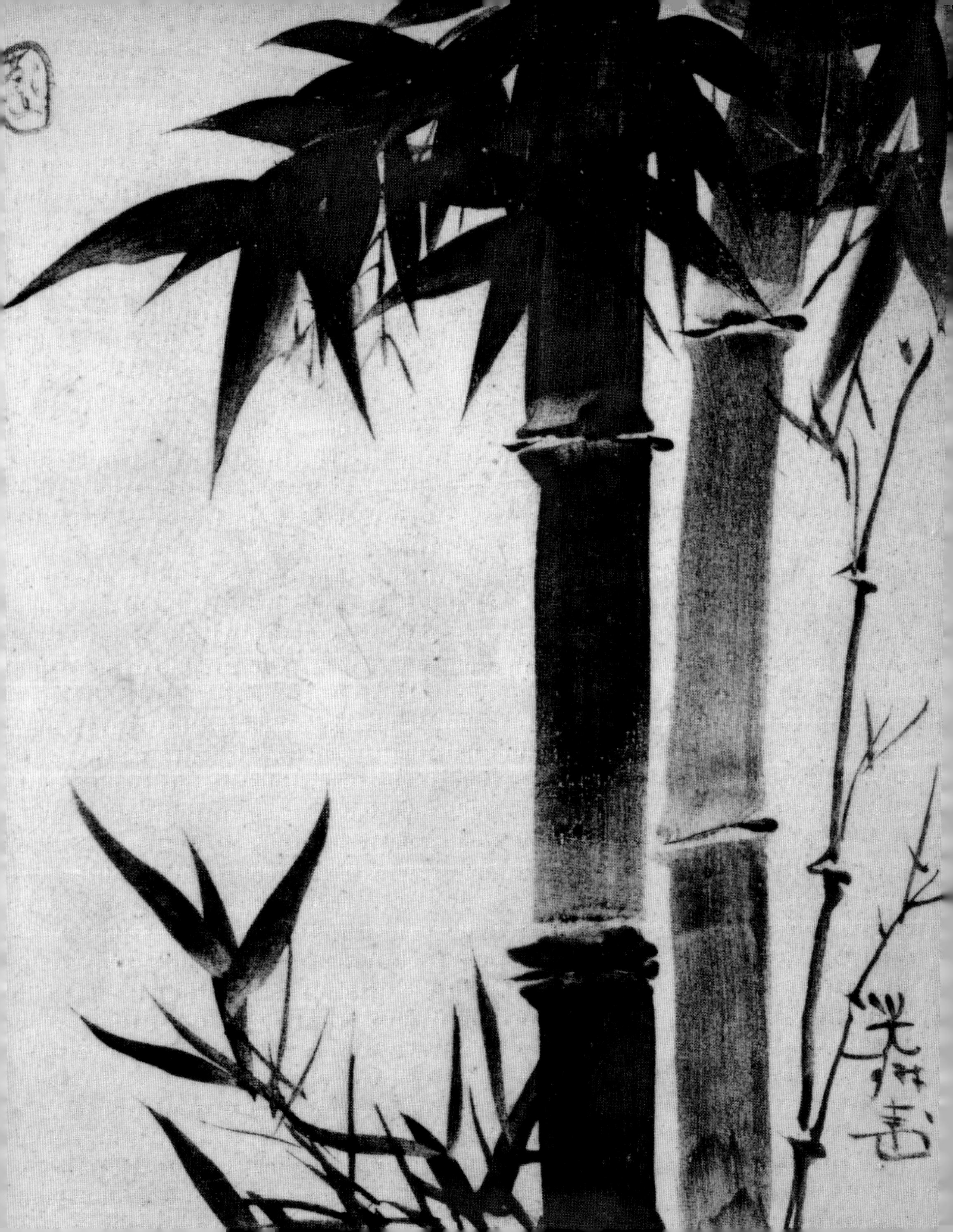

5 Beyond Ink

Ceramics by Kōrin and Kenzan

When Kuranosuke was at the height of his splendor, he frequently summoned the painter Kōrin. One time, Kuranosuke told Kōrin that his wife was soon to join a picnic at Higashiyama. Since a certain [rival] lady was also to participate, [he had] decided [their] encounter should be dazzling. . . . Kōrin contemplated this for a while and told Kuranosuke [his idea]. . . . When Kuranosuke's wife stepped out of her palanquin, all that were present gasped in awe. Her *obi* and *habutae* both were black in color while beneath she was entirely clad in white. Her garments consisted of many layers and when she smoothly exited [her palanquin] and calmly arrived at her seat it felt beyond everyone's imaginations.

—Kanzawa Tokō in the novella *Pasqueflower* (*Okina gusa*), 1791

Shortly after his return to Kyoto in 1709, Kōrin made his way to the residence of his aristocratic friend and supporter Nijō Tsunahira.[1] As Kōrin and Tsunahira sat together conversing in the heat of summer, the artist likely told unflattering stories of life in Edo. The city had strained his energy and pride. In spite of the exhaustion he felt toward the end of his time in Edo, Kōrin returned to Kyoto with an enterprising spirit and artistic inspiration. He channeled these newfound resources into a period of noteworthy creativity.

Sometime soon after returning from Edo, Kōrin began to collaborate in making ceramics with his brother, the potter Kenzan (fig. 84).[2] Starting around 1709, during the final five years or so of his life, Kōrin painted so-called *sabi-e,* literally "rustic pictures" in iron-oxide pigment onto vessels coated in white slip that were made at Kenzan's kiln. Kōrin used brushwork and an aesthetic sense that closely followed his works in ink. As he placed quick, sweeping strokes on Kenzan's ceramic dishes, the two artists combined the practice of ink painting and pottery.

Throughout his life, Kōrin avidly painted with ink, a genre in which he received part of his earliest artistic training. As he experimented with styles ranging from the early seventeenth-century monk painter Shōkadō Shōjō to the

Detail of fig. 90

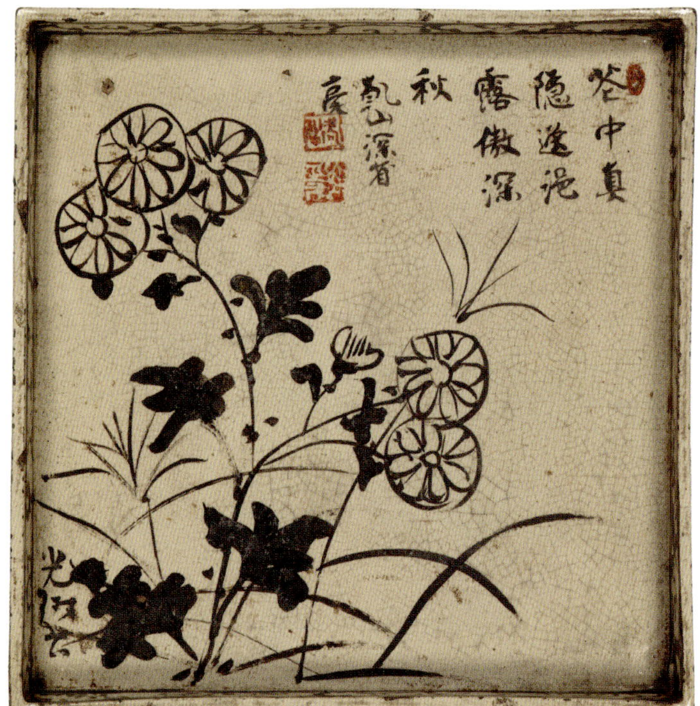

FIGURE 84
Ogata Kōrin (painting) and Ogata Kenzan (dish and calligraphy), *Square Dish with Design of Chrysanthemums,* early 18th century. Buff clay with iron pigment under transparent lead glaze. Yamato Bunkakan, Nara.

Kano and the medieval master Sesshū, he adopted and adapted specific inspirations in ink during overlapping phases of his career. In the process of digesting, reinterpreting, and expanding, Kōrin merged the various uses of ink into an eclectic blend that transcended the boundaries of the genre's material definition. As a result, the traditional perception of ink monochrome—ink applied by brush on paper or silk—became just one aspect of a larger heterogeneity in which Kōrin and Kenzan reinterpreted the techniques and materials of this tradition.

RUSTIC PICTURES

Sabi-e, the practice of painting iron-oxide pictures on ceramics covered in white slip, existed in Japan at least since the late sixteenth or early seventeenth century, a time to which Kōrin often referred in his art. Shino ware, for example, began using abstracted iron-oxide imagery by the sixteenth century (fig. 85). Also, a fashion of sabi-e found in Karatsu ware is similar to that produced by Kōrin and Kenzan around the beginning of the eighteenth century. A jar with an abstracted, hand-painted design of what appears to be a persimmon or plum tree is dated to the cusp of the seventeenth century (fig. 86).[3] Karatsu potters in northern Kyūshū enjoyed easy access to the important trade port in Nagasaki, and they may have adapted such monochromatic techniques from Korean ceramics. Other Japanese wares followed this precedent.[4] Iron-oxide

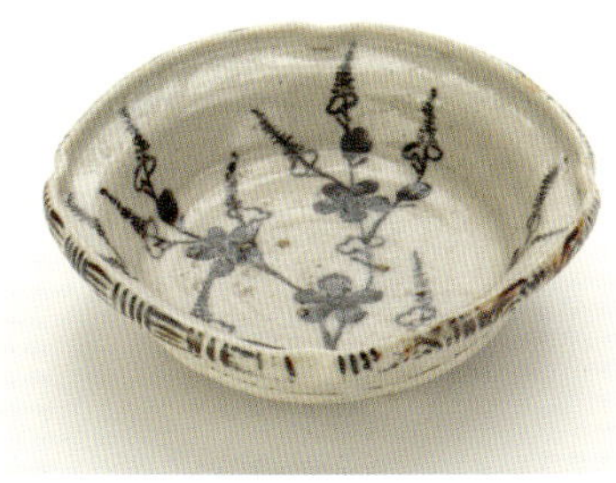

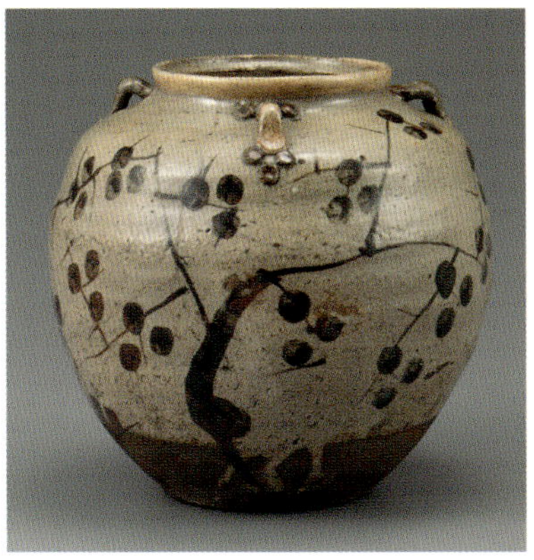

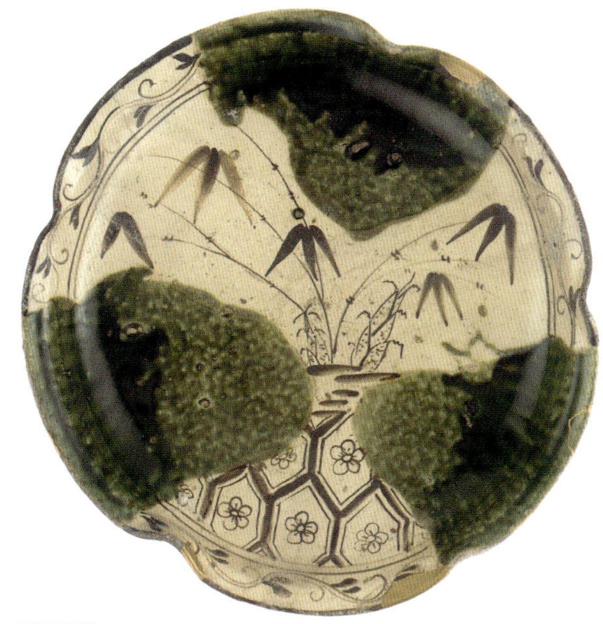

FIGURE 87
Serving Dish with Design of "Three Friends of Winter," 1615–24, Mino ware, Oribe type; stoneware with Oribe glaze and iron decoration under clear glaze; gold lacquer repairs. Freer Gallery of Art, Smithsonian Institution, Washington, D.C.: Purchase—Charles Lang Freer Endowment, F1973.6a–e.

FIGURE 85
Individual Serving Dish with Design of Flowering Quince, 1607–15. Mino ware, Shino type; stoneware with iron pigment under feldspathic glaze. Freer Gallery of Art, Smithsonian Institution, Washington, D.C.: Purchase—Charles Lang Freer Endowment, F1962.20.

FIGURE 86
Jar with Decor of Plum Blossoms or Persimmons, late 16th or early 17th century. Karatsu ware; stoneware clay with iron pigment and ash glaze. Idemitsu Museum of Arts, Tokyo.

décor also became an established feature of Oribe ware, which dates to the early seventeenth century (fig. 87). As a result, sabi-e were made part of the repertoire for Kyoto wares in the seventeenth century. Kōrin and Kenzan eventually participated in creating this type of iron-oxide pictures.[5]

While the concept of adding iron-oxide designs onto ceramics was hardly new, the way in which the Ogata brothers made their sabi-e marked a change. Sabi-e designs created by potters before Korin and Kenzan share a level of stylization and a deemphasis on painterliness that distinguishes them from the brothers' works. Kōrin and Kenzan, by contrast, made motifs that visibly celebrate the versatility of the brush. Many sabi-e works produced by Kōrin and Kenzan are square dishes, with the occasional exceptions of braziers and hexagonal plates. A dish depicting a bridge and iris flowers illustrates the essence of the Ogata brothers' sabi-e works and marks a noteworthy extension of Kōrin's signature theme, the ninth chapter of the *Tales of Ise* (fig. 88). Its underglaze image—a technical feature customary to their sabi-e—is painted with a brush onto a ground layer of white slip. After the picture was added, the work was fired, then coated with clear glaze, and fired again. The borders of the dish are raised at a ninety-degree angle, creating a clearly defined central surface onto which Kōrin brushed his painting. The reverse side carries a large Kenzan signature, highlighting how the potter incorporated Kōrin's painting style into his ceramic practice.

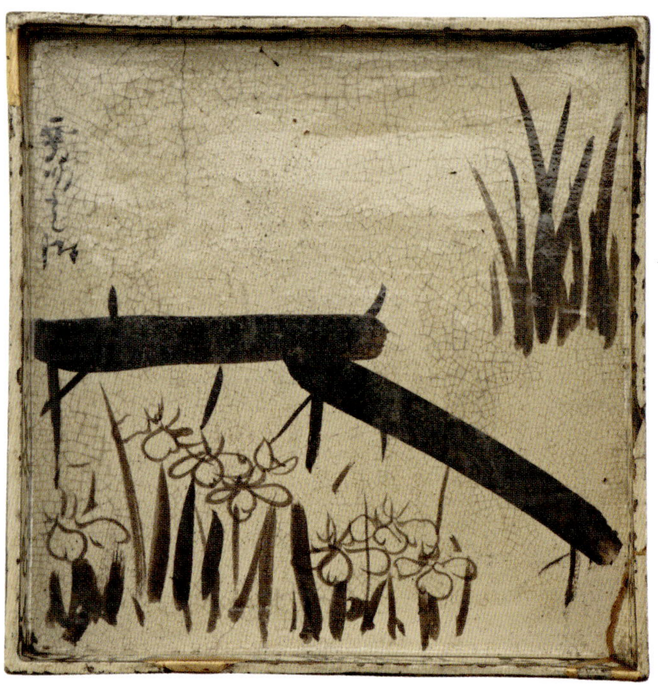

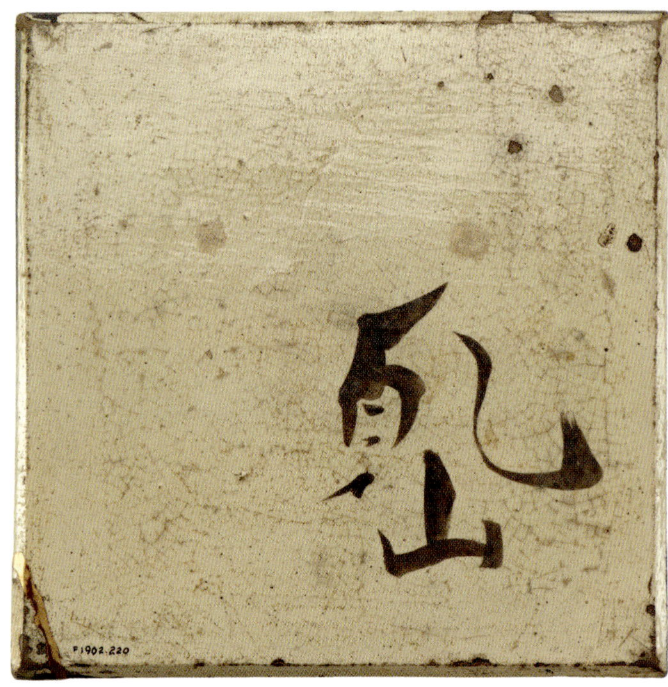

FIGURE 88
Ogata Kōrin (painting) and Ogata Kenzan (dish), *Square Dish with Design of Eight-Plank Bridge, from the Tales of Ise* (left: front; right: verso), 1712–16. Buff clay with iron pigment under transparent lead glaze; gold lacquer repairs. Freer Gallery of Art, Smithsonian Institution, Washington, D.C.: Gift of Charles Lang Freer, F1902.220.

The picture is done in quick strokes in a consistently dark hue of iron oxide. Each element of the irises and bridge is composed of single lines, emphasizing speed and visual economy. The brushwork and the dark blackish-brown hue of the iron-oxide mixture Kōrin used resemble ink. Transposing the aesthetics of ink paintings on paper or silk onto ceramics put his ability as an artist to the test. Appreciating ink paintings depended on seeing the painter's hand in each brushstroke, thus making the movement of the artist's brush visible in perpetuity. In his images on ceramics, Kōrin set out to convey the palpable presence of the artist by shifting the speed and movement of the brush. In his sabi-e Kōrin did just that, translating the appearance of ink paintings into ceramics.

Through his sabi-e, Kōrin demonstrates that the visual and thematic traits of ink paintings need not be limited to paper or silk. Having mastered the complicated process of brushing ink onto gold—a ground essentially as impermeable as ceramics—Kōrin applied his experiences to sabi-e. *Plum and Bamboo,* a screen on which the artist created a quintessential ink painting in terms of both technique and subject matter, exemplifies how Kōrin may have seen technical and aesthetic commonalities between ink paintings on gold and iron-oxide paintings on ceramics (fig. 89). The plum branch and bamboo stalks, two age-old topics in East Asian ink painting, find their direct equivalent in some of his sabi-e (figs. 90, 91). The screen *Plum and Bamboo* bears a Masatoki seal, a

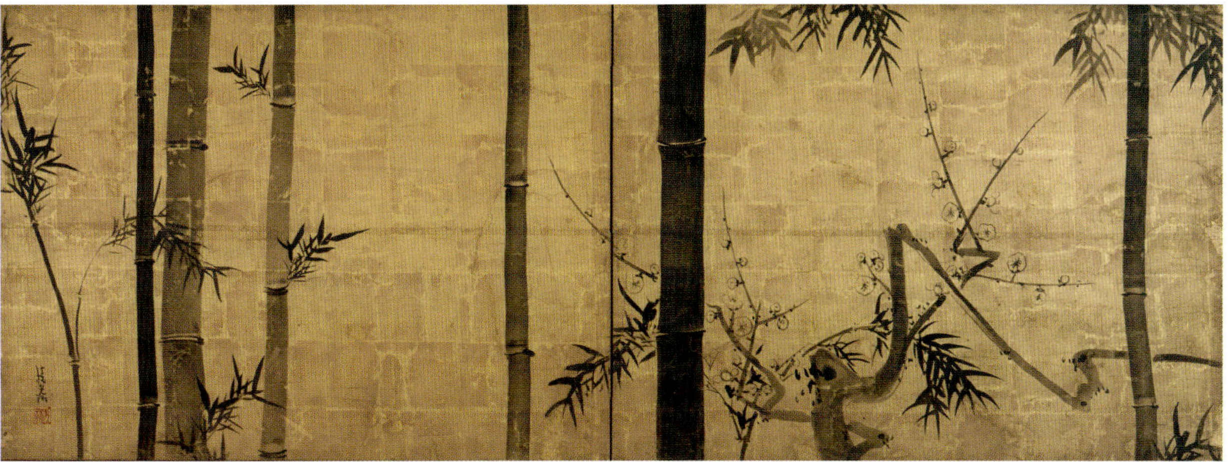

FIGURE 89
Ogata Kōrin, *Plum and Bamboo,* early 18th century. Two-panel folding screen; ink on gilded paper. Tokyo National Museum, Image: TNM Image Archives.

pseudonym common to his late works. The work was likely made in the 1710s during the height of Kōrin and Kenzan's sabi-e collaboration. Kōrin used the same method to render bamboo stalks in the screen as he did in his sabi-e bamboo dish. He set his brush down at a horizontal angle, pulled it upward, and then retraced the same line downward before stopping a little above each bamboo joint. Also, the bamboo leaves, done in a faintly curvy swing of the brush, correspond in screen and dish. A similar correlation exists between the gilded screen and sabi-e in Kōrin's idiosyncratic rendering of plum blossoms. The way he transposed the characteristics of painting to sabi-e reveals his stylistic and technical template for applying key aspects of ink techniques to ceramics.

In addition, when considered from a different angle, the small, two-panel screen painting looks like a magnified view of details taken from a larger composition. The screen's vertically narrow and horizontally elongated dimensions resemble those of a handscroll. Similar close-up subjects are seen in Kōrin's sabi-e dishes. Their square format required a keen awareness of space and composition, a skill Kōrin displayed throughout his career. To retain a sense of balance within the quadrilateral space, Kōrin often placed his motifs slightly off-center or in either corner of the picture. Many times, he included a diagonal element, such as an arching bridge or a leaf, to imbue the scene with a feeling of spatial congruity. Such basic compositional devices, introduced through Chinese small-format paintings in Japan's medieval period (fig. 92), differ from the mannered two-dimensionality of earlier sabi-e by Oribe and Karatsu potters.

The times in which Kenzan and Kōrin flourished as artists offered a variety of incentives that may have prompted them to take ink paintings as their point of reference for sabi-e. In fact, during the middle of the Edo period, paintings on ceramics constituted part of a larger trend that expanded and

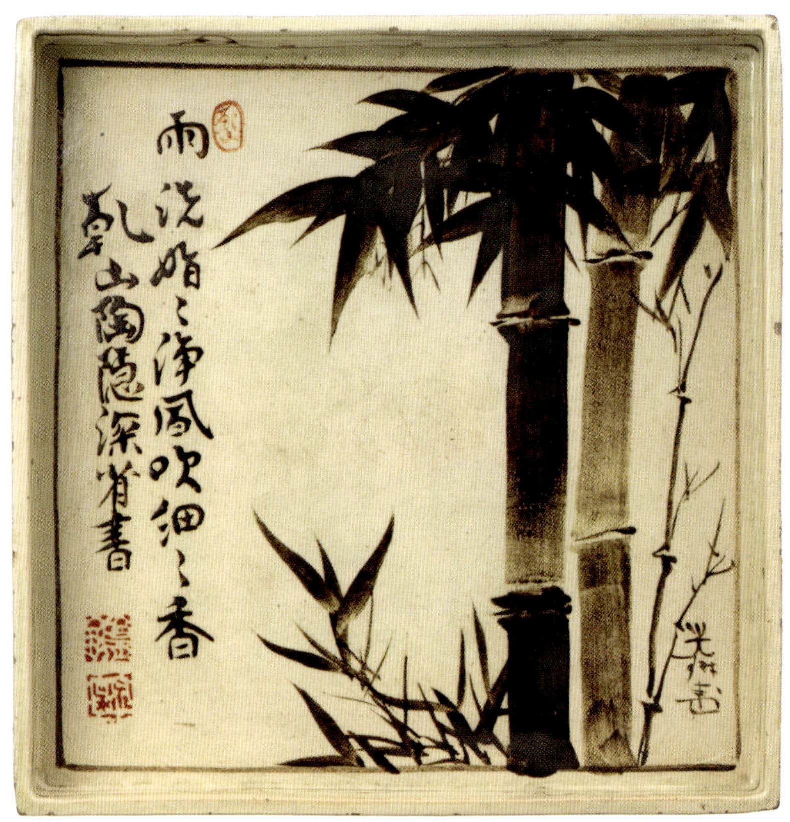

FIGURE 90

Ogata Kōrin (painting) and Ogata Kenzan (dish and calligraphy), *Square Dish with Design of Bamboo,* early 18th century. Buff clay with iron pigment under transparent lead glaze. Idemitsu Museum of Arts, Tokyo.

FIGURE 91

Ogata Kōrin (painting) and Ogata Kenzan (dish and calligraphy), *Square Dish with Design of Plum Blossoms,* early 18th century. Buff clay with iron pigment under transparent lead glaze. Nezu Museum, Tokyo.

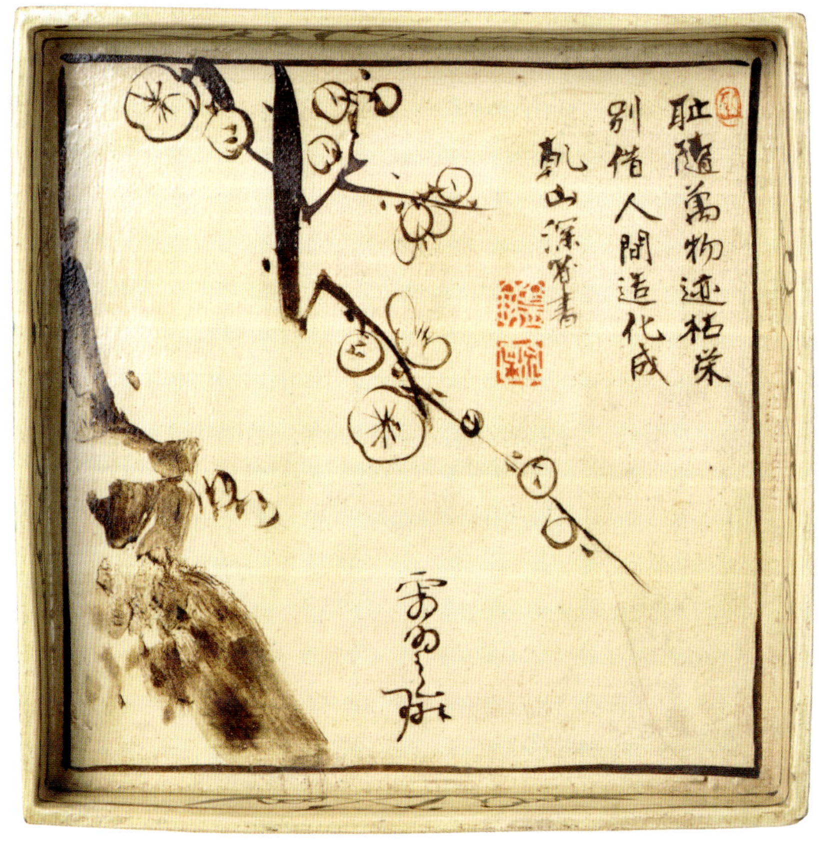

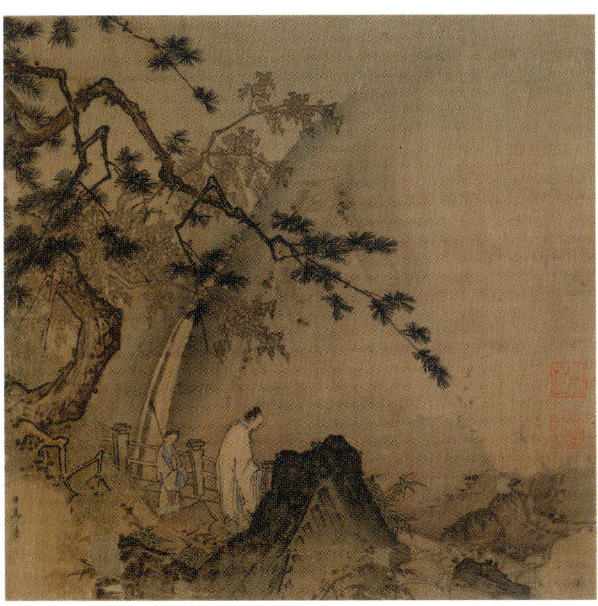

FIGURE 92

Ma Yuan (active late 12th–early 13th century), *Scholar Viewing a Waterfall*, late 12th–early 13th century. Album leaf; ink and color on silk. The Metropolitan Museum of Art, New York, Ex coll.: C. C. Wang Family, Gift of The Dillon Fund, 1973, 1973.120.9.

FIGURE 93

Nonomura Ninsei, *Ceramic Box in Shape of a Bamboo Flute*, 17th century. Stoneware with enamel over white glaze. Idemitsu Museum of Arts, Tokyo.

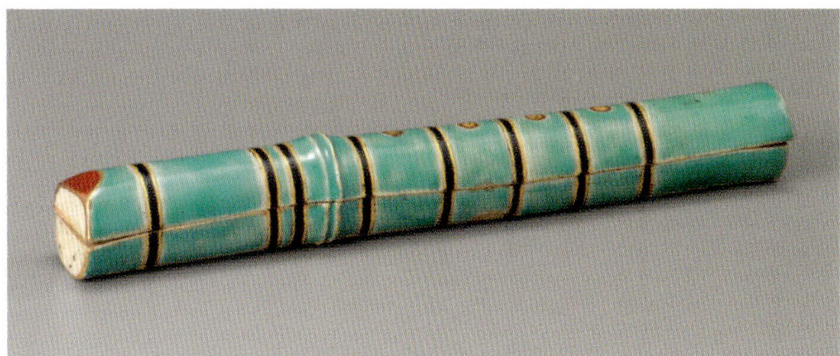

altered traditional notions of materials and definitions of media. The production of sabi-e by Kōrin and Kenzan occurred against the backdrop of experiments with the visual and physical effects of cross-mediality that had developed during the seventeenth century and continued after it. In addition to other representations of different materials in ceramics, Kenzan's alleged teacher Nonomura Ninsei excelled in producing ceramic vessels that punned on other objects, such as his box in the shape of a bamboo *shakuhachi* flute (fig. 93). The sabi-e of Kōrin and Kenzan arose from such trends in pottery, where methods were devised to transform ceramics into approximations of other things whose shapes and aesthetics had once been alien to the medium. In the process, distinctions between different media and genres gradually blurred.

BLACK AND WHITE

Kenzan's foray into making sabi-e began a decade before he collaborated with his brother Kōrin. In fact, Kenzan laid the path for producing monochromatic sabi-e shortly after he established his first kiln at Narutaki to the northwest of Kyoto in 1699. A bowl for steeped tea (*sencha*) is considered one of his most important early works (fig. 94).[6] Like Kōrin's sabi-e a decade later, the sencha bowl adapts the subjects and aesthetics of traditional ink painting. Kenzan's sabi-e benefited from the inspiration he took from early seventeenth-century trends in tea culture, in particular those created at Ninsei's kiln.

Kanamori Sōwa (1584–1656), an influential tea connoisseur, helped determine the selection of styles and aesthetics in Ninsei's early ceramics.[7] Sōwa

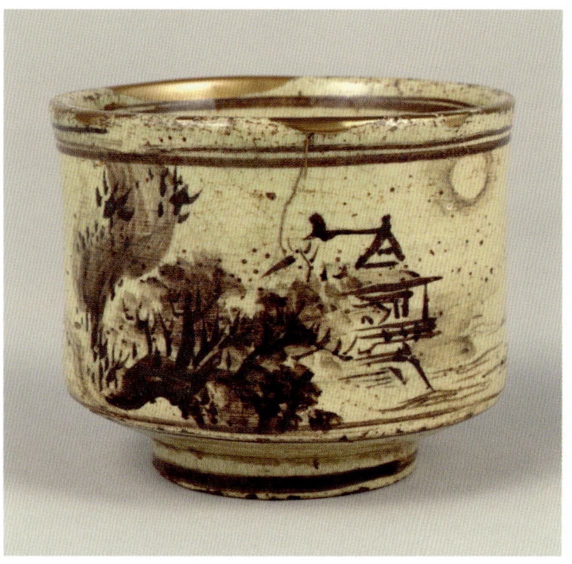

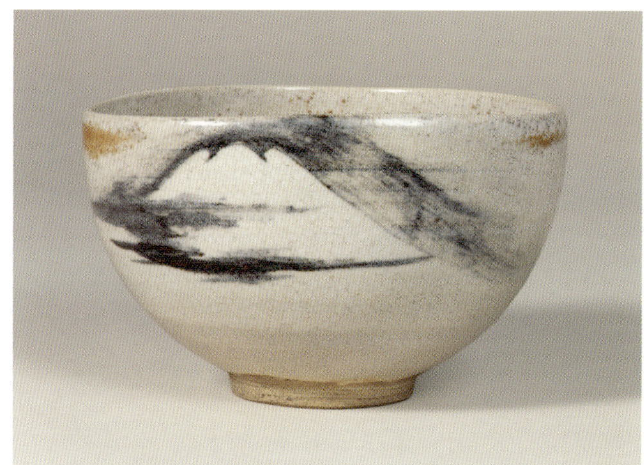

FIGURE 94
Ogata Kenzan, *Sencha Tea Bowl with Landscape Design,* early 18th century. Buff clay with iron pigment under transparent lead glaze. Nezu Museum, Tokyo.

FIGURE 95
Nonomura Ninsei, *Tea Bowl with Design of Mt. Fuji,* 17th century. Stoneware with iron pigment and gold over white glaze. Idemitsu Museum of Arts, Tokyo.

infused Ninsei's wares with the contemporary trends of tea culture and disseminated them among elite clients, thus making sabi-e a staple of salons in the capital. Sōwa's tea journal records dozens of so-called Omuro ware objects from 1650 to 1656, the time span between the establishment of Ninsei's Omuro kiln and Sōwa's death. The tea master obviously admired Ninsei's ceramics and sought to endorse them.[8] Tea bowls, trays, and vessels to serve food made by Ninsei found their way into Sōwa's gatherings, perhaps in an attempt to publicize and market the potter's Omuro ware.

Sōwa's journal contains the earliest mention of Omuro objects adorned with sabi-e paintings. In 1651 the tea master served fish in a Ninsei-made vessel with a sabi-e of plum blossoms. Later that same year a tea bowl with a sabi-e of plum blossoms under the moon is described.[9] The same tea bowl, or a different one with a similar design, was used at a gathering held almost precisely one year later.[10] Ninsei adorned his tea bowls and other ceramics with simple sabi-e that refer to various traditional ink painting subjects. One such example depicts Mount Fuji against a contrasting white ground (fig. 95). The mountain's three-peaked shape, for example, was ubiquitous in early modern ink painting and is reminiscent of Kōrin's dream painting in ink of 1699.[11] All of these décors emulate more or less successfully the modality of ink paintings, albeit in a more stylized manner than in Kōrin and Kenzan's sabi-e.

In general, sabi-e at Omuro were painted designs in a characteristically blackish-brown hue applied with a brush either by Ninsei himself or by a specially hired painter. Before the designs were added, the clay body was covered in a layer of slip and bisque fired at a temperature high enough to strengthen the clay body and sufficiently adhere the slip. Once the sabi-e was painted, the

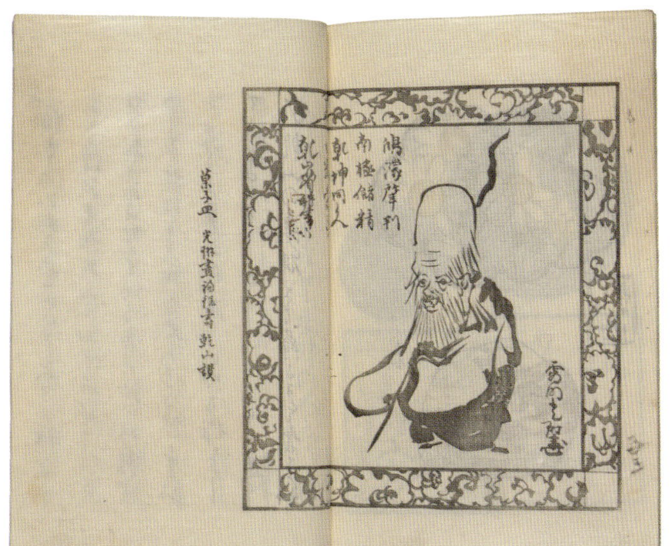

FIGURE 96
Sakai Hōitsu, *Traces of Kenzan's Brush* (*Kenzan iboku*), 1823. Woodblock-printed book; ink on paper. Freer Gallery of Art and Arthur M. Sackler Gallery Library/ Smithsonian Libraries Rare Book Collection (ND1059.O35 A4 1823).

vessel was coated with a thin layer of transparent glaze and fired again at the high temperature needed to melt the glaze.[12] The glaze not only prevented the slip and pigment from flaking off but also added a lustrous glossiness. This is essentially the same procedure Kenzan used in his sabi-e production.

The aesthetic of sabi-e in the tradition of Ninsei and Sōwa garnered a following among seventeenth-century tea practitioners. Sōwa himself reigned at the center of that culture, maintaining friendships with such high-level connoisseurs as the Rokuonji abbot Hōrin Jōshō (1593–1668). Serving akin to an agent, Sōwa procured tea wares, such as those by Ninsei, for the abbot.[13] Sōwa's involvement in creating Ninsei's aesthetic and establishing it as a major part of his tea gatherings prompted the speedy rise in popularity of Omuro ware. In the process sabi-e became an essential feature of upscale salons from the mid-seventeenth century onward—and Kōrin and Kenzan responded to that style and demand. The use of sabi-e in tea culture is mentioned in Sakai Hōitsu's *Traces of Kenzan's Brush* (*Kenzan iboku*) of 1823. The book contains printed reproductions of paintings and ceramics by Kenzan. Among them is an image of Kōrin's sabi-e dish depicting Jurōjin (fig. 96). Hōitsu's annotation calls the dish a "tray for sweets" (*kashi bon*), a key accoutrement in tea culture. Kanamori Sōwa's promotion of Ninsei's ceramics among tea circles in the early seventeenth century preceded this use of works decorated with sabi-e.

Ninsei's Omuro kiln that existed until the late seventeenth century outside the gates of the temple Ninnaji in the northwestern outskirts of Kyoto and, later, Kenzan's Narutaki kiln were virtually neighbors. Before building his kiln, Kenzan had established a hermitage, Hall of Mastering Tranquility (Shūseidō), near the Omuro kiln in 1689, a geographic proximity that enabled easy transmission of aesthetics and techniques.[14] Although Ninsei had already made sabi-e a feature of his wares, Kenzan refined the method to include not just the visual but also the technical faculties of ink paintings. Kenzan's sencha bowl has an off-white surface that creates a ground similar to the look of paper. Onto this surface Kenzan himself or a hired professional painter applied a Chinese landscape in iron oxide that clearly was intended to reproduce the brushwork of landscape paintings in ink.[15] In his notes on making ceramics, titled *Essentials of the Potter* (*Tōkō hitsuyō*) of 1737, Kenzan refers to sabi-e as "black pictures" (*kuro-e*).[16] Others, such as Kenzan's adopted son Ihachi (active ca. 1720–1760), also labeled Kōrin's sabi-e with the same term.[17] Within Kenzan's color vocabulary, the brownish hue of iron oxide seems to have been considered a variation of black, a chromatic association likely supported by the resemblance of sabi-e paintings to ink. On the other hand, white to Kenzan could be a white hue as well as a transparent glaze. In *Essentials of the Potter,* he uses the term *shiro,* or white, to denote both transparent glaze and white enamel.[18] Traditional paintings share this double semantic association, where negative space could mean whiteness in the same way as could areas of white pigment, such as shell-white. The juxtaposition of black and white, or solid and void, is as old as the medium of ink painting itself. It played a defining role in Japanese art from the medieval period onward, when ink became one of the prime means of painterly expression. The visual and technical hallmarks of sabi-e—especially the blackish hue and ability to convey the individual hand of a painter—provided Kōrin and Kenzan with a solution to the challenge of how to fuse the aesthetic of paintings with ceramics.

Kenzan's writings illustrate his quest for the right hue of white. Ultimately, he engineered a particular kind of white slip to look like sized paper. It became a defining feature of his ceramics by the first decade of the eighteenth century, the time leading up to his collaboration with Kōrin.[19] Using slip made from a blend of clays originating in different regions in Japan, Kenzan created surfaces that to him neared white, the veneer he considered most suitable for applying colors. In *Essentials of the Potter,* Kenzan declares that white clay from Aikawa in Bungo Province, in Kyūshū—dried, finely ground, and mixed with animal glue (*nikawa*)—provides the purest hue of white.[20] What is more, Kenzan explains that Aikawa residents traditionally use the same clay to whiten paper. In essence, the potter created a white ground by employing a component of papermaking and thereby directly linking the inherently different qualities of ceramics and paper. This relationship illustrates the intimate connection between Kenzan's method for producing whitish ceramic surfaces and the hue of paper used for painting and writing.

BROTHERLY BONDS

Building on Kenzan's early work, Kōrin adapted the technical aspects of his brother's ceramic décor for their collaborative sabi-e. The extensive palette of Kenzan's output at Narutaki and at the kiln he rented in Kyoto's urban Nijō Chōjiyamachi neighborhood after 1712 provided Kōrin with a broad selection of materials and styles. Perhaps encouraged by Kenzan's experience, Kōrin used monochromatic sabi-e as the basis for collaborating with his brother. In Kōrin's final years, the Ogata brothers joined forces as two accomplished artists.

In the designs, each of the brothers contributed his respective forte. Their teamwork reflects a reciprocity that existed between the siblings throughout much of their lives. Kōrin and Kenzan were close, and just as Kenzan was invested in Kōrin's financial, social, and physical well-being, so Kōrin abided by his younger brother's opinions and intellect. After giving Kōrin financial advice in the late 1690s, Kenzan helped broker the mortgage on Kōrin's estate at Nakamachi Yabunouchichō in 1703. Later, in 1713, Kenzan again issued the full repayment of that mortgage on Kōrin's behalf. Their relationship was further nurtured through their appreciation for Noh performances and their participation in the circle of the aristocrat Nijō Tsunahira and other esteemed men of culture in Kyoto.

Tsunahira, one of Kōrin's main supporters, played an important part in Kenzan's life as well, and both brothers enjoyed equal favors from the courtier throughout the 1690s and early 1700s. For example, a 1693 entry in the Nijō family records notes that Kenzan sent a basket of strawberries to Tsunahira. Ill at the time, Kenzan dispatched the gift to thank Tsunahira for worrying about his health. Four days later, Tsunahira held a get-together to celebrate Kenzan's recovery.[21] The year before, Tsunahira had stopped by Kenzan's Hall of Mastering Tranquility hermitage. According to these records, the Ogata brothers maintained close ties to Tsunahira and his group of acquaintances. In fact, it was Tsunahira who in 1694 granted Kenzan the land in Narutaki that the potter used five years later to build his kiln. The lot was part of Tsunahira's country estate.[22]

Kenzan's first years at Narutaki coincided with a surge in commissions for Kōrin. During that time, Kōrin churned out screens, fans, hanging scrolls, and lacquer works. As Kōrin sought to establish himself as a painter, Kenzan attempted to do so as a potter. The first evidence of their efforts to help each other during their initial steps as artists dates to sometime between 1699 and 1701. In a letter quoted in chapter 1, Kōrin informed Nishimura Seiiku, the art dealer who managed some of Kōrin's earliest commissions, that Kenzan had completed an order for a sake ewer, and he was ready to send it to Seiiku's unnamed client.[23] This evidence indicates that Kōrin took charge of some initial sales of Kenzan's ceramics, and both brothers used their respective advantages to gain traction in the art world.

That being said, however, it appears that Kōrin and Kenzan limited their early cooperation to practical matters, such as the logistics of long-distance sales, and initiated their creative collaboration only later. Each brother was busy making a name for himself in the early 1700s, leaving little time or space for the level of inspired teamwork that led to their sabi-e works a decade later. In 1709, Kōrin returned to Kyoto after his successful activities in Edo left his atelier flourishing. Artistic collaboration between the two brothers surged at that time. Kenzan also became more invested in Kōrin's professional identity. In addition to supplying the ceramics for sabi-e, Kenzan suggested a set of pseudonyms for his brother.[24] He probably drafted the list of elegant sobriquets around the time Kōrin returned from Edo and at the height of their sabi-e collaboration. Kenzan's input resonated with Kōrin, and the painter followed his brother's advice by adopting two of the names, Jakumei Kōrin and Seisei Kōrin. All of this illustrates the vivacity of Kōrin and Kenzan's fraternal alliance.

PAINTING DISHES

While Kōrin's prominence as a painter exerted a deep influence on Kenzan ware, the brothers' sabi-e production also reveals the opposite: Kōrin's repertoire was expanded through the participation of his brother. In addition, Kōrin's time in Edo and his exposure to the Kano aesthetic had left him with a heightened awareness of the capabilities of ink. His experiences in eastern Japan provided a mental and technical roadmap for his creation of sabi-e on Kenzan's ceramics.

Among the stylistic luggage that Kōrin carried home from Edo was his study of the work of the late medieval painter Sesson Shūkei.[25] While in Edo, Kōrin gained access to Sesson's works through the collections of daimyo patrons, and he copied some of their paintings (figs. 97, 98). Kōrin even owned a seal that read "Sesson" (fig. 99). Even though the seal can be found on only two known Sesson paintings (including the one Kōrin copied) and may have been carved by Kōrin himself, it is a sign of his veneration for the sixteenth-century master. Aside from making careful copies of paintings by Sesson, Kōrin absorbed and reformulated their style and motifs into Sesson-esque paintings of his own. An example is Kōrin's paintings of Jurōjin, a subject to which he frequently turned. The archetype for Kōrin's renderings of Jurōjin during the last years of his life may have been works by Sesson, such as a large hanging scroll that Kōrin could have seen in Edo (fig. 100).[26] The work was once in the collection of the Sakai family, one of Kōrin's main Edo patrons, and it is possible that he examined the painting when he served the Sakai from around 1705 and

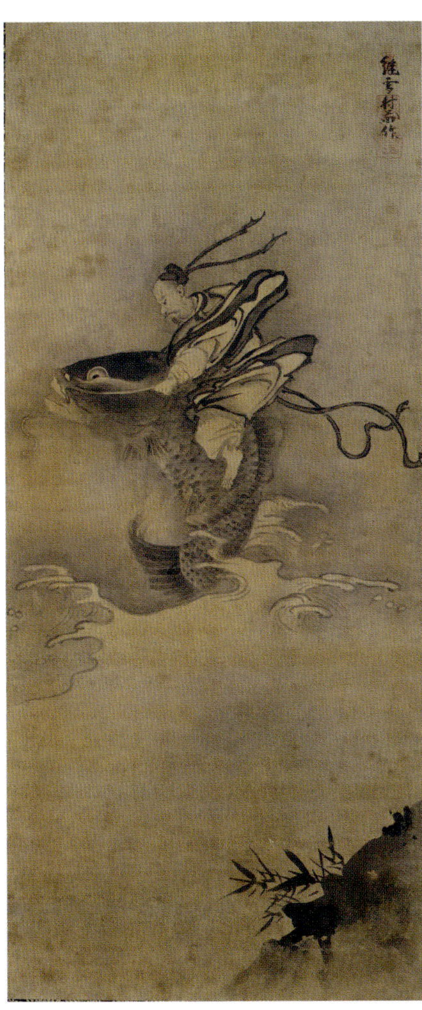

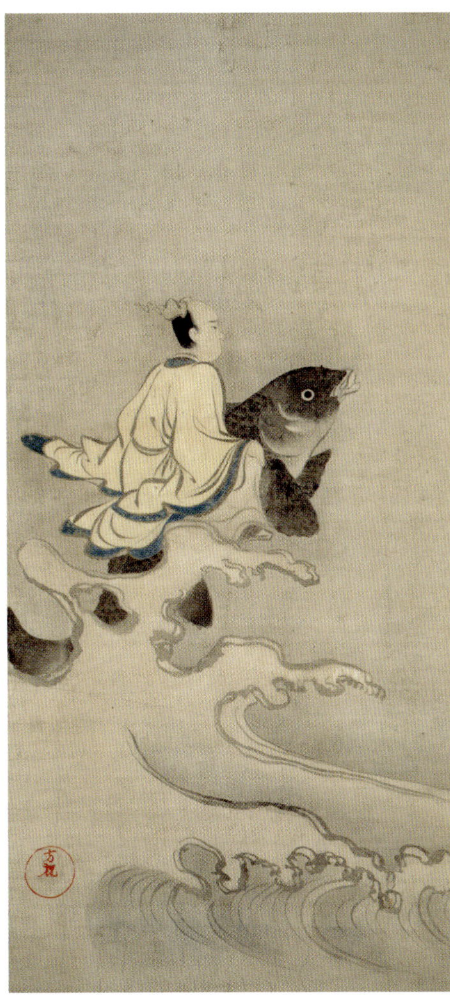

FIGURE 97
Sesson Shūkei, *Qin Gao Riding a Carp,* 16th century. Hanging scroll; ink on paper. Kyoto National Museum.

FIGURE 98
Ogata Kōrin, *Qin Gao Riding a Carp,* early 18th century. Hanging scroll; ink and color on paper. MOA Museum of Art, Atami.

FIGURE 99
Ogata Kōrin, *Square Relief Seal Reading "Sesson,"* early 17th century. Konishi Family Archive, Kyoto National Museum.

later. The peculiar position, squat physique, and body proportions of Jurōjin in Sesson's painting are evident in Kōrin's numerous renderings of the subject, suggesting some tangible stylistic connection between those works (fig. 101).

Kōrin, however, tailored his Jurōjin figures after his personal approach to painting, and he did not slavishly follow the model provided by Sesson or any other artist. While adopting the composition and physical aspects of the figure in the medieval work, Kōrin employed mannerisms he had learned from Shōkadō Shōjō's works during his early painting endeavors in the 1690s. For example, in his sabi-e of Jurōjin the deity has the same posture and physique as in Sesson's painting, but the rendering of the hair and the dark hues used for the clothing are a direct nod to Shōkadō—they do not appear as such in Sesson's works. Just as in *Hotei Playing Kemari,* one of his earliest paintings, Kōrin's works in multiple media fuse references to artists who are removed in time but still maintain a degree of aesthetic overlap. Shōkadō's own art referred to

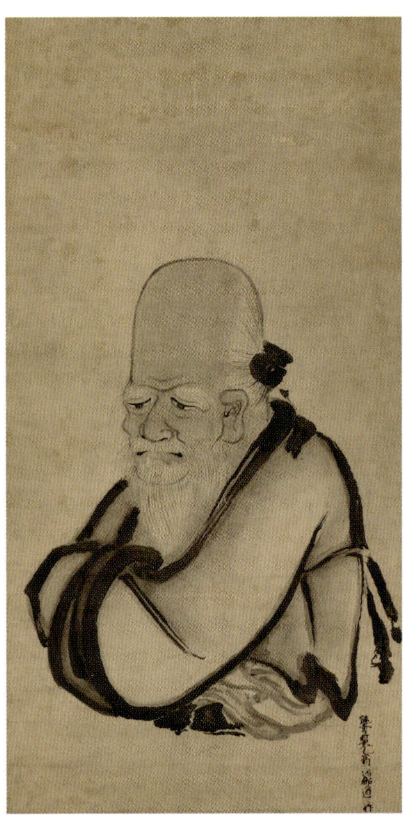

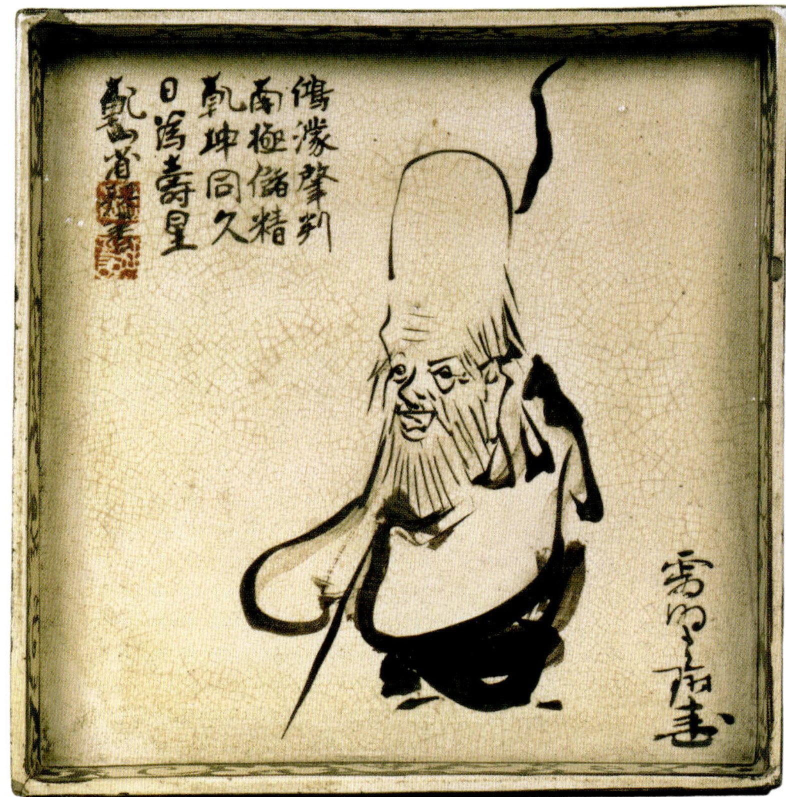

FIGURE 100
Sesson Shūkei, *Image of Jurōjin,* 16th century. Hanging scroll; ink on paper. Freer Gallery of Art, Smithsonian Institution, Washington, D.C.: Purchase—Charles Lang Freer Endowment, F2015.6a–d.

FIGURE 101
Ogata Kōrin (painting) and Ogata Kenzan (dish and calligraphy), *Square Dish with Design of Jurōjin,* early 18th century. Buff clay with iron pigment under transparent lead glaze. MOA Museum of Art, Atami.

medieval ink paintings—the time of Sesson—and by adopting his mode, Kōrin linked himself to a canonized retrospection of Japan's artistic past. Those two painters thus supplied Kōrin with a practical combination of references to the medieval and early modern periods and provided the cultural authority needed for his ink and sabi-e paintings.

The use of the Jakumei signature on Kōrin's sabi-e of Jurōjin assigns the date of that work to circa 1709.[27] Appearing exclusively on Kōrin's ink paintings and sabi-e, the name Jakumei conveys an intellectualized, continental air and serves to group his monochromatic works under one intellectual and artistic rubric. Having been suggested by his brother, the sobriquet shares this characteristic with the pseudonym Kenzan, a reference to the northwestern mountains bordering the capital and the location of his kiln. Kōrin placed his signature where Sesson did in his painting of Jurōjin, that is, to the lower right of the picture. This whimsical positioning makes it seem as if Jurōjin has turned his back on the name of the painter. As in *Hotei Playing Kemari* and other early works, Kōrin took great care incorporating his signature into a painting's overall composition. Here, too, its placement seems cautiously calculated.

Kōrin's sabi-e dishes create close views of their subjects on square spaces that resemble shikishi.[28] Kenzan had employed the square format since at least

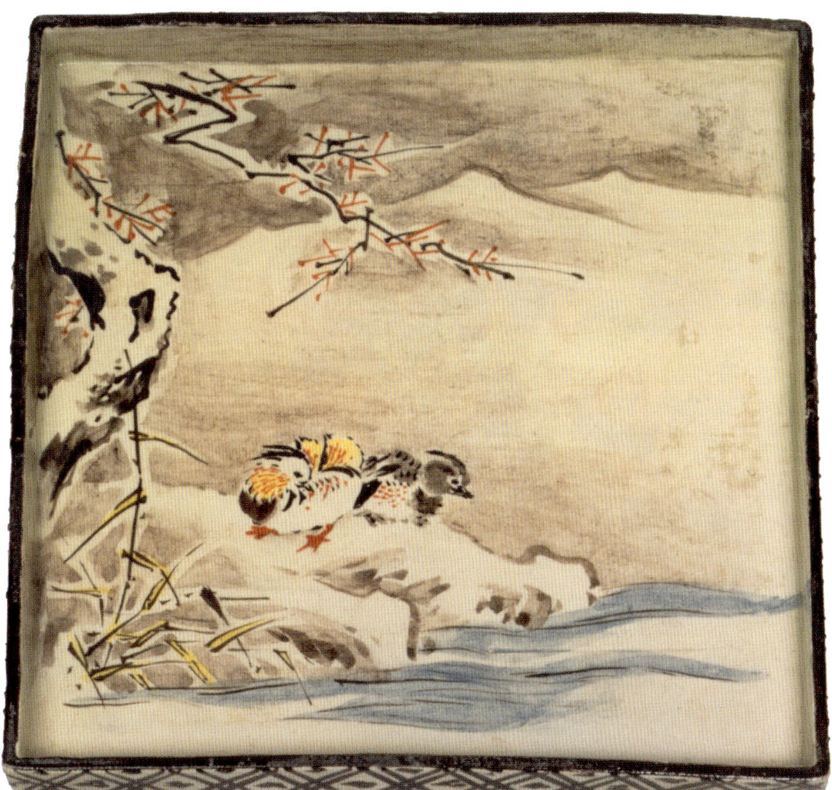

FIGURE 102
Ogata Kenzan, *Twelve Months After Fujiwara Teika* (*Twelfth Month*), circa 1702. Buff clay with pigment under transparent lead glaze. MOA Museum of Art, Atami.

1702 but with more complex pictures than Kōrin's sabi-e (fig. 102). The shikishi-shaped dishes of Kōrin and Kenzan's sabi-e bring to mind a classical practice in which poetry was inscribed on the clearly defined square spaces of shikishi that were pasted onto painted screens or admired in albums.[29] Kenzan's 1702 set also follows this principle by pairing pictures of the twelve months with accompanying poems on the back of the plates, thus visually separating writing from pictures. Later, in collaboration with Kōrin, Kenzan used the square dishes as grounds for sabi-e and began to combine calligraphy and imagery by adding his inscriptions directly onto the front of his dishes.

The shikishi-inspired format of many of Kōrin and Kenzan's plates served above all to showcase the paintings they carry. This practice is reminiscent of shikishi produced by Tawaraya Sōtatsu's atelier. Kōrin had access to examples of the Tawaraya-made leaves depicting scenes from the *Tales of Ise,* and the shikishi and ceramic plates by Kōrin and Kenzan correspond conceptually. Both pair images with calligraphic inscriptions that relate to and enhance the pictorial content. Writing was added directly onto the picture, granting more or less equal visual significance to both elements. The same holds true for the brothers' sabi-e dishes. Furthermore, many of their dishes were produced in sets that establish loose associations among each other, a strategy also pursued in the Tawaraya shikishi of the *Tales of Ise.*[30] Kenzan conceived of a number of his objects in groups, a common practice in ceramics. He and Kōrin made at least some sabi-e in sets, probably over extended periods of time. The same was true for the Tawaraya shikishi set, which was compiled over several decades.[31]

Parts of the Tawaraya shikishi are connected through stylistic and chromatic correspondence. Similarly, Kōrin and Kenzan's sabi-e dishes are linked by their distinct matching rims. Their use of recurring motifs—Hotei, Jurōjin, chrysanthemums, and bamboo—establishes another correlating element. A further characteristic that unifies the sabi-e oeuvre produced by Kōrin and Kenzan is the focus on monochrome. This type of association is seen in the Tawaraya shikishi, where the repetitive use of azurite and malachite establishes a chromatic connection within the set that persists even though the individual pieces were often painted by different artists.

Producing the sabi-e fused the brothers' respective skills of painting and calligraphy. Kōrin instilled his sabi-e with stylistic and thematic elements that emphasize his exposure to ink paintings in Edo. Through this process, the brothers looked back to the sixteenth and early seventeenth centuries for inspiration. By transposing the aesthetics of late medieval ink paintings onto ceramics—a novelty at the time—they imbued their sabi-e with an innovative dimension. In other words, the old provided the framework for the new. Although their transposition of the aesthetics of ink to ceramics was at the cutting edge, their reliance on medieval ink painting was not. By referring to such retrospective styles, Kōrin and Kenzan tapped into a time-honored metaframework that lent the cultural gravitas of old ink modes to their explorations of sabi-e. Despite the daring quality of their innovation, the brothers remembered to stay within an orthodox, recognizable chassis that imbued their works with cultural validity. The poems that Kenzan inscribed onto a considerable number of dishes with Kōrin's sabi-e amplified that strategy.

PAINTING POETRY

By the time Kōrin and Kenzan began to collaborate, Kenzan ware had achieved considerable name recognition.[32] This is best illustrated by the prominent Kenzan and Shinsei signatures that the potter added next to his inscriptions or sometimes on the verso of his pieces. Following the fashion of his time, Kenzan sought to present himself as a noble recluse, a practice from the medieval period that gained widespread momentum in early modern Japan.[33] In 1689 Kenzan moved into his Hall of Mastering Tranquility outside Ninnaji. In doing so, he followed in the footsteps of his maternal ancestor Hon'ami Kōetsu, who relocated from Kyoto to rural Takagamine to the same region of the capital, making

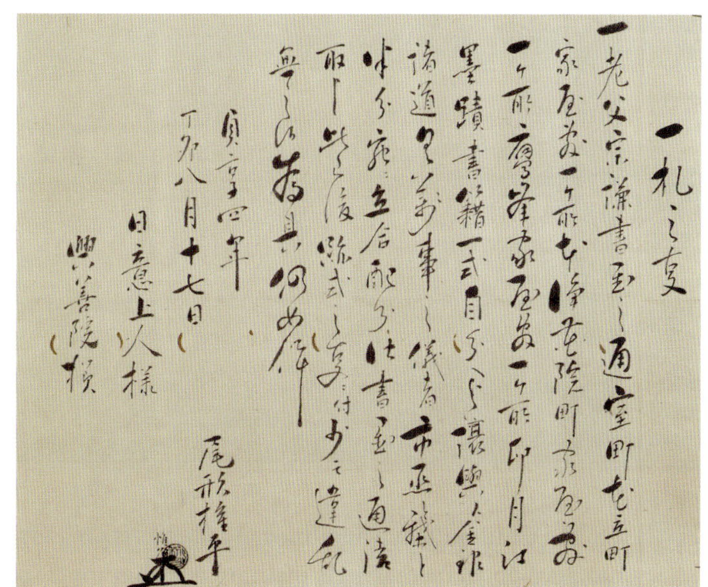

FIGURE 103
Ogata Kenzan, *Letter Accepting His Father's Bequest*, 1687. Konishi Family Archive, Kyoto National Museum.

sure to be close enough to the city for convenience but still far enough away to qualify as a recluse. The same could be said of the site of Kenzan's Narutaki kiln, which he established in the same hilly area just outside of Kyoto. The poems Kenzan selected to complement Kōrin's sabi-e were part of his attempts to endow Kenzan ware with the alternative, intellectual aura of the age-old interaction between lyrical word and virtuoso pictures.

At first sight, their ceramic dishes suggest a communicative interaction between the inscriptions and their accompanying paintings. Adhering to the seemingly free-spirited nature of the sabi-e by Kōrin, Kenzan sought to enhance this image via a combination of writing and painting that was intended to suggest spontaneous communication between the two. Calligraphy, a revered form of individual expression, provided an ideal means to project this unrehearsed air. The impromptu style of the pictures and the expressive, individualized calligraphy camouflaged the meticulous process that formed the backdrop of their sabi-e. Kenzan's inscriptions with Kōrin's sabi-e were in fact the product of carefully selected, repetitive references that were intended to exude an extempore feeling.

From a young age Kenzan expressed a personal approach to calligraphy. In a document dated to 1687, his calligraphy already diverged from that of his father and two brothers (fig. 103). Contrary to Kenzan, Ogata family members largely followed the elegant, curvy writing style of their famous ancestor Kōetsu. Yet in its thick, stubby horizontal strokes, Kenzan's early writing showed signs of the bold calligraphy that later became his trademark. Kenzan's enthusiasm led his father to bequeath him a calligraphy collection that contained a piece attributed

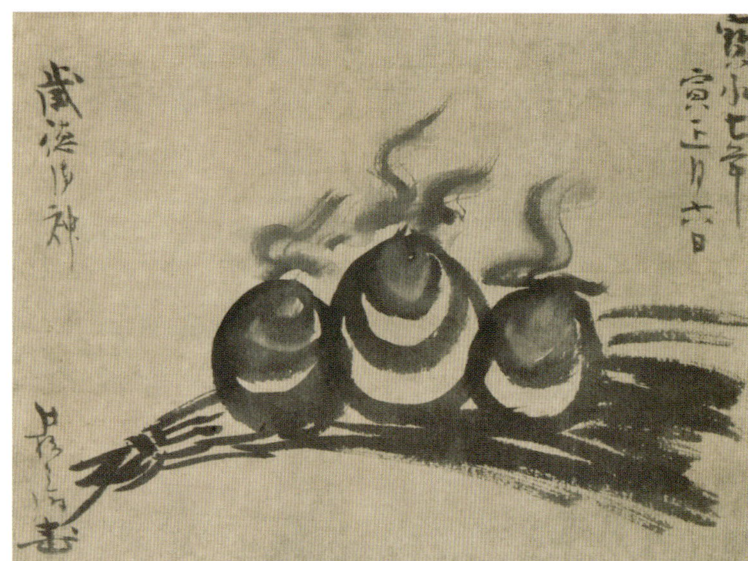

FIGURE 108 Ogata Kōrin, *Cintamani Jewels,* 1710. Hanging scroll; ink on paper. Private collection.

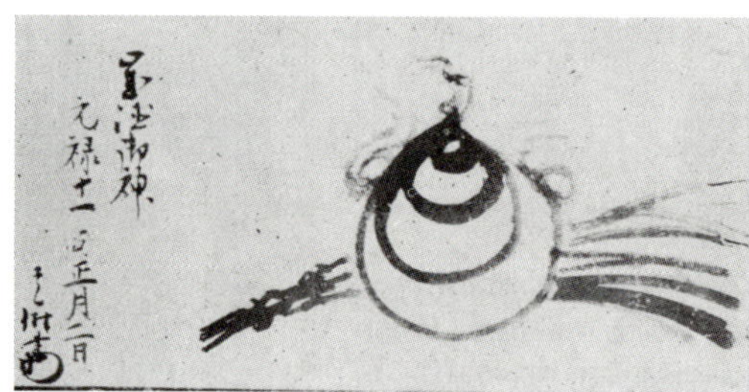

FIGURE 109 Ogata Kōrin, *Cintamani Jewel,* dated 1699. Hanging scroll; ink on paper. Present location unknown (published in an auction catalogue accompanying the sale of parts of the estate of the Aoji family, held at the Tokyo Bijutsu Club in March 1920, p. 107). Image Courtesy: Tokyo National Research Institute for Cultural Properties.

Templates of Kōrin's general approach to ink—and by extension his sabi-e—include his New Year's paintings. A piece depicting three wish-granting *cintamani* jewels arranged on a bundle of bamboo branches is an auspicious subject commonly presented as a gift celebrating the New Year (fig. 108). The painting records the date of the sixth day of the first month of 1710, when the brothers were busy collaborating on sabi-e. Paintings of similar auspicious motifs, such as treasure ships (*takarabune*) that Kōrin also painted, were established themes for New Year's painting performances.[40] The date inscribed on Kōrin's cintamani jewels also confirms this idea. Kōrin signed the New Year's painting "Hokkyō Kōrin" and included a cypher (*kaō*) that reads *ju* or *kotobuki* (luck or long life). The same cypher appears on many of his sabi-e and in similarly abbreviated, swiftly made ink paintings, linking the two genres.[41] Kōrin's use of this cypher on ceramic dishes and his impromptu New Year's paintings suggests that he viewed the two as belonging to the same conceptual category. The cintamani painting also embraces an array of stylistic peculiarities that Kōrin transferred to his sabi-e. His sabi-e of plum blossoms and Jurōjin were created with noticeably rapid brushwork. In this swift, ad hoc mode, Kōrin carefully included "flying white" (Chinese, *feibai;* Japanese, *hihaku*), washes, and other markers of his virtuosity in ink, making sabi-e displays of his painterly acumen. Areas of washes gracing the upper portion of the cintamani in the ink painting and the lower trunk of the sabi-e plum correspond, thus demonstrating the extent to which the brothers managed to merge ink and ceramics.

Although the cintamani painting was produced after Kōrin's return from Edo, he made similar pieces confirming that such painting practices were an established facet of his oeuvre (fig. 109).[42] The composition is more or less identical, yet Kōrin's brushwork in the 1699 and 1710 pieces differs slightly. As might be expected, the 1710 work is closer in style to his sabi-e paintings, while the 1699 work resembles his earlier efforts. Both pieces subtly show how Kōrin moved from a straightforward, steady painting style to the eclectic, technique-heavy visual language that he transferred to his sabi-e. Eventually, toward the end of his life, the concepts of sabi-e and ink paintings were unified in Kōrin's body of work.

TOWARD A BRAND OF POTTERY

The distinctive language of Kōrin and Kenzan's sabi-e demonstrates their attempt to establish a visual recognizability that eventually became a core element of Kenzan ware. From his early days as a potter, Kenzan's tendency to experiment and innovate was geared at setting Kenzan ware apart from the products of other Kyoto pottery workshops. A proximity to painting was at the heart of this endeavor. Kenzan's own dishes with landscapes show elements—namely, boats and figures, as well as conspicuous strokes used to add texture to the mountains—found in model books for painting, such as *Genealogy of Eight Types of Painting* (*Hasshu gafu*) (figs. 110, 111). The manual, originally published

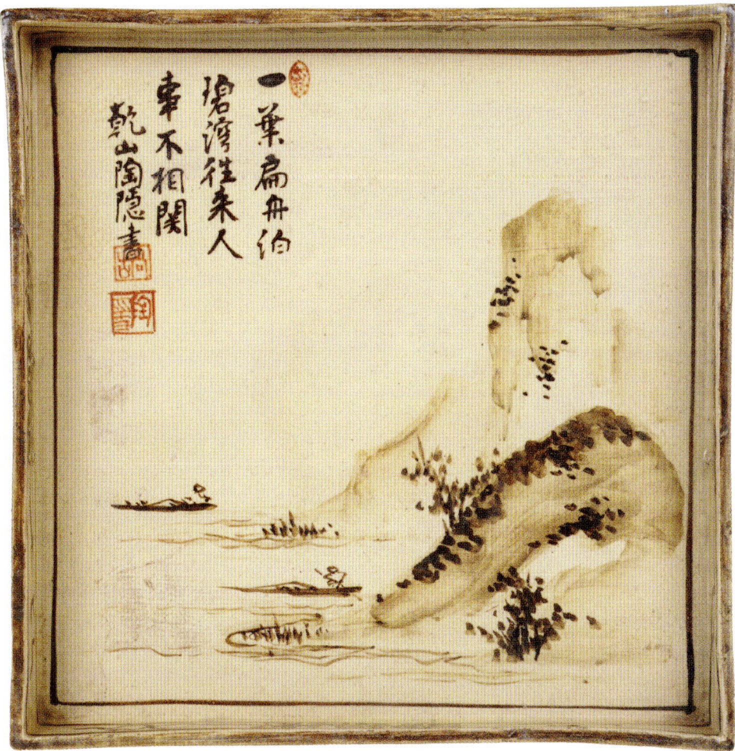

FIGURE 110
Ogata Kenzan, *Square Dish with Design of a Landscape with Figures,* early 18th century. Buff clay with iron pigment under transparent lead glaze. Nezu Museum, Tokyo.

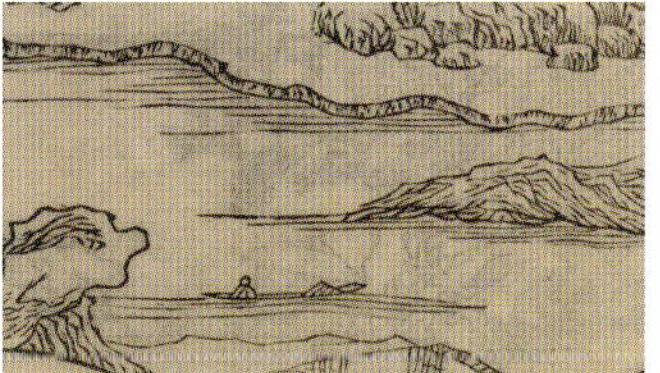

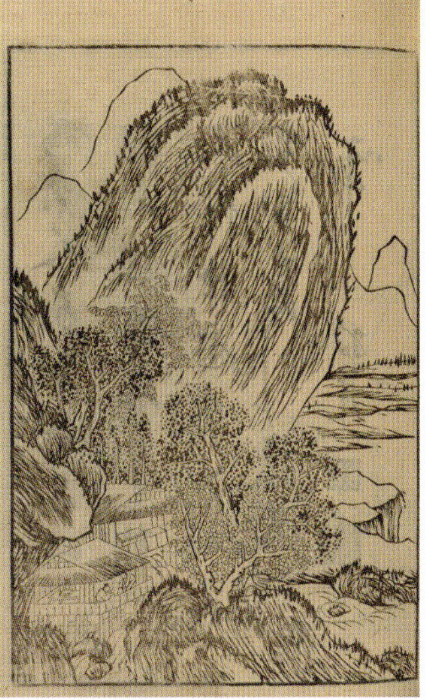

FIGURE 111
Genealogy of Eight Types of Painting (*Hasshu gafu*) (details), early 18th century. Woodblock-printed book; ink on paper. Freer Gallery of Art and Arthur M. Sackler Gallery Library/Smithsonian Libraries Rare Book Collection (752.1 .H25).

in China and reprinted in Japan in 1672, was likely accessed by the sinophile Kenzan. The practice of using printed painting manuals for ceramics was by then an established tradition.[43] While the dishes are by Kenzan, it is far from certain whether he was the painter, rather than the artistic manager who chose the subjects and guided the production.[44] The prominent Kenzan signatures should be read less as a personal signature and more as a pottery trademark.

Pictures associated with Kenzan ware can be divided into two categories: composite pictures by anonymous secondary painters contracted by Kenzan's atelier and succinct, prominently signed images designed by Kōrin. None of Kenzan's workshop painters signed their sabi-e. Only an obscure figure named Watanabe Soshin is known. Kenzan recorded the painter's name on the back of a single surviving work.[45] Kōrin, by contrast, never failed to add his signature to his sabi-e. It seems that, to Kenzan, Kōrin alone was celebrated enough to justify adding his name directly on Kenzan ware.

Eventually, this joint venture became so popular and the demand for Kōrin's work was so profitable in the years after his death that Kenzan sought to align his ceramics with his famous deceased brother. In 1737 he wrote in his pottery manual *Ceramic Techniques* (*Tōji seihō*): "I took care of technical aspects and patterns by consulting with Kōrin. The first pictures [on my ceramics] were all painted by Kōrin himself. The style of my pictures now follows Kōrin, but I also instilled them with new ideas of my own."[46] This claim likely contains little truth, since Kōrin added pictures to Kenzan's wares only a decade after he opened his first kiln. It does, however, reflect Kenzan's attempt to use Kōrin's artistic clout as a way to market his pottery. The statement also reveals his pride in the brothers' achievements. Above all, Kenzan's declaration in *Ceramic Techniques* plays on the momentum of Kōrin's art, especially after the painter's death. When Kenzan wrote the manual, Kōrin's works and persona had generated substantial popular acclaim. Kenzan proudly employed his brother's fame for his own business, so much so that he adopted Kōrin's particular sabi-e style to create his own painted pottery.

By merging his brother's style with his own, Kenzan absorbed Kōrin's free-spirited brushwork into an eclectic pictorial language. Works dating to the middle of Kenzan's Nijō Chōjiyamachi kiln period—that is, in the 1720s or early 1730s—often conflate the brothers' distinctive modes into a bricolage of Kōrin's sabi-e repertoire. Such works unite the most straightforward features of their sabi-e, signaling how Kōrin's style eventually became part of a calculated amalgam incorporated into later Kenzan ware (fig. 112).

In fact, Kōrin encouraged his brother to embrace his sabi-e style in Kenzan ware, a fact confirmed by a small handscroll. In monochrome ink on paper, Kōrin provided several motifs for paintings on ceramics and labeled

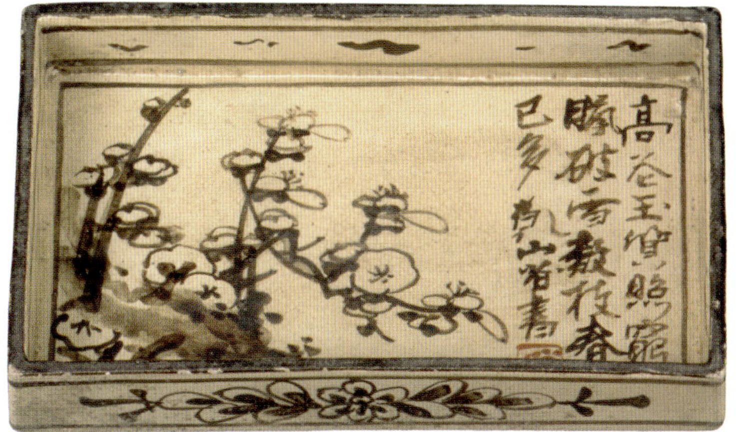

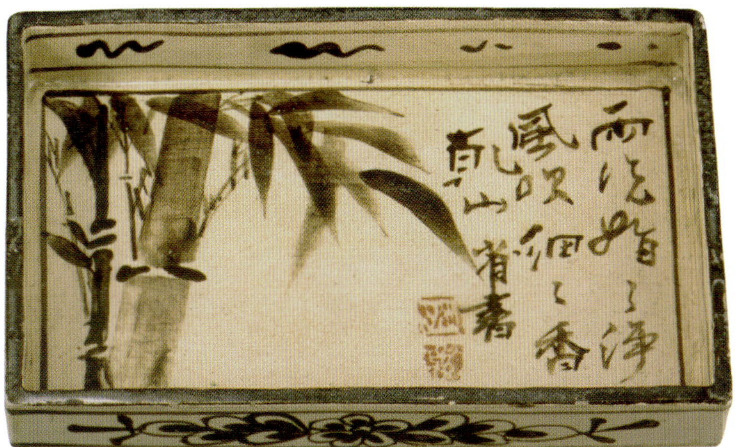

FIGURE 112
Ogata Kenzan, *Rectangular Dishes with Designs of Plum Blossoms and Bamboo* (from a set of ten), circa 1720s and 1730s. Buff clay with iron pigment under transparent lead glaze. Private collection.

them "model book for Kenzan's tea bowls, by Seisei [Kōrin]" (fig. 113). Their subjects of horses, Hotei, plum blossoms, and pines largely represent traditional motifs for ink paintings. Kōrin created the images with the nonchalant air typical of his sabi-e. The scroll reaffirms the style and efficacy of traditional ink painting subjects as well as how Kōrin brushed his images on Kenzan's ceramics. As such, the model scroll is symbolic of Kōrin and Kenzan's accomplishment to connect ink and sabi-e, and it provided a template for Kenzan to reference beyond Kōrin's lifetime.

The sketches left Kenzan with the subjects and brushwork of Kōrin's painterly practice, both of which became hallmarks of Kenzan ware. They also suggest that Kenzan's incorporation of his brother's artistic peculiarities into his later pottery brand was initiated when Kōrin was still alive. Kōrin's models range from specific to referential. For example, the scroll opens with images

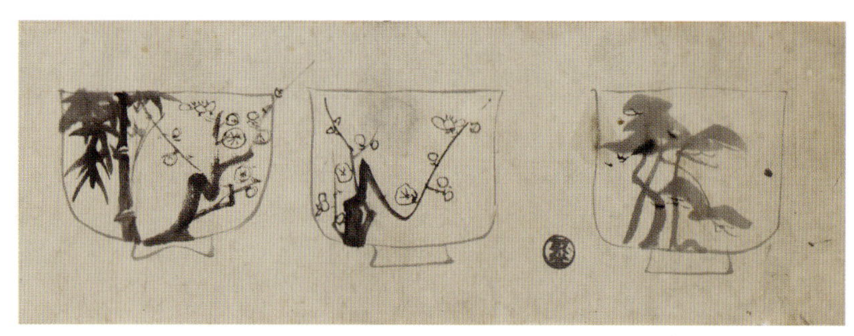

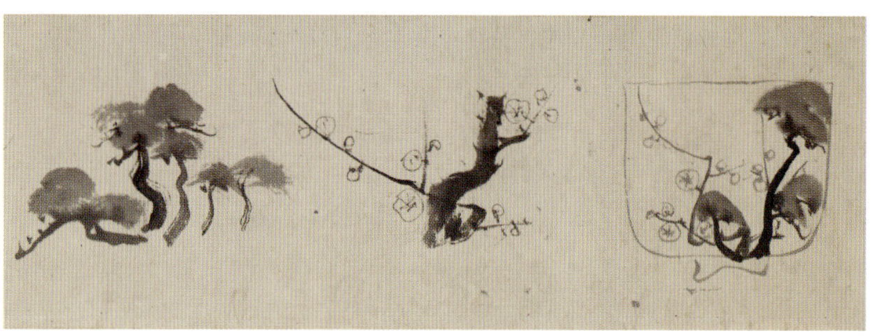

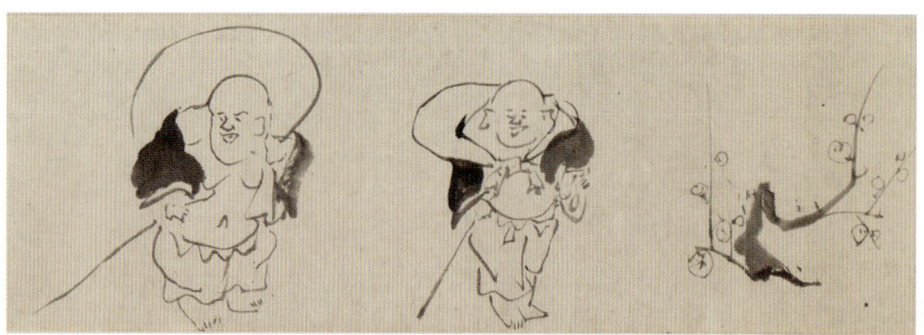

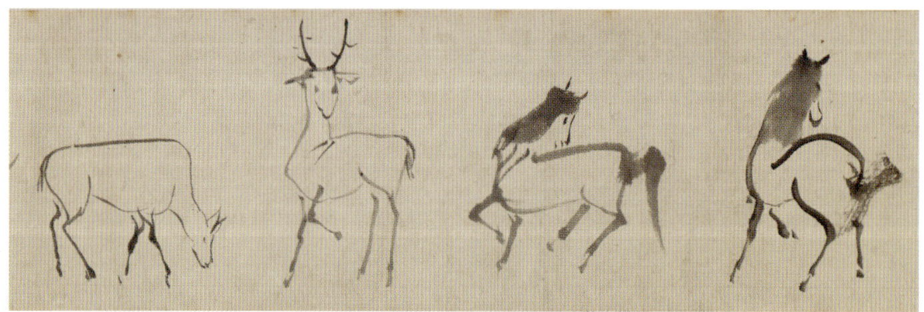

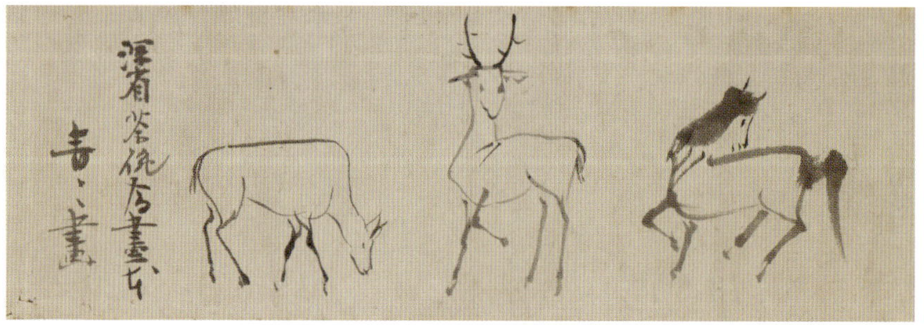

FIGURE 113 Ogata Kōrin, *Designs for Tea Bowls,* early 18th century. Handscroll; ink on paper. Idemitsu Museum of Arts, Tokyo.

of plum blossoms painted directly into the outlines of tea bowls so as to create a sense of space and proportion in the three-dimensional medium. In spite of Kōrin's labeling as a model book for tea bowls, most of the designs are less concretely placed and may have also functioned as broadly defined sources of reference that could be modified to fit a number of vessels, from tea bowls and dishes to braziers and other objects—in short, Kenzan's full repertoire. The designs all follow the brushwork and general manner that Kōrin employed consistently in his sabi-e and that Kenzan made a part of his aesthetic identity afterward.

The undated scroll in many ways represents the pinnacle of Kōrin and Kenzan's artistic collaboration and bonds of brotherhood. From the early days of Kenzan's ceramics and Kōrin's first steps as a painter both artists joined forces in aiding each other in selling their works and in sculpting their respective artistic identities. Kenzan provided Kōrin with counsel on life choices and pseudonyms and likely encouraged him to work on his ceramics. Kōrin helped Kenzan ship and sell his first pieces and later lent his name and skill to embellish his brother's popular ceramics. The second and third sons of one of Kyoto's waning upper-class houses, Kōrin and Kenzan made their names through the arts, an onerous yet inspirational path that the two brothers chose to walk together. Perhaps their biggest joint accomplishment is the unison of painting and ceramics.

❖ ❖ ❖

In popular reception during the Edo period, Kōrin came to be associated with a free-handed, virtuoso brushwork in ink. He gained recognition for his expertise in that medium, which he deployed in his sabi-e. Conspicuously labeled "black pictures" and applied to ceramic surfaces meant to resemble white paper, sabi-e emulate the aesthetic of works of art in ink. Kōrin's sabi-e are a culmination of a lifelong process of honing his skills in painting and translating that aptitude into a variety of media. With Kenzan's collaboration, Kōrin applied his painterly prowess to turning sabi-e into simulacra of traditional paintings that expanded the scope of ink to ceramics. As a result, during the last decade of Kōrin's life, the brothers diversified the definition of ink paintings and ceramics, effectively obfuscating the boundaries between the two media.

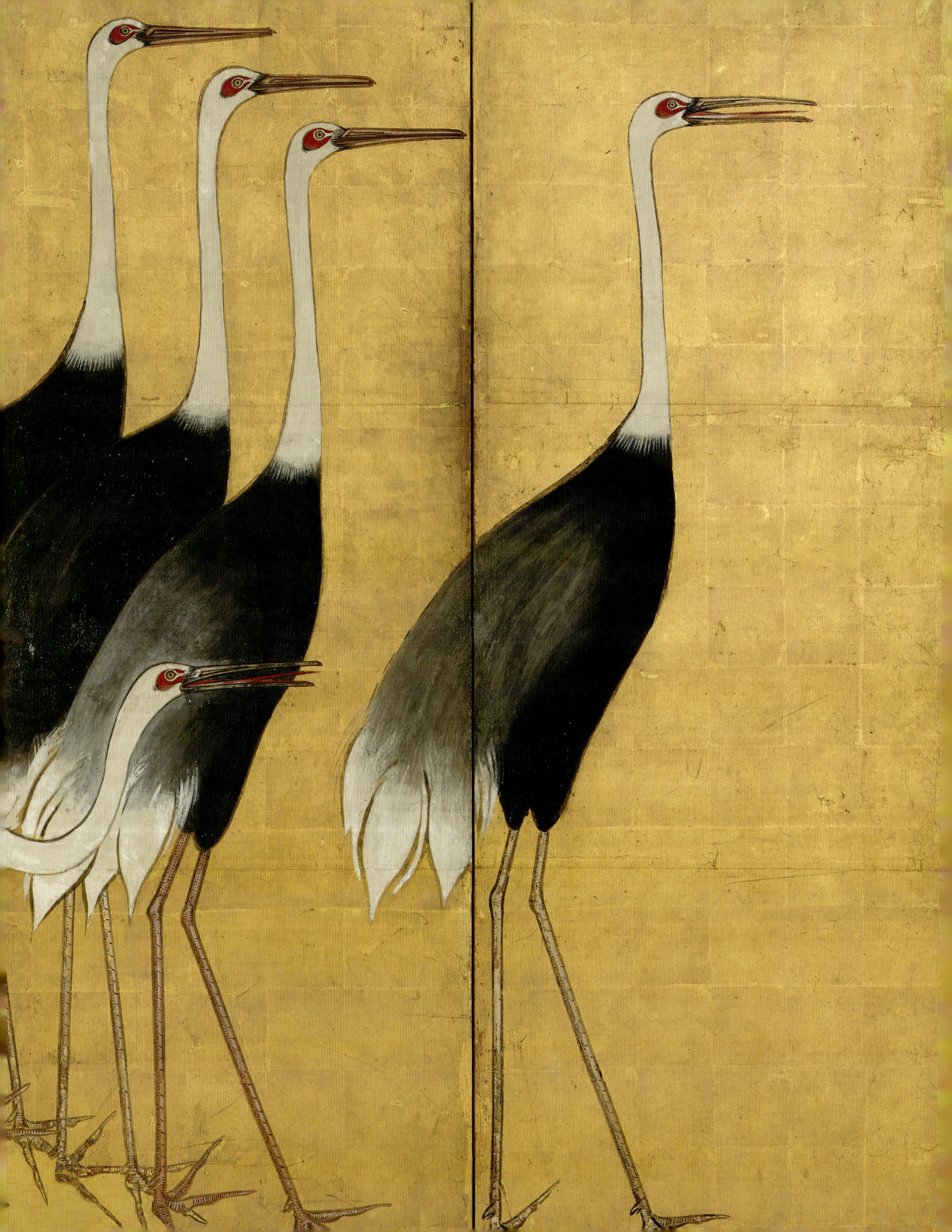

6 Toward the End

Kōrin's Late Work

> I ask you to . . . guard the memory of our ancestors. This is important to me. You are my flesh and blood. But since I lack a family business, it was hard [for me] to provide security [for you].
>
> —Ogata Kōrin in his two wills, 1713

The last works of an artist often become the subject of mystification. In the case of Kōrin, we are captivated by the winding path of his prowess, and we follow with fascination his road from the time he first took up the brush to his final works. The "old-age" or mature style encompasses the culmination of a lifetime's achievement that is paired with the decline in the artist's physical aptitude and the necessary adjustments in his way of making art.[1] In this way, the works produced during that time contain important messages about the painter's strategy of creating and selling art. Edward Said argued that late works gain in intricacy and profundity and are often freer and unleash a stronger creative force when the end is nigh.[2] At the same time, they offer a window onto shifting levels of health and possible expansion of studio involvement in increasingly sprawling ateliers. In many ways, the late work of a painter is the summation of a life lived, a style formed, and a legacy established. All of this is true of Kōrin's final paintings.

Kōrin's last works were also the threshold to something new and everlasting. The paintings he made during the final five or so years after his return from Edo had perhaps the most profound impact on his posthumous reception and role in the history of Japanese art. The relatively brief span of frenzied creativity brought forth works that still hold iconic status in Japan today. One painting exemplifies the dusk of Kōrin's life and the culmination of his two-and-a-half decades as a painter: *Red and White Plum Blossoms* (fig. 114) is considered not only one of Kōrin's final pictures but also one of his signature accomplishments.

The pair of two-panel screens illustrates Kōrin's idiosyncratic approach to form and composition. It also offers evidence of the ways in which Kōrin

Detail of fig. 119

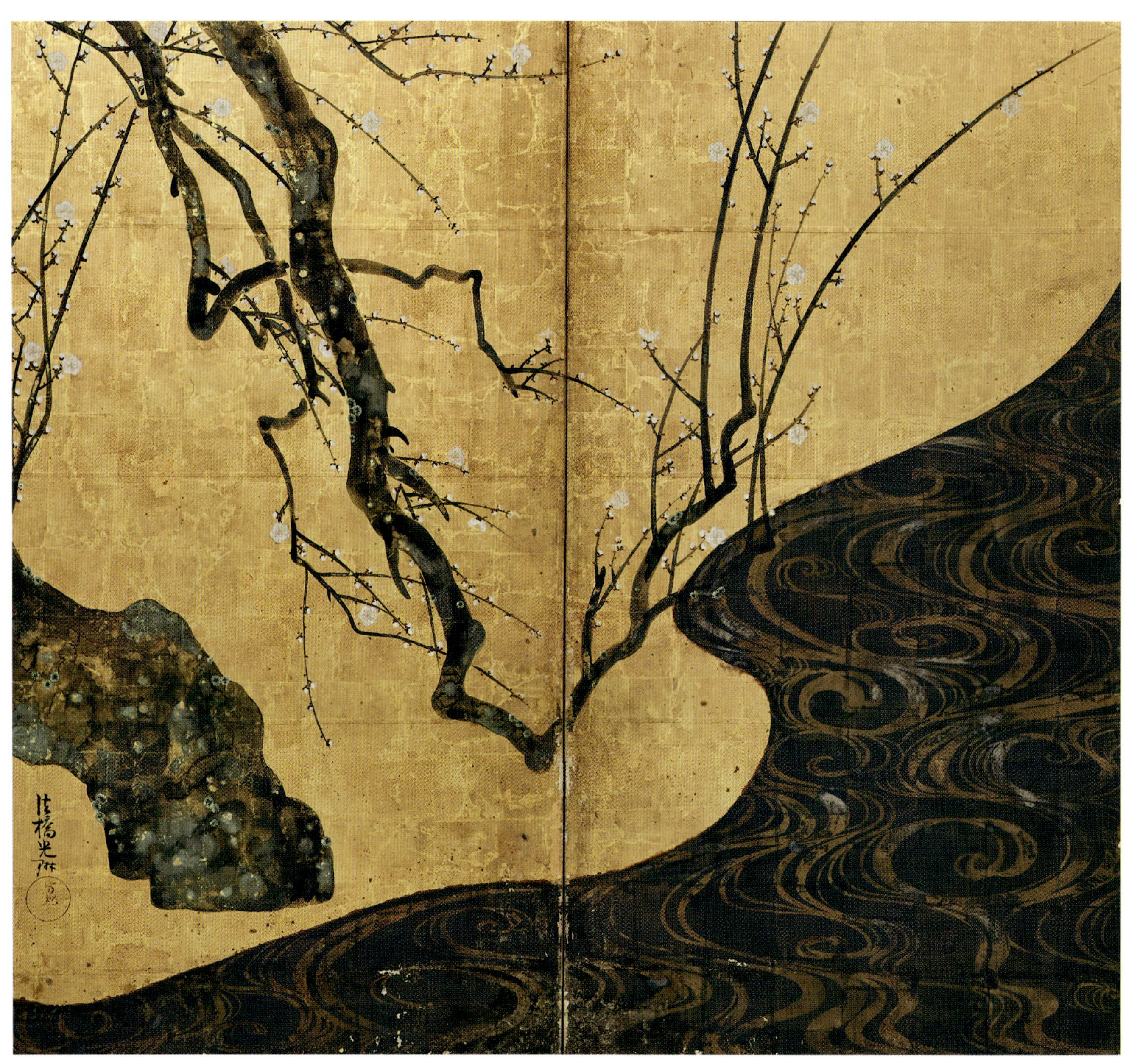

FIGURE 114 Ogata Kōrin, *Red and White Plum Blossoms,* early 18th century. Pair of two-panel folding screens; ink, color, silver, gold, and unidentified materials on paper. MOA Museum of Art, Atami.

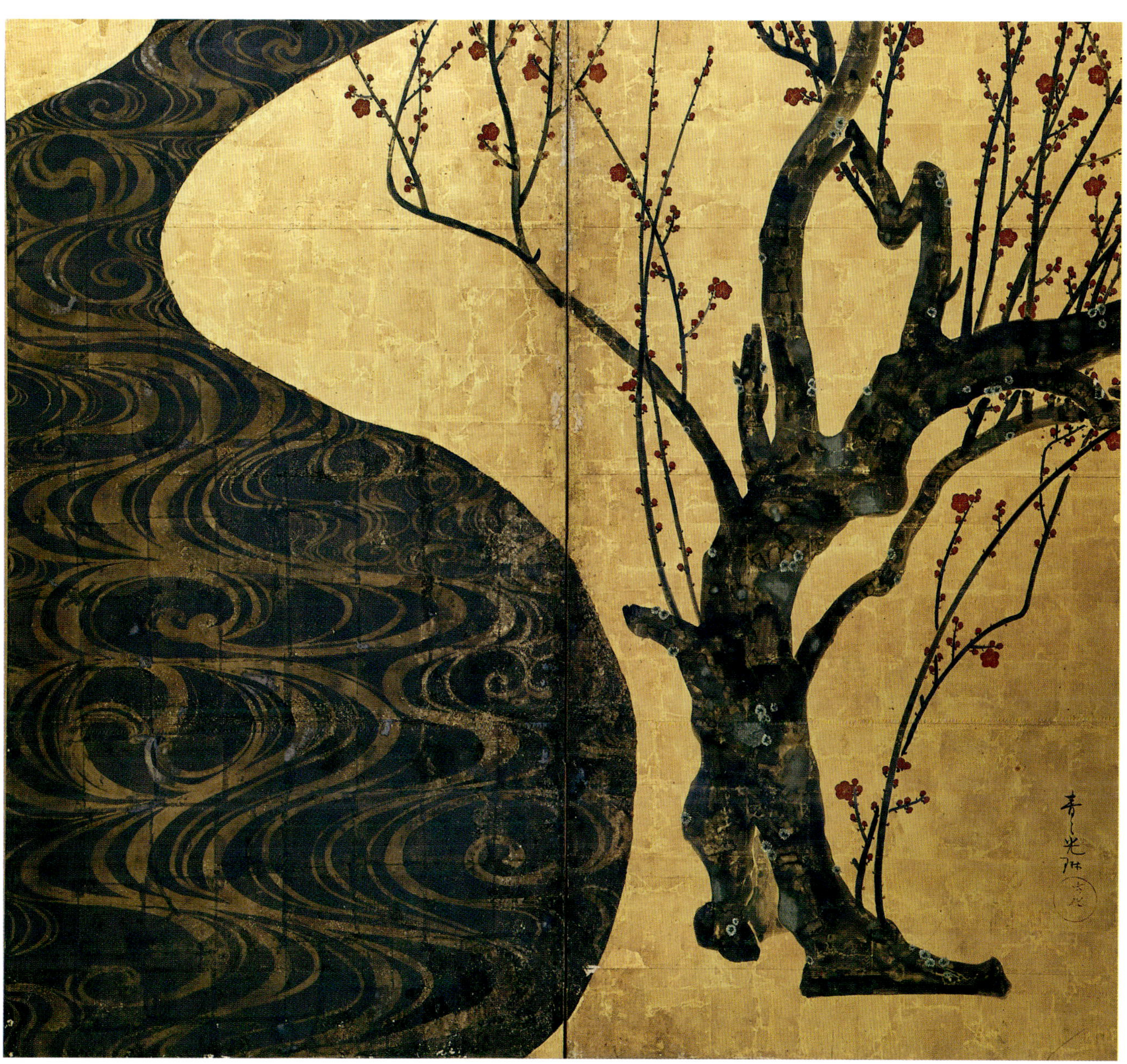
青々光琳

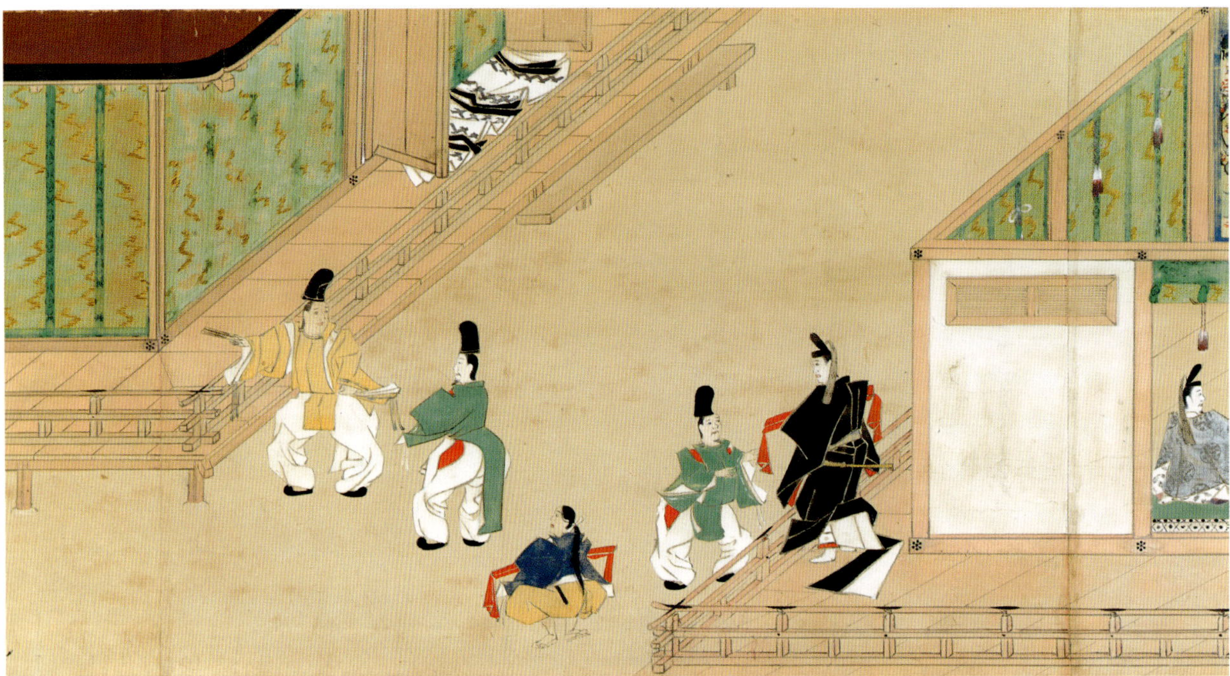

FIGURE 115
Tawaraya Sōtatsu, *Illustrated Life of Saigyō* (detail), 1630. Handscroll; ink and color on paper. Idemitsu Museum of Arts, Tokyo.

tailored his oeuvre toward a diverse clientele whose demand for his artworks had proliferated with his growing public fame. *Red and White Plum Blossoms* makes apparent Kōrin's ailing physical state and, possibly, an increase in the role of assistants in the production of many works made during his final years. Further, the screens provide an ultimate case in point for Kōrin's use of visual effect for creating allusive cultural meaning. Responding to his penchant for reconfiguring age-old subjects in a new visual guise, later painters adopted Kōrin's novel ways of expression from his works. They searched for and found in his works an experimental style that emphasized unorthodox forms and inventive technique. This key principle of Kōrin's oeuvre was a beacon for later artists in their own quests to imbue their paintings with cultural potency and established Kōrin's long-lasting stamp on Japanese art.

LIQUID TREES

The simple title given to the work today conveys a humility that fails to communicate the profound impact of the painting itself. The understated name conceals the vast array of interpretations that scholars have thrust upon this peculiar work of art in attempts to make sense of it. *Red and White Plum Blossoms* has been read variously as representing a trifold relationship between Kōrin, a man, and a woman, Kōrin's dark psyche at the end of his life, and the lens of

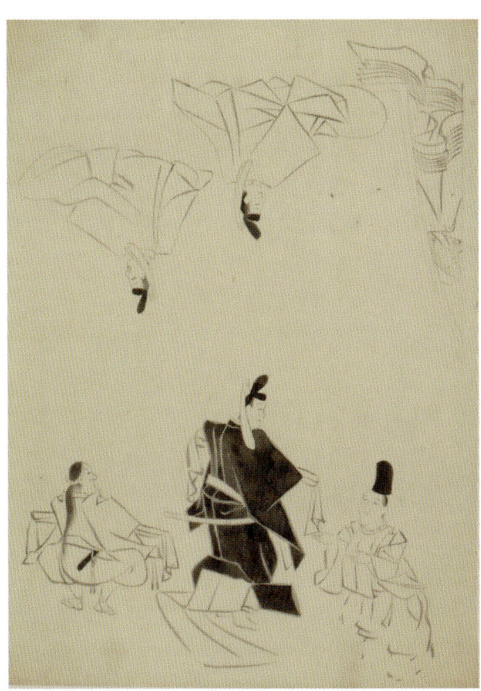

FIGURE 116
Ogata Kōrin, *Sketch of Illustrated Life of Saigyō,* early 18th century. Ink on paper. Konishi Family Archive, Kyoto National Museum.

Chinese poetry and the Noh theater, among other analyses—virtually every major Kōrin scholar has offered a reading of this painting.[3] But as often happens with Kōrin's works of art, specific personal interpretations are hard to assign to a painting whose subject—plum blossoms—was painted countless times in the history of Japanese art. By way of their ubiquitous role as a symbol for winter and the new year alone do plum blossoms carry deep-seated cultural significance. Such omnipresence presented painters with substantial leeway in interpreting the subject. For Kōrin, too, the most pronounced way in which the screens differ from other plum paintings is the same as in many other works by Kōrin: how he painted it. Kōrin's prime achievement lies in his reformulating of an orthodox subject into a mystifying work of art.

The right screen of the pair bears the signature Seisei Kōrin, while the left screen is signed Hokkyō Kōrin. Beneath both signatures, Kōrin placed a round relief seal reading Masatoki. The Seisei Kōrin imprimatur was one of a number of signatures suggested to Kōrin by his brother Kenzan, probably after his return from Edo in 1709. Masatoki is considered Kōrin's latest pseudonym and can regularly be found on works made during the final half-decade of the artist's life.[4] The screens juxtapose a tree with red blossoms in the right screen with white blossoms on the left. The red-flowering tree is recognizably slender, less ancient than the thick, gnarling trunk seen in the left screen. A single bulky branch of the white-flowered tree extends like an elephant's trunk from the upper left of the screen and is supported by a second branch that forks out into two zigzagging limbs. The stark diagonality of the left tree is contrasted with the gentle rightward bent of the tree on the right. The trees seem to be reaching out toward each other across a creek of heavily stylized water that descends downward from the upper right screen in a delicately curving motion, akin to silk billowing in a gentle breeze. *Red and White Plum Blossoms* is striking in that Kōrin translated the solid trunks of trees into liquid forms while transforming the river into an artificial pattern that is constrained by the winding body of the stream—in Kōrin's painting, fluidity and solidity are reversed.

The genesis of *Red and White Plum Blossoms* may lie within two other works that Kōrin made during his final years. After his return from Edo, Kōrin produced a set of handscrolls depicting the life of the monk-poet Saigyō (1118–1190)—the work bears the same Hokkyō Kōrin signature and Masatoki seal as the plum screens. Kōrin's handscrolls are copies of copies that Tawaraya Sōtatsu made of a set of medieval handscrolls in the imperial collections. The whereabouts of the original are unknown, but Sōtatsu's copies survive (fig. 115).[5] Kōrin made his version at a time when he produced more or less faithful duplicates of several Sōtatsu paintings, including the screens *Gods of Wind and Thunder.* Kōrin studied Sōtatsu's set of handscrolls closely and sketched a number of details (fig. 116). These examples make clear that Kōrin's turn to Sōtatsu's style, which began in the late 1690s, amplified considerably during the last years of his life. From Sōtatsu's Saigyō handscrolls, Kōrin seems to have selected an inconspicuous tree and made it the template for his red plum tree in the right screen of *Red and White Plum Blossoms.* In essence, a prop in the handscroll becomes the protagonist of the screen (fig. 117).

The approach of isolating a detail from a larger narrative and magnifying it at the center of a screen painting was an established mechanism in Kōrin's oeuvre, and he did so in some of his most important works, such as the *Hakurakuten* screens. Their central image is probably an adaptation from a section of a fifteenth-century handscroll called *Illustrated Miracles of Vajrapani* (*Shukongōjin engi*), a work at Tōdaiji that was also copied by other Kyoto painters such as Kōrin's older contemporary Tosa Mitsuoki. The practice of highlighting a detail extends beyond paintings with an identifiable source. The *Irises* screens, for example, do not find their origin in illustrated handscrolls. Yet the iris flower, which would commonly be one feature of a larger whole, was magnified and made the center of a large-format work of art. This simple yet potent strategy was a cynosure of Kōrin's artistry, one that he adhered to until his very last breath. In this way, *Red and White Plum Blossoms* is a facet reenvisioned as a totality and turned into a tour de force in style and composition.

The stylized rivulet at the center of the screens is equally referential. Kōrin most likely took inspiration from lacquer designs. In chapter 3 we encountered Kōrin's suzuribako with a design of hollyhocks in mother-of-pearl and lead on a black lacquer ground. The flowers float on a winding pattern in gilded lacquer that is akin to threads of gold meandering alongside each other, sometimes touching, sometimes recoiling. The possible prototype for this sophisticated pattern survives in a rectangular sketch (fig. 118). The sketch and lacquer design find their twin in the water pattern in *Red and White Plum Blossoms.*

Kōrin applied his experience in lacquer onto his late work as a painter. In a pair of screens depicting cranes, Kōrin chose a similarly swirling stream to frame his composition of repetitive birds (fig. 119). The work represents a fusion of Kōrin's approach to the repetition in *Irises* and the stylization in *Red and White Plum Blossoms.* In spite of their spurious signatures, the *Cranes* screens were likely painted after his return from Edo by combining the recurrent, slightly alternating shapes of the cranes with the mannered swirling motion of the water.[6] In that way, the *Cranes* screens link Kōrin's early work in *Irises* with

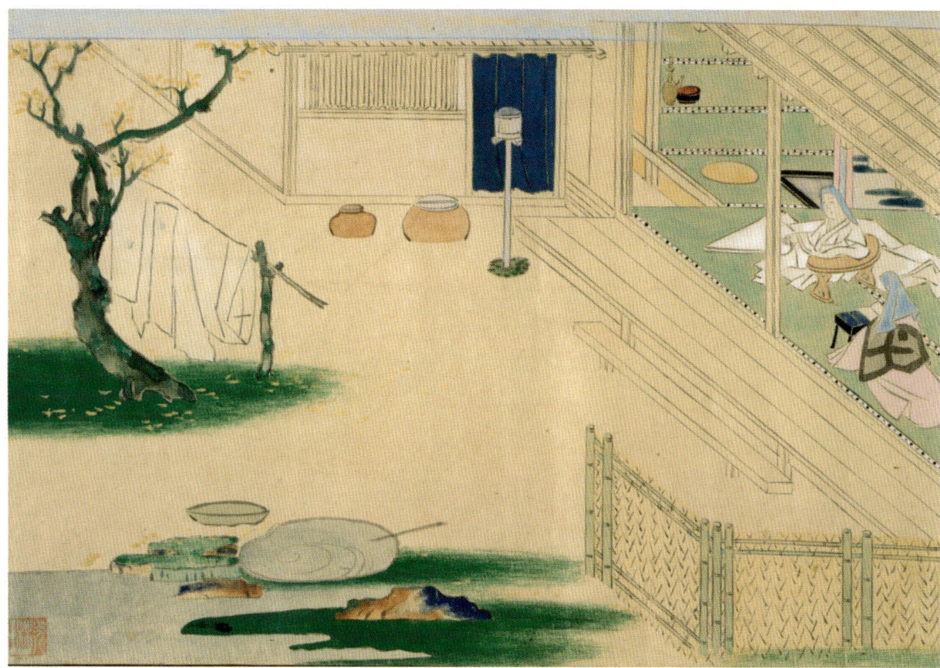

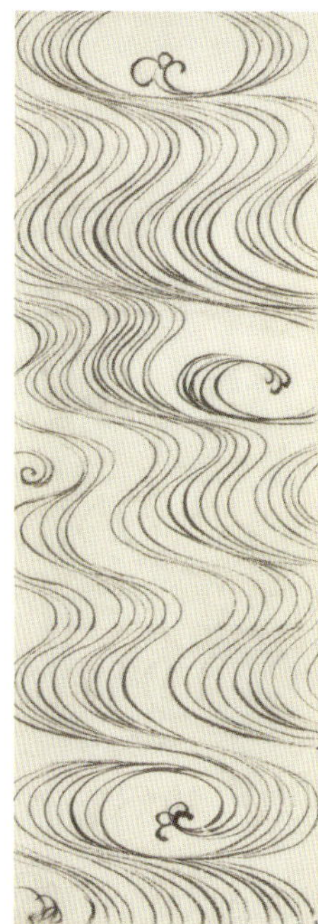

FIGURE 117
Ogata Kōrin, *Illustrated Life of Saigyō* (detail), early 18th century. Handscroll; ink and color on paper. Museum of the Imperial Collections, Sannomaru Shōzōkan, Tokyo.

FIGURE 118
Ogata Kōrin, *Sketch of Water Pattern,* late 17th or early 18th century. Ink on paper. Konishi Family Archive, Kyoto National Museum.

his final crescendo, *Red and White Plum Blossoms.* In their totality, the screens are an oblique, cleverly constructed homage to Tawaraya Sōtatsu and the visual potency of his mode, paired with the decorative motifs in lacquer. The painting creates a hybrid between two genres—painting and lacquer—and two forms of expression—liquid, painterly trees with ornate, stylized water.

The arresting effect of Kōrin's painting is contrasted by his puzzling use of materials. More than any other work by Kōrin, *Red and White Plum Blossoms* has mystified scholars and scientists with its unprecedented and unusual use of pigments. To date, the material used to paint the swirling water pattern remains unknown. Through age and damage, the screens' appearance today differs from its original state. Modern scholars before World War II originally commented on a blue sheen they detected in Kōrin's water pattern.[7] Following water damage incurred during the war, the blue color is all but lost. The stream at the center may have originally appeared less dark and gloomy than it is now. Responding to the changed aesthetic, some postwar commentators argued that Kōrin painted the water pattern in sizing (*dōsa*) mixed with animal glue (nikawa) onto a silver ground that has darkened with age.[8] A range of other complicated processes has also been proposed to solve the riddle surrounding Kōrin's enigmatic materials. Yet a scientific analysis conducted in the years 2002 and 2003 suggests that the water pattern—believed to be oxidized silver—is not actually silver but a blend of black and brown pigments with miniscule quantities of silver pigment applied throughout.[9] The consistency of the black and brown pigments remains unknown. Adding to the confusion, the areas of gold leaf that form the screens'

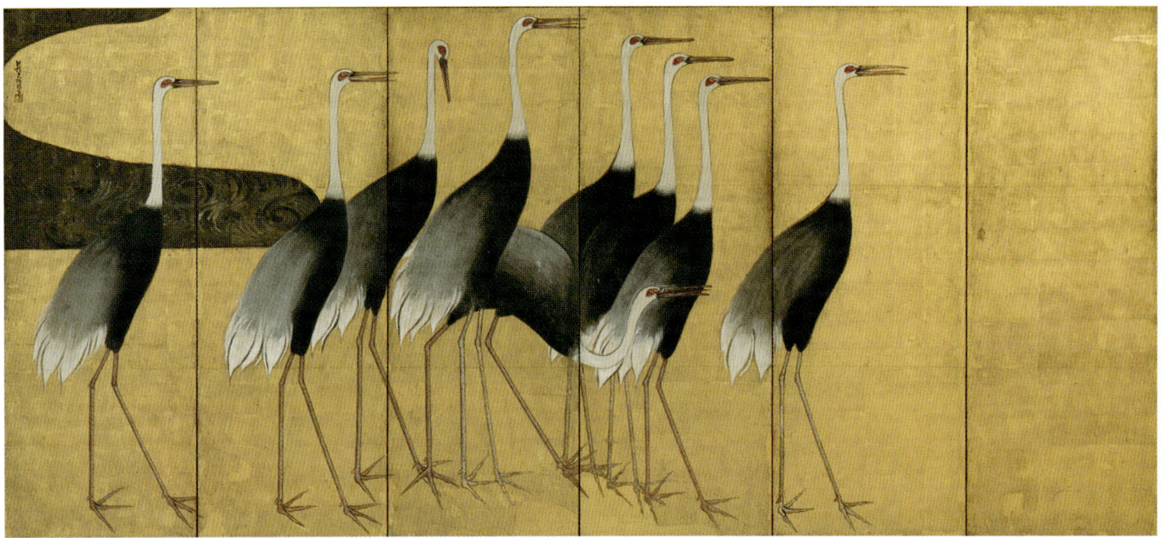

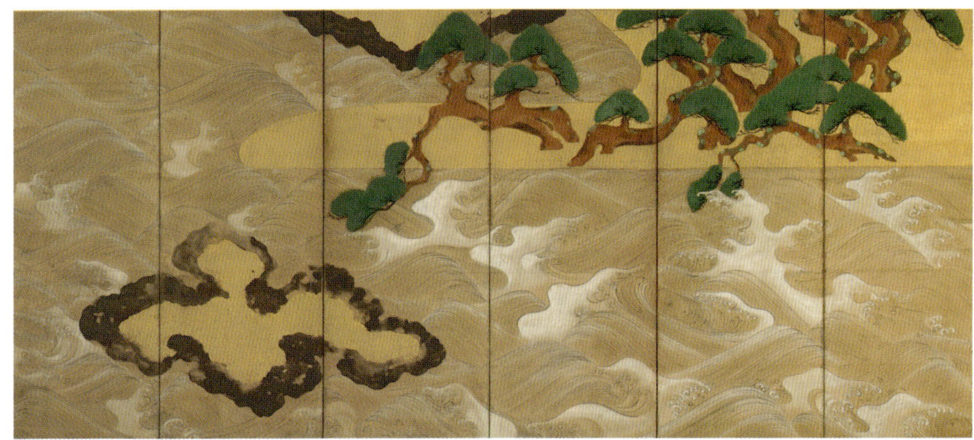

FIGURE 119
Ogata Kōrin, *Cranes,* early 18th century. Pair of six-panel folding screens; ink, color, gold, and silver on paper. Freer Gallery of Art, Smithsonian Institution, Washington, D.C.: Purchase—Charles Lang Freer Endowment, F1956.20–21.

FIGURE 120
Tawaraya Sōtatsu, *Waves at Matsushima* (right screen), early 17th century. Pair of six-panel folding screens; ink, color, gold, and silver on paper. Freer Gallery of Art, Smithsonian Institution, Washington, D.C.: Gift of Charles Lang Freer, F1906.231–232.

background contain only tiny amounts of actual gold, which is unusual for early modern paintings. Analysis of the water pattern yielded no findings of gold at all. The only considerable quantities of silver anywhere in the screens can be detected in the outer rim of the river, where Kōrin seems to have tried to silhouette the body of water. This aesthetic choice is reminiscent of a trope found in some of Tawaraya Sōtatsu's works, such as the amorphous, cloudlike shape in the left screen of *Waves at Matsushima* (fig. 120).

Rather than precious metals like gold and silver—a staple of early modern painting—Kōrin seems to have resorted to ink and a range of other less costly and less orthodox pigments to paint the screens. The trees are the only straightforward part of the paintings; they were painted in ink with elements of malachite green to represent moss. In short, in spite of extensive scientific analysis, a definitive conclusion on materials used in *Red and White Plum Blossoms* remains to be found. The screens continue to be an enigma in meaning and matter.

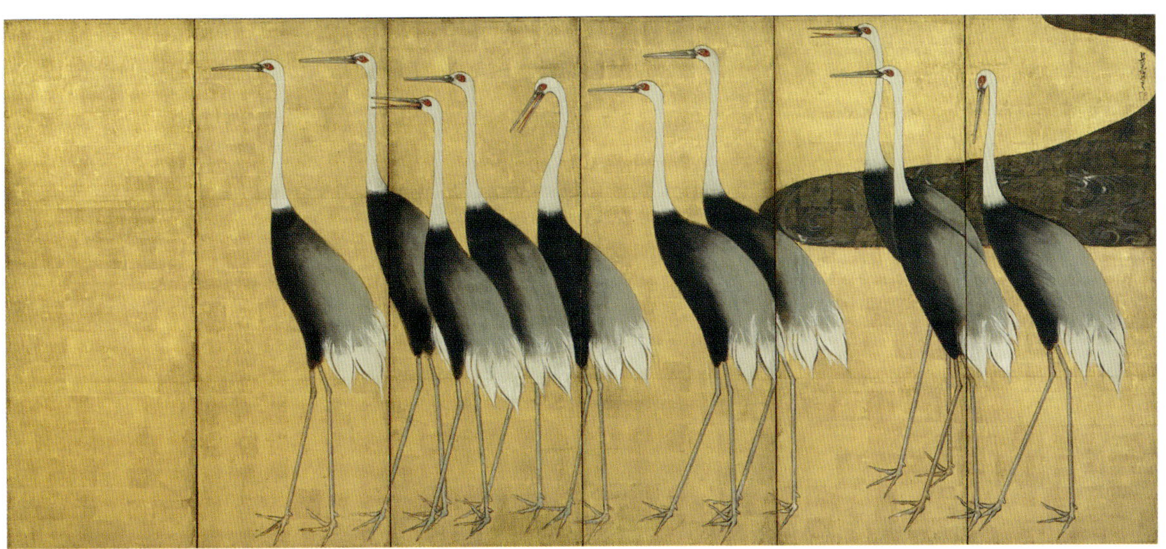

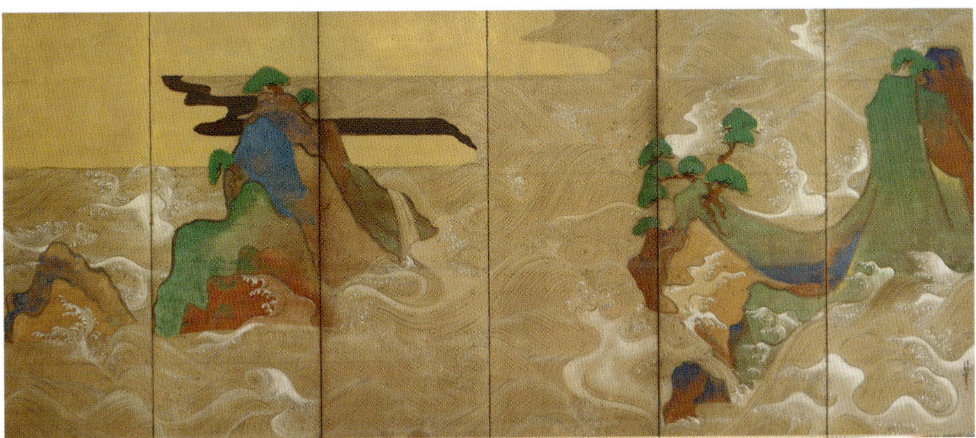

DRIPPING IN AGAIN

Kōrin painted the prunus flowers in his screens in the idiosyncratic round shape that he devised early on in his career. The flowers became a trademark feature of his style and were absorbed into popular garment patterns from around the 1710s onward. The tree bark similarly becomes a symbol for Kōrin's visuality in that he turned it into a spectacle of his powerful command of tarashikomi. In its totality, *Red and White Plum Blossoms* is an homage to the visual force of the technique. The tree trunks seem to dissolve into themselves. The molten appearance of the mix of ink and malachite in the bark endows the work with a sense of perpetual wetness.[10] By contrast, the mannered shapes of the red and white flowers seem like solid forms floating on the edges of flexuous trees.

As we have seen, the first five years or so of the eighteenth century marked Kōrin's intensive adoption of the style of Tawaraya Sōtatsu and his atelier. The beginning of this process can be gleaned from the still awkward use of

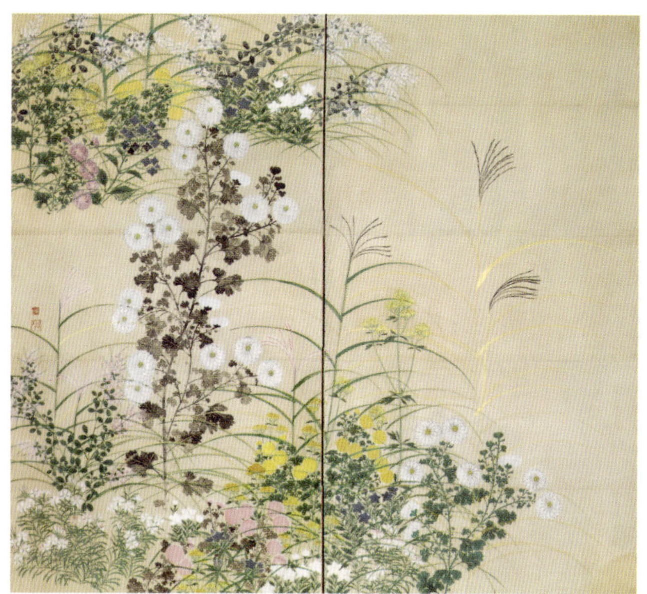

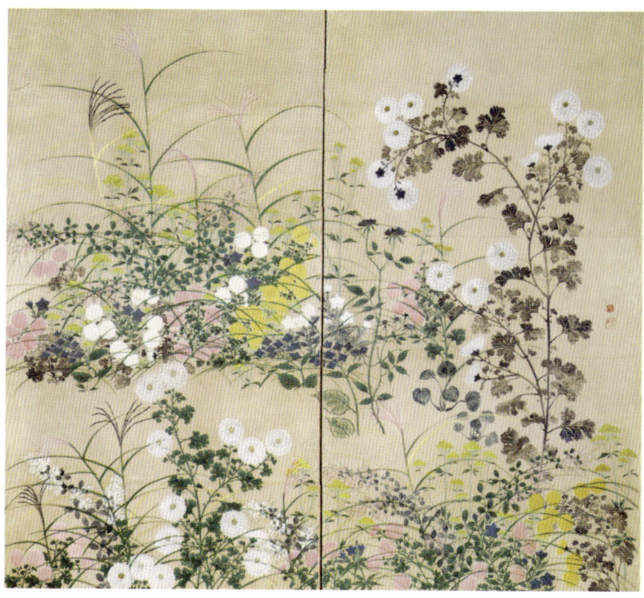

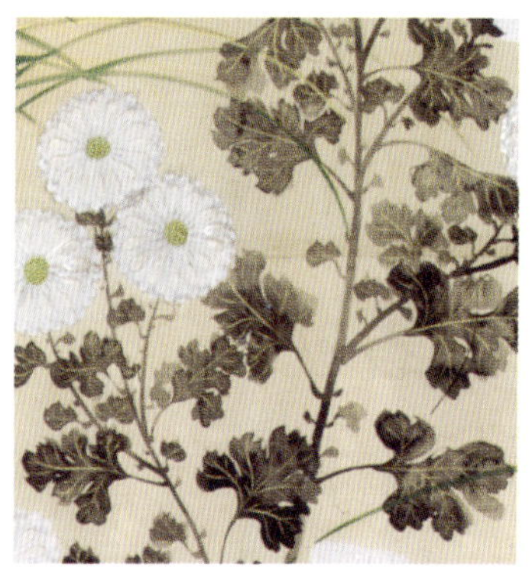

FIGURE 121
Ogata Kōrin, *Plants of Autumn* (top: left and right screens; bottom: detail, left screen), late 17th century. Pair of two-panel folding screens; ink, color, and gold on paper. Suntory Museum of Art, Tokyo.

tarashikomi in *Plants of Autumn* (fig. 121). The pair of two-panel screens appears to be an unfinished painting and carries two square Kansei seals, the nom de plume that Kōrin assumed during the early eighteenth century. References to Sōtatsu's artistry in paintings like *Red and White Plum Blossoms* provide evidence that Kōrin's exposure and perpetual attraction to the early seventeenth-century artist's legacy amplified toward the end of his life. Works like the Saigyō scrolls provided signed, immediate templates of Sōtatsu's style, use of space, and choice of subjects that informed the last stage of Kōrin's practice.

In Kōrin's lifelong quest for artistic reformulation of older traditions, the early seventeenth-century technique tarashikomi enabled him to be cutting edge and rooted in tradition at the same time. For example, the countless offshoots of Sōtatsu's tradition had perpetuated the pooling of ink and malachite in depictions of plants in early modern visual culture. From the early eighteenth century onward, Kōrin paired the abstraction that was emblematic of Sōtatsu's paintings with the naturalism he learned while apprenticing with the Kano school. Traces of the Tawaraya-Kano fusion survive in *Red and White Plum Blossoms* in the form of round patches of moss rendered in a circle of azurite with a perimeter of shell-white that are scattered across the bark of the plum trees (fig. 122). These speckles are an aspect often found in Kano paintings. In *Red and White Plum Blossoms,* they provide evidence that deep into his final years Kōrin kept expanding the repertoire he absorbed from other artists.

Red and White Plum Blossoms reflects a referential strategy, where Kōrin would take artists like Sōtatsu as his model and modify their painting manners in his own image. As a result, the screens create a synergy between Kōrin's

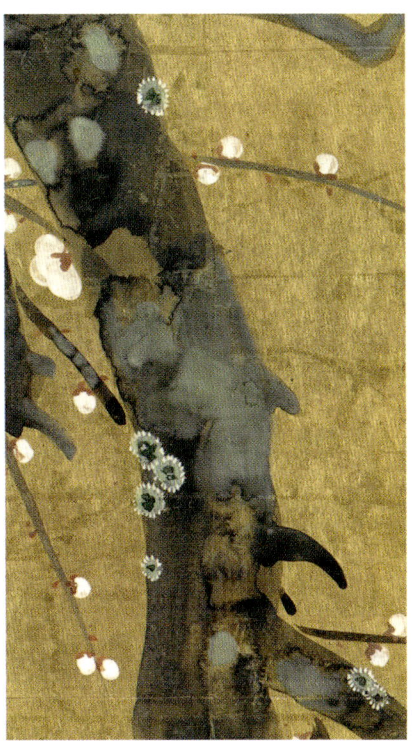

FIGURE 122
Detail, fig. 114.

use of the Kano style in the 1690s (and after) and his artistic embrace of the Tawaraya in the early 1700s. *Red and White Plum Blossoms* is the result of a lifelong quest for artistic innovation, accomplished through careful study and reshuffling of the past and by fusing painting with the aesthetics of other, previously unrelated media, such as lacquer. In this way, *Red and White Plum Blossoms* is Kōrin's final product of decades challenging the boundaries of Japanese painting.

EDO OWNERSHIP

Kōrin had initially turned to Sōtatsu's manner as part of his preparations for moving to Edo—Sōtatsu and his Tawaraya atelier were closely tied to Kyoto culture, which Kōrin hoped would appeal to Edo clients. In spite of early struggles, his strategy eventually paid off. A majority of his paintings made during the final half decade of his life incorporate tarashikomi as a key visual feature. The lion's share of these paintings entered the possession of Edo-based merchants and daimyo: Kōrin's *Irises at Yatsuhashi* was owned by the Fuyuki family of lumber merchants and *Red and White Plum Blossoms* was in the collection of the Tsugaru family, lords of Hirosaki Domain in present-day Aomori Prefecture of northern Japan. Kōrin had made another work that entered Tsugaru ownership, a scroll with flowers in ink and light colors on paper that is dated to 1705 and makes heavy use of tarashikomi. The work opens with a prominent image of a peony—the flower that graces the Tsugaru family crest—an indicator that the work may have been originally painted for the clan.[11]

Still, in spite of attempts by scholars to link *Red and White Plum Blossoms* to the Tsugaru family, as with practically all of Kōrin's artworks, a tangible connection of provenance is lacking. The work was introduced in the art historical journal *Kokka* in 1902 as "plum blossom screens" (*baika zu byōbu*) by Kōrin.[12] The article also mentions the screens' Tsugaru ownership. The screens were again featured as Tsugaru family property a year later in the *Collection of Paintings by the Kōrin School* (*Kōrin-ha gashū*), a lavish multivolume publication that lists the work for the first time under its present title, *Red and White Plum Blossoms* (*Kōhakubai zu byōbu*).[13] As with all other Kōrin works, the painting's premodern history of ownership, however, remains a matter of conjecture.

Kōrin's 1705 flower scroll—if indeed made for the Tsugaru—offers a link between the clan and *Red and White Plum Blossoms.* Some have recognized stylistic similarities in both works, such as an abundance of tarashikomi and *horinuri,* literally "carved lacquer," a painting method where parts of pigmented areas are scraped off or left blank in order to create sharp outlines (fig. 123).[14] The frequency of both techniques in the two Tsugaru-owned works draws a stylistic link that might indicate how both were made to order after the tastes of the clan's leadership during Kōrin's time. Although Kōrin had returned to Kyoto by the time he made *Red and White Plum Blossoms,* his commissions from Edo did not cease, and he seems to have continued to ship a substantial number works there from his studio.

FRAIL HEALTH

The abundant productivity of Kōrin's final years stands in contrast with evidence of his failing health. Kōrin lived an extravagant lifestyle, which may have left its mark on his physical well-being. However, regardless of life choices, Kōrin appears to have suffered from stomach pains for much of his adult life. In an undated letter from early in Kōrin's adulthood, Suma, a woman with whom he had an amorous liaison, discloses an instance where the artist displayed such an ailment: "You say you are suffering from abdominal pain. It seems you are feeling quite distressed, so I would like to call on you and see how you are."[15] Colic pains stand out as the one affliction that Kōrin mentions on several occasions, and Suma's letter reveals that Kōrin may have been troubled by a chronic malady for an extensive period of time. In his personal notebook (*oboegaki*) on an unspecified date, he records the following recipe for a potion.

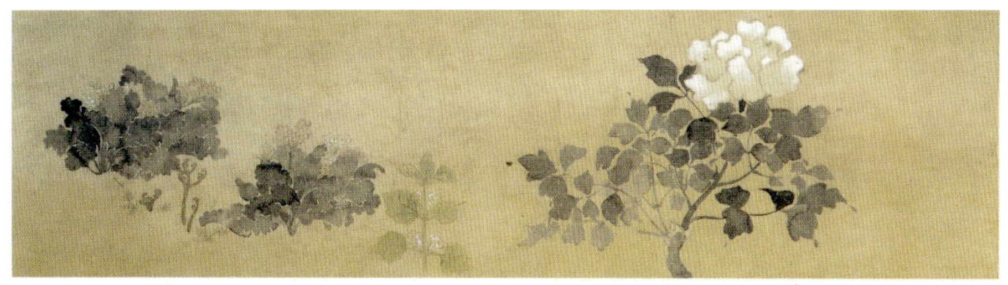

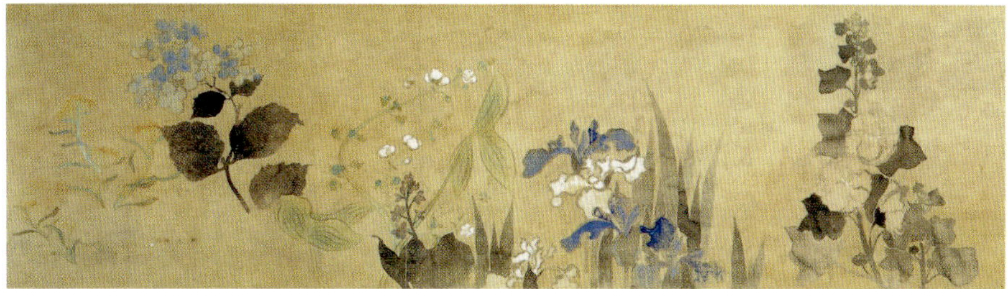

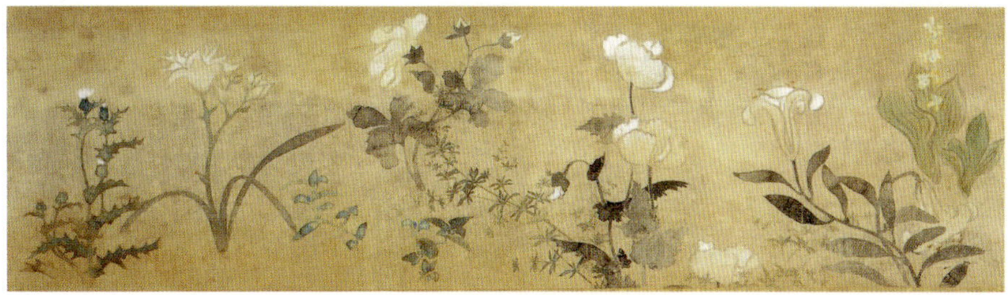

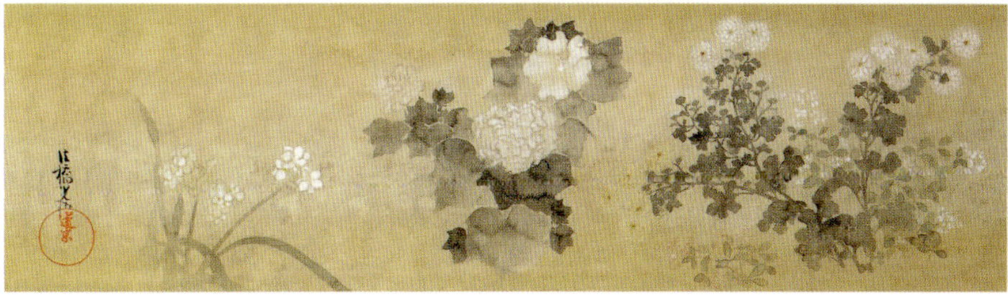

FIGURE 123
Ogata Kōrin, *Plants of the Four Seasons,* 1705. Handscroll; ink and color on paper. Private collection. (Originally conceived as a handscroll, the work has been cut up into fragments.)

> I have been suffering from colic pains in my stomach for many years, so I received this remedy from Arima Jōhaku: [Dissolve] the following ingredients in *sencha* [steeped tea] water and immediately add plenty of honey.
>
> Three *bu*[16] of chestnuts — Three *bu* of cinnamon
> Six *bu* of a tincture from Chinese peonies — Two *bu* of licorice
> Two pieces of jujube
>
> Add two *bu* of ginger to the tea water.[17]

In his notes, Kōrin wrote down a second list of ingredients for medication against stomach aches. The elixir is a broth made by soaking soft rice cakes (*mochi*) stuffed with red beans in hot salted water.[18] Adding to what appears to have been a lifelong colic affliction, hard work also deteriorated the painter's physical strength. In the letter to Ueshima Gennojō, introduced in chapter 4 and written around the final year or so of Kōrin's activities in Edo, the artist complains: "When I work at night, my hands and legs grow numb—signs of old age, I think. Now I have [no more than] a decade to live. It pains me that [life] passes by like this."[19] Kōrin laments exhaustion and failing health, admitting his struggle to meet the demands of his patrons during his final half decade. The resilience and enterprising spirit of his earlier days have given way to resignation in the face of declining fitness.

Kōrin's frail health is at odds with the surging numbers of commissions that he received toward the end of his life: the majority of screens and other large-format paintings that survive by Kōrin date to the small window between his final return from Edo in 1709 and his death in 1716. During Kōrin's final years, we see increased studio production among his output of paintings.

THE ARTIST'S STUDIO

After his return from Edo in 1709, Kōrin seems to have presided over a small but prolific atelier. The floorplan of his last house provides some physical indication for an increase in workshop involvement during Kōrin's final years. Located in Kyoto's Shinmachi Nijōkudari area, the artist erected a comfortable two-story building in 1711 after his own designs, presumably with money gained while in Edo (fig. 124).

On entering the property through the main gate, a visitor seeking a work of art from Kōrin would have passed by the outside walls of Kōrin's study (*shoin*) before reaching the entrance area on the righthand side. The high ceiling of the entrance, omitting the second story and soaring up to the roof, surely made an impression. To visit the atelier, the visitor would have been guided up a flight of steep wooden stairs onto the second floor, where Kōrin and his assistants occupied two rooms totaling roughly thirty square meters—a substantial work area in relation to the total size of the house and by far the largest suite of rooms in the building. The amount of space alone suggests that Kōrin did not labor there in solitude but, instead, maintained at least one or two assistants working on different artworks simultaneously. We have seen how a few years earlier, in a letter from Edo to his friend Ueshima Gennojō, Kōrin mentions the presence of an unidentified pupil who accompanied him to the eastern city: "Kō[ken?] is also well and I take him along to appointments [with clients] to paint."[20] The person appears nowhere else in surviving documents. Although the second character of the name is illegible, the first character corresponds with that of Kōrin's own name, insinuating a teacher-pupil relationship. It was customary practice in Japan to adopt a character of one's teacher's nom de plume.

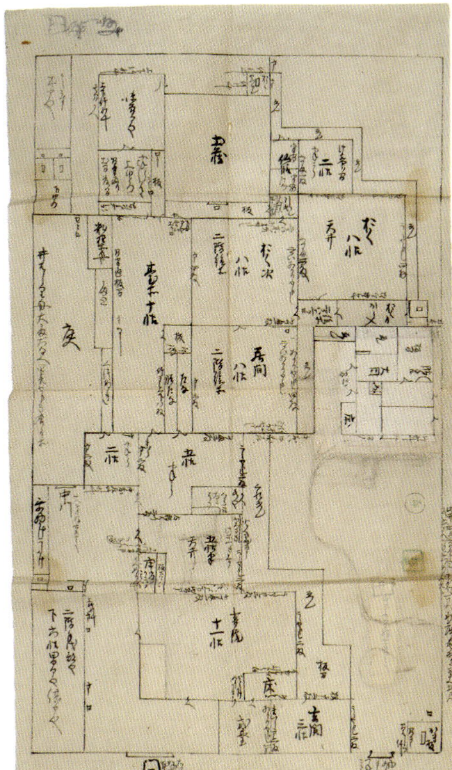

FIGURE 124

Ogata Kōrin, *Floor Plan of His Nijō Shinmachi Residence,* circa 1711. Ink on paper. Konishi Family Archive, Kyoto National Museum.

Kōrin may also have been at work creating reference materials for himself and affiliated painters, a fact that is reflected in the large number of sketches that survive. We also learn that his work remained diverse in terms of themes and media. In a letter dated to around 1715 and 1716, Kōrin requests the loan of a screen depicting chrysanthemums, a favorite subject, to cross-check with his sketchbook.

> Please also give my best to Chihō.[21] It has been a while and I hope everything is going well. For my part, since a day or two I have started to get better, so please don't worry.
> Concerning one of the three inrō [we discussed] the other day, the frontal design of camellias (*tsubaki*) and young pines should reach around to the backside. The other two were sent back and I will make new ones instead.
>
> Could you lend me the single six-panel screen with chrysanthemums that you have, so I can compare it with my sketchbook? Kindly send it today, so I receive it tomorrow. It is an old screen.
> Second month, eleventh day.
> The Karasumaru ware piece I promised should be ready by tomorrow.
>
> To Konishi Juichirō Ogata Kōrin[22]

In his final years, Kōrin evidently collaborated with Juichirō, his son, who helped with the mediation and sale of his works. We are told how transporting large works like screens from one place to another appears to have been a common practice, as Kōrin hastily demands to receive the six-panel work at his residence. Evidently, the artist was generating a referential system for himself and perhaps for other painters in his orbit.

The quantity and quality of extant paintings dating to the final years of Kōrin's life—for example, those bearing his Masatoki seal and signatures like Seisei Kōrin, among others—far exceed the number of works made earlier in his career. In fact, a survey of the artworks Kōrin made during his last half decade or so vis-à-vis his earlier output shows that his late paintings make up roughly half of his total surviving works.[23] In other words, Kōrin's last seven years were by far the most productive period in his three decades as a painter. He not only worked for high-ranking clients in Edo but also catered to patrons closer to home and of his own class. For example, sometime after 1709, he wrote to the art dealer Tachibana Ihei, referring to him by his shop's name, Tachibanaya, about an order of a painting for a Kyoto townsman referred to only as Kichimonji.

> To Tachibanaya Ihei [From] Ogata Kōrin
>
> [My apologies for] being brief last evening. I am at Kichimonji's now. Please come here to discuss his order for a painting, so I can start working on it. Sincerely. Ninth month, twentieth day.[24]

The reasons that so many late works survive go beyond pure happenstance and the better care that owners surely devoted to preserving works made during the peak of Kōrin's public fame: Kōrin simply made more works of art in this time. Kōrin's productivity during the period after he returned from Edo in 1709 is also compelling in its diversity of subjects and formats. Alongside hanging scrolls, ceramics, fans, and virtually all other small formats, Kōrin churned out the biggest number of screen paintings of his career. In addition to *Red and White Plum Blossoms,* for example, Kōrin produced masterpieces like *Irises at Yatsuhashi.* Similar large-format orders clustered around the same time. In earlier years, aside from outstanding commissions like the *Irises* screens, most paintings signed by Kōrin were single two-panel screens, hanging scrolls, and fans. Conversely, the density of large orders during his final years, in addition to Kōrin's failing health and advanced age, makes it improbable that he was the only artist responsible for their production. Kōrin probably enlisted the help of assistants, such as the mysterious pupil who accompanied him to Edo. On returning to Kyoto, Kōrin could staff his atelier with helpers to meet the high demand for his artworks.

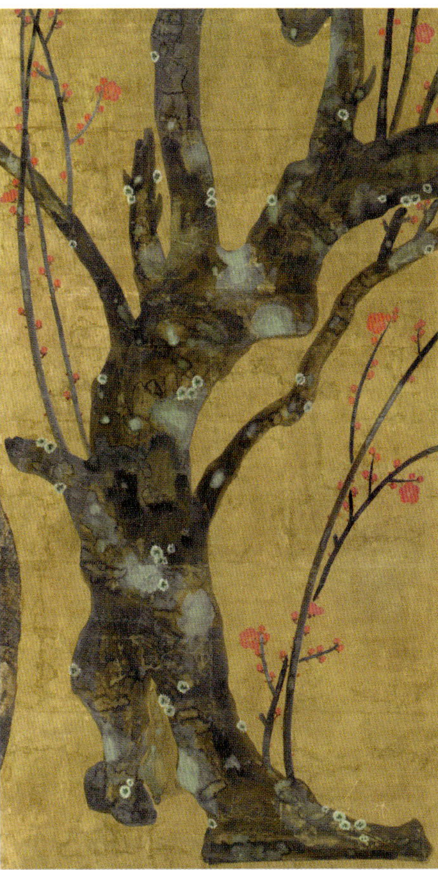

FIGURE 125
Left: Detail, fig. 114;
Below: Detail, fig. 25.

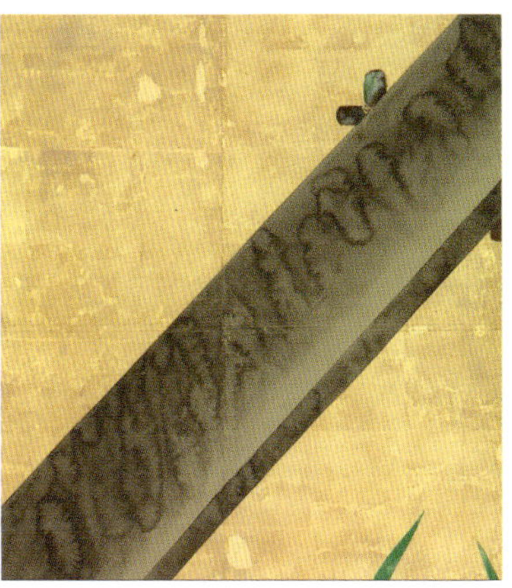

That a growing number of hands were likely involved in Kōrin's late commissions as opposed to his earlier works in no way diminishes their artistic value. On the contrary, masterpieces like *Red and White Plum Blossoms* and *Irises at Yatsuhashi* would have been unimaginable without Kōrin's personal agency. More than ever before, Kōrin's ingenuity and idiosyncrasy are front and center in virtually all of the artist's late paintings. Studio production was a reality for most major painters of early modern Japan. Indeed, the teamwork of an atelier enabled Kōrin to unleash his creative force in a way that was inconceivable earlier in his life, when he toiled largely by himself or with a pupil in tow.

Traces of Kōrin's hand are present throughout his most important late works. Consider, for example, the tarashikomi in *Red and White Plum Blossoms* and *Irises at Yatsuhashi*. Examination of both paintings discloses a repeating modus operandi for applying Kōrin's signature technique (fig. 125). Even though tarashikomi is a painting technique that is partly accidental, Kōrin's application reveals certain habits that keep reappearing in his works. When applying a blend of malachite and ink, for example, the artist often did so by forming concentric, roundish areas. When dripping in water onto still-wet ink, in contrast, Kōrin frequently created noticeably oblong shapes. Kōrin used the latter technique repeatedly in some of his major late works: *Red and White Plum Blossoms, Irises at Yatsuhashi,* and *Gods of Wind and Thunder.*

The finesse and consistency with which tarashikomi was applied in several of these late paintings insinuates that Kōrin himself did it. Generally speaking, in traditional Japanese "built-up pictures" (*tsukuri-e*), the head painter of a workshop would outline the composition before other hands would add colors. Finally, that same artist would redraw the ink outlines and facial features of the figures. In short, the most senior painter was in charge of the most crucial elements of the painting. Similarly, in Kōrin's case, it is easy to assume that he would have determined the composition and executed at least his signature technique tarashikomi, the most central factors of many of his late paintings, himself.

Perhaps emboldened by the help of assistants and a diverse pool of patrons, Kōrin thrived in experimentation. *Red and White Plum Blossoms* and *Irises at Yatsuhashi* diverge drastically in their respective materials. The blossoms in *Irises at Yatsuhashi* were painted in expensive mineral pigments onto a layer of shell-white on gold leaf, a textbook example of an early modern painting technique. By contrast, in *Red and White Plum Blossoms* Kōrin employs a hodge-podge of materials, ranging from impure gold and silver to mysterious pigments that are yet to be identified. In spite of such differences, both works reside firmly in the canon of Kōrin's accomplishments. The two paintings share an approach to flatness and stylization of forms—an approach to space and composition that Kōrin continued to perfect from the beginnings of his career as an artist. The use of tarashikomi is a key aesthetic component in both pairs of screens, as well as in other major paintings made during his final years. In this way, this surge of creativity and productivity is also marked by stylistic consistency, if not overlap in materials. It was that aesthetic reliability that established certain tropes of Kōrin's practice within the broader cultural memory of the Edo period.

Although Kōrin most likely did not produce his final commissions entirely by himself, his atelier must have been small. Certain tasks, such as constructing the frames of folding screens and, eventually, gilding them, had to be outsourced. In his personal notebook, Kōrin records his order for the frame of a folding screen from a specialized workshop in the Shimo-Tachiuri neighborhood of Kyoto: "I ask you to build the screen with a width of five *shaku,* nine *sun,* and three *bu* [about 1.8 meters]."[25] Thus, we learn that building the hardware for Kōrin's paintings required help from outside the atelier. In the same log, Kōrin records the address of a brush maker. The notebook also contains Kōrin's instructions to an artisan for a lacquer box, indicating that Kōrin's late workshop adhered to his lifelong tendency of diversified production of artworks.

Kōrin himself provides evidence that his atelier was too small to be turned into a full-fledged painting enterprise that would be able to continue beyond his death. In his will to his son Konishi Juichirō, Kōrin admits that his profession is insecure and his business unstable.

> Will
>
> You are my flesh and blood. But since I lack a family business, it was hard [for me] to provide security [for you]. We were in an unfortunate [situation] until, luckily, Nakamura Kuranosuke took pity and [arranged for you] to be adopted into the family of Konishi Hikokurō. Nakamura Kuranosuke then gave you his daughter, Katsu,[26] as your wife. [The privilege that] you will succeed as head and heir to the Konishi family, [we owe] above all to Kuranosuke's generosity. You should pay him respect and follow his wishes. Katsu herself is [a woman] without flaw.
>
> My house[27] and various implements I leave to my widow Tayo. Upon Tayo's death, your younger brother Katsunojō[28] will receive [the house]. Since he will inherit my family name [Ogata], you shall help him [manage] my estate, so as to avoid any complications.[29]
>
> As part of his inheritance, one *wakizashi* and screen[(s)] shall be given to your brother Katsunojō. Please support him.
>
> Shōtoku 3 [1713], [Year of the] Water-Snake, first month,
> twenty-fifth day. Ogata Kōrin
> [round relief seal:] Hosei Masatoki
>
> To Konishi Juichirō[30]

The will dates to 1713 and shows how, three years before his death, Kōrin must have anticipated that his end was nigh. Evidently, in spite of the adoption into another family, Kōrin saw Juichirō as his favorite son, entrusting him with the execution of his will. In the opening sentence, Kōrin effectively prophesied the discontinuation of his painting business on his death, a conjecture that became reality. Although a younger son, Katsunojō, is mentioned as the successor to the Ogata name and inheritor of the house with Kōrin's studio, there is no clause about passing on the leadership of Kōrin's atelier, nor is his profession addressed in any concrete manner. The workshop was apparently not meant to be continued. Instead, Kōrin's style was embraced by generations of successive painters, creating a lineage through indirect transmission of Kōrin's works after his death.

AN ARTIST'S TWILIGHT

Kōrin died on the second day of the sixth month in 1716.[31] At the beginning of that year, the artist made his final known public appearance when he delivered New Year's greetings to his old acquaintance and supporter Nijō Tsunahira.[32]

The artist was undoubtedly frail, and the gathering must have been a somber affair. Tsunahira had accompanied Kōrin's fortunes throughout his three decades as an artist. Seven years earlier, in 1709, the aristocrat had welcomed Kōrin back to Kyoto with a celebratory feast. The two men grew closer after Kōrin's return from Edo; in 1715 alone Kōrin visited the minister of the left twenty-three times. Just a few days before the 1716 New Year event, on the twenty-seventh day of the twelfth month, Kōrin entertained Tsunahira for the last time by performing his ultimate otogi. The performance celebrated the courtier's ascension to junior first rank (*juichi'i*), the second-highest aristocratic tier, on that day. Surely, the two men knew that Kōrin's death was coming. The artist had spoken of declining health on numerous occasions before. In a late letter to Juichirō, Kōrin reports on his brief recovery from illness.[33]

Kōrin's death at age fifty-nine by the Japanese count concluded an eventful life, one that in many ways is summarized in the will that Kōrin wrote for his wife, Tayo, in 1713. Kōrin speaks of extramarital children, real estate issues, daimyo debts, and artworks, all of which had been determining factors for much of his life.

> [Tayo, you shall receive] two properties: the current house [at Shinmachi Nijōkudari] with a southward width of eleven *ken*[34] and extending inward for twenty-four *ken* [along with the other house] at Higashimachi with a front width of two *ken* and extending inward for fifteen *ken*, along with various furnishings. In addition, I leave you the invoices of money loaned to daimyo lords that I inherited from my father, Sōken. You shall receive their full amounts in case of repayment.[35] You may sell the houses should you wish to do so. In that case, you will be in charge of that money and receive its interest. This way you should be able to lead a comfortable life.
>
> [My] secondary house I give to [my son] by the name of Katsunojō and his mother. Since he is my flesh and blood, my family shall take him in and raise him. He shall carry the name Ogata and, upon coming of age, he shall succeed to the legacy of [our] ancestors.
>
> To Katsunojō's mother, Aya, I leave altogether two houses, the small house in northern [Shinmachi Nijōkudari] that is rented out to Kohei, as well as the house in northern Higashimachi, alongside various furnishings from the secondary house [the one given to Katsunojō].[36] With this inheritance, she should be in a good position to find a suitable partner. Since Katsunojō's mother is [a woman] of reputable stature and does not give in to trivial pursuits, please try to get along well together.
>
> I have been unable to provide for [my son] Konishi Juichirō, so it was no difficult decision to have him adopted by the Konishi family. Once Juichirō came of age, I told him the details of my reasoning. I leave to him [a] *wakizashi* and screen[(s)].[37]

> Although I would also like to leave him a house, he already has one [as the heir to the Konishi family]. Thus, I am leaving it to Katsunojō. I ask you to guide and advise Juichirō. Make him guard the memory of our ancestors. This is important to me, so I entrust this [to you and him].[38]
>
> Shōtoku 3 [1713], [Year of the] Water-Snake, first month, twenty-fifth day.
> Ogata Kōrin
> [round relief seal:] Hosei Masatoki
> For Tayo[39]

Since, on the same day, Kōrin also composed a will for his son Juichirō, he anticipated his death years before it happened, a reminder of his failing health during his later years. Different from the will to Juichirō, which is filled with fatherly advice, the bequest for Tayo is a synopsis of Kōrin's assets, worries, and hopes. With a comparatively humble number of items to bestow, the artist had much less to offer than what he received from his father in 1687. Yet Kōrin had managed to defy the odds and create a comfortable life for himself and those he held dear. The mortgage-free residence at Shinmachi Nijōkudari is a notable step up from the debt-laden life that the artist had led before his work in Edo. Clearly, Kōrin's last years provided more revenue than at any other time in his career.

❖ ❖ ❖

In spite of having offered Juichirō for adoption into the Konishi family, Kōrin implores Tayo to make his son preserve "the memory of our ancestors," the Ogata family. The request put him in charge of safekeeping the physical and spiritual memory of his bloodline, a responsibility that established what is now known as the Konishi Family Archive, the prime resource on Kōrin's life. Juichirō also received screens and sketches, presumably made by Kōrin, thereby also assigning him with keeping Kōrin's artistic memory. Kōrin apparently was mindful of the discontinuity of his atelier and, unlike many other Japanese artists, instigated the creation of a repository of his sketches, letters, hobbies, and business documents. In a sense, the fleeting nature of Kōrin's family and atelier reinforced the need to conserve his memory through the Konishi family's agency. That memory survived in the documents, in his artworks, and in the public realm. Numerous painters, lacquer artists, potters, and textile designers turned to Kōrin for inspiration. In this way, he lived on even without having established, as he says, a "family business." Perhaps unwittingly, Kōrin had entered the artistic memory of Japan.

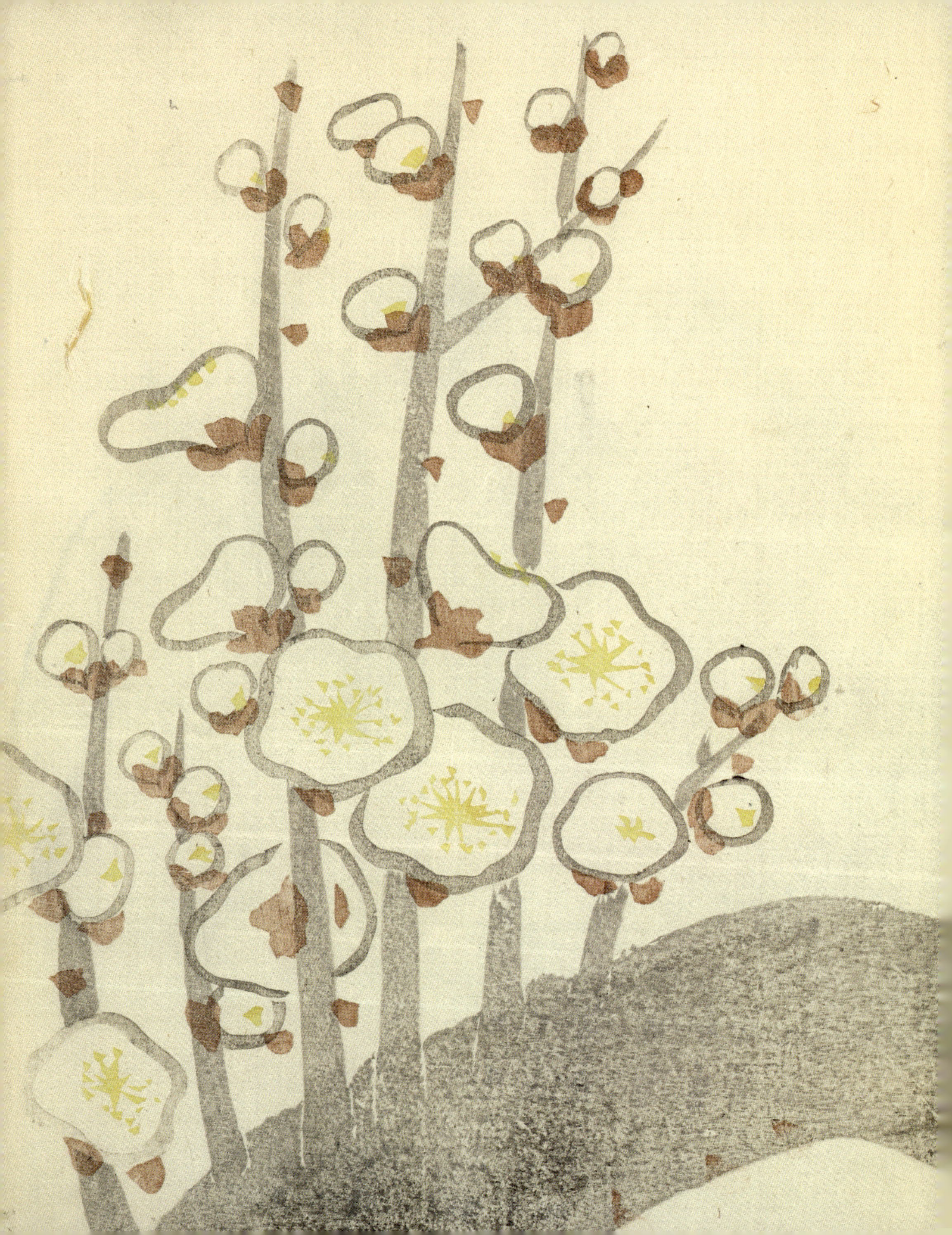

Epilogue

By the time of Kōrin's passing, his legacy had already become a part of the mainstream of Edo period art. Although no direct pupil or successor to Kōrin's atelier can be identified for certain, a range of painters followed in his footsteps, revealing how Kōrin, initially a reluctant and struggling painter, had transformed into a coveted role model. Alongside his popular reception in pattern books as a designer of textiles and lacquer objects, a major part of Kōrin's afterlife was channeled through his paintings. The painter Kōrin affected artists in various ways, but it was above all his tarashikomi and specific subjects such as the iris that were received enthusiastically over centuries. In the case of tarashikomi, artists of the late eighteenth and early nineteenth centuries associated the technique indiscriminately with Kōrin, even though Sōtatsu had actually devised it a hundred years before.

AFTER KŌRIN

Fukae Roshū (1699–1757), a painter thought to have studied under Kōrin, and Tatebayashi Kagei (active mid-eighteenth century), who apprenticed with Kōrin's brother Kenzan, used tarashikomi copiously in their works (figs. 126, 127). Roshū was the son of the silver mint official Fukae Shōzaemon.[1] Such a professional relationship makes Roshū's connection to the Ogata brothers more tangible than that of other alleged students of Kōrin. After all, Fukae Shōzaemon's colleague, the bureaucrat Nakamura Kuranosuke, was one of Kōrin's main benefactors throughout the early eighteenth century. Roshū's gravestone mentions his pseudonym Seihakudō, a possible reference to Kōrin's artistic name Seisei.[2] However, Roshū was born in 1699, and any apprenticeship with Kōrin—if there was one—could have lasted only for a few years around the end of the master's life, perhaps as part of his late atelier. Speculations about the relationship were complicated a hundred years later by Sakai Hōitsu, who included the name Roshū as one of Kōrin's own pseudonyms in his *Concise Chronology of Seals of the Ogata School* of 1815. Hōitsu seems to have mistaken

Detail of fig. 129

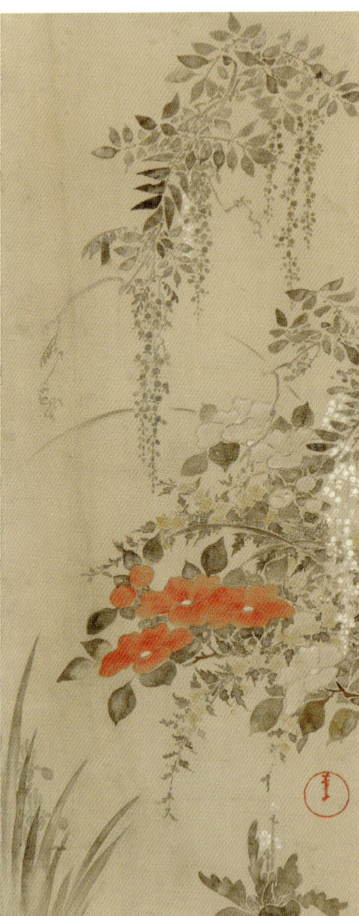

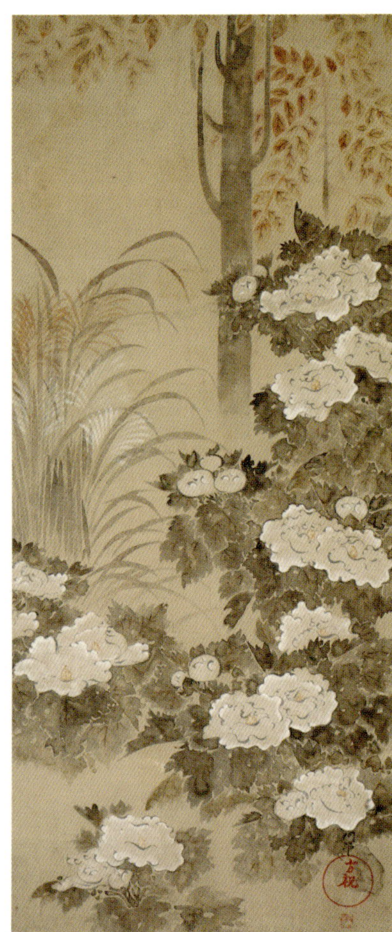

FIGURE 126
Fukae Roshū, *Wisteria and Other Flowers,* 18th century. Hanging scroll; ink and color on paper. Freer Gallery of Art, Smithsonian Institution, Washington, D.C.: Purchase—Charles Lang Freer Endowment, F1958.12.

FIGURE 127
Tatebayashi Kagei, *Flowers and Foliage of Autumn,* 18th century. Hanging scroll; ink and color on paper. Cleveland Museum of Art, Worcester R. Warner Collection, 1964.105.

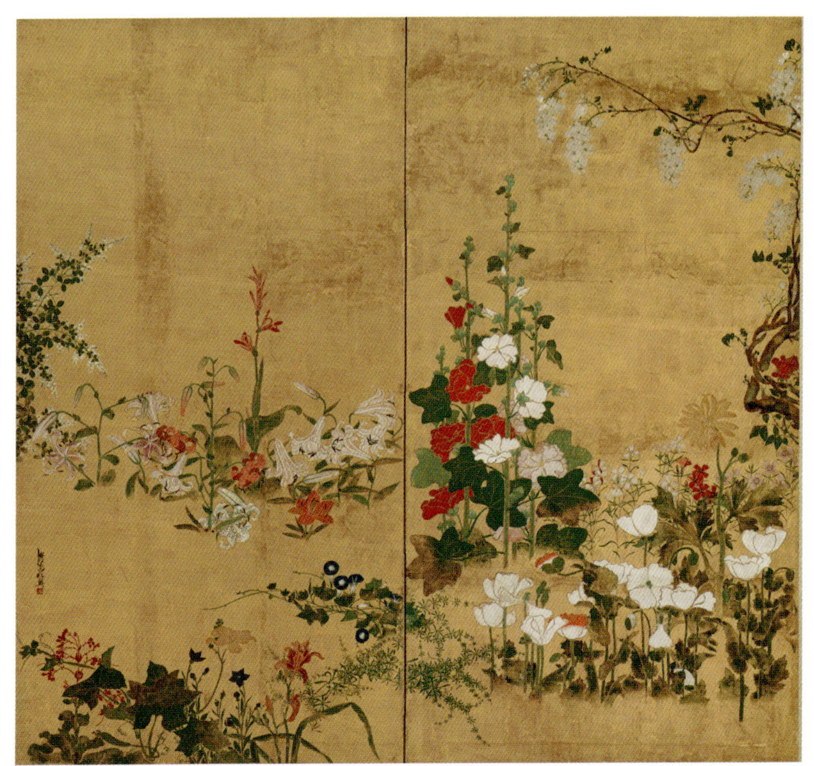

FIGURE 128
Watanabe Shikō, *Flowers,* 18th century. Two-panel folding screen; color and gold on paper. Freer Gallery of Art, Smithsonian Institution, Washington, D.C.: Gift of Charles Lang Freer, F1903.238.

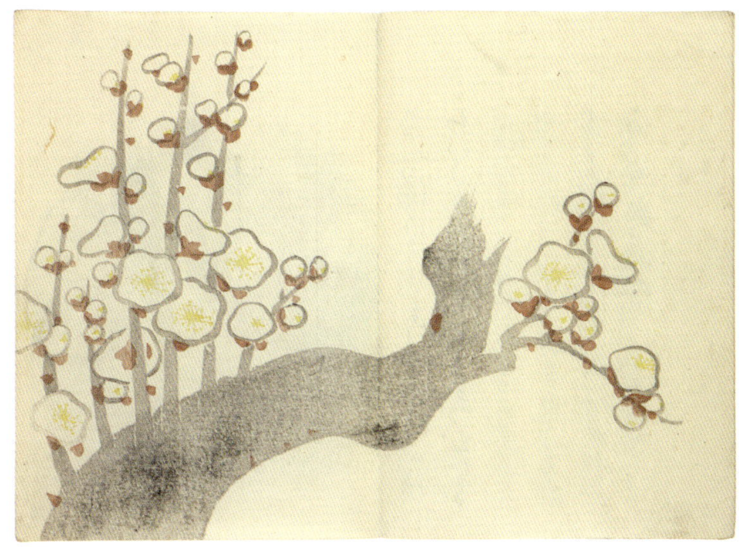

FIGURE 129
Nakamura Hōchū, *Genealogy of Kōrin's Paintings* (*Kōrin gafu*), 1802. Woodblock-printed book with hand colorations; ink and color on paper. Freer Gallery of Art, Smithsonian Institution, Washington, D.C.: Purchase, The Gerhard Pulverer Collection—Charles Lang Freer Endowment, Friends of the Freer and Sackler Galleries and the Harold P. Stern Memorial fund in appreciation of Jeffrey P. Cunard and his exemplary service to the Galleries as chair of the Board of Trustees (2003–2007) FSC-GR-780.436.1–2.

Roshū's paintings for those by Kōrin. The book also mentions Watanabe Shikō as Kōrin's pupil—albeit without evidence—making clear how much Hōitsu's interpretations have influenced modern scholarship on Kōrin's life and work. As we have seen, Shikō had a penchant for Kōrin's approach to painting, as his renderings of figures and flowers show (fig. 128). A direct apprenticeship, however, lacks conclusive corroboration. It has been speculated that Shikō was the identity of Watanabe Soshin, an otherwise unknown artist who added, for example, a painting of orchids on one of Ogata Kenzan's ceramics.[3] This, however, remains guesswork, relying more on semantic association and their mutual if common surname, Watanabe, than on documentary evidence or significant stylistic overlap.[4]

Yet direct apprenticeship was not necessary to adopt Kōrin's way of art-making. By the end of Kōrin's life, his style was part of the public realm, mainly by way of widely circulating catalogues for kimono patterns that had absorbed features of Kōrin's artistic practice.[5] Other genres, such as reference works for lacquer, soon followed suit and made access to the idiosyncrasies of Kōrin's works widely accessible. In the same way, a number of painters drew works with conscious and unconscious associations to Kōrin's oeuvre.

Nakamura Hōchū (d. 1819) was similar to Roshū and Kagei in that he made tarashikomi a core element of his painting style. In his *Genealogy of Kōrin's Paintings* (*Kōrin gafu*) of 1802, the painter presents his interpretation of Kōrin in a combination of print and hand-colored elements (fig. 129).[6] The subjects and their rendering are less of a faithful reproduction than a free-spirited homage to Kōrin by way of Hōchū's imagination. With his abundant use of

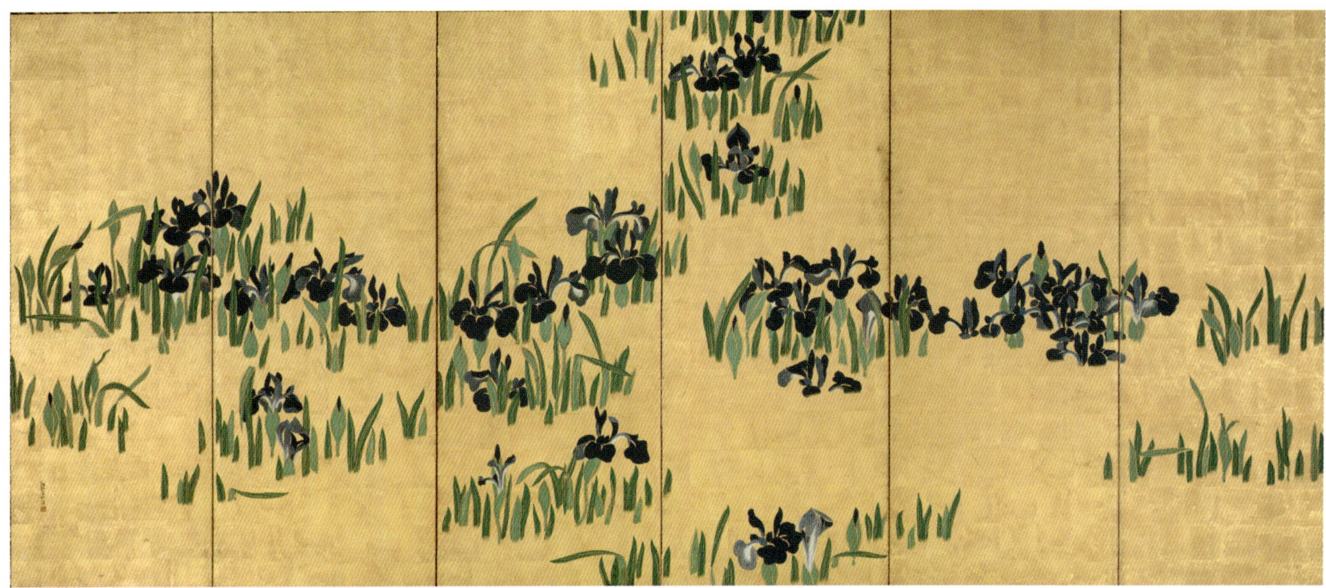

FIGURE 130
Watanabe Shikō, *Irises,* 18th century. Pair of six-panel folding screens; ink and color on gilded paper. Cleveland Museum of Art, Gift of The Norweb Foundation, 1954.603.

tarashikomi in a publication that carries Kōrin's name, *Genealogy of Kōrin's Paintings* symbolizes how the technique was an integral part of the artist's afterlife. Hōchū's publication also marks a symbiosis of two major avenues of Kōrin's posthumous reception. The plump, round forms in *Genealogy of Kōrin's Paintings* are reminiscent of the kimono patterns that Kōrin's name was already associated with during his lifetime. Hōchū, a painter, seems to have discovered Kōrin through a combination of the artist's popular reception and the study of his actual paintings. By doing so, Hōchū was one of the first artists to bring together the two sides of Kōrin's posthumous reception—popular and elite—that determine the painter's afterlife to this day.

In terms of subjects, irises became one of the themes through which posterity recognized and appreciated Kōrin's oeuvre. By way of his *Irises* screens, and by extension *Irises at Yatsuhashi,* Kōrin effectively established a new genre that later painters embraced. The screens instituted a trope and a tradition that were inextricably linked to Kōrin. The novel use of color, space, and effect in *Irises* and *Irises at Yatsuhashi* resonated with painters over centuries. Shortly after Kōrin died, Watanabe Shikō produced his own version of the irises described in the ninth chapter of the *Tales of Ise* (fig. 130). The work differs from Kōrin's famous screens in that Shikō showed his flowers largely submerged in a sea of gold. The towering stalks and bulging blossoms of Kōrin's larger-than-life irises are replaced with smaller, more slender forms that betray Shikō's botanical studies.[7]

Had Shikō seen Kōrin's work? The contrasting visual effect of their paintings almost makes it seem as if Shikō tried to create a counterstatement to his

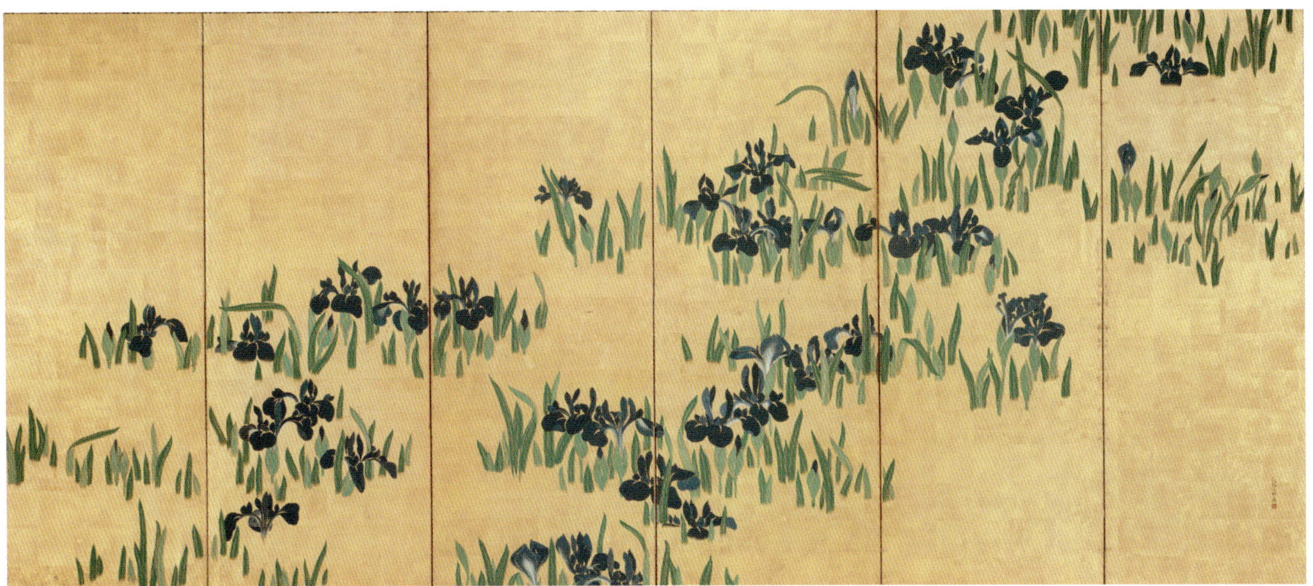

forebear's screens, even though he used a similar color palette. Although Shikō's life overlapped with that of Kōrin by three decades, no proof of a face-to-face interaction has been found. The many paintings by Shikō that allude to Kōrin, however, illustrate how he sought out works by the master and modeled part of his style after him. Until documentary evidence is unearthed about Shikō's visit to Nishi Honganji or proof of the affection of his patron, the courtier Konoe Iehiro (1667–1736), for Kōrin's *Irises* is found, we have no way of knowing whether Shikō made the screens in response to Kōrin's work. The chromatic and conceptual relationship between them suggests some palpable connection, raising the possibility that Kōrin's many renderings of the iris flower in one way or another inspired artists like Shikō during the eighteenth century.

The longevity of this impact is felt most strongly in the work of Sakai Hōitsu. Born into a wealthy and influential daimyo family, Hōitsu responded to and galvanized a resurgence of interest in Kōrin's work in the early nineteenth century. His home base in Edo afforded Hōitsu with relatively easy access to works by or attributed to Kōrin. The fluid nature of the early modern art market, with artworks frequently moving between Kyoto and Edo, made paintings by Kōrin a part of many collections in the eastern city. The general antiquarian interest—especially in works with roots in the ancient capital of Kyoto or in other regional centers—during the late eighteenth and early nineteenth centuries triggered a spike in the popular fascination with Kōrin, an artist who was considered to be at once innovative and conservative.

Hōitsu's endeavors to access, understand, and absorb Kōrin's oeuvre explicate this seemingly paradoxical understanding of the master. He held a

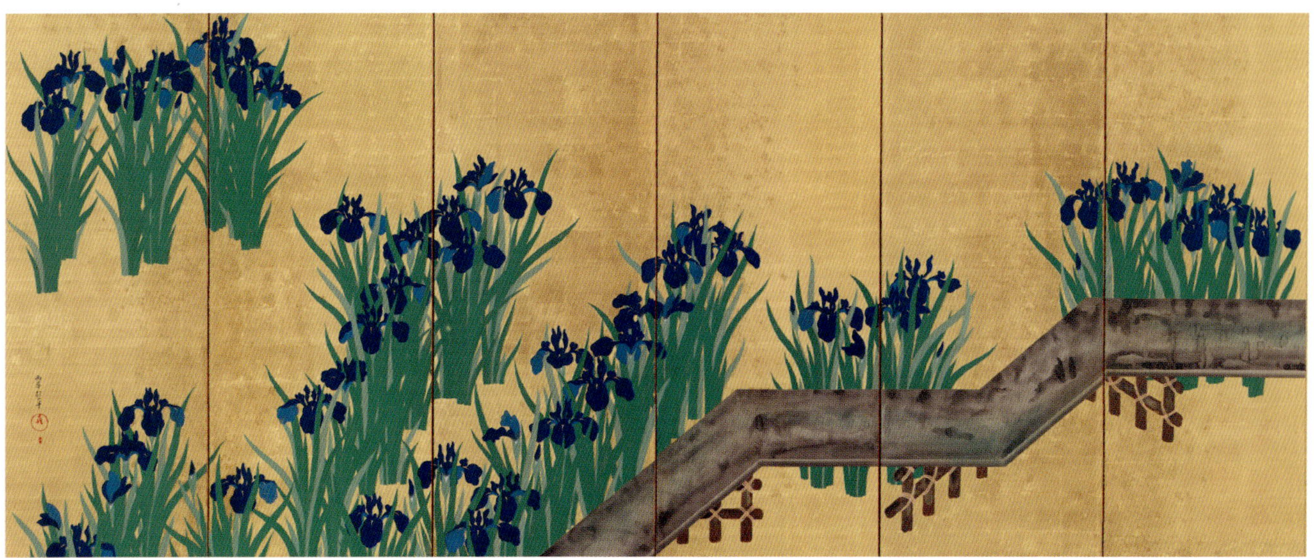

FIGURE 131

Sakai Hōitsu, *Irises at Yatsuhashi, from the Tales of Ise,* early 19th century. Pair of six-panel folding screens; ink and color on gilded paper. Idemitsu Museum of Arts, Tokyo.

memorial exhibition for Kōrin in 1815 and published the first edition of *One Hundred Pictures by Kōrin* shortly after. The first volume carries a preface by the poet and scholar Kameda Bōsai (1752–1826) that encompasses Hōitsu's understanding of Kōrin.

> Ogata Kōrin was proficient at painting. For a long time, he turned away from the set patterns and shortcomings of court painting, and he brought forth fresh forms. He painted from life and captured their spirit, revealing the nature [of things] under his brush. His insects and flowers on paper are infused with feelings.[8] [His] paintings' character is extraordinary, [their] vigor and appeal are distinct and brilliant. As such, he stood out in his time and was claimed to be divine and untrammeled. Later generations have not had the ability to succeed in his footsteps. Hōitsu Shōnin alone mastered his brush method and perfected his delicate and enchanting [style]. The second day in the sixth month of Bunka 12 [1815] was the hundredth anniversary of [Kōrin's] death. [Hōitsu] Shōnin gathered elites of the time and secretly performed rites of remembrance and blessing. On that occasion, works by Kōrin were brought together from collections near and far, and copies were made of them during the gathering, resulting in one hundred paintings. Thereupon, printed reproductions of [the paintings] were made to pass them on to [future] generations. Alas! This act alone expresses the sincerity of [Hōitsu] Shōnin's long affection [for Kōrin]. If the dead could know, [Hōitsu] Shōnin took Kōrin to be a soulmate whom he encountered ever so briefly [through his works].
> Kameda Bōsai [two seals:] Chōkyō wain, Hōsai Mōto

Bōsai's exuberant text demonstrates how artists and other men of culture read Kōrin during the early nineteenth century—as a painter who mastered and

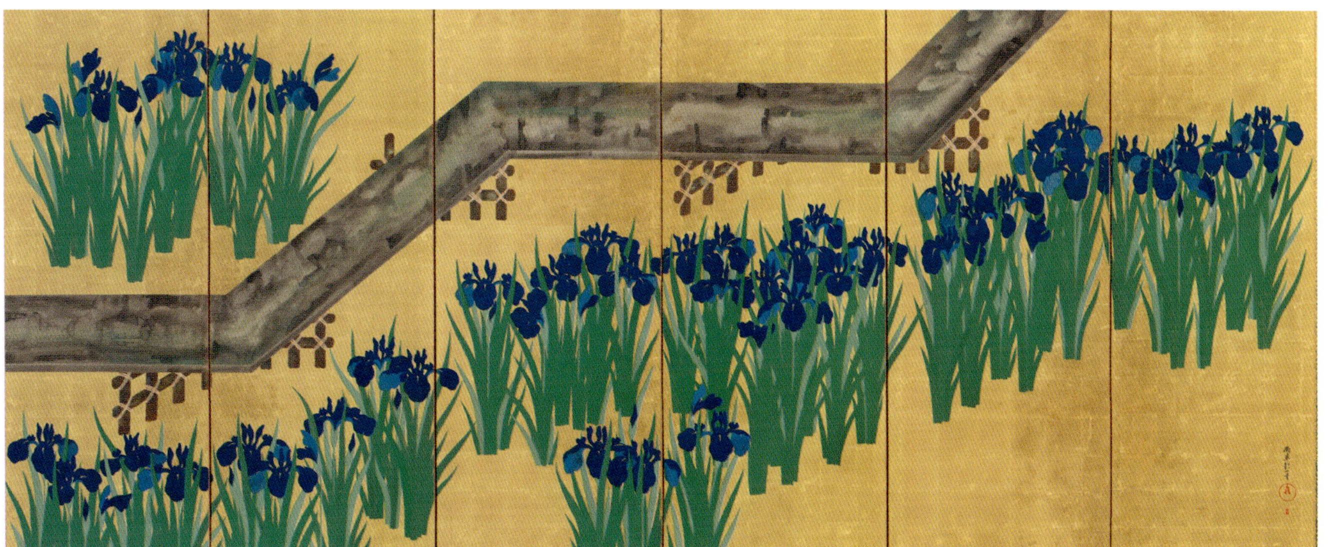

transcended tradition, an accomplishment that endowed Japanese painting with a renewed vigor. Through his *One Hundred Pictures by Kōrin,* Hōitsu made himself the ex cathedra conduit for Kōrin's reputation. The second, expanded edition of the book, published in 1826, underscored this ambition.

If the first edition was a testing ground for Hōitsu's efforts to render himself as Kōrin's legitimate successor, the second edition, produced eleven years later, was the climax to that endeavor. In the first edition, Hōitsu drew mainly from works in the collections of his connections in Edo. For the second, he orchestrated a concerted effort among his pupils and acquaintances to seek out and sketch works by Kōrin, many of which have been linked to exalted collections in Edo and elsewhere. Hōitsu also reproduced Kōrin's screens *Irises at Yatsuhashi,* which were then in the collection of the Edo-based Fuyuki family. The work's image extends over six full pages—a space larger than for any other work in both editions of *One Hundred Pictures by Kōrin.* Hōitsu clearly assigned great importance to the painting. As is the case with many reproductions in the two editions of *One Hundred Pictures by Kōrin,* the image is not an exact copy of the original work but rather an interpretation. Discrepancies resulted from the inherent difficulties of transferring the qualities of one medium to another.

Hōitsu annotated his sketch with the words "gilded screens, six panels with paper ground, each six *shaku* (about two meters) irises in rich color." He made a point of adding similar details to all the black-and-white illustrations in *One Hundred Pictures by Kōrin,* underscoring the publication's purpose as a means to picture, study, and copy Kōrin's style. Hōitsu himself did so with a range of famous paintings by Kōrin. He eventually made his own version of irises and an eightfold bridge on the basis of Kōrin's work (fig. 131). In his

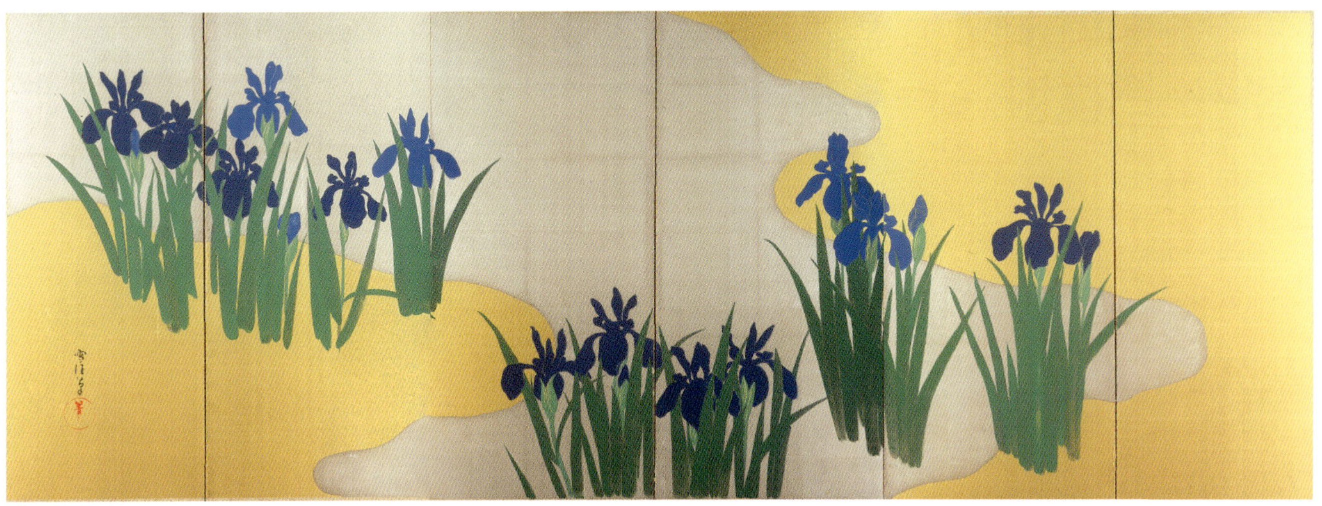

FIGURE 132
Kamisaka Sekka, *Irises,* first half of 20th century. Pair of six-panel folding screens; color on gold and silver ground on silk. Okada Museum of Art, Hakone.

homage to Kōrin's iconic painting, Hōitsu betrays his close study of the original. Not only is his manner of naturalistic blossoms growing atop straight, emphatically vertical stalks a direct reference to Kōrin's work, but Hōitsu also employed a similar technique when he applied the pigment, one that could only be replicated by close study of the original. In the same way as Kōrin, Hōitsu first created a ground layer of shell-white onto which he applied costly azurite and malachite, resulting in hues that resemble Kōrin's screens. In this way, Hōitsu's *Irises at Yatsuhashi* adapted compositional, technical, and chromatic formulas from a painting created more than a hundred years earlier. Moving much further than Watanabe Shikō before him, Hōitsu drew an unmistakable link to his revered Kōrin, illustrating how the artist's influence endured not through direct transmission but by means of later rediscoveries of his oeuvre.

Each rebirth of a painting by Kōrin through the hands of another artist carried Kōrin's style into posterity while naturally including personalized touches. Hōitsu's own *Irises at Yatsuhashi* is about twenty centimeters shorter and twenty centimeters wider than Kōrin's painting. The ink bridge also appears less steep, creating a more gentle, horizontal image that resembles the illustration in *One Hundred Pictures by Kōrin.* Hōitsu clearly tried to balance his veneration for Kōrin with creativity—a dualism also evident in Kameda Bōsai's preface. Hōitsu was mindful of Kōrin's use of modularity to repeat the similar shapes of the irises throughout his pair of screens. He did not, however, reiterate entire clusters of flowers as Kōrin did to link his early *Irises* screens with his later *Irises at Yatsuhashi.* Evidently, Hōitsu understood Kōrin's trademark repetition in a different, more straightforward manner. Rather than embedding and concealing modular shapes within the work as Kōrin had done, Hōitsu

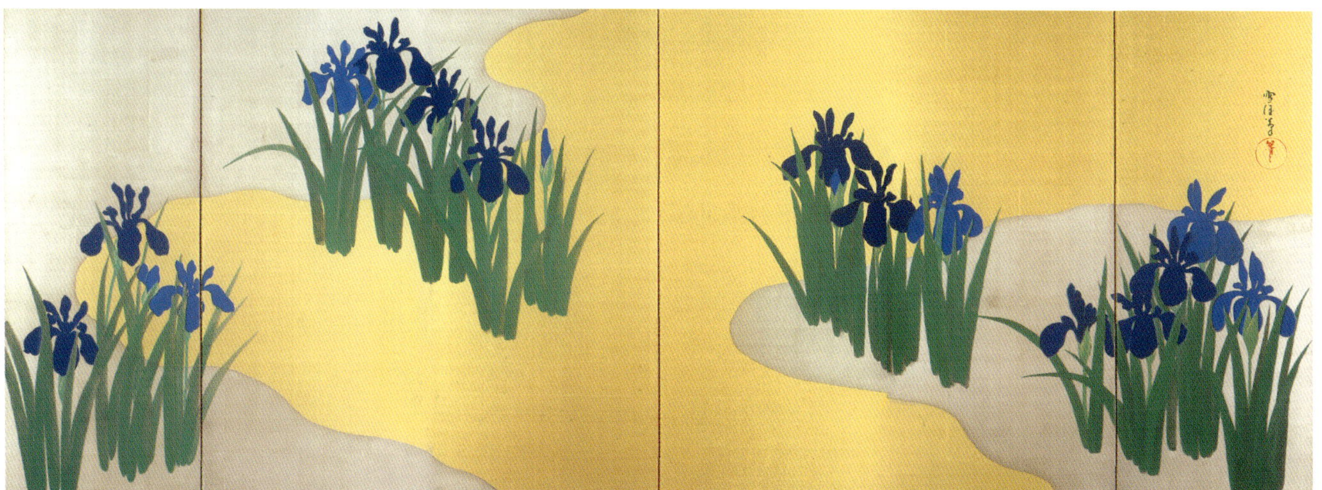

made his entire painting a symphony composed of repetitive forms. As a result, Hōitsu's amplified, candid use of repetition became a quality that posterity also came to associate with Kōrin.

Hōitsu's pair of screens is the final crescendo in the early modern tradition of iris paintings that looked back to Kōrin. The increasing accessibility to original works by Kōrin during the modern age diffused the rigidity of earlier, indirect transmission from one painter to another. Even Hōitsu had no access to or even knowledge of Kōrin's *Irises* screens, a work hidden from view at Nishi Honganji. Modern painters, such as Kamisaka Sekka (1866–1942), carried on the torch of Kōrin's artistry and translated his work into new concepts of painting, design, and graphic illustration.[9] Sekka, who studied Kōrin's manner early on, synthesized his impressions into works of his own (fig. 132). Paintings like Kōrin's *Irises* that were hidden for centuries also became available for public viewing when Nishi Honganji sold the screens alongside other treasures in 1917, when Sekka saw the screens. With rising opportunities for direct study of Kōrin's works as they increasingly circulated in the popular realm, Sekka and artists of his generation disrupted Hōitsu's claim as the ultimate successor to Kōrin. Esoteric transmission and publications like *One Hundred Pictures by Kōrin* were no longer the sole conduits for later painters to adopt Kōrin's style, as secretive collections became more and more publicly accessible. The varied ways by which artists approached and absorbed Kōrin's oeuvre speak of the diversity and differing zeitgeists of the respective traditions he posthumously established and of the longevity of his arresting style.

❖ ❖ ❖

Kōrin's shadow looms large to this day. The bold forms and colorful palette of his paintings are cited in countless pieces of early modern and modern art and are often invoked as the quintessence of Japanese-style paintings. Kōrin's name resonates in Japan's traditional arts, such as flower arrangement and confectionery. The name has become synonymous with traditional Japan in ways that few early modern painters can claim. Kōrin's striking style and its hybridity of tradition and innovation have installed this bon vivant painter at the very core of Japanese culture. The name Kōrin is more a public brand today than it was three hundred years ago. Driven by boundless creativity and the urgent need to make a living, Kōrin transformed from a happy-go-lucky heir to one of Japan's most revered cultural assets, a metamorphosis crowned by the image of *Irises* on the five-thousand-yen bill issued in 2004 and a set of 2017 Japanese postal stamps. Kōrin's legacy is alive and thriving, a legacy continued by countless artists, both professional and amateur, who turned to Kōrin for inspiration. His works of art and innumerable homages have carried him through the centuries and have immortalized the man and his work, making him a symbol of Japanese painting.

NOTES

Introduction

1. A number of documents with orders and designs for the retired empress Tōfukumon'in and other court ladies survive. See Yamane, *Konishi-ke kyūzō,* 46–75, 293–308. On Tōfukumon'in, see Lillehoj, "Tōfukumon'in."

2. See Tachibana Chikage's preface to Nakamura Hōchū's *Genealogy of Kōrin's Paintings* (*Kōrin gafu*) of 1802.

3. For analyses of Kōrin's work in relation to the Noh theater, see, e.g., Fukui, "Kōrin-kō 1"; Kōno, "Kōrin to nō"; and Emura, "Kōrin-ga ni okeru nō no eikyō ni tsuite." While making the case that Kōrin was affected by Noh, Emura acknowledges that a direct connection between the Noh theater and Kōrin's works is difficult to draw.

4. Kobayashi, "Kōrin to Kenzan."

5. Sakazaki, *Nihon gadan taikan,* 1037.

6. Sakazaki, 1063.

7. Translated by Melanie Trede in "Terminology and Ideology."

8. See, e.g., Oyama, *Kōrin moyō;* and Feltens, "Sartorial Identity."

9. See, e.g., Lillehoj, *Critical Perspectives;* Sakomura, *Poetry as Image;* and Sakomura, "Pictured Words and Codified Seasons."

10. On Tawaraya Sōtatsu, see Lippit, "Tawaraya Sōtatsu: Five Perspectives," 23–42. See also Yamane, *Sōtatsu kenkyū ichi;* and Yamane, *Sōtatsu kenkyū ni.*

11. In different family trees that Juichirō drafted throughout his life he mostly focused on the Ogata line, rather than that of the Konishi.

12. The Konishi Family Archive also became a repository of the Konishi family's own heritage. For example, it contains several family chronologies, letters, business papers, and a copy of the eighth-century Japanese classic *Nihon shoki,* handwritten by Juichirō himself.

13. See Kōno, "Hōitsu no denki," 19; and McKelway, *Silver Wind,* 18.

14. The document is transcribed in Yamane, *Konishi-ke kyūzō,* 202–3.

15. Aimi, "Ogata Kōrin narabi ni Ogata-ke no koto"; Fukui, "Kōrin kō 1"; Fukui, "Kōrin kō 2"; Fukui, "Kōrin kō 3."

16. A number of letters and sketches from the Konishi Family Archive are scattered across other private collections and museums, such as the Yamato Bunkakan, Nara.

17. Tanaka's publications are: "Konishi-ke kyūzō Kōrin kankei shiryō (jō)"; "Konishi-ke kyūzō Kōrin kankei shiryō (chū)"; "Konishi-ke kyūzō Kōrin kankei shiryō (ge no 1)"; and "Konishi-ke kyūzō Kōrin kankei shiryō (ge no 2)."

18. Kano, *Kōrin geijutsu no kisō.*

19. On Sōtatsu, see, e.g., Lippit and Ulak, *Sōtatsu;* and on Kōetsu, see Fischer, *Arts of Hon'ami Kōetsu.*

Chapter 1. Before Painting

Epigraph: Perzynski, *Kōrin und Seine Zeit,* 1.

1. See also Feltens, "Ogata Kōrin."

2. Yamane, *Konishi-ke kyūzō,* 84. Furnishings or implements (*dōgu*) usually included furniture and interior outfitting, such as tatami, screens, paper sliding doors (*shōji*), and *sugito,* outer sliding doors made from cypress wood that were often painted.

3. Yamane, 82–83.

4. Kosugi Kazuo was the first to point out the repetition of irises in Kōrin's screens and linked them to textile-making. See Kosugi, "Kakitsubata zu byōbu ni mirareru kata no shiyō."

5. Yoshida, *Kōshoku fumi denju,* 324.

6. Yamane, *Konishi-ke kyūzō,* 149–50.

7. Two kan silver is roughly 7.5 kilograms, and one monme amounts to 3.75 grams of silver.

8. Yamane, *Konishi-ke kyūzō,* 140.

9. Sakakibara Toranosuke, also named Masakuni, was initially the daimyo of the Murakami Domain in Echigo Province. In 1704 he was named lord of Himeji Domain, which in 1749 ceded to the control of the Sakai family, one of Kōrin's main patrons based in Edo.

10. This employment as overseer of Sakakibara Toranosuke's rice storage facilities in Osaka does not appear in other surviving documents. It is unclear how much work Kōrin devoted to this position or how much responsibility, if any, he had.

11. Yamane, *Konishi-ke kyūzō,* 118–19.

12. The elders of the two districts where Tsune and Kōrin resided joined forces to make a decision in the case.

13. The district where Tsune's family, the Hosoi, maintained their residence.

14. Kōrin's official residence at the time.

15. Yamane, *Konishi-ke kyūzō,* 142.

16. Yamane Yūzō suggested that Kōrin's affair with Suma occurred in the early 1690s, given that Kōrin had changed his name from Ichinojō to Kōrin sometime between 1689 and 1691. See Yamane, *Kōrin kenkyū ichi,* 13.

17. Yamane, *Konishi-ke kyūzō,* 143.

18. Yamane, 144.

19. By describing her suffering, Suma suggests that her sickness is a result of Kōrin's attempts to avoid meeting her and acknowledging their relationship.

20. The letter is unsigned, but judging from its relation to those written by Suma or concerning her, she was probably its author. The letter shares the same handwriting with the previous document.

21. Yamane, *Konishi-ke kyūzō,* 144–45.

22. Yamane, 120–21.

23. Kōken was the son of the daughter of Takatsukasa Norihira (1609–1668) and Reizei Tamemitsu (1559–1619). Norihira himself was a grandson of emperor GoYōzei (1571–1617). See Igarashi, *Kinsei Kyōto gadan no nettowāku,* 92.

24. The performance took place on the twenty-third day of the seventh month in 1675. My translation follows the transcription provided in Igarashi, 131.

25. On the ninth day of the eighth month in 1675, only Kōrin's elder brother Tōzaburō, the prospective heir to the Kariganeya, performed Noh with Kenzan and Shibuya Shichizaemon. The Ogata might have used this occasion to introduce the youngest son, Kenzan, to the temple. Igarashi, 131.

26. Igarashi, 131–32.

27. *Shimai* are relatively short dances that rely on passages and keywords in a full play to signal the actor when to change positions and to coordinate movements during the performance. For the nights of the seventh and eighth days of the tenth month and again the twenty-second and twenty-third days of the same month, the Sanbōin records mention that both brothers slept in the Daigoji's priest quarters. Igarashi, 133–35.

28. Yamane, *Konishi-ke kyūzō,* 171–74.

29. Miyamoto, *Kamigata nōgakushi no kenkyū,* 82.

30. The priestly journal of the temple, *Kan'ei hinamiki,* records Sōtatsu's completion of an order of Genji screens (*Genji onbyōbu*) for the thirteenth day of the ninth month in 1631. See Igarashi, "Sanbōin Kakutei to Sōtatsu."

31. According to early research by Kuwada Tadachika, the term itself initially meant simply "to gather people" or "to spend the night away." Itō Shingo is careful to differentiate between otogi and recitals of stories on the basis of *emaki* and *monogatari zōshi,* vernacular tales of fiction, which were popular at court during the Muromachi period. The debut of *otogishū,* the collective term for performers of otogi in aristocratic circles, dates back to GoYōzei and GoMizuno'o, two emperors who played a significant cultural role in seventeenth-century Japan. See Kuwada, *Daimyō to otogishū,* 2–3, 136–43. On the basic role of otogi performers to provide diversion, see also Matsubayashi, "Kanze Matajirō oboegaki," 32–45; and Itō, "Kinsei shoki no kugeshū to otogi."

32. Kamimichi, "Kōrin kankei shiryō," 46.

33. Kamimichi, 46–53.

34. The painter Yamamoto Soken first appears in the Nijō records on the ninth day of the ninth month in 1700 and was made to perform otogi during his next visits on the thirteenth day of the fifth month, the first day of the sixth month, and the sixteenth day of the sixth month in 1701. Only after he had performed otogi several times did Tsunahira commission paintings from him. In the same way as with Kōrin, summons for otogi directly preceded orders for paintings. Soken, however, seems to have displayed less talent in storytelling than Kōrin, since Tsunahira called on Soken far less for otogi. See Kamimichi, "Kōrin kankei shiryō," 53–57.

35. Shinjōsaimon'in, also called Fusako, was a sister of the wife of shogun Tokugawa Tsunayoshi (1646–1709), one of the customers of the Ogata's family business, the Kariganeya. See Kamimichi, 47. See also Igarashi, *Kinsei Kyōto gadan no nettowāku,* 164; and Emura, "Neoi no bungen," 273, 278.

36. One of Kōrin's early sources of stylistic inspiration, Kano Eikei (1662–1702), the fourth head of the Kyoto-based Kano atelier, also brought a fan painted by him as a present to Nijō Tsunahira when they were introduced. See Igarashi, "Kano Eikei no kenkyū," 11.

37. Kamimichi, "Kōrin kankei shiryō," 48.

38. Jakunyo also had close family ties to Tsunahira. The abbot was the nephew of Kujō Kaneharu (1641–1677), the biological father of Tsunahira. Such family connections cemented Tsunahira's instrumental role in linking Kōrin with the highest tiers of Nishi Honganji.

39. Yamane, "Ogata Kōrin hitsu Sōgi-zō," 23.

40. On the third day of the first month in 1703 and on the second day of the first month in 1704, Kōrin gave sets of shikishi as New Year's presents, while he chose fans on the third day of the first month in 1699 and the fourth day of the first month in 1701. See Kamimichi, "Kōrin kankei shiryō," 51, 53, 55.

41. Yamane, *Konishi-ke kyūzō,* 121.

42. *Bu* is a weight unit, measuring about 0.34 grams.

43. This note seems to have been added after the initial letter was written.

44. Nagato Province, or Chōshū, encompassed the western half of today's Yamaguchi Prefecture. The domain was ruled by the Mōri family, and Kenzan here probably refers to a debt repaid by Mōri Tsunamoto (1651–1709), lord of the domain until 1697. Lord Tosa is more difficult to identify—this title was carried by a number of people simultaneously. One possibility is Yamauchi Toyomasa (1641–1700), lord of Tosa Domain.

45. Nagai Naotoki (1638–1680) was lord of the Takatsuki Domain in present-day Osaka Prefecture.

46. A man named Hinoya Jirō sent a different letter that also deals with borrowed money to Kōrin. He seems to have acted as a major creditor for Kōrin during the 1690s.

47. It is unclear whether Kenzan refers to a work by himself or by Kōrin, or whether the screen was part of their inheritance. During the 1690s, Kōrin pawned or sold several works that appear to have been bequeathed to him by Sōken, so this work might have been inherited as well.

48. Yamane, *Konishi-ke kyūzō,* 122.

49. Yamane, 125–26.

50. Emura, *Neoi no bungen,* 279–80.

Chapter 2. Of Poets and Flowers

Epigraph: Okamoto, "Ogata Kōrin," 49.

1. On *karamonoya,* see Oka, "Karamonoya oboegaki"; and Oka, "Kan'ei bunka no naka no karamonoya."

2. Yamane dates the letter to circa 1700 and 1701, shortly after Kenzan opened his first kiln at Narutaki in 1699. See Yamane, *Kōrin kenkyū ichi,* 70–71.

3. Wilson and Ogasawara, *Ogata Kenzan,* 125–26.

4. On Kōrin's relationships with art dealers, see Noguchi, "Kōrin gagyō no kenkyū."

5. Wakisaka, *Kyō-Gano no kenkyū,* 77.

6. My translation is based on Kobayashi and Kōno, *Teihon Nihon kaigaron taisei,* 10.

7. Translation after Sugimoto, "Kyō no machi eshi," 73–74.

8. Yamane, "Ogata Kōrin hitsu Sōgi-zō."

9. Nakabe, "Ogata Kōrin to Shōkadō Shōjō."

10. Xiaojin Wu has argued that Shōkadō emphatically turned his subjects into literati figures. This notion also befits Sōgi's posthumous persona. See Wu, "Innumerable Embodiments of Hotei."

11. Yazaki, "Shōkadō Shōjō no gadai," 31.

12. Yazaki, 30–31.

13. Tani, *Chakaiki no kenkyū,* 117–42.

14. Sasaki and Sasaki, "Shōkadō Shōjō no kaiga," 113.

15. Etō, *Sadō bijutsu zenshū,* 128.

16. Etō, 144.

17. Aimi, "Kōetsu gaji no mondai," 24.

18. See volume 2 of Ban, *Kinsei kijin den.*

19. Koresawa, *Kan'ei no sanpitsu,* 9.

20. Yamane argued that Kōrin used the Kansei seal until around 1704 or 1705. He admits, however, that Kōrin may have used different seals simultaneously, making it difficult to pinpoint exact periods of usage. See Yamane, *Kōrin kenkyū ichi,* 119–23.

21. Kōrin's portrait of Nakamura Kuranosuke at the Yamato Bunkakan carries the Kansei seal. By way of its inscription, the work can be dated to 1704. Kōrin had a different alias, Dōsū, divined in 1704, possibly for use in Edo from that time to circa 1709. It seems he abandoned his use of Kansei within a year or two after he adopted the Dōsū seal.

22. Since at least the time of Japan's earliest poetic anthology, the eighth-century *Collection of Ten Thousand Leaves* (*Man'yōshū*), irises and their variant *ayamegusa,* or Siberian iris, were associated with summer. The twelfth-century *Emperor Horikawa's One Hundred Poets* (*Horikawa hyakushu*) instigated a long-lasting distinction between irises as a poetic trope of summer and *ayamegusa* as a symbol for the fifth month and the Tango Festival (*Tango no sekku*), one of the five major ceremonies conducted annually at the imperial court. See Shirane, *Japan and the Culture of the Four Seasons,* 52–53.

23. The first printed edition of the *Tales of Ise* was published in two illustrated volumes in 1608 as part of the so-called Saga-bon, books printed in movable type. The 1608 edition has a postscript by the aristocrat Nakanoin Michikatsu (1556–1610), whose calligraphy was used for the printed book.

24. Hayashi, "Azuma kudari kankei shōdan," 310.

25. The *Tales of Ise* give illicit love and idleness as an explanation for why Narihira leaves the capital at the beginning of chapters 7 and 8. In chapter 9, the reason for Narihira's departure from the capital is not specified. Medieval commentaries, among them Sōgi's influential *Commentaries on the Tales of Ise Heard by Shōhaku,* commonly offer the reason of idleness (*yō nashi,* lit. "nothing to do" or "idle"). See Hayashi, 314–17.

26. Ichihara Sunao has drawn attention to the fast narrative pace of the *azuma kudari* chapters—a feat that enhances the feeling of transience in this travel section of the *Tales of Ise.* See Ichihara, *Ise monogatari kaishakuron,* 230–31.

27. See Tsuruta, "Ganryō no rekishi," 49–50.

28. Kosugi, "Kakitsubata zu byōbu ni mirareru kata no shiyō."

29. Scholars have emphasized the relationship between *Irises* and the use of stencils among the Kariganeya. See, e.g., Nakabe, "Kakitsubata zu byōbu no kokusaisei," 88–89.

30. The idea of using stencils in *Irises* was first proposed by Kosugi Kazuo and subsequently taken up by other scholars. See Kosugi, "Kakitsubata zu byōbu ni mirareru kata no shiyō," 35; and, e.g., Yamane, *Kōrin kenkyū ni,* 192.

31. See Yamane, *Sōtatsu,* 240.

32. The objects seem to have been sold off in some sort of salonlike setting, where a group of potential clients was presented with a selection of artworks to choose from. Such gatherings were common venues for the sale of antiques and newer artworks during the early modern period.

33. One bu equals one tenth of one monme, so circa 0.375 grams.

34. Yamane, *Konishi-ke kyūzō,* 125–26.

35. For example, in the year 1630 Sōtatsu is mentioned in a letter written by the courtier Ichijō Kanetō (1605–1672) to an attendant of emperor GoMizuno'o, informing the monarch that Sōtatsu completed an order of three pairs of screens. In the same year, the aristocrat Karasumaru Mitsuhiro (1579–1638) wrote a postscript for Sōtatsu's copy of a now-lost handscroll in the imperial collection. On Sōtatsu's ties to the court, see, e.g., Yamane, *Sōtatsu kenkyū ichi,* 52–88; and Lippit, "Tawaraya Sōtatsu: Five Perspectives," 23–42.

36. One theory maintains that works like screens with arrangements of poppies that resemble *Irises* may have played a part in conceiving Kōrin's work. However, such paintings frequently lack the repetition of the same flowers in one screen. See Kōno, *Ogata Kōrin,* 100; and Kōno, "Kōrin futatsu daikessaku no gensen to tokushitsu," 25.

37. Yamane, *Konishi-ke kyūzō,* 121–22.

38. Yamane has argued that the screens were produced within the window of just one or two years after Kōrin received the *hokkyō* title in 1701. See Yamane, *Kōrin kenkyū ni,* 187–88; and Igarashi, *Kyōto gadan no nettowāku,* 167.

39. See, e.g., Yamane, *Kōrin kenkyū ichi,* 127–36, 182–217.

40. See Noguchi, "Yatsuhashi zu byōbu ni kan suru oboegaki," 79–80; and Noguchi, "Yatsuhashi zu byōbu kō," 58–65.

41. Scientific analysis conducted by the Metropolitan Museum of Art has unveiled how Kōrin applied a ground layer of shell-white (*gofun*) onto which he added azurite. See Leona and Perry, "Beneath the Blue," 129–39; and Carpenter, *Designing Nature,* 24–25.

42. See Sakazaki, *Nihon kaigaron taikei,* 5:35.

43. The pair of screens with plants of autumn was introduced by Yamane, who dated them to the late 1690s. Their present whereabouts are unknown. Yamane, "Kōrin hitsu Akikusa zu byōbu ni tsuite."

44. A scientific analysis of *Red and White Plum Blossoms* was conducted by the National Research Institute of Cultural Properties in 2002 and 2003. See MOA Bijutsukan and Tōkyō Bunkazai Kenkyūjo, *Kokuhō Kōhakubai zu byōbu.*

45. Igarashi, *Kyoto gadan no nettowāku,* 131–47; and Kamimichi, "Kōrin kankei shiryō."

46. See, e.g., Yamane, *Kōrin kenkyū ni,* 210–12; Kōno, "Kōrin to nō," 53–56; and Emura, "Kōrin-ga ni okeru nō no eikyō ni tsuite," 19, 24.

47. Arntzen and Ito, *Sarashina Diary,* 104.

48. The play was translated into English in Klein, *Allegories of Desire,* 430–58.

49. Klein, 433–34.

50. The dishes were originally owned by the Maeda family, lords of Kaga Domain (present-day Ishikawa Prefecture), a clan renowned for their zeal for the Noh theater and patronage of descendants of Tawaraya Sōtatsu's atelier. Hon'ami Kōetsu was close to the Maeda, as is evident from a number of letters where Kōetsu and the Maeda retainer Imaeda Shigenao converse about Noh practice. On the provenance of Kenzan's set, see Idemitsu Bijutsukan, *Ninsei Kenzan,* 117.

51. Translation in Klein, "Allegories of Desire," 450.

52. An auction catalogue from 1 April 1917 records *Irises* as a "famous treasure" (*meibutsu*) of Nishi Honganji. On that occasion, the work was sold to the industrialist Nezu Kaichirō (1860–1940), whose collection formed the foundation for today's Nezu Museum. Scholars now believe that *Irises* was commissioned for Nishi Honganji and remained at the temple from Kōrin's day until the wake of Japan's modernity. See Noguchi, "Yatsuhashi zu byōbu kō," 56–57.

53. Fenollosa writes: "In Japan great Kōrin screens are many, but among the finest are the great iris screens on gold, shown in 1882 by the Nishi Honganji temple at the first loan exhibition of the art club." Fenollosa, *Epochs of Chinese and Japanese Art,* 514. See also Nakabe, "Kakitsubata zu byōbu no kokusaisei," 86.

54. See, e.g., Yamane, *Kōrin kenkyū ichi,* 216–18.

55. Kamimichi, "Kōrin kankei shiryō," 46.

56. Kōrin's *Dream Fuji* was first introduced in 1920 by Fukui Rikichirō. The whereabouts of the work, however, are unknown and its authenticity is uncertain. See Fukui, "Kōrin no yume."

57. Kōno, "Kōrin futatsu daikessaku no gensen to tokushitsu," 24; Murase, "Ogata Kōrin Kakitsubata zu to Yatsuhashi zu wo megutte," 13–14.

58. The two works are mentioned in auction records of March and May 1917, respectively.

59. On Sakai Hōitsu in English, see McKelway, *Silver Wind.* Research of Hōitsu in Japanese was spearheaded by Tamamushi Satoko. See Tamamushi, *Toshi no naka no e.*

60. Tamamushi, *Tawaraya Sōtatsu kingin no kazari no keifu,* 380–83.

61. The layout of the bridge in Busei's rough sketch and the arrangement of the iris flowers are compellingly close to *Irises at Yatsuhashi.* See Tamamushi, "Shashi to tōjin he no akogare," 73–96.

62. Tamamushi, however, has argued that the signatures in *Record of Glancing at the Past* and *Irises at Yatsuhashi* are not exact matches and therefore defy a direct connection. See her *Toshi no naka no e,* 82–83, and "Shashi to tōjin he no akogare," 85–87.

63. The modern provenance of the screens is complicated by the fact that in the 1919 auction catalogue of their sale, *Irises at Yatsuhashi* is said to have been owned by the Ikeda family of Tottori Domain. The Ikeda and Matsudaira families were closely linked by marriage, and the Ikeda appear to have kept *Irises at Yatsuhashi* at the time of the auction but did not own it. An entry in the diary of Takahashi Yoshio (1861–1937), who attended the auction, notes Matsudaira Narimitsu (1897–1974), the son of Naritami, as the owner. He writes: "Among the Ikeda family pieces, displayed in the large room on the second floor, were Kōrin's Siberian iris screens (*ayame no byōbu*), owned by Lord Matsudaira Narimitsu." See Takahashi, *Manzōroku Takahashi Sōan nikki,* 203; and Noguchi, "Yatsuhashi zu byōbu kō," 56–57.

64. Aimi Kōu was the first to provide evidence for Kōrin's early tea studies with Sōsa. Other major Kōrin scholars, including Yamane Yūzō and Kōno Motoaki, repeated this proposal. See Aimi, "Kōrin azuma kudari kō (naka no ichi)," 28–29; Yamane, "Zoku Kōrin to Nakamura Kuranosuke," 20; Yamane, *Kōrin kenkyū ichi,* 148; and Kōno, "Kōrin to Tsugaru-ke," 4.

65. Yamane, "Ogata Kōrin hitsu Shiraji akikusa moyō byakue kosode," 24.

66. See Sen, *Kōshin Sōsa chasho,* 87, 200.

67. Aimi, "Kōrin azuma kudari," 32–33. Ishizuka, "Kiba Fuyuki-ke kō," esp. 32–35.

Chapter 3. Art and Family

Epigraph: Translation based on Yasuda, "Edo jidai ni okeru Kōrin-zō no hensen ni tsuite (chū)," 93.

1. See, e.g., Gonse, *L'Art japonais,* 2:102–3, 204–8.

2. Lacquer sap is toxic when wet but loses that quality once it dries.

3. Yamane initially suggested Kōrin adopted the first syllable in reference to Kōetsu but did not elaborate any reasons beyond Kōrin's possible reverence for his great-granduncle. Yamane, *Kōrin kenkyū ichi,* 4–6, 59.

4. Yamane, *Konishi-ke kyūzō,* 182.

5. Yamane, 174.

6. Emura Tomoko has shown that, in 1714, a suzuribako by Kōetsu with motifs of pine and camellia was valued at four kan and 697 monme. Another suzuribako by him, with a design of a boat among reeds, went for two kan and 250 monme. Emura, "Kōrin no maki-e seisaku to kaiga ni tsuite," 114.

7. On Kōetsu-style calligraphy and contemporaneous followers, see, e.g., Hatano, "Kōetsu no sho wo chūshin toshite Momoyama Edo no sho wo miru."

8. See Nakamachi, "Kōrin no monogatari zu ni tsuite," 48.

9. Here, Kōrin's great-granduncle collaborated with aristocrats, including Nakanoin Michikatsu, who provided the postscript to Kōetsu's printed edition of *Commentaries on the Tales of Ise Heard by Shōhaku.* See Gotō Bijutsukan, *Kōetsu: Momoyama no koten,* 210.

10. Takeuchi and Itō, *Yakimono to fureau.*

11. Hayashiya, *Kōetsu,* 131; Masuda, *Kōetsu no tegami,* 135.

12. Masuda, *Kōetsu no tegami,* 135.

13. Uchida, *Kōrin maki-e no kenkyū,* 183–200.

14. The letter accompanies a sutra box with floral designs in mother-of-pearl, but it seems to refer to a different, now lost piece. The document is frequently quoted in discussions of Kōetsu's lacquer works. See, e.g., Hayashiya, *Kōetsu,* 132–33.

15. Uchida, *Kōrin maki-e no kenkyū,* 183.

16. Uchida, 185.

17. Okada, "Kōetsu no maki-e," 125–40; Uchida, *Kōrin maki-e no kenkyū,* 187–200.

18. Yamane proposes that this neighbor might be Jūichiya Tokuemon, who resided next to Kōrin's residence in the district of Nakamachi Yabunouchichō. This neighbor is mentioned in another letter by Kōrin to the art dealer Nishimura Seiiku. Yamane, *Kōrin kenkyū ichi,* 67.

19. Yamane, 66–68.

20. Uchida Tokugo argued that the suzuribako mentioned here is either the work with a décor of *mizuaoi* at the MOA Museum of Art or a box with *beniaoi* (both species of hollyhock) at the Hatakeyama Memorial Museum of Fine Art. Both works fit the elongated shape described in the letter. See Uchida, *Kōrin maki-e no kenkyū,* 219–20.

21. In a letter dated to the fifteenth day of the fifth month in 1701, he was called, together with the official Ikeda Denshichi, to report on the amount of copper kept at the mint's storage facility at Izumiya. The letter also discloses that Kuranosuke, along with Kōrin and other officials, were busy inspecting the copper mint's Osaka mansion and other properties a little later that same year. See Yamane, "Kōrin to Nakamura Kuranosuke," esp. 17–18.

22. One sheet (*mai*) equaled one *ryō* gold. See Yamane, "Kōrin maki-e nidai," 15.

23. *Oshū,* the district council of elders. Townspeople commonly sought their advice and approval on business transactions. Yamane takes this as evidence that Kōrin and Seiiku perhaps lived in the same district of Kyoto. Yamane, *Kōrin kenkyū ichi,* 72.

24. The letter is dated to around 1701 to 1703. It accompanies a lacquer writing box (suzuribako) with mizuaoi by Kōrin, now in the MOA Museum of Art, Atami. It is possible that the letter refers to this particular box. See Yamane, "Kōrin maki-e nidai," 14–18.

25. Yamane, *Konishi-ke kyūzō,* 182.

26. Yamane, "Kōrin maki-e nidai," 12.

27. Yasuda, "Edo jidai ni okeru Kōrin-zō," 95.

28. Quoted after Uchida, *Suzuribako no bi,* 88.

29. The poem inscribed in Kōetsu's characteristic calligraphy reads: "Crossing the pontoon bridge / in Sano along the eastern route / no one knows of / my deep memories." Translation after Uchida, 78–79.

30. Yamane, *Kōrin kenkyū ichi,* 80–81.

31. Haino, *Ogawa Haritsu.*

32. Translated after Yoshida, *Kōshoku fumi denju,* 324.

33. See Milhaupt, *Kimono,* 32–54.

34. Uchida, *Kōrin maki-e no kenkyū,* 212.

35. Emura, "Kōrin no maki-e seisaku," 115–18.

36. A section of Sōtatsu and Kōetsu's deer scroll, which is now cut into individual pieces, at the Seattle Art Museum carries Sōtatsu's Inen seal at the end, along with Kōetsu's signatures Tokuyūsai and Kōetsu hitsu (written by Kōetsu). Sōtatsu also painted a similar example with a décor of cranes, now at the Kyoto National Museum, among other works. Kōrin's sketches of this particular type of crane are preserved among the Konishi Family Archive. On Kōrin's sketches of lacquer designs see, e.g., Kano, *Kōrin Geijutsu no kisō,* 59–64, 67. Emura Tomoko has shown how a variety of Kōrin's sketches for lacquer works, preserved as part of the Konishi Family Archive, corresponds with printed mica designs used as paper décor in Kōetsu's Noh libretti. See Emura, "Kōrin no maki-e seisaku," 111–24.

37. See Uchida, *Kōrin maki-e no kenkyū,* 212.

38. Yamane, *Kōrin kenkyū ichi,* 95–96.

39. Sugimoto, "Kyō no machi eshi," 68.

40. Emura, "Kōrin no maki-e seisaku," 113.

41. See Fukui, "Kōrin no shi toshite no Yamamoto Soken," 136–38; and Yasuda, "Edo jidai ni okeru Kōrin-zō," 95.

42. Emura, "Kōrin maki-e seisaku," 112.

Chapter 4. Heading East

1. Bashō famously immortalized the joys and perils of his journey to the northern regions of Japan's Honshū island in his *Narrow Road to Oku.* For an English translation, see Keene, *Narrow Road to Oku.*

2. On Kano Tan'yū and seventeenth-century Kano practice, see, e.g., Gerhart, *The Eyes of Power: Art and Early Tokugawa Authority;* Lippit, *Painting of the Realm;* and Fischer and Kinoshita, *Ink and Gold.*

3. On Kōrin's trips to Edo, see Nakamachi, "Kōrin no Edo kudari no seika to imi."

4. Kamimichi, "Kōrin kankei shiryō," 58.

5. Kōrin's poem and the feeling of farewell it evokes suggest that Kōrin sent the letter after his second departure for Edo, around the third month of 1705. The fourth month is too early for the letter to have been written when Kōrin first departed for Edo in 1704. Yamane, *Kōrin kenkyū ichi,* 80–81.

6. Yamane, *Konishi-ke kyūzō*, 174–75.

7. The mortgage allowed the creditor, Kawai Heiemon, to move into the estate. The contract stipulated that the property would enter Heiemon's permanent ownership if Kōrin failed to repay the debt. See Yamane, *Konishi-ke kyūzō*, 126–27, 139.

8. Kamimichi, "Kōrin kankei shiryō," 54–55.

9. Kōrin is said to have studied tea with Masachika before the 1690s. Although the Fuyuki ran a business in Edo, until Masachika's death their family temple was located in Kyoto. See Ishizuka, "Kiba Fuyuki-ke kō," esp. 33–34.

10. Igarashi, *Kinsei Kyōto gadan no nettowāku*, 159.

11. Kuranosuke and Kōrin may have begun associating sometime around 1700. See Yamane, "Kōrin to Nakamura Kuranosuke," 7–22.

12. In 1915 Fukui Rikichirō was the first scholar to scrutinize the relationship between Kōrin and Kuranosuke. He drew attention to the 1702 contract to give Kuranosuke's daughter into Kōrin's fosterage and the importance of Kuranosuke as Kōrin's patron. See Fukui, "Ogata Kōrin no shōgai ni tsuite," 96–97, 102. Fukui's piece was originally published in the journal *Mitsukoshi* in 1915.

Later, Aimi Kōu showed that the close relationship between Kōrin and Kuranosuke might have affected the artist's activities in Edo from 1704 to 1709. He argued that Kuranosuke paved the way for Kōrin with introductions to various high-ranking warriors, such as Ogiwara Shigehide (1658–1713), a commissioner of the shogunate, and the Sakai and Tsugaru daimyo clans. The two families, especially the Sakai, are assumed to be among Kōrin's major patrons in Edo. See Aimi, "Kōrin azuma kudari kō (naka no ichi)," 28–29.

13. Yamane, *Konishi-ke kyūzō*, 146.

14. Kōrin's will of 1713 mentions Nakamura Kuranosuke as the person who arranged Juichirō's adoption into the Konishi family. See Yamane, 148–49.

15. In light of Kōrin's many visits to Nijō Tsunahira's mansion and their close relationship, Fukui argued that the Nijō were instrumental in supporting Kōrin's receipt of the hokkyō title. Fukui, "Ogata Kōrin no shōgai ni tsuite," 95.

Kōrin continued to conduct courtesy calls on Tsunahira during special annual festivities and, for instance, when he returned briefly from Edo on the twentieth day of the third month in 1705. Kamimichi, "Kōrin kankei shiryō," 56.

16. The audience is recorded for the twenty-sixth day of the twelfth month in 1703. Kamimichi, 55.

17. See Yamane, "Kōrin to Nakamura Kuranosuke"; and Yamane, "Zoku Kōrin to Nakamura Kuranosuke."

18. On Sōtatsu's shikishi of the *Tales of Ise*, see Hagoromo Kokusai Daigaku Nihon Bunka Kenkyūjo, *Sōtatsu Ise monogatari zu shikishi*. Timon Screech has discussed the use of the art of Sōtatsu and Kōrin in the self-fashioning of the urban elite of Kyoto. See Screech, "Rinpa and the Space of Dreams," 42–55; and Screech, *Obtaining Images*, 222–28.

19. Yamane, "Zoku Kōrin to Nakamura Kuranosuke," 22.

20. Tayo did not travel to Edo until 1707.

21. This provides evidence that Kōrin had accepted pupils by the early 1700s and took at least one of them to Edo.

22. Ueshima Gennojō. See Yamane, *Rinpa kaiga zenshū Kōrin-ha ichi*, 66–67.

23. In a separate letter to Ueshima Gennojō, Kōrin gives him instructions on painting.

24. Janice Katz discusses the Maeda's patronage of artists, such as Tawaraya Sōsetsu. See Katz, "Collecting and Patronage of Art in Seventeenth Century Japan."

25. While modern scholarship has built uncritically on Fukui's early assumption, another pioneer of the study of Kōrin's art, Aimi Kōu, gave Soken little presence in his own analyses. At most, he says, Kōrin might have been influenced by Soken in his choice of colors, though he leaves the implications of this rather vague. See Aimi, "Kōrin," 113; and Fukui, "Kōrin no shi," 138–41.

26. Fukui gives an overview of the different premodern theories on possible teachers of Kōrin. See Fukui, "Kōrin no shi toshite no Yamamoto Soken," 136–45. Fukui's piece was originally published in 1916, in the journal *Geibun*.

27. Fukui, "Kōrin no shi," 139–40.

28. Kōno, "Kōrin suibokuga no tenkai to gensen," 57.

29. Kōno, 141.

30. Kamimichi, "Kōrin kankei shiryō," 55.

31. Tan'yū entered the service of Tokugawa shoguns and at a young age moved to Edo, where he established the Kajibashi Kano atelier and helped shape the visual aesthetic of the city. On Kano Tan'yū and his practice, see Lippit, *Painting of the Realm*, esp. 20–21, 145–49.

32. On Kōrin's bird studies, see Nakamachi, "Kinsei zenki no chōjū shasei"; and Nishimoto, "Kōrin hitsu Chōjū shasei zukan ni tsuite."

33. Tan'yū's bird studies are discussed in Katō, "Kano Tan'yū Shasei ron"; and Tsuji, "Kano Tan'yū hitsu Chōrui shasei chō mohon."

34. See Yamane, *Kōrin kenkyū ichi*, 96–97. Kōrin's signature in the letter resembles that of a brazier at the Yamato Bunkakan, which Kōrin and Kenzan made together during the last half-decade of Kōrin's life. See Emura, "Ogata Kōrin no kaiga gakushū to gafū keisei ni tsuite," 8–9.

35. See Shimao, "Haboku sansui zu no ga to shi"; and Lippit, "Of Modes and Manners in Japanese Ink Painting."

36. Tani, *Chakaiki no kenkyū*, 117–42.

37. Sakazaki, *Nihon gadan taikan*, 1058.

38. Lippit, *Painting of the Realm*, 196–97.

39. Lippit, 78–82, 196–98.

40. Yamane, *Kōrin kenkyū ichi*, 82–84.

41. Kyōto Kokuritsu Hakubutsukan, *Tan'yū shukuzu ge*, 97–99, 202.

42. This account of tarashikomi is indebted to Yukio Lippit and Sandy Kita's scholarship. Lippit describes the tarashikomi technique's technical features in "Tawaraya Sōtatsu and the Watery Poetics of Japanese Ink Painting," 57–60. See also Kita, "Bulls of Chōmyōji."

43. This project is recorded in the journal of the Maeda retainer Yamada Shirōemon, *Mitsubo kikigaki*. See Murashige,

"Kitagawa Sōsetsu to kusabana zu," 26; and Ishikawa Ken Bijutsukan, *Sōsetsu Sōsetsu ten,* 1–3. See also Katz, "Collecting and Patronage," 120.

44. In lieu of a brush, the painter uses a slightly burned wooden stick. This technique was often employed for underdrawings.

45. Yamane, *Kōrin kenkyū ichi,* 82–84.

46. Nakamachi Keiko discusses these works in her "Kōrin no Edo kudari," 44, and in English in "Patrons of Tawaraya Sōtatsu and Ogata Kōrin."

47. Tamamushi, *Toshi no naka no e,* 339–96.

48. See Nakamachi, "Fūjin Raijin zu byōbu to Sōtatsu, Kōrin."

49. Arakawa, "Gayū no tō," esp. 14.

50. Munetada was the fourth son of shogun Tokugawa Yoshimune. On the Hitotsubashi Tokugawa clan, see Takeshi, "Gosankyō no kashindan kōzō."

51. Takahashi, *Edo no barokku,* 164–84.

52. Yamane, "Zoku Kōrin to Nakamura Kuranosuke," 26.

53. Translated after Kōno, "Kōrin to Tsugaru-ke," 4–5.

54. Tamamushi, *Toshi no naka no e,* 34.

55. Nakagawa, *Ninsei,* 92–93.

56. Tamamushi, *Toshi no naka no e,* 34; and Tamamushi, "Hōitsu-ga no teihen," 62–63.

57. Kawai Heiemon's de facto purchase of Kōrin's Nakamachi Yabunouchichō estate—Shichibei was the district elder in charge of approving the transaction—dates to 1703 and 1704, not 1705, the date given in the document here. Considering this discrepancy, the transfer of Kōrin's Nakamachi Yabunouchichō property to Kawai Heiemon was probably finalized in 1705.

58. Yamane, *Konishi-ke kyūzō,* 139.

Chapter 5: Beyond Ink

Epigraph: Translation based on Sugimoto, "Kyō no machi eshi," 69–70. A *habutae* is equivalent to a *haori,* a shorter garment resembling a jacket that is worn over a kimono. It is often used in reference to a haori in saturated black.

1. Kamimichi, "Kōrin kankei shiryō," 59.

2. Initially, scholars argued that Kōrin was involved in adding paintings to Kenzan's ceramics from 1699 onward. By focusing on the signatures used by Kōrin in ceramic paintings, many of which omit the hokkyō sobriquet, scholars concluded that those paintings predate the artist's receipt of the title in 1701. Yamane later proposed, through stylistic analysis and the discovery of new pieces bearing dates after 1701 (though with signatures that lack hokkyō), Kōrin could not have collaborated with Kenzan before circa 1709. Historians of ceramics, such as Takeuchi Jun'ichi, have endorsed that theory. See Yamane, "Kōrin to Kenzan yaki nidai"; and Takeuchi, "Chawan sandai."

3. Arakawa Masaaki argued that the jar depicts plum blossoms instead of persimmons. See his "E-Karatsu Kaki mon sanjiko."

4. Satō, *Karatsu,* 63.

5. On Ninsei's role among the pottery traditions of Kyoto, see Oka, *Kinsei Kyōyaki no kenkyū,* 124–241.

6. Arakawa suggested that sencha culture in Ming China used similar tea bowls with high rims to better preserve the heat. Arakawa, "Gayū no tō," 16. On sencha culture in Japan, see Graham, *Tea of the Sages.*

7. On the relationship of Ninsei and Sōwa, see Oka, *Kokuhō Ninsei no nazo,* 126–56.

8. On Omuro ware objects in Sōwa's tea diary, see Tani, *Kanamori Sōwa chasho,* 261–87, 294–97, 304–6.

9. The gathering took place on the sixteenth day of the fourth month in 1651. Nishida Hiroko suggested that the tea bowl, now lost, might have been close to an example of the same subject in sabi-e at the MOA Museum of Art. See Nishida, *Ninsei no chawan,* 48. On the entry in Sōwa's tea diary, see Tani, *Kanamori Sōwa chasho,* 263–64.

10. Tani, 265–66.

11. See Arakawa, "Fujisan wo egaita Hizen jiki," 31–33.

12. The white slip was applied with a broad brush, a technical aspect that the technique shares with sizing paper. Takeuchi, "Kenzan yaki chawan kō," 5–6.

13. On an account of the life of Sōwa, see Oka, "Kanamori Sōwa," 52–55.

14. Oka, *Kokuhō Ninsei,* 167–74; Kenzan's contemporary Gettan Dōchō records his 1690 visit to the Shūseidō, drawing the picture of a paradisiacal place with a lush garden and all the amenities of a study, an extensive library, and other perks that a scholar would need. Tanaka, "Shūseidōki ni tsuite," 324–26.

15. Richard Wilson argued that Kenzan largely worked as a designer for his wares, rather than producing ceramics with his own hands. Thus, works with such intricate pictures as the Narutaki tea bowl may have been painted by artists employed by Kenzan. See Wilson, *Art of Ogata Kenzan,* 71–96.

16. See, e.g., Mizuo, "Ogata Kōrin Kenzan saku Ume zu kakuzara," 36.

17. Wilson, "Kenzan yaki no keifu," 131. Although he was not married, Kenzan ambiguously calls Ihachi his son in *Tōji seihō.* Sahara Kiku'u (1762–1832) specifies that Ihachi was Kenzan's adopted child and the second son of Nonomura Ninsei. See Wilson, *Art of Ogata Kenzan,* 163.

18. Wilson, *Art of Ogata Kenzan,* 221–30.

19. Arakawa, "Gayū no tō," 19.

20. Kenzan writes how he initially followed Ninsei and used white clay from Kurodani, near Kyoto, as well as Bizen clay. After years of trying out different clays, he was unable to find a better white than that found at Aikawa. He made this clay part of his personal method to create a ground that came as close to white as possible. Wilson, *Art of Ogata Kenzan,* 219–20, 227, 229.

21. Kamimichi, "Kōrin kankei shiryō," 45.

22. The site, called Narutaki no chaya, housed a Nijō-owned estate used for tea gatherings and other salon activities. See Arakawa, "Gayū no tō," 13.

The records of Ninnaji, *Omuro gyoki,* mention the establishment of Kenzan's Narutaki kiln in the eighth month of 1699. Like Kōrin, Kenzan was a late bloomer. He was already thirty-seven years old at the time. Tanaka, "Shūseidōki ni tsuite," 330–31.

23. Yamane, *Kōrin kenkyū ichi,* 70–71.

24. The list is part of Kōrin's personal notes, written on a separate sheet by Kenzan himself. Yamane, *Konishi-ke kyūzō,* 180–82. Yamane dates the list to around the late Hōei and early Shōtoku eras (1711–16), since the catalogue of pseudonyms is followed by a separate sheet with the alias Masatoki, which Yamane believes Kōrin adopted by 1712. Yamane, *Kōrin kenkyū ichi*, 62, 129.

25. The most thorough study on Sesson's life and work in English was accomplished by Barbara Ford in her dissertation, "A Study of the Painting of Sesson Shūkei."

26. On the painting's provenance in the Sakai family, see Tanaka, "Sesson hitsu Enkō zu," 51–57; and Shimao, "Sesson hitsu Jurō zu," 26–29.

27. Yamane has proposed that Kōrin adopted the alias Jakumei sometime around the late Hōei era. See Yamane, *Kōrin kenkyū ichi*, 62–63.

28. See, e.g., Mitsuoka, "Kenzan iro-e Teika kachō waka shikishi zara," 111–12.

29. Kōrin and Kenzan's great-granduncle Hon'ami Kōetsu, for example, was a virtuoso in inscribing shikishi that have been attributed to the Tawaraya atelier under Sōtatsu. During the last years of his life, Kōrin again came back to his great-granduncle Hon'ami Kōetsu, whose cultural leverage he had used during his early years as a painter.

30. See Kasashima, "Sōtatsu Ise monogatari zu shikishi wo megutte," 120; Nakamachi, "Shinshutsu no Sōtatsu-ha Ise monogatari-e shikishi ni tsuite," 13; and Kawada, "Sōtatsu Ise monogatari zu shikishi no genjō."

31. Igarashi, "Sōtatsu Ise monogatari zu shikishi no jintekina nettowāku."

32. Scholars have suggested that Kenzan's ceramics became increasingly commercial and brandlike after he rented a kiln at Nijō Chōjiyamachi. See Hayashiya, "Kōetsu Kenzan no tōgei"; and Takeuchi, "Kenzan yaki."

33. On medieval practices of urban reclusion, see Parker, "Hermit at Court."

34. Richard Wilson and Ogasawara Saeko have discovered that much of the poetry inscribed by Kenzan on his pottery refers to complete poems or fragments of poems in *Enki kappō*. See Wilson and Ogasawara, "Kenzan yaki."

35. Wilson and Ogasawara, 2–5.

36. Wilson and Ogasawara, 26.

37. I refer here to a copy of *Complete Perfect Means*, published in 1672 or 1673, now housed in the Waseda University Library.

38. *Fluttering of a Snipe's Wing* includes an array of different Japanese poetry sequences, such as the Thirty-Six Poet Immortals and the poems of the twelve months after Teika, among others. Kōrin's personal notes in the Konishi Family Archive include direct copies of the Teika poems in *Fluttering of a Snipe's Wing*. The proximity of Kenzan's poetic inscriptions on the reverse of the MOA Museum of Art set of twelve dishes, dated to 1702, suggests that the brothers had access to a copy around that time.

39. I am grateful to Amanda Imai for her advice in translating this poem.

40. Alexander Hofmann's book offers the only cohesive study of performed paintings in the early modern period. In response to the frequent absence of written records, Hofmann has proposed a methodology to discern painting performances by means of their visual qualities. Broadly speaking, *sekiga*, or paintings on the spot, were mainly done in ink on paper using conspicuously abbreviated brushwork. Such works often emphasize auspicious, easily understood motifs. Hofmann states that certain performances, such as the established tradition of the first painting of the New Year (*on'e hajime*), symbolized the trust and devotion of painters and patrons. Hofmann, *Performing/Painting*.

41. The dish depicting bamboo at the Idemitsu Museum of Arts is signed Kōrin, together with the kotobuki cypher. The Nezu dish with plum blossoms is signed Jakumei Kōrin and also includes that cypher, just as in the Jurōjin dish at the MOA Museum of Art.

42. The piece bears the date of the second day of the first month of 1699. The work is published in an auction catalogue that accompanied the sale of parts of the estate of the Aoji family, held at the Tokyo Bijutsu Club in March 1920, p. 107.

43. Arakawa Masaaki has illustrated the importance of the painting manual *Hasshu gafu* in the painted decorations of Kokutani ware. Arakawa, "Hizen jiki to Hasshu gafu."

Richard Wilson also suggested the possibility that Kenzan may have referred to *Hasshu gafu* for some of his sabi-e. See Wilson and Ogasawara, "Kenzan yaki," 8.

44. See Nishimoto, *Kōrin Kenzan*, esp. 121–23; and Oka, *Kokuhō Ninsei*, 204–33. See also Wilson, *Art of Ogata Kenzan*, 77–96.

45. The identity of Watanabe Soshin is unclear, but one theory maintains that he was the painter Watanabe Shikō, who adapted Kōrin's style, among others. See, e.g., Mitsuoka, *Kenzan*, 5.

46. Translated after Kawahara, *Kenzan*, 22–23.

Chapter 6. Toward the End

1. David Rosand has discussed the late styles of artists in his "Style and the Aging Artist."

2. Said, *On Late Style*.

3. See Kobayashi, *Kōrin to Kenzan;* Kōno, "Kōrin to nō"; Fukui, "Ogata Kōrin no shōgai ni tsuite"; Matsushita, "Kōrin no Kōhakubai zu byōbu"; Yamane, *Sōtatsu to Kōrin*, 237–39; and Hayashi, "Haru no raigo," 37–55.

4. See, e.g., Yamane, *Kōrin kenkyū ichi*, 63, 128–36.

5. From a postscript by the courtier Karasumaru Mitsuhiro (1579–1638) in the fourth and final scroll of Sōtatsu's set, dated to 1630, we learn that the painter copied the works on the basis of works in the palace collection. Sōtatsu's copy was commissioned by Honda Tomimasa (1572–1649), the chief retainer of the lords of Fukui Domain on the western coast. The scrolls were given to the Mōri clan of Chōshū Domain in western Honshū. See Yamane, *Sōtatsu*, 238–40.

6. The signatures on both screens in the pair are apocryphal and probably represent later additions. The style and the general dominance of large-format works during Kōrin's last half-decade indicate that the screens were probably made during that time.

7. Tajima, *Rinpa gashū dai ikkan;* Hamada, "Ogata Kōrin hitsu Baika zu byōbu ni tsuite," 569; Matsushita, "Kōrin no nami," 7–9; and Chizawa, *Kōrin*, esp. 107.

8. Nakamura, "Rinpa no gihō ni tsuite," 24–34.

9. The findings of the scientific analysis conducted by the MOA Museum of Art and the National Research Institute for Cultural Properties, Tokyo, in 2002 and 2003 are published in MOA Bijutsukan and Tōkyō Bunkazai Kenkyūjo, *Kokuhō Kōhakubai zu byōbu*. Some parts of the original findings of the study were reassessed in a subsequent publication. See Uchida, "Kokuhō Kōhakubai zu byōbu," 34–46.

10. This effect was also commented on in relation to Tawaraya Sōtatsu's *Bulls* at the temple Chōmyōji, a key work for understanding the efficacy of tarashikomi. See Lippit, "Tawaraya Sōtatsu and the Watery Poetics of Japanese Ink Painting"; and Kita, "Bulls of Chōmyōji."

11. See Kōno, "Kōrin to Tsugaru-ke."

12. Hamada, "Ogata Kōrin hitsu Baika zu byōbu ni tsuite," 569.

13. Tajima, *Kōrin-ha gashū dai ikkan*.

14. Kōno, "Kōrin to Tsugaru-ke," 6.

15. Yamane, *Konishi-ke kyūzō*, 144.

16. About one gram.

17. Yamane, *Konishi-ke kyūzō*, 182.

18. Yamane, 183.

19. Yamane, *Kōrin kenkyū ichi*, 54, 82–84.

20. Yamane, 79.

21. Chihō was Konishi Juichirō's adoptive mother.

22. The letter is dated to 1715 or 1716, the last years of Kōrin's life. It appears that he was not well at the time of writing. Yamane, *Kōrin kenkyū ichi*, 95–96.

23. Yamane, 109–37.

24. Dated to after 1709. Yamane, 89.

25. Yamane, *Konishi-ke kyūzō*, 182.

26. The same Katsu whom Kōrin raised under his roof from 1702 to 1706.

27. Kōrin's last residence at Shinmachi Nijōkudari, built in 1711.

28. One of Kōrin's illegitimate sons. Since Kōrin refers to Katsunojō as Juichirō's younger brother, he was born later, probably sometime after Kōrin's return to Kyoto from Edo around 1709. In Kōrin's will to his wife, Tayo, a woman named Aya is given as Katsunojō's mother. She also gave birth to another son, Saijirō. See Yamane, *Kōrin kenkyū ichi*, 6–7; and Yamane, "Zoku Kōrin to Nakamura Kuranosuke," 34.

29. This passage gives evidence that Katsunojō must have been quite young when Kōrin drafted this will in 1713. Kōrin effectively installed Juichirō as the manager of his estate until Katsunojō came of age.

30. The will is important because it explains how Nakamura Kuranosuke brokered the adoption of Kōrin's son Juichirō (formerly named Shinjirō) into the Konishi family. Konishi Hikokurō, Shinjirō's adopted father, like Kuranosuke was a silver mint official. The possibility of Kuranosuke's involvement was first raised by Fukui Rikichirō in 1915. See Fukui, "Kōrin no shusatsu ni tsuite."

31. Yamane, *Kōrin kenkyū ichi*, 36.

32. Kamimichi, "Kōrin kankei shiryō," 63.

33. Yamane, *Kōrin kenkyū ichi*, 95–96.

34. One *ken* is a length of slightly less than two meters.

35. This indicates that Kōrin still hoped these debts, already more than thirty years old in 1713, would be repaid someday.

36. It seems that Aya was allowed to live in a smaller house on the same property as Tayo.

37. In a later letter, Kōrin asked for Juichirō to return screens with paintings of chrysanthemums. The screens mentioned here may have been those works.

Kōrin instructed Juichirō to give the *wakizashi* and screen to his brother Katsunojō once he came of age. This clause is also mentioned in the will to Juichirō of the same year.

38. Here, Kōrin likely refers to the assortment of sketches, letters, and other documents that now constitute the Konishi Family Archive.

39. Yamane, *Konishi-ke kyūzō*, 149–50.

Epilogue

1. Yamane, "Hara Sankei kyūzō," 35, 41.

2. Aimi, "Fukae Roshū no funbo hakken wo megutte."

3. Nishimoto, "Hōitsu no Kōrin kenshō," 55. See, e.g., Yamane, *Sōtatsu to Kōrin*, 228; Kōno, *Ogata Kōrin*, 117; Yamane, *Kōrin kenkyū ichi*, 136; and Yamane, *Kōrin kenkyū ni*, 36, 119, 221, among others.

4. For example, it has been suggested that the first character of the name Soshin derives from that of Yamamoto Soken, presumably Kōrin's first painting teacher, indicating a master-pupil relationship. The validity of this claim remains inconclusive in the absence of documentary proof and significant stylistic correspondence between Soshin's ceramic pictures and the paintings by Soken and Shikō. See Aimi, "Watanabe Shikō to Kenzan," 66–71.

5. Feltens, "Sartorial Identity," 125–36.

6. On *Kōrin gafu*, see Keyes, *Ehon*, 148; and McKelway, *Silver Wind*, 78–79.

7. See Lee, "Watanabe Shikō's Irises," 63–67; and Guth, "Watanabe Shikō's Irises," 240–51.

8. No paintings of plants and insects by Kōrin are extant. Hōitsu, on the other hand, painted many works of this genre. This expression might also be a phrase that Bōsai adopted from Chinese art criticism. References to insects in relation to life-likeness are frequently found in poetry.

9. On Kamisaka Sekka's study of Kōrin and related artists, see, e.g., Tamamushi, *Rinpa to dezain sōshoku kazari*, 45, 73–75; see also Trinh, *Kamisaka Sekka*.

BIBLIOGRAPHY

Abe Tomoe. "Muromachi jidai ni okeru baika Jurō zu no imēji sekai." *Bijutsu kenkyū* 59 (October 2005): 125–45.

Aimi Kōu. "Ogata Kōrin narabi ni Ogata-ke no koto." *Shoga kottō zasshi* 85 (July 1915): 2–19.

——. "Kōrin shoki no shūsaku ga." *Yamato bunka* 19 (March 1956): 1–9.

——. "Kenzan Jūnikagetsu kachō uta-e." *Yamato bunka* 21 (October 1956): 23–33.

——. "Watanabe Shikō to Kenzan." *Yamato bunka* 23 (June 1957): 66–71.

——. "Fukae Roshū no funbo hakken wo megutte." *Yamato bunka* 31 (October 1959): 16–29.

——. "Rinpa sōdan." In *Aimi Kōu shū* 1, Nihon shoshigaku taikei 45 (1), 11–17. Musashimurayama-shi: Seishōdō Shoten, 1985.

——. "Kōetsu gaji no mondai." In *Aimi Kōu shū* 1, Nihon shoshigaku taikei 45 (1), 18–30. Musashimurayama-shi: Seishōdō Shoten, 1985.

——. "Kōrin azuma kudari kō (naka no ni)." *Yamato bunka* 33 (September 1960): 28–34.

——. "Daikyoan no nijū geijutsu." In *Aimi Kōu shū* 1, Nihon shoshigaku taikei 45 (1), 31–36. Musashimurayama-shi: Seishōdō Shoten, 1985.

——. "Hon'ami keizu no kōsatsu." In *Aimi Kōu shū* 1, Nihon shoshigaku taikei 45 (1), 37–43. Musashimurayama-shi: Seishōdō Shoten, 1985.

——. "Sōtatsu Fūjin Raijin to Myōkōji." In *Aimi Kōu shū* 1, Nihon shoshigaku taikei 45 (1), 44–49. Musashimurayama-shi: Seishōdō Shoten, 1985.

——. "Sōsetsu, Sōsetsu to Sōsen." In *Aimi Kōu shū* 1, Nihon shoshigaku taikei 45 (1), 63–78. Musashimurayama-shi: Seishōdō Shoten, 1985.

——. "Kōrin." In *Aimi Kōu shū* 1, Nihon shoshigaku taikei 45 (1), 101–64. Musashimurayama-shi: Seishōdō Shoten, 1985.

——. "Kōetsu Kōrin no koto." In *Aimi Kōu shū* 1, Nihon shoshigaku taikei 45 (1), 159–64. Musashimurayama-shi: Seishōdō Shoten, 1985.

——. "Ogata Kōrin no Ōishi Ryōga-zō." In *Aimi Kōu shū* 1, Nihon shoshigaku taikei 45 (1), 223–26. Musashimurayama-shi: Seishōdō Shoten, 1985.

——. "Tenka taihei no Kenzan." In *Aimi Kōu shū* 1, Nihon shoshigaku taikei 45 (1), 335–38. Musashimurayama-shi: Seishōdō Shoten, 1985.

——. "Hōitsu Shōnin nenpu kō." In *Aimi Kōu shū* 1, Nihon shoshigaku taikei 45 (1), 395–541. Musashimurayama-shi: Seishōdō Shoten, 1985.

——. "Hōitsu ryaku nenpu." In *Aimi Kōu shū* 1, Nihon shoshigaku taikei 45 (1), 543–47. Musashimurayama-shi: Seishōdō Shoten, 1985,

——. "Hōchū mandan." In *Aimi Kōu shū* 1, Nihon shoshigaku taikei 45 (1), 548–54. Musashimurayama-shi: Seishōdō Shoten, 1985.

Allan, Sarah. "The Identities of Taigong Wang in Zhou and Han Literature." *Monumenta Serica* 30 (January 1972): 57–99.

Alpers, Svetlana. "Ekphrasis and Aesthetic Attitudes in Vasari's Lives." *Journal of the Warburg and Courtauld Institutes* 23, no. 3/4 (July 1960): 190–215.

——. "Describe or Narrate? A Problem in Realistic Representation." *New Literary History* 8, no. 1 (October 1976): 15–41.

——. *The Art of Describing: Dutch Art of the Seventeenth Century.* Chicago: University of Chicago Press, 1983.

——. "Interpretation without Representation; or, The Viewing of Las Meninas." *Representations,* no. 1 (February 1983): 31–42.

Aoki Shizuko. "Ise monogatari kyūchūron josetsu: Ichijō Kanera to Sōgi to." *Joshidai bungaku kokubunhen* 37 (March 1986): 38–52.

Aoyagi Keisuke. "Tōfukumon'in Masako." *Shūbi* 4 (Summer 2012): 95–97.

Arakawa Masaaki. "Fujisan wo egaita hizen jiki." *Idemitsu bijutsukan kenkyū kiyō* 3 (1997): 21–39.

——. "Nihon tōki ni okeru uwanagashi no keifu: Sōshoku ishō toshite no yūyaku." *Idemitsu bijutsukan kenkyū kiyō* 4 (1998): 67–99.

——. "Hizen jiki to Hasshu gafu: Kokutani yōshiki ni okeru jinbutsu ishō no haikei." *Idemitsu bijutsukan kenkyū kiyō* 5 (1999): 161–89.

——. "Gayū no tō: Narutaki jidai no Kenzan yaki wo chūshin toshite." In *Kenzan no geijutsu to Kōrin,* 11–20. Tokyo: NHK Puromōshon, 2007.

——. "Narutaki jidai ni okeru Kenzan yaki no sakufū tenkai." *Idemitsu bijutsukan kenkyū kiyō* 13 (2007): 13–31.

——. "E-Karatsu Kaki mon sanjiko." *Kokka* 1388 (June 2011): 38–42.

Ariyoshi Tamotsu, Inaoka Kōji, and Shimazu Tadao, eds. *Kinsei no waka.* Waka bungaku kōza 8. Tokyo: Benseisha, 1994.

Arntzen, Sonja, and Moriyuki Ito, trans. *The Sarashina*

Diary: A Woman's Life in Eleventh-Century Japan. New York: Columbia University Press, 2014.

Asaoka Okisada. *Zōtei Koga bikō.* 4 vols. Kyoto: Shibunkaku Shuppan, 1970.

Asō Isoji and Fuji Akio, eds. *Taiyaku Saikaku zenshū.* Vol. 12. Tokyo: Meiji Shoin, 1974.

——. *Taiyaku Saikaku zenshū.* Vol. 4. Tokyo: Meiji Shoin, 1978.

Ban Kōkei. *Kinsei kijin den.* Tokyo: Iwanami Shoten, 2004.

Berry, Mary Elizabeth. *The Culture of Civil War in Kyoto.* Berkeley: University of California Press, 1994.

Blanchon, Flora, ed. *La question de l'art en Asie orientale. Collection Asie; Variation: Asies (Centre de recherche sur l'Extrême-Orient de Paris-Sorbonne).* Paris: Presses de l'Université Paris–Sorbonne, 2008.

Bowring, Richard. "The Ise Monogatari: A Short Cultural History." *Harvard Journal of Asiatic Studies* 52, no. 2 (December 1992): 401–80.

Brecher, W. Puck. "Kōetsumura: Of Rhythms and Reminiscence in Hon'ami Kōetsu's Commune." *Japan Review,* no. 22 (January 2010): 31–57.

Brinker, Helmut, Hiroshi Kanazawa, and Andreas Leisinger. "ZEN Masters of Meditation in Images and Writings." *Artibus Asiae* Supplementum 40 (January 1996): 3–384.

Brock, Karen L. "The Shogun's 'Painting Match.'" *Monumenta Nipponica* 50, no. 4 (December 1995): 433–84.

Brown, Kendall. "Shokado Shojo as 'Tea Painter.'" *Chanoyu Quarterly* 49 (1987): 7–40.

——. "Re-Presenting Teika's Flowers and Birds." In *Word in Flower: The Visualization of Classical Literature in Seventeenth-Century Japan,* 33–53. New Haven: Yale University Art Gallery, 1989.

Bush, Susan, and Christian F. Murck, eds. *Theories of the Arts in China.* Princeton, N.J.: Princeton University Press, 1983.

Bush, Susan, and Hsio-yen Shih, eds. *Early Chinese Texts on Painting.* Cambridge, Mass.: Harvard University Press, 1985.

Bussotti, Michela, and Jean-Pierre Drège, eds. *Chine-Europe: Histoires de livres.* Geneva: Droz, 2007.

Butler, Lee. *Emperor and Aristocracy in Japan, 1467–1680: Resilience and Renewal.* Harvard East Asian Monographs 209. Cambridge, Mass.: Harvard University Asia Center, 2002.

Cahill, James F. "The Six Laws and How to Read Them." *Ars Orientalis* 4 (January 1961): 372–81.

Carpenter, John. *Designing Nature: The Rinpa Aesthetic in Japanese Art.* New York: Metropolitan Museum of Art, 2012.

Carter, Steven D. "Three Poets at Yuyama: Sogi and Yuyama Sangin Hyakuin, 1491." *Monumenta Nipponica* 33, no. 3 (October 1978): 241–83.

Casal, U. A. "Japanese Art Lacquers." *Monumenta Nipponica* 15, no. 1/2 (April 1959): 1–11.

——. "The Lore of the Japanese Fan." *Monumenta Nipponica* 16, no. 1/2 (April 1960): 53–117.

Chadō Shiryōkan, ed. *Senke sadō ten Genroku ki no chanoyu.* Kyoto: Chadō Shiryōkan, 1980.

Chiba Yutaka. "Kenzan Shōgoin kama Kyōto daigaku byōin kōnai no hakkutsu chōsa kara." In *Kōrin dezain,* 192–97. Kyoto: Tankōsha, 2005.

Chino Kaori. *Emaki Ise monogatari-e.* Nihon no bijutsu 301. Tokyo: Shibundō, 1991.

——. "Yamato-e no keisei to sono imi." In *Nihon no bijutsu—geijutsu gaku fōramu* 5, 104–20. Tokyo: Keisō Shobō, 1994.

Chizawa Teiji. "Kōrin no hito to geijutsu." In *Kōrin,* 8–17. Tokyo: Nihon Keizai Shinbunsha, 1959.

——. *Kōrin.* Nihon no bijutsu 53. Tokyo: Shibundō, 1970.

——. "Rinpa no sōsetsu." In *Sōritsu hyakunen kinen tokubetsuten Rinpa,* 3–15. Tokyo: Tōkyō Kokuritsu Hakubutsukan, 1972.

Chizawa Teiji and Yamaji Shōzō. "Kiitsu ga no tenbō." *Museum* 261 (December 1972): 4–18.

Clark, Sue Cassidy. "Ogata Korin: Personal Visions of Classic Traditions." M.A. thesis, Columbia University, 1989.

Cort, Louise Allison. "A Tosa Potter in Edo." In *The Artist as Professional in Japan,* 103–12. Stanford, Calif.: Stanford University Press, 2004.

Cosgrove, Denis E., and Stephen Daniels, eds. *The Iconography of Landscape: Essays on the Symbolic Representation, Design, and Use of Past Environments.* Cambridge Studies in Historical Geography 9. Cambridge: Cambridge University Press, 1988.

Croissant, Doris. *Sōtatsu und der Sōtatsu-Stil: Untersuchungen zu Repertoire, Ikonographie und Ästhetik der Malerei des Tawaraya Sōtatsu (um 1600–1640).* Wiesbaden: F. Steiner, 1978.

——, ed. *Splendid Impressions: Japanese Secular Painting, 1400–1900, in the Museum of East Asian Art, Cologne.* Leiden: Hotei, 2011.

Cunningham, Michael R. "Byōbu: The Art of the Japanese Screen." *Bulletin of the Cleveland Museum of Art* 71, no. 7 (September 1984): 223–32.

Deal, William E. *Handbook to Life in Medieval and Early Modern Japan.* New York: Oxford University Press, 2007.

Dei, Luigi, Andreas Ahle, Piero Baglioni, Daniela Dini, and Enzo Ferroni. "Green Degradation Products of Azurite in Wall Paintings: Identification and Conservation Treatment." *Studies in Conservation* 43, no. 2 (January 1998): 80–88.

D'Etcheverry, Charo Beatrice. *Love After the Tale of Genji: Rewriting the World of the Shining Prince.* Harvard East Asian Monographs 286. Cambridge, Mass.: Harvard University Asia Center, 2007.

Dobbins, James C. "The Biography of Shinran: Apotheosis of a Japanese Buddhist Visionary." *History of Religions* 30, no. 2 (November 1990): 179–96.

Dore, R. P. "Talent and the Social Order in Tokugawa Japan." *Past and Present,* no. 21 (April 1962): 60–72.

Dunn, Michael. *Traditional Japanese Design: Five Tastes.* New York: Japan Society and Abrams, 2001.

Eck, Caroline van, and Stijn Bussels, eds. *Theatricality in Early Modern Art and Architecture.* Chichester, West

Sussex: Wiley-Blackwell, 2011.

Egami Yasushi. "Heike nōkyō to Sōtatsu." In *Kōetsu sho Sōtatsu kingindei-e kenkyūhen*, 121–42. Tokyo: Asahi Shinbunsha, 1978.

Emura Tomoko. "Kōrin-ga ni okeru nō no eikyō ni tsuite: Seikadō bunko bijutsukan shozō Ubune zu wo chūshin ni." *Bijutsushi kenkyū* 34 (December 1996): 19–38.

——. "Ogata Kōrin no suiboku jinbutsuga no gafū seiritsu ni tsuite: Yuima zu wo chūshin ni." *Kajima bijutsu zaidan nenpō* 18 (2000): 413–25.

——. "Kōrin no maki-e seisaku to kaiga ni tsuite." *Bijutsushi* 55, no. 1 (October 2005): 111–24.

——. "Kōrin to mon: Kōrin no ishōsei to Kōrin kankei shiryō." In *Kokuhō Kakitsubata zu: Kōrin Genroku no isai*, 96–108. Tokyo: Nezu Bijutsukan, 2005.

——. "Ogata Kōrin no kaiga gakushū to gafū keisei ni tsuite." *Musashino bijutsu daigaku kenkyū kiyō* 36 (2005): 5–14.

——. "Neoi no bungen, egaki he no michi: Ogata Kōrin wo torimaku kankyō to sakuhin seisaki ni tsuite." *Bijutsu kenkyū* 392 (September 2007): 270–90.

——. "Ogata Kōrin no Edo zaijū to gafū tenkan: Frīa bijutsukan shozō Hakubai zu byōbu wo chūshin ni." *Bijutsu kenkyū* 421 (March 2017): 183–202.

Endō Motoko. "Yamamoto Soken hitsu Jūnikagetsu kachō zu byōbu no seisaku jijō: San Furanshisuko Ajia bijutsukan bon ni okeru Konoe Iehiro no yakuwari." *Museum* 597 (August 2005): 7–25.

Endō Moto'o. "Chūsei ni okeru kōgeishiteki shomondai (jō)." *Gasetsu* 17 (May 1938): 467–74.

——. "Chūsei ni okeru kōgeishiteki shomondai (ge)." *Gasetsu* 18 (June 1938): 502–15.

Etō Shun. *Sadō bijutsu zenshū* 12. Edited by Sen Sōshitsu. Kyoto: Tankōsha, 1973.

Faure, Bernard. *The Red Thread: Buddhist Approaches to Sexuality*. Princeton, N.J.: Princeton University Press, 1998.

Feltens, Frank. "Ogata Kōrin (1658–1716) and the Possibilities of Painting in Early Modern Japan." Ph.D. diss., Columbia University, 2016.

——. "Sartorial Identity: Early Modern Japanese Textile Patterns and the Afterlife of Ogata Kōrin." *Ars Orientalis* 47 (2017): 117–57.

——. "Ogata Kōrin: Stumbling into His Artistic Legacy." *Impressions* 40 (2019): 163–83.

Fenollosa, Ernest F. *Epochs of Chinese and Japanese Art: An Outline History of East Asiatic Design*. Berkeley, Calif.: Stone Bridge Press, 2007.

Fischer, Felice. *The Arts of Hon'ami Kōetsu, Renaissance Master*. Philadelphia: Philadelphia Museum of Art, 2001.

Fischer, Felice, and Kyoko Kinoshita, eds. *Ink and Gold: Art of the Kano*. Philadelphia: Philadelphia Museum of Art, 2015.

Fleming, Stuart. "Pigments in History: The Growth of the Traditional Palette." *Archaeology* 37, no. 4 (July 1984): 68–69.

Flueckiger, Peter Andrew. "Poetry, Culture, and Social Harmony in Eighteenth-Century Japanese Literary Thought: The Sorai School and Its Critics." Ph.D. diss., Columbia University, 2003.

Forbes, Edward W. "Materials Used in Japanese Painting." *Bulletin of the Fogg Art Museum* 1, no. 3 (March 1932): 48–52.

Ford, Barbara B. "The Self-Portrait of Sesson Shūkei." *Archives of Asian Art* 35 (1982): 6–26.

——. "A Study of the Painting of Sesson Shūkei." Ph.D. diss., Columbia University, 1982.

——. "The Arts of Japan." *Metropolitan Museum of Art Bulletin* 45, no. 1 (July 1987): 1–56.

Fujiki Kayoko. "Machishū tesarugaku ni tsuite." *Shiron* 13 (March 1965): 46–62.

Fujita Tsuneyo, ed. *Kōkan bijutsu shiryō zokuhen*. Vol. 2. Tokyo: Kōkanbijutsu Shiryō Zokuhen Kankōkai, 1985.

Fukui Rikichirō. "Kōrin kō 1." *Geibun* 6, no. 6 (June 1915): 61–90.

——. "Kōrin kō 2." *Geibun* 6, no. 7 (July 1915): 65–99.

——. "Kōrin kō 3." *Geibun* 6, no. 8 (August 1915): 42–79.

——. "Meiji izen ni okeru Sōtatsu Kōrin ga no kanshō ichi." *Geibun* 7 (1920): 73–106.

——. "Sōtatsu to Kōrin." In *Rikichirō bijutsushi ronshū jō*, 109–42. Tokyo: Chūō Kōron Bijutsu Shuppan, 1998.

——. "Kōrin no shi toshite no Yamamoto Soken." In *Rikichirō bijutsushi ronshū ge*, 133–49. Tokyo: Chūō Kōron Bijutsu Shuppan, 2000.

——. "Kōrin no shusatsu ni tsuite." In *Rikichirō bijutsushi ronshū ge*, 176–84. Tokyo: Chūō Kōron Bijutsu Shuppan, 2000.

——. "Kōrin no yume." In *Rikichirō bijutsushi ronshū ge*, 197–209. Tokyo: Chūō Kōron Bijutsu Shuppan, 2000.

——. "Ogata Kōrin no shōgai ni tsuite." In *Rikichirō bijutsushi ronshū ge*, 84–102. Tokyo: Chūō Kōron Bijutsu Shuppan, 2000.

Furuta Ryō. *Tawaraya Sōtatsu: Rinpa no so to shinjitsu*. Tokyo: Heibonsha Shinsho, 2010.

——. "Waves at Matsushima and Mount Fuji." In *Sōtatsu*, 251–52. Washington, D.C.: Freer Gallery of Art and Arthur M. Sackler Gallery, 2015.

Furuya Aiko. "Kōrin mon'yō no seiritsu to tenkai: Kosode moyō wo chūshin ni." *Fukushoku bigaku*, no. 33 (September 2001): 33–47.

Gage, John. "Black and White and Red All Over." *RES: Anthropology and Aesthetics*, no. 16 (October 1988): 51–53.

——. *Colour and Meaning: Art, Science and Symbolism*. London: Thames and Hudson, 1999.

——. *Color in Art*. World of Art. New York: Thames and Hudson, 2006.

Genjō Masayoshi. "Kōetsu maki-e." In *Kōgei to Rinpa kankaku no tenkai*, 120–28. Rinpa Bijutsukan 4. Tokyo: Shūeisha, 1993.

——. "'Honchō Gashi' and Painting Programs: Case Studies of Nijō Castle's Ninomaru Palace and Nagoya Castle's Honmaru Palace." *Ars Orientalis* 27 (January 1997): 67–97.

Gerhart, Karen M. *The Eyes of Power: Art and Early Tokugawa Authority*. Honolulu: University of Hawai'i Press, 1999.

——. "Kano Tan'yū and Hōrin Jōshō: Patronage and Artistic Practice." *Monumenta Nipponica* 55, no. 4 (December 2000): 483–508.

——. "Issues of Talent and

Training in the Seventeenth-Century Kano Workshop." *Ars Orientalis* 31 (January 2001): 103–28.

Goff, Janet Emily. *Noh Drama and the Tale of Genji: The Art of Allusion in Fifteen Classical Plays.* Princeton Library of Asian Translations. Princeton, N.J.: Princeton University Press, 1991.

Gonse, Louis. *L'Art japonais.* 2 vols. Paris: A. Quantin, 1883.

Goshima Kuniharu. "Bunmei nenkan no dairi te-sarugaku ni tsuite." *Geinōshi kenkyū,* April 1991, 15–37.

Gotō Bijutsukan, ed. *Kōetsu: Momoyama no koten.* Tokyo: Gotō Bijutsukan, 2013.

Graham, Patricia Jane. *Tea of the Sages: The Art of Sencha.* Honolulu: University of Hawai'i Press, 1998.

Guth, Christine. "Watanabe Shikō's Irises." *Bulletin of the Cleveland Museum of Art* 71, no. 7 (September 1984): 240–51.

——. "Varied Trees: An I'nen Seal Screen in the Freer Gallery of Art." *Archives of Asian Art* 39 (January 1986): 48–61.

Hagoromo Kokusai Daigaku Nihon Bunka Kenkyūjo, ed. *Ise monogatari emaki ehon taisei.* Tokyo: Kadokawa Gakugei Shuppan, 2007.

——, ed. *Sōtatsu Ise monogatari zu shikishi.* Tokyo: Shibunkaku Shuppan, 2013.

Haino Akio. *Ogawa Haritsu: Edo kōgei no iki.* Nihon no bijutsu 389. Tokyo: Shibundō, 1998.

Hamachiyo Kiyoshi. *Renga: Kenkyū to shiryō.* Tokyo: Ōfūsha, 1988.

Hamada Seiryō. "Ogata Kōrin hitsu Baika zu byōbu ni tsuite." *Kokka* 201 (February 1907): 569.

Hatakeyama Kinenkan, ed. *Rinpa yoshū aigan.* Tokyo: Hatakeyama Kinenkan, 2011.

Hatano Yukihiko. "Kōetsu no sho wo chūshin toshite Momoyama Edo no sho wo miru." In *Kōetsu no sho: Keichō Genna Kan'ei no meihitsu,* 276–82. Osaka: Ōsaka Shiritsu Bijutsukan, 1990.

Hayashi Kōhei. "Azuma kudari kankei shōdan." In *Ise monogatari no hyōgenshi,* 310–21. Tokyo: Kasama Shoin, 2004.

——. "Ise monogatari no dokusharon." In *Ise monogatari no hyōgenshi,* 43–59. Tokyo: Kasama Shoin, 2004.

Hayashi Susumu. "Zuhan kaisetsu." *Yamato bunka* 81 (March 1989): 43–59.

——. *Nihon Kinsei kaiga no zuzōgaku: Shukō to shin'i.* Tokyo: Yagi Shoten, 2000.

——. "Masuda-ke bon Sōtatsu Ise monogatari zu shikishi no seiritsu." In *Sōtatsu Ise monogatari zu shikishi,* 163–77. Tokyo: Shibunkaku Shuppan, 2013.

——. "Sōtatsu o kenshō suru: Sōtatsu no kyojūchi oyobi Sōtatsu no shakaiteki kiso ni tsuite." *Kōbe daigaku bijutsushi kenkyūkai bijutsushi ronshū* 13 (February 2013): 17–33.

Hayashiya Seizō. "Kōetsu Kenzan no tōgei." *Museum* 260 (November 1972): 13–23.

——. *Ninsei Kenzan.* Nihon no tōji 12. Tokyo: Chūō Kōronsha, 1974.

——. *Ninsei.* Nihon no bijutsu 138. Tokyo: Shibundō, 1977.

——. *Chanoyu: Japanese Tea Ceremony.* New York: Japan Society, 1979.

——. "Kenzan yaki ni tsuite." In *Kenzan no tōgei,* 114–18. Tokyo: Gotō Bijutsukan, 1987.

Hayashiya Tatsusaburō. *Cha.* Dentō geijutsu kōza 6. Tokyo: Kawade Shobō, 1955.

——. *Kōetsu.* Tokyo: Daiichi Hōki Shuppan Kabushiki Gaisha, 1964.

——. *Machishū.* Tokyo: Chūō Kōronsha, 1964.

——. *Machishū: Kyōto ni okeru "shimin" keiseishi.* Chūō shinsho 59. Tokyo: Chūō Kōronsha, 1964.

——. *Cha no bijutsu.* Nihon No Bijutsu 15. Tokyo: Heibonsha, 1965.

——. *Rekishi, Kyōto, geinō.* Tokyo: Asahi Shinbunsha, 1969.

——. *Chūsei no Nihon.* Vol. 3. Shinshū kyōdai Nihon shi. Osaka: Sōgensha, 1970.

——, ed. *Kodai chūsei geijutsuron.* Nihon shisō taikei 23. Tokyo: Iwanami Shoten, 1973.

——. *Suminokura Sōan.* Asahi hyōdensen 19. Tokyo: Asahi Shinbunsha, 1978.

——. *Kyōto bunka no zahyō.* Kyoto: Jinbun Shoin, 1985.

——. *"Za" no kankyō.* Nihon geinō shiron 1. Kyoto: Tankōsha, 1986.

——. *"Te" no geijutsu.* Nihon geinō shiron 3. Kyoto: Tankōsha, 1986.

——. *Kindai no mosaku.* Nihon shi ronshū 6. Tokyo: Iwanami Shoten, 1988.

Hickman, Money L., ed. *Japan's Golden Age: Momoyama.* New Haven: Yale University Press in association with Dallas Museum of Art, 1996.

Hida Kōzō. "Genroku jidai no shomin geinō." In *Kamigata no bunka Genroku no bungaku to geinō,* 139–88. Kamigata bunko 6. Osaka: Izumi Shoin, 1989.

Hirayama Ikuo, Kayama Matazō, and Murashige Yasushi, eds. *Sōtatsu Kōrin.* Suibokuga no kyoshō 6. Tokyo: Kōdansha, 1994.

Hiroshima Susumu. "Saikaku to Ise monogatari." In *Ise Monogatari: Kyōju no tenkai,* 317–33. Tokyo: Chikurinsha, 2010.

Hofmann, Alexander. *Performing/Painting in Tokugawa Japan: Artistic Practice and Socio-Economic Functions of Sekiga (Paintings on the Spot).* Hammonds Foundation Monograph Series on Asian Art. Berlin: Reimer, 2011.

Hoga Koshiro. "Kakemono no rekishi." In *Sadō shūkin,* 9:81–89. Tokyo: Shōgakukan, 1984.

Honda Mitsuko. "Tawaraya no ōgi-e: Kyū Hara-ke bon senmen chirashi byōbu wo miru." *Shūbi* 7 (Spring 2013): 38–49.

Hong Sŏn-p'yo. *Chōsen ōchō no kaiga to Nihon: Sōtatsu, Taiga, Jakuchū mo mananda ringoku no bi.* Osaka: Yomiuri Shinbun Ōsaka Honsha, 2008.

Hori, Sachiko Yasunaka. "The Thirty-Six Immortal Poets of Ogata Korin and the Rimpa Artists." M.A. thesis, Columbia University, 1983.

Horiguchi Yasuo. "Te-sarugaku Shibuya no nihyakunen zen." *Geinōshi kenkyū* 41 (April 1973): 1–11.

——. "Te-sarugaku Shibuya no nihyakunen go." *Geinōshi kenkyū* 43 (October 1973): 27–39.

——. "Shibuya ato'oi (te-sarugaku)." *Joshidai bungaku kokubunhen* 26 (February 1975): 44–58.

Horiuchi Yūko. "Sōtatsu-ha no Genji-e: Kogamen shūgō keishiki byōbu ni okeru bamen kōseihō wo chūshin ni." In *Rinpa daiyonkan jinbutsu,* 246–49. Kyoto: Shikōsha, 1991.

Horton, H. Mack. "Renga Unbound: Performative Aspects of Japanese Linked

Verse." *Harvard Journal of Asiatic Studies* 53, no. 2 (December 1993): 443–512.

Hosono Masanobu. "Kakitsubata zu byōbu." *Kobijutsu* 39 (December 1972): 42–45.

Hyōgo Kenritsu Rekishi Hakubutsukan, ed. *Kano Einō: Sono tasai naru gagyō.* Himeji-shi: Hyōgo Kenritsu Rekishi Hakubutsukan, 2004.

Ichihara Sunao. *Ise monogatari kaishakuron.* Tokyo: Kazama Shobō, 2001.

Ichikawa Akira. "Kano Eikei hitsu Jūnikagetsu kai zu byōbu ni tsuite." *Suzaku* 23 (2011): 63–72.

Idemitsu Bijutsukan, ed. *Ninsei Kenzan: Kyō no kōgei.* Tokyo: Idemitsu Bijutsukan, 2014.

Igarashi Kōichi. "Einō sakuhin no seisaku nendai." *Jinkai* 11 (1999): 3–23.

——. "Kano Eikei no kenkyū." *Kajima bijutsu zaidan nenpō* 18 (2000): 11–23.

——. "Kano Einō to Nijō-ke." *Bijutsushi ronsō* 21 (2005): 23–47.

——. "Sanbōin Kakutei to Sōtatsu." *Kokka* 1319 (September 2005): 32–35.

——. "Kenzan no ichikiroku." In *Kenzan no geijutsu to Kōrin,* 185–87. Tokyo: NHK Puromōshon, 2007.

——. "Kōetsu to Sōtatsu wo tsunagu sen." *Jinkai* 18 (2007): 32–39.

——. "Omuro gyoki no naka no Ogata Kenzan to Kano Eikei." *Jinkai* 20 (2009): 3–10.

——. *Kinsei Kyōto gadan no nettowāku: Chūmonnushi to eshi.* Tokyo: Yoshikawa Kōbunkan, 2010.

——. *Kyō-Gano sandai ikinokori no monogatari: Sanraku, Sansetsu, Einō to Kujō Yukiie.* Tokyo: Yoshikawa Kōbunkan, 2012.

——. "Sōtatsu Ise monogatari zu shikishi no jintekina nettowāku." In *Sōtatsu Ise monogatari zu shikishi,* 156–62. Tokyo: Shibunkaku Shuppan, 2013.

Ihara Hanae, Ōyama Kazuya, Kumagai Kazum, et al. "Nakanoin Michishige 'Miraiki Uchūgin Kikigaki' Honkoku (1)." *Kyoto daigaku kokubungaku ronsō* 21 (April 2009): 47–56.

Ihara Saikaku. *Kōshoku ichidai otoko.* Edited by Yokoyama Shigeru. Tokyo: Iwanami Bunko, 2008.

Iijima Isamu. "Gyobutsu Senmen chirashi byōbu ni tsuite." *Museum* 4 (July 1951): 19–21.

Ijichi Tetsuo, ed. *Rengaron shinshū.* Vol. 2. Tokyo: Koten Bunko, 1960.

Ikawa Jōkei. "Shōkadō Shōjō no kōyū kankei." *Bukkyō daigaku kenkyū kiyō* 52 (March 1968): 1–15.

Ikegami, Eiko. *Bonds of Civility: Aesthetic Networks and the Political Origins of Japanese Culture.* Cambridge: Cambridge University Press, 2005

Inada Toshinori. "Hatakeyama shōsakutei shika no shohon to seiritsu ni tsuite." *Waka bungaku kenkyū* 23 (June 1968): 33–43.

Inoue Muneo. *Chūsei kadanshi no kenkyū Muromachi zenki.* Tokyo: Kazama Shobō, 1961.

——. *Chūsei kadanshi no kenkyū Muromachi kōki.* Tokyo: Meiji Shoin, 1987.

Ishikawa Ken Bijutsukan, ed. *Sōsetsu Sōsetsu ten: Sōtatsu to Kōrin o tsunagu hitobito.* Kanazawa: Ishikawa Ken Bijutsukan, 1975.

Ishikawa Kenritsu Bijutsukan, ed. *Tawaraya Sōtatsu to Rinpa.* Kanazawa: Ishikawa Kenritsu Bijutsukan, 2013.

Ishikawa Tsunehiko. *Shūi gusō kochū jō.* Chūsei no bungaku. Tokyo: Miyai Shoten, 1983.

——. *Shūi gusō kochū chū.* Chūsei no bungaku. Tokyo: Miyai Shoten, 1986.

——. *Shūi gusō kochū ge.* Chūsei no bungaku. Tokyo: Miyai Shoten, 1989.

Ishizuka Seiga. "Kiba Fuyuki-ke kō." *Kokka* 889 (April 1966): 29–39.

Itabashi Kuritsu Bijutsukan. *Karasumaru Mitsuhiro to Tawaraya Sōtatsu.* Tokyo: Itabashi Kuritsu Bijutsukan, 1982.

Itō Shingo. "Kinsei shoki no kugeshū to otogi." *Denshō bungaku kenkyū* 58 (April 2009): 1–11.

Itō Toshiko. "Den Kōetsu hitsu utaibon to Kanze Kokusetsu." *Kokka* 922 (June 1970): 5–22.

——. *Kōetsu shikishi harimaze byōbu.* Tokyo: Heibonsha, 1974.

——. "Kōetsu no shoseki." In *Kōetsu sho Sōtatsu kingindei-e kenyūhen,* 91–120. Tokyo: Asahi Shinbunsha, 1978.

——. *Ise monogatari-e.* Tokyo: Kadokawa Shoten, 1984.

——. *Tegami wo yomu: Kan'ei bunkajintachi.* Tokyo: Heibonsha, 1998.

Itō Yoshiaki. "Kenzan yaki no sōzō he no apurōchi." In *Kōrin dezain,* 144–57. Kyoto: Tankōsha, 2005.

Izumi Yoshinaga, ed. *Edo jidai shomin bunko: Edo shomin no seikatsu wo shiru.* Tokyo: Ōzorasha, 2012.

Jansen, Marius B. *China in the Tokugawa World.* Cambridge, Mass.: Harvard University Press, 1992.

Jōichi Mariko. *Muromachi suibokuga to Gozan bungaku.* Kyoto: Shibunkaku Shuppan, 2012.

Jungmann, Burglind. *Painters as Envoys: Korean Inspiration in Eighteenth-Century Japanese Nanga.* Princeton, N.J.: Princeton University Press, 2004.

Kagotani Machiko. *Geinōshi no naka no Honganji: Nō, kyōgen, chanoyu, hana no bunkashi.* Kyoto: Jishōsha Shuppan, 2005.

Kakimoto Mutsuo. "Bashō no azuma kudari: Ise monogatari no zanshō." In *Ise monogatari: kyōju no tenkai,* 288–316. Tokyo: Chikurinsha, 2010.

Kamei-Dyche, Andrew T. "The History of Books and Print Culture in Japan: The State of the Discipline." *Book History* 14 (January 2011): 270–304.

Kamens, Edward. "The Past in the Present: Fujiwara Teika and the Traditions of Japanese Poetry." In *Word in Flower: The Visualization of Classical Literature in Seventeenth-Century Japan,* 16–31. New Haven: Yale University Art Gallery, 1989.

——. *Utamakura, Allusion, and Intertextuality in Traditional Japanese Poetry.* New Haven: Yale University Press, 1997.

Kamimichi Setsuko. "Kōrin kankei shiryō: Nijō-ke nainai gobansho hinamiki shōroku." *Yamato bunka* 33 (September 1960): 43–66.

——. "Kōrin shokan." *Yamato bunka* 33 (September 1960): 35–37.

Kanazawa Hiroshi. "Kanzan Jittoku zu." *Kobijutsu* 27 (September 1969): 33–44.

Kanechiku Nobuyuki. "Nakanoin Michishige no 'Shūi gusō' chūshaku." *Kokubungaku kenkyū* 84 (October 1984): 54–65.

Kaneko Kinjirō. *Sōgi renga kochū*. Chūsei bungei sōsho 1. Hiroshima: Hiroshima Chūsei Bungei Kenkyūkai, 1965.

Kano Hiroyuki. "Edo ni okeru Rinpa no juyō to tenkai." In *Hōitsu to Edo Rinpa*, 5–12. Rinpa bijutsukan 3. Tokyo: Shūeisha, 1993.

——. "Rinpa no yūmoa kankaku." In *Kōrin to Kamigata Rinpa*, 112–20. Rinpa bijutsukan 2. Tokyo: Shūeisha, 1993.

——. "Rinpa to shasei." In *Kōgei to Rinpa kankaku no tenkai*, 101–8. Rinpa bijutsukan 4. Tokyo: Shūeisha, 1993.

——. *Hyūman, imēji wareware ha ningenwo donoyōni hyōgen shite kita no ka?* Kyoto: Kyōto Kokuritsu Hakubutsukan, 2001.

——. *Kōrin geijutsu no kisō: Konishi-ke kyūzō shiryō wo chūshin ni*. Nihon no bijutsu 462. Tokyo: Shibundō, 2004.

——. *Edo kaiga no futsugōna shinjitsu*. Chikuma Sensho. Tokyo: Chikuma Shobō, 2010.

Kano Hiroyuki, Okudaira Shunroku, Katagiri Yayoi, and Kimura Shigekazu. *Kōrin to Kamigata Rinpa*. Rinpa bijutsukan 2. Tokyo: Shūeisha, 1993.

Kano Hiroyuki, Okudaira Shunroku, and Nakabe Yoshitaka. *Sōtatsu to Rinpa no genryū*. Rinpa bijutsukan 1. Tokyo: Shūeisha, 1993.

Kasashima Tadayuki. "Sōtatsu Ise monogatari zu shikishi wo megutte: Shinshiryō kara no hitotsu shiron." *Idemitsu bijutsukan kenkyū kiyō* 12 (2007): 107–22.

Kashiwagi Mari. "Ogata Kōrin Kenzan gassaku sabi-e shōkin zu kadozara." *Kokka* 1324 (February 2006): 29–31.

Katagiri Yayoi. "Kakefuku monogatari-e no jidai." In *Kōrin to Kamigata Rinpa*, 101–11. Rinpa bijutsukan 2. Tokyo: Shūeisha, 1993.

Katagiri Yōichi. *Ise monogatari no kenkyū kenykūhen*. Tokyo: Meiji Shoin, 1968.

——. *Ise monogatari no kenkyū shiryōhen*. Tokyo: Meiji Shoin, 1969.

——. *Ise monogatari no shinkenkyū*. Tokyo: Meiji Shoin, 1987.

——. "Genroku jidai no Ise monogatari." In *Kamigata no bunka Genroku no bungaku to geinō*, 113–38. Kamigata bunko 6. Osaka: Izumi Shoin, 1989.

Katagiri Yōichi and Yamamoto Tokurō, eds. *Ise monogatari kochūshaku taisei*. Vol. 4. Tokyo: Kasama Shoin, 2009.

——, eds. *Ise monogatari kochūshaku taisei*. Vol. 5. Tokyo: Kasama Shoin, 2010.

Katō Etsuko. "Chūsei yamato-e ni okeru kaboku hyōgen no kenkyū: Idemitsu bijutsukan zō Shiki kaboku zu byōbu ni tsuite." *Kajima bijutsu kenkyū* 28 (2011): 108–17.

Katō Hiroko. "Kano Tan'yū shasei ron: Chōjū to jinbutsu wo chūshin ni." *Kokka* 1386 (April 2011): 5–18.

——. "Noda Tōmin hitsu Chōrui shasei zu: Ogata Kōrin hitsu chōrui shasei zu to no kankei." *Bijutsushi* 162 (March 2007): 338–55.

Katsura Matasaburō. "Ninsei to banshū Hayashida yaki." *Tōsetsu* 186 (September 1968): 17–20.

Katz, Janice. "Collecting and Patronage of Art in Seventeenth Century Japan: The Maeda Daimyo." Ph.D. diss., Princeton University, 2004.

——, ed. *Beyond Golden Clouds: Japanese Screens from the Art Institute of Chicago and the Saint Louis Art Museum*. Chicago: Art Institute of Chicago; and St. Louis, Mo.: Saint Louis Art Museum, 2009.

Kawada Masayuki. "Sōtatsu Ise monogatari zu shikishi no genjō." In *Sōtatsu Ise monogatari zu shikishi*, 149–55. Tokyo: Shibunkaku Shuppan, 2013.

——. "Sōtatsu Ise monogatari zu shikishi no kashoku gihō to kōzu." In *Sōtatsu Ise monogatari zu shikishi*, 178–98. Tokyo: Shibunkaku Shuppan, 2013.

Kawahara Masahiko. *Kyōyaki*. Tōji taikei 48. Tokyo: Heibonsha, 1974.

——. *Kenzan*. Nihon no bijutsu 154. Tokyo: Shibundō, 1979.

Kawai Masatomo. "Kōrin hitsu Shiki kusabana zukan ni tsuite." In *Rinpa kaiga zenshū Kōrin-ha ichi*, 31–35. Tokyo: Nihon Keizai Shinbunsha, 1979.

——. "Sōtatsu Kōrin-ha no suibokuga." In *Rinpa daiyonkan jinbutsu*, 250–54. Kyoto: Shikōsha, 1991.

——. "Kaiga to ōcho bunka no shiten kara." In *Kokuhō Kakitsubata zu byōbu: Hozon shūri shunkō kinen*, 98–114. Tokyo: Nezu Bijutsukan, 2005.

——. "Ogata Kōrin: Sono geijutsu no shimesu mono." In *Kokuhō Kakitsubata zu: Kōrin Genroku no isai*, 74–83. Tokyo: Nezu Bijutsukan, 2005.

Kawasaki Hiro. "Sagabon Ise monogatari no sashi-e sakusha ni tsuite." *Kokka* 1258 (August 2000): 26–30.

Keene, Donald, trans. *The Narrow Road to Oku*. New York: Kodansha USA, 1997.

——. *Essays in Idleness*. New York: Columbia University Press, 1998.

Keyes, Roger S. *Ehon: The Artist and the Book in Japan*. [New York]: New York Public Library; and Seattle: University of Washington Press, 2006.

Kichizawa Chū. "Shōkadō Shōjō hitsu Kamo no Chōmei-zō." *Kokka* 917 (August 1968): 33.

Kimborough, Keller, and Satoko Shimazaki, eds. *Publishing the Stage: Print and Performance in Early Modern Japan*. Boulder: University of Colorado Center for Asian Studies, 2011.

Kim Jeong Ah. "Sōtatsu-ha Ise monogatari-e shikishi no kōsatsu." *Bijutsushi* 139 (February 1996): 12–30.

Kimura Shigekazu. "Nakamura Hōchū ni tsuite." In *Kōrin to Kamigata Rinpa*, 121–30. Rinpa bijutsukan 2. Tokyo: Shūeisha, 1993.

Kinoshita, Kyoko. "The Advent of Movable-Type Printing: The Early Keichō Period and Kyoto Cultural Circles." In *The Arts of Hon'ami Kōetsu, Renaissance Master*, 56–73. Philadelphia: Philadelphia Museum of Art, 2001.

Kirihata Ken. "Hinagata bon ni miru Kōrin mon'yō: Funpon toshite no hinagata." *Ōtemae joshi daigaku ronshū* 29 (1995): 69–84.

Kita, Sandy. "The Bulls of Chōmyōji: A Joint Work by Sotatsu and Mitsuhiro." *Monumenta Nipponica* 47, no. 4 (December 1992): 495–519.

Kitagawa, Joseph M. "The Career of Maitreya, with Special Reference to Japan." *History of Religions* 21, no. 2 (November 1981): 107–25.

Kitakōji Ken. "Sakai Hōitsu jihitsu kushū Keikyokan kusō ni tsuite." *Museum* 261 (December 1972): 19–23.

Klein, Bettina, and Carolyn Wheelwright. "Japanese Kinbyōbu: The Gold-Leafed Folding Screens of the Muromachi Period (1333–1573); Parts II–IV." *Artibus Asiae* 45, no. 2/3 (January 1984): 101–73.

Klein, Susan Blakeley. "Allegories of Desire: Kamakura Period Commentaries and the Noh." Ph.D. diss., Cornell University, 1994.

——. *Allegories of Desire: Esoteric Literary Commentaries of Medieval Japan.* Harvard-Yenching Institute Monograph Series 55. Cambridge, Mass: Harvard University Asia Center for the Harvard-Yenching Institute, 2002.

Knowlton, Helen M. "The Painting of Landscape." *Modern Art* 4, no. 1 (January 1896): 11–15.

Kobayashi Seki. *Nōgaku daijiten.* Tokyo: Chikuma Shobō, 2012.

Kobayashi Tadashi. "Tawaraya Sōri ni tsuite." *Museum,* no. 260 (November 1972): 4–12.

——. "Tawaraya Sōtatsu shita-e Hon'ami Kōetsu sho Tsuru zu shita-e waka shokan." *Kobijutsu* 39 (December 1972): 38–41.

——. "Tawaraya kōbōron: Hōgen Heiji monogatari senmenga wo chūshin ni shite." In *Rinpa kaiga zenshū Sōtatsu-ha ichi,* 61–67. Tokyo: Nihon Keizai Shinbunsha, 1977.

——. *Edo kaiga shiron.* Tokyo: Ruri Shobō, 1983.

——. *Sumi-e no fu: Nihon no suiboku gakatachi.* Tokyo: Perikansha, 1991.

——. *Edo no kaiga.* Tokyo: Geika Shoin, 2010.

Kobayashi Tadashi and Kōno Motoaki, eds. *Teihon Nihon kaigaron taisei daiyonkan.* Tokyo: Perikansha, 1997.

Kobayashi Tadashi and Murashige Yasushi. *Sōtatsu to Kōrin.* Nihon bijutsu zenshū 18. Tokyo: Kōdansha, 1990.

Kobayashi Taichirō. "Kōrin to Kenzan." In *Kōrin to Kenzan,* 15–199. Kobayashi Taichirō chosakushū 6. Kyoto: Tankōsha, 1974.

——. "Kenzan Kyōto hen." In *Kōrin to Kenzan,* 203–442. Kobayashi Taichirō chosakushū 6. Kyoto: Tankōsha, 1974.

——. "Kenzan 'Ōtotsuka wo yogiru no ki' yakuchū kōshō." In *Kōrin to Kenzan,* 445–508. Kobayashi Taichirō chosakushū 6. Kyoto: Tankōsha, 1974.

Kodama Kōta. *Genroku jidai.* Nihon no rekishi 16. Tokyo: Chūō Kōron Shinsha, 2005.

Kokkasha, ed. *Kōetsu sho Sōtatsu kingindei-e kenyūhen.* Tokyo: Asahi Shinbunsha, 1978.

——, ed. *Kōetsu sho Sōtatsu kingindei-e zurokuhen.* Tokyo: Asahi Shinbunsha, 1978.

Kokuristsu Nōgakudō, ed. *Ise monogatari to nō.* Tokyo: Kokuritsu Nōgakudo, 2001.

——, ed. *Hosomi korekushon Rinpa ni miru nō.* Tokyo: Kokuritsu Nōgakudō, 2009.

Komatsu Shigemi. *Karasumaru Mitsuhiro.* Tokyo: Shōgakukan, 1982.

Kondō Taketsune. "Gyobutsu Sōtatsu senmen chirashi byōbu no denrai ni tsuite no goden." *Kobijutsu* 33 (March 1971): 78–82.

Kōno Motoaki. *Ogata Kōrin.* Nihon bijutsu kaiga zenshū 17. Tokyo: Shūeisha, 1976.

——. "Kōrin suibokuga no tenkai to gensen." In *Kōetsu Sōtatsu Kōrin,* 53–66. Suiboku bijutsu taikei fukyūhan 10. Tokyo: Kōdansha, 1977.

——. "Hōitsu no denki." In *Rinpa kaiga zenshū Hōitsu-ha,* 15–29. Tokyo: Nihon Keizai Shinbunsha, 1978.

——. "Kōrin futatsu daikessaku no gensen to tokushitsu." In *Rinpa kaiga zenshū Kōrin-ha ichi,* 21–30. Tokyo: Nihon Keizai Shinbunsha, 1979.

——. "Kenzan to Teika: Jūnikagetsu kachō waka no sekai." In *Rinpa daiikkan kachō ichi,* 236–44. Kyoto: Shikōsha, 1989.

——. "Fukurokuju, Sansui zu." *Kokka* 1167 (February 1993): 51–52.

——. "Hakubai akikusa zu." *Kokka* 1167 (December 1993): 49–51.

——. "Kōrin to nō." *Bijutsushi ronsō* 10 (1994): 42–72.

——. "Ogata Kōrin hitsu Baichiku zu uchiwa." *Kokka* 1227 (January 1997): 32–33.

——. "Kōrin to Tsugaru-ke." *Kokka* 1251 (January 2000): 3–12.

——. "Kōrin ga Rōkaku sansui zu hibachi (Kenzan mei)." *Kokka* 1285 (November 2002): 18–24.

——. "Tawaraya Sōtatsu hitsu Ise monogatari zu shikishi." *Kokka* 1325 (March 2006): 25–26.

——. "Sōtatsu-ha Hōgen Heiji monogatari-e senmen." *Kokka* 1333 (November 2006): 32–34.

——. "Kenzan to Kōrin: Kyōdai gyakuten shiron." In *Kenzan no geijutsu to Kōrin,* 6–10. Tokyo: NHK Puromōshon, 2007.

——. "Rinpa to nō." In *Hosomi korekushon Rinpa ni miru nō,* 4–7. Tokyo: Kokuritsu Nōgakudō, 2009.

——. "Tawaraya Sōtatsu Genji monogatari zu shikishi." *Shūbi* 7 (Spring 2013): 82–85.

——. "Kenzan bunjinga shiron." *Kokka* 1419 (February 2014): 14–23.

Koresawa Kyōzō. *Kan'ei no sanpitsu.* Nihon no bijutsu 150. Tokyo: Shibundō, 1978.

"Kōrin." *Kokka* 70 (July 1895): 430.

"Kōrin." *Kokka* 81 (June 1896): 642.

"Kōrin." *Kokka* 88 (January 1897): 67.

"Kōrin." *Kokka* 89 (February 1897): 92–93.

"Kōrin." *Kokka* 102 (March 1898): 113.

"Kōrin." *Kokka* 113 (September 1899): 167–68.

"Kōrin." *Kokka* 125 (June 1900): 92–94.

"Kōrin." *Kokka* 127 (September 1900): 121–22.

"Kōrin ga Haritsuke tebako kai." *Kokka* 558 (May 1937): 134–39.

"Kōrin hitsu Yuima zu." *Bijutsu kenkyū* 37 (January 1935): 28–29.

Kornicki, Peter F. *The Book in Japan: A Cultural History from the Beginnings to the Nineteenth Century.* Honolulu: University of Hawai'i Press, 2001.

——. "Unsuitable Books for Women? 'Genji Monogatari' and 'Ise Monogatari' in Late Seventeenth-Century Japan." *Monumenta Nipponica* 60, no. 2 (July 2005): 147–93.

Kosugi Kazuo. "Kakitsubata zu byōbu ni mirareru kata no shiyō." *Sansai* 130 (September 1960): 35–38.

Koyama Hiroshi and Satō Ken'ichirō, eds. *Yōkyokushū.* Vol. 2. Shinpen Nihon koten bungaku zenshū. Tokyo: Shōgakukan, 1997.

Kumakura Isao. "Kan'ei Culture." *Chanoyu Quarterly* 42 (January 1985): 12–23.

——. *Kan'ei bunka no kenkyū.* Tokyo: Yoshikawa Kōbunkan, 1988.

——. "Chanoyu no rengateki seikaku." *Kokubungaku* 43, no. 14 (December 1998): 106–12.

——. *GoMizuno'o tennō.* Tokyo: Chūō Kōron Shinsha, 2010.

Kuroda, Taizō. *Worlds Seen and Imagined: Japanese Screens from the Idemitsu Museum of Arts.* New York: Asia Society Galleries, 1995.

Kyōto Kokuritsu Hakubutsukan, ed. *Tan'yū shukuzu jō.* Kyoto: Dōhōsha Shuppan, 1980.

——, ed. *Tan'yū shukuzu ge.* Kyoto: Dōhōsha Shuppan, 1981.

Lee, Sherman E. "Watanabe Shikō's Irises." *Bulletin of the Cleveland Museum of Art* 42, no. 4 (April 1955): 63–67.

——. "Sōsetsu and Flowers." *Bulletin of the Cleveland Museum of Art* 57, no. 8 (November 1970): 263–71.

Lee, Soyoung. "Interregional Reception and Invention in Korean and Japanese Ceramics, 1400–1800." Ph.D. diss., Columbia University, 2014.

Leona, Marco, and Jennifer Perry. "Beneath the Blue: A Scientific Analysis of Kōrin's Irises at Yatsuhashi." *Impressions* 37 (March 2016): 129–39.

Levine, Gregory, and Yukio Lippit. *Awakenings: Zen Figure Painting in Medieval Japan.* New York: Japan Society, 2007.

Lillehoj, Elizabeth. "Tōfukumon'in: Empress, Patron, and Artist." *Woman's Art Journal* 17, no. 1 (April 1996): 28–34.

——, ed. *Critical Perspectives on Classicism in Japanese Painting, 1600–1700.* Honolulu: University of Hawai'i Press, 2004.

——, ed. *Acquisition: Art and Ownership in Edo-Period Japan.* Warren, Conn.: Floating World Editions, 2007.

——. *Art and Palace Politics in Early Modern Japan, 1580s–1680s.* Leiden: Brill, 2011.

Linhartová, Věra. *Sur un fond blanc: Écrits japonais sur la peinture du IXe au XIXe siècle.* Paris: Gallimard, 1996.

Lippit, Yukio. "The Birth of Japanese Painting History: Kano Artists, Authors, and Authenticators of the Seventeenth Century." Ph.D. diss., Princeton University, 2003.

——. "Tawaraya Sōtatsu and the Watery Poetics of Japanese Ink Painting." *RES: Anthropology and Aesthetics* 51 (April 2007): 57–76.

——. "Of Modes and Manners in Japanese Ink Painting: Sesshū's 'Splashed Ink Landscape' of 1495." *Art Bulletin* 94, no. 1 (March 2012): 50–77.

——. *Painting of the Realm: The Kano House of Painters in Seventeenth-Century Japan.* Seattle: University of Washington Press, 2012.

——. "Tawaraya Sōtatsu: Five Perspectives." In *Sōtatsu,* 23–42. Washington, D.C.: Arthur M. Sackler Gallery, Smithsonian Institution, 2015.

Ludwig, Theodore M. "The Way of Tea: A Religio-Aesthetic Mode of Life." *History of Religions* 14, no. 1 (August 1974): 28–50.

——. "Before Rikyū: Religious and Aesthetic Influences in the Early History of the Tea Ceremony." *Monumenta Nipponica* 36, no. 4 (December 1981): 367–90.

MacDuff, William. "Beautiful Boys in Nō Drama: The Idealization of Homoerotic Desire." *Asian Theatre Journal* 13, no. 2 (October 1996): 248–58.

Machida Shiritsu Kokusai Hanga Bijutsukan, ed. *Rinpa: Han to kata no tenkai.* Machida-shi: Machida Shiritsu Kokusai Hanga Bijutsukan, 1992.

Maruyama Nobuhiko. *Edo mōdo no tanjō: Mon'yō no ryūkō to sutā eshi.* Tokyo: Kadokawa Gakugei Shuppan, 2008.

Masaki Tokuzō, ed. *Hon'ami gyōjōki to Kōetsu.* Tokyo: Chūō Kōron Bijutsu Shuppan, 1993.

Masuda Katsuhiko. "Ogata Kōrin ga Kōhakubai zu wo egaku tame no eranda ryōshi." *Shūbi* 6 (Winter 2013): 118–19.

Masuda Takashi. *Kōetsu no tegami.* Tokyo: Kawade Shobō Shinsha, 1980.

——. "Shōkadō Shōjō no sho." *Sadō bunka kenkyū* 4 (October 1998): 67–103.

Matsubayashi Yasuaki. "Kanze Matajirō oboegaki: Sono otogishūteki kankyō ni tsuite." *Aosugahara* 24 (May 1982): 32–45.

Matsuo Tomoko and Okano Tomoko, eds. *Sakai Hōitsu to Edo Rinpa no zenbō.* Tokyo: Kyūryūdō, 2011.

Matsushita Takaaki. "Kenzan hitsu Jūnikagetsu waka kachō zu ni tsuite." *Bijutsu kenkyū* 184 (January 1956): 66–72.

——. "Kōrin no nami." *Museum* 58 (January 1956): 7–9.

——. "Iwayuru Matsushima zu byōbu ni tsuite." *Museum* 259 (October 1972): 10–15.

——. "Kōrin no Kōhakubai zu byōbu." *Mita hyōron* 790 (March 1979).

McCausland, Shane, and Matthew P. McKelway. *Chinese Romance from a Japanese Brush: Kano Sansetsu's Chōgonka Scrolls in the Chester Beatty Library.* London: Scala, 2009.

McCullough, Helen Craig, trans. *Tales of Ise.* Stanford, Calif.: Stanford University Press, 1968.

McKelway, Matthew P. *Traditions Unbound: Groundbreaking Painters of Eighteenth-Century Kyoto.* San Francisco: Asian Art Museum—Chong-Moon Lee Center, 2005.

——. *Capitalscapes: Folding Screens and Political Imagination in Late Medieval Kyoto.* Honolulu: University of Hawai'i Press, 2006.

——. *Silver Wind: The Arts of Sakai Hōitsu (1761–1828).* New York: Japan Society, 2012.

Milhaupt, Terry Satsuki. *Kimono: A Modern History.* London: Reaktion Books, 2014.

Minamoto Toyomune. "Ōgiya Tawaraya Sōtatsu." *Kobijutsu* 1, no. 2 (August 1950): 51–55.

——. "Kōrin no geijutsu." *Nihonshi kenkyū* 40 (February 1959): 697–706.

——. "Sōtatsu no sumi-e." *Sansai* 142 (September 1961): 7–19.

——. "Nihon bijutsu ni okeru sōshokusei." *Nihon bijutsu kōgei* 403 (April 1972): 15–23.

——. "Hon'ami Kōetsu nenpyō." *Bokubi* 227 (January 1973): 57–58.

——. "Sōtatsu to sono shūhen." *Nihon bijutsu kōgei* 428 (May 1974): 12–14, 15–23.

——. *Tawaraya* Sōtatsu. Nihon bijutsu kaiga zenshū 14. Tokyo: Shūeisha, 1977.

——. "Nihon bijutsu ni okeru kachōga." *Nihon bijutsu kōgei* 580 (January 1987): 15–20.

———. "Tawaraya Sōtatsu." In *Minamoto Toyomune chosakushū Nihon bijutsushi ronkyū 6 Momoyama Genroku,* 178–233. Kyoto: Shibunkaku Shuppan, 1990.

———. "Sōtatsu no geijutsu." In *Minamoto Toyomune chosakushū Nihon bijutsushi ronkyū 6 Momoyama Genroku,* 234–61. Kyoto: Shibunkaku Shuppan, 1990.

———. "Kōrin no shōgai." In *Minamoto Toyomune chosakushū Nihon bijutsushi ronkyū 6 Momoyama Genroku,* 300–308. Kyoto: Shibunkaku Shuppan, 1990.

———. "Kōrin to Nihon bijutsu no kōgeisei." In *Minamoto Toyomune chosakushū Nihon bijutsushi ronkyū 6 Momoyama Genroku,* 326–32. Kyoto: Shibunkaku Shuppan, 1990.

———. "Kōetsu no geijutsu." In *Minamoto Toyomune chosakushū Nihon bijutsushi ronkyū 6 Momoyama Genroku,* 348–70. Kyoto: Shibunkaku Shuppan, 1990.

Minamoto Toyomune, Tanaka Ichimatsu, and Mizuo Hiroshi. "Heike nōkyō to Sōtatsu." *Kokka* 994 (September 1976): 3–15, 17–32.

Minear, Richard H. "Ogyū Sorai's Instructions for Students: A Translation and Commentary." *Harvard Journal of Asiatic Studies* 36 (1976): 5–81.

Mitsuoka Tadanari. *Kenzan.* Tōki zenshū 7. Tokyo: Heibonsha, 1958.

———. "Kenzan iro-e Teika kachō waka shikishi zara." *Kobijutsu* 26 (June 1969): 111–12.

Miyajima Shin'ichi. "Suibokuga kara sumi-e he." In *Nihon no bijutsu—Geijutsugaku fōramu* 5, 133–48. Tokyo: Keisō Shobō, 1994.

Miyamoto Keizō. "Nō tayū Kobatake Ryōtatsu to sono ichizoku." *Geinōshi kenkyū* 157 (April 2002): 17–42.

———. *Kamigata nōgakushi no kenkyū.* Osaka: Izumi Shoin, 2005.

Miyazaki Enjun, Okada Jō, and Horie Tomohiko. *Nishi Honganji: Sono bijutsu to rekishi.* Kyoto: Tankō Shinsha, 1961.

Mizuo Hiroshi. "Senmen kōzu ron: Sōtatsu ga kōzu kenkyū e no joron." *Kokka* 785 (August 1957): 245–51.

———. "Ogata Kōrin hitsu Ryūko zu." *Kokka* 788 (October 1957): 361–62.

———. "Ogata Kōrin hitsu Shiraji akikusa moyō kaki-e kosode." *Kokka* 814 (January 1960): 18–25.

———. "Sōtatsu byōbu gakō zuron." *Kokka* 814 (January 1960): 13–18.

———. *Sōtatsu Kōrin-ha senmen gashū.* Kyoto: Kōrinsha, 1965.

———. "Ogata Kōrin hitsu Take ni tora zu." *Kokka* 865 (April 1967): 17.

———. "Ogata Kōrin hitsu Chikubai zu byōbu." *Kokka* 868 (July 1967): 18.

———. "Ogata Kōrin hitsu Hakubai zu kōzutsumi." *Kokka* 884 (November 1968): n.p.

———. "Ogata Kōrin to kusabana-e: Kusabana zukan wo chūshin ni shite." *Kokka* 889 (April 1969): 9–15.

———. *Edo Painting: Sotatsu and Korin.* Heibonsha Survey of Japanese Art 18. New York: Weatherhill, 1972.

———. "Shiki kusabana zu byōbu." *Kokka* 969 (May 1974): 22–29.

———. "Kōetsu sho Sōtatsu kingindei-e no suii." In *Kōetsu sho Sōtatsu kingindei-e kenyūhen,* 71–90. Tokyo: Asahi Shinbunsha, 1978.

———. "Ogata Kōrin hitsu Haen zu." *Kokka* 1127 (October 1989): 53–55.

———. "Yatsuhashi akikusa zu." *Kokka* 1167 (February 1993): 49.

———. "Ogata Kōrin hitsu Ryo Dōhin zu." *Kokka* 1172 (July 1993): 29–30.

———. "Ogata Kōrin hitsu Setsuro shiragiku zu uchiwa." *Kokka* 1213 (December 1996): 22.

———. "Ogata Kōrin Kenzan saku Yanagi tsubame zu kadozara Tsuta zu kadozara." *Kokka* 1220 (June 1997): 20–25.

———. "Ogata Kōrin Kenzan saku Ume zu kakuzara." *Kokka* 1297 (November 2003): 30–36.

MOA Bijutsukan, ed. *Kōetsu to nō: kareinaru utaibon no sekai.* Atami: MOA Bijutsukan, 1999.

———, ed. *Kōrin dezain.* Kyoto: Tankōsha, 2005.

MOA Bijutsukan and Tōkyō Bunkazai Kenkyūjo, eds. *Kokuhō Kōhakubai zu byōbu.* Tokyo: Chūō Kōron Bijutsu Shuppan, 2005.

Moriya Takeshi. "Mountain Dwelling in the City." *Chanoyu Quarterly* 56 (1988): 7–21.

Mostow, Joshua S. "Female Readers and Early Heian Romances: The 'Hakubyō Tales of Ise Illustrated Scroll Fragments.'" *Monumenta Nipponica* 62, no. 2 (July 2007): 135–77.

———. *Courtly Visions: The Ise Stories and the Politics of Cultural Appropriation.* Leiden: Brill, 2014.

Mostow, Joshua S., and Royall Tyler, trans. *The Ise Stories: Ise Monogatari.* Honolulu: University of Hawai'i Press, 2010.

Mrázek, Jan, and Morgan Pitelka, eds. *What's the Use of Art? Asian Visual and Material Culture in Context.* Honolulu: University of Hawai'i Press, 2008.

Munakata Shinsaku. "Den Tawaraya Sōtatsu hitsu Tsuki ni akikusa zu byōbu shōkō." *Idemitsu bijutsukan kenkyū kiyō* 16 (2010): 109–27.

———. "Kitagawa Sōsetsu hitsu Shiki kusabana zu haritsuke byōbu." *Kokka* 1390 (August 2011): 26–33.

Murai Atsushi. *Kanjō bugyō Ogiwara Shigehide no shōgai: Arai Hakuseki ga shitto shita tensai keizai kanryō.* Tokyo: Shūeisha, 2007.

Murai Yasuhiko. "The Development of Chanoyu: Before Rikyū." In *Tea in Japan: Essays on the History of Chanoyu,* 3–32. Honolulu: University of Hawai'i Press, 1994.

Murase Hiroharu. "Tawaraya Sōtatsu to Rinpa he no aratana shiten: Kangaeru koto no fukken." In *Tawaraya Sōtatsu to Rinpa,* 115–39. Kanazawa: Ishikawa Kenritsu Bijutsukan, 2013.

Murase, Miyeko. "Japanese Screen Paintings of the Hōgen and Heiji Insurrections." *Artibus Asiae* 29, no. 2/3 (January 1967): 193–228.

———. "Farewell Paintings of China: Chinese Gifts to Japanese Visitors." *Artibus Asiae* 32, no. 2/3 (January 1970): 211–36.

———. "Fan Paintings Attributed to Sōtatsu: Their Themes and Prototypes." *Ars Orientalis* 9 (January 1973): 51–77.

———. *Emaki, Narrative Scrolls from Japan.* New York: Asia Society, 1983.

———. *Iconography of the Tale of Genji: Genji Monogatari Ekotoba.* New York: Weatherhill, 1983.

Sōwa: Omuro kaiyō izen wo chūshin ni." *Geinōshi kenkyū* 114 (July 1991): 37–60.
——. "Karamonoya oboegaki: Ōhira Gohei to Katsurayama Chōji." In *Kan'ei bunka no nettowāku: Kakumeiki no sekai,* 199–208. Kyoto: Shibunkaku Shuppan, 1998.
——. *Kokuhō Ninsei no nazo.* Tokyo: Kadokawa Shoten, 2001.
——. "Kyōyaki ni okeru Kenzan Kōrin ishō no keishō to fukkō." In *Kōrin dezain,* 178–91. Kyoto: Tankōsha, 2005.
——. "Kan'ei bunka no naka no karamonoya: Bijutsushō no kigen wo megutte." In *Bijutsushō no hyakunen: Tōkyō bijutsu kurabu hyakunenshi,* 59–88. Tokyo: Tōkyō Bijutsu Kurabu, 2006.
——. *Kinsei Kyōyaki no kenkyū.* Kyoto: Shibunkaku Shuppan, 2011.
Okamoto Tarō. "Ogata Kōrin." *Chanoyu Quarterly* 2, no. 2 (Summer 1971): 48–49.
Okudaira Shunroku. "Kōrin yume moyō." In *Kōrin to Kamigata Rinpa,* 5–12. Rinpa bijutsukan 2. Tokyo: Shūeisha, 1993.
——. "Sōtatsu no inyōkatsu: suibokuga wo chūshin ni." In *Sōtatsu to Rinpa no genryū,* 110–21. Rinpa bijutsukan 1. Tokyo: Shūeisha, 1993.
——. *Tawaraya Sōtatsu.* Shinchō Nihon bijutsu bunko 5. Tokyo: Shinchōsha, 1997.
Ōmi Shōji. "Te-Sarugaku no ikkōsatsu: shōmoji no te-sarugaku ni tsuite." *Kokushigaku* 71 (March 1960): 105–14.
Omote Akira. *Kōzan bunko-bon no kenkyū: Utaibon no bu.* Tokyo: Wan'ya Shoten, 1965.
——. *Kita-ryū no seiritsu to tenkai.* Tokyo: Heibonsha, 1994.
——. *Yamato sarugaku shi sankyū.* Tokyo: Iwanami Shoten, 2005.
Onishi, Hiroshi. "Chinese Lore for Japanese Spaces." *Metropolitan Museum of Art Bulletin* 51, no. 1 (July 1993): 3–47.
Ono-Descombes, Yasuko. *Kenzan potier ermite: Regards sur un artiste japonais de jadis.* Paris: L'Harmattan, 2011.
Ōoka Makoto, ed. *Nihon no iro.* Tokyo: Asahi Shinbun Shuppankyoku, 1976.
Ōtani Setsuko. "Ise monogatari to nō." In *Ise monogatari to nō,* 30–37. Tokyo: Kokuritsu Nōgakudō, 2001.
——. "Nō Kakitsubata no kōzō: Zenchiku no hōhō." In *Ise monogatari: kyōju no tenkai,* 380–94. Tokyo: Chikurinsha, 2010.
Ōtani Shunta. "GoMizuno'o to Nakanoin, Karasumaru-ke no hitobito." In *Kinsei no waka,* 29–46. Waka bungaku kōza 8. Tokyo: Benseisha, 1994.
Ōta Shōko. *Tawaraya Sōtatsu hitsu Matsushima zu byōbu.* E ha kataru 9. Tokyo: Heibonsha, 1995.
Ōta Takahiko. "Suibokuga no tenkai." In *Nihon no bijutsu—geijutsugaku fōramu* 5, 149–65. Tokyo: Keisō Shobō, 1994.
——. "Ōoka Shunboku ga kataru Edo jidai chūki no bijutsu dōkō: Wakan meihitsu ehon tekagami Wakan meigaen no dōjidai bijutsuron." *Bigaku geijutsugaku* 17 (2001): 1–32.
——. "Shunboku no chōsen Ehon tekagami ga kataru Muromachi jidai no gakatachi." *Bijutsu fōramu* 21, no. 10 (Summer 2004): 41–46.
Ōtsu Yūichi. *Ise monogatari kochūshaku no kenkyū.* Tokyo: Yagi Shoten, 1986.
Ōyama Kazuya, Nakashima Mari, and Nakamura Takeshi. "Nakanoin Michishige 'Miraiki uchūgin kikigaki' honkoku (3)." *Kyoto daigaku kokubungaku ronsō* 23 (March 2010): 61–71.
Ōyama Kazuya, Kobayashi Yūichi, and Nakamura Takeshi. "Nakanoin Michishige 'Miraiki uchūgin kikigaki' honkoku (2)." *Kyoto daigaku kokubungaku ronsō* 22 (September 2009): 51–70.
Oyama Yuzuruha. *Kōrin moyō.* Nihon no bijutsu 524. Tokyo: Gyōsei, 2010.
Perzynski, Friedrich. *Kōrin und Seine Zeit.* Die Kunst 63–64. Berlin: Marquardt, 1907.
Phillips, Quitman E. "Honchō Gashi and the Kano Myth." *Archives of Asian Art* 47 (January 1994): 46–57.
——. *The Practices of Painting in Japan, 1475–1500.* Stanford, Calif.: Stanford University Press, 2000.
Pilgrim, Richard. "Zeami and the Way of Nō." *History of Religions* 12, no. 2 (November 1972): 136–48.
——. "The Artistic Way and the Religio-Aesthetic Tradition in Japan." *Philosophy East and West* 27, no. 3 (July 1977): 285–305.
Pitelka, Morgan, ed. *Japanese Tea Culture: Art, History, and Practice.* London: Routledge, 2003.
——. *Handmade Culture: Raku Potters, Patrons, and Tea Practitioners in Japan.* Honolulu: University of Hawai'i Press, 2005.
Priest, Alan. "Korin and the Iris Screens." *Metropolitan Museum of Art Bulletin* 13, no. 7 (March 1955): 209–12.
Raku Bijutsukan Kenkyūshitsu, ed. *Godai Sōnyū: Raku rekidai.* Kyoto: Raku Bijutsukan, 1982.
Rath, Eric C. "Legends, Secrets, and Authority: Hachijō Kadensho and Early Modern Noh." *Monumenta Nipponica* 54, no. 2 (July 1999): 169–94.
Rosand, David. "Ekphrasis and the Generation of Images." *Arion* 1, no. 1 (January 1990): 61–105.
——. "Style and the Aging Artist." *Art Journal* 46, no. 2 (July 1987): 91–93.
Rousmaniere, Nicole Coolidge, ed. *Kazari: Decoration and Display in Japan, 15th–19th Centuries.* New York: Japan Society; and London: British Museum Press, 2002.
Ruch, Barbara, ed. *Zaigai Nara ehon.* Tokyo: Kadokawa Shoten, 1981.
Said, Edward. *On Late Style: Music and Literature Against the Grain.* New York: Vintage, 2007.
Saitō Kikutarō. "Ko-Kutani sansui zu to Hasshu gafu (1)." *Tōsetsu* 186 (September 1968): 11–16.
——. "Ko-Kutani Sansui zu to Hasshu gafu (2)." *Tōsetsu* 187 (October 1968): 26–38.
Sakazaki Tan, ed. *Nihon gadan taikan.* Tokyo: Mejiro Shoin, 1917.
——. *Nihon garon taikan jōkan.* Tokyo: Arusu, 1927.
——. *Nihon garon taikan chūkan.* Tokyo: Arusu, 1929.
——. *Nihon kaigaron taikei.* Vol. 1. Tokyo: Meicho Fukyūkai, 1979.
——. *Nihon kaigaron taikei.* Vol. 5. Tokyo: Meicho Fukyūkai, 1979.
Sakomura, Tomoko. "Pictured Words and Codified Seasons: Visualizations of Waka Poetry in Late Sixteenth- and Early Seventeenth-Century Japan." Ph.D. diss., Columbia University, 2007.

———. *Poetry as Image: The Visual Culture of Waka in Sixteenth-Century Japan*. Japanese Visual Culture 16. Leiden: Brill, 2015.

Sanari Kentarō, ed. *Yōkyoku taikan*. Vol. 2. Tokyo: Meiji Shoin, 1982.

Sanford, James H., William R. LaFleur, and Masatoshi Nagatomi, eds. *Flowing Traces: Buddhism in the Literary and Visual Arts of Japan*. Princeton, N.J.: Princeton University Press, 1992.

Sano Midori. "Sōtatsu no kingindei wakakan shita-e." In *Rinpa daiikkan kachō ichi*, 227–35. Kyoto: Shikōsha, 1989.

———. "Santori Bijutsukan zō Ise monogatari shikishi haritsuki byōbu wo megutte." *Kokka* 1245 (July 1999): 15–40.

Suntory Bijutsukan, ed. *Kaga, Nōtō no gakatachi: Tōhaku, Morikage, Sōsetsu ten*. Tokyo: Suntory Bijutsukan, 1992.

Sasaki Jōhei and Sasaki Masako. "Shōkadō Shōjō no kaiga: Senren no bigaku." *Sadō bunka kenkyū* 4 (October 1998): 105–20.

Sasaki Kōzō. "Shin Rinpa ron: Tawaraya Sōtatsu ni tsuite." *Kobijutsu* 39 (December 1972): 25–34.

Satō Masahiko. *Karatsu*. Nihon tōji zenshū 17. Tokyo: Chūō Kōronsha, 1976.

Satō Miki. "Kinsei shoki Nihon bijutsu ni okeru ishōsei: Waka shudai no zōkeika wo tegakari ni." *Kajima bijutsu zaidan nenpō* 18 (2000): 294–303.

Satō Ryō. *Kōrin*. Tōyō bijutsu bunko 12. Tokyo: Atoriesha, 1939.

Satō Torao. *Shōkadō*. Tōyō bijutsu bunko 37. Tokyo: Atoriesha, 1939.

Sato, Yasuko. "Neither Past nor Present: The Pursuit of Classical Antiquity in Early Modern and Modern Japan." Ph.D. diss., University of Chicago, 2002.

Sayre, Charles Franklin. "Japanese Court-Style Narrative Painting of the Late Middle Ages." *Archives of Asian Art* 35 (January 1982): 71–81.

Screech, Timon. "Rinpa and the Space of Dreams." In *Nihon bijutsu no kūkan to keishiki: Kawai Masatomo kyōju kanreki kinen ronbunshū*, 42–55. Tokyo: Kawai Masatomo Kyōju Kanreki Kinen Ronbunshū Kankōkai, 2003.

———. *Obtaining Images: Art, Production and Display in Edo Japan*. London: Reaktion Books, 2012.

Sen Masayoshi. "Tawaraya Sōtatsu hitsu Hasuike suikin zu shiron." In *Nihon bijutsu no kūkan to keishiki: Kawai Masatomo kyōju kanreki kinen ronbunshū*, 229–47. Tokyo: Kawai Masatomo Kyōju Kanreki Kinen Ronbunshū Kankōkai, 2003.

Sen Sōsa, ed. *Kōshin Sōsa chasho*. Tokyo: Shufu-no-tomo Sha, 1998.

Sen Sōshitsu, ed. *Sadō koten zenshū*. Vol. 4. Kyoto: Tankōsha, 1956.

———. *Sadō koten zenshū*. Vol. 2. Kyoto: Tankōsha, 1958.

———. *Sadō koten zenshū*. Vol. 5. Kyoto: Tankōsha, 1958.

———. *Sadō koten zenshū*. Vol. 7. Kyoto: Tankōsha, 1959.

———. *Sadō koten zenshū*. Vol. 12. Kyoto: Tankōsha, 1962.

———. *Sadō koten zenshū*. Vol. 9. Kyoto: Tankōsha, 1967.

Sheldon, Charles D. "Merchants and Society in Tokugawa Japan." *Modern Asian Studies* 17, no. 3 (January 1983): 477–88.

Shimada Shūjirō. "Hotei zu." *Kokka* 730 (January 1953): 12.

Shimada Shūjirō, and Iriya Yoshitaka, eds. *Zenrin gasan: Chūsei suibokuga wo yomu*. Tokyo: Mainichi Shinbunsha, 1987.

Shimada Tsukuba. "Fuyuki enkakushi." In *Shimada Tsukuba shū ge*, 602–30. Musashimurayama-shi: Seishōdō Shoten, 1976.

Shimao Arata. "The Stewards of Art in Muromachi Japan: Nōami, Geiami, and Sōami." *Chanoyu Quarterly* 84 (1996): 7–36.

———. "Haboku sansui zu no ga to shi." *Tenkai toga* 3 (2000): 32–46.

———. "Sesson hitsu Jurō zu." *Kokka* 1340 (June 2007): 26–29.

———. "Sesson hitsu Shōki giko zu." *Kokka* 1390 (August 2011): 22–25.

Shimazu Tadao. "Kinsei waka no sekai." In *Kinsei no waka*, 7–28. Waka bungaku kōza 8. Tokyo: Benseisha, 1994.

———. *Shinkei to Sōgi*. Shimazu Tadao chosakushū 4. Osaka: Izumi Shoin, 2004.

Shimizu, Yoshiaki. *Masters of Japanese Calligraphy: 8th–19th Century*. New York: Asia Society Galleries—Japan House Gallery, 1984.

Shimizu, Yoshiaki, and Carolyn Wheelwright, eds. *Japanese Ink Paintings from American Collections: The Muromachi Period; An Exhibition in Honor of Shūjirō Shimada*. Princeton, N.J.: Art Museum, Princeton University, 1976.

Shimohara Miho. "Genroku ki ni okeru Teika tomi tsukinami kachō uta-e ni tsuite no kōsatsu: Mitsuoki-bon, Tan'yū-bon, Gukei-bon wo chūshin to shita hikaku." *Bijutsushi* 146 (March 1999): 285–301.

Shinbo Tōru, ed. *Kōrin meigafu*. Tokyo: Nihon Shinbunsha, 1978.

———. *Kōrin chōrui shasei chō*. Tokyo: Iwasaki Bijutsusha, 1983.

———. "Chanoyu ni okeru kake-e: Sono gaka to sakuhin." In *Sadō shūkin*, 9:217–27. Tokyo: Shōgakukan, 1984.

Shirahata Yoshi. "Ise monogatari shita-e bonjikyō kō." *Bijutsu kenkyū* 15, no. 2 (May 1948): 1–20.

Shirahata Yoshi and Kirihata Ken, eds. *Mitsui-ke denrai Maruyama-ha ishōga*. Kyoto: Shikōsha, 1975.

Shirane, Haruo. *The Bridge of Dreams: A Poetics of the Tale of Genji*. Stanford, Calif.: Stanford University Press, 1987.

———. "Matsuo Bashō and the Poetics of Scent." *Harvard Journal of Asiatic Studies* 52, no. 1 (June 1992): 77–110.

———. *Traces of Dreams: Landscape, Cultural Memory, and the Poetry of Bashō*. Stanford, Calif.: Stanford University Press, 1998.

———, ed. *Early Modern Japanese Literature: An Anthology, 1600–1900*. Translations from the Asian Classics. New York: Columbia University Press, 2002.

———. "Performance, Visuality, and Textuality: The Case of Japanese Poetry." *Oral Traditions* 20, no. 2 (2005): 217–32.

———, ed. *Traditional Japanese Literature: An Anthology, Beginnings to 1600*. Translations from the Asian Classics. New York:

Columbia University Press, 2007.
——, ed. *Envisioning the Tale of Genji: Media, Gender, and Cultural Production.* New York: Columbia University Press, 2008.
——. *Japan and the Culture of the Four Seasons: Nature, Literature, and the Arts.* New York: Columbia University Press, 2012.
Shirane, Haruo, and Tomi Suzuki, eds. *Inventing the Classics: Modernity, National Identity, and Japanese Literature.* Stanford, Calif.: Stanford University Press, 2002.
Shively, Donald H. "Buddhahood for the Nonsentient: A Theme in Nō Plays." *Harvard Journal of Asiatic Studies* 20, no. 1/2 (June 1957): 135–61.
"Shōkadō Shōjō hitsu Sōgi-zō kai." *Kokka* 506 (January 1933): 25.
"Shōkadō Shōjō jiga zō kai." *Kokka* 552 (November 1936): 318–23.
Silbergeld, Jerome. "Chinese Concepts of Old Age and Their Role in Chinese Painting, Painting Theory, and Criticism." *Art Journal* 46, no. 2 (July 1987): 103–14.
Smith, Henry D. "Japaneseness and the History of the Book." *Monumenta Nipponica* 53, no. 4 (December 1998): 499–515.
"Sōgi-zō." *Bijutsu kenkyū* 26 (February 1934): 32–33.
Solomon, Michael. "Kinship and the Transmission of Religious Charisma: The Case of Honganji." *Journal of Asian Studies* 33, no. 3 (May 1974): 403–13.
Sugahara Hisao. "Bokuseki no kanshō." In *Sadō shūkin*, 9:106–14. Tokyo: Shōgakukan, 1984.
Suganuma Teizō. "Kōrin hitsu Nakamura Kuranosuke-zō." *Yamato bunka* 5 (March 1952): 20–27.
Sugihara Atsuko. "Sōtatsu hitsu Matsushima zu byōbu no shudai ni tsuite." *Bijutsushi kenkyū* 30 (December 1991): 145–60.
Sugimoto Yoshihisa. "Kyō no machi eshi: Ogata Kōrin no ishōsei to Kōrin mon'yō." *Kurokawa kobunkan kenkyūjo kiyō Kobunka kenkyū* 7 (February 2008): 57–79.
"Sumiyoshi-ke kanteikō ichi." *Bijutsu kenkyū* 38 (February 1935): 79–94.
"Sumiyoshi-ke kanteikō ni." *Bijutsu kenkyū* 39 (March 1935): 137–44.
Suntory Bijutsukan, ed. *Kenzan, Kenzan! Chakusō no maesutoro.* Tokyo: Suntory Bijutsukan, 2015.
Tajima Shiichi. *Rinpa gashū dai ikkan.* Tokyo: Shinbi Shoin, 1903.
Takahashi Hiromi. "Nakane Genkei to Ogyū Sorai." *Bungei kenkyū* 109 (May 1985): 54–64.
——. *Edo no barokku: Sorai-gaku no shūhen.* Tokyo: Perikansha, 1997.
Takahashi Yoshio. *Manzōroku Takahashi Sōan nikki.* Vol. 7. Kyoto: Shibunkaku Shuppan, 1990.
Takeda Kōichi. "Kōrin hyakuzu shuppan no shūhen: Hōitsu to Bunchō no kōyū." In *Rinpa: Han to kata no tenkai*, 18–23. Machida-shi: Machida Shiritsu Kokusai Hanga Bijutsukan, 1992.
Takeda Yōjirō, Eguchi Tsuneaki, and Kamata Junko. *Kinsei goyō eshi no shiteki kenkyū: Bakuhansei shakai ni okeru eshi no mibun to joretsu.* Kyoto: Shibunkaku Shuppan, 2008.
Takemoto Mikio, ed. *Nōgaku shiryōshū.* Vol. 21. Tokyo: Waseda Daigaku Shuppanbu, 1988.
Takeno Megumi. "Kinsei no okeru Teika yomi tsukinami kachō uta-e no tenkai: Yoshimura Kōkei sakuhin wo chūshin ni." *Museum* 414 (September 1985): 4–17.
Takeoka Masao. *Ise monogatari zenhyōshaku: Kochūshaku jūisshu shūsei.* Tokyo: Yūbun Shoin, 1987.
Takeshi Hiromi. "Gosankyō no kashindan kōzō: Hitotsubashi Tokugawa wo jirei toshite." *Gakushūin shigaku* 49 (March 2011): 46–62.
Takeuchi Jun'ichi. "Kenzan yaki chawan kō." *Yamato bunka* 81 (March 1989): 1–15.
——. "Chawan sandai to Kenzan yaki seisaku nendai ni tsuite." *Kokka* 1169 (April 1993): 9–28.
Takeuchi Jun'ichi and Itō Yoshaki. *Yakimono to fureau.* Tokyo: Shinchōsha, 1996.
Takeuchi, Melinda, ed. *The Artist as Professional in Japan.* Stanford, Calif.: Stanford University Press, 2004.
Tamamushi Satoko. "Hōitsu-ga no teihen: Hōitsu geijutsu seiritsu no dojō ni tsuite." In *Rinpa kaiga zenshū Hōitsu-ha*, 61–66. Tokyo: Nihon Keizai Shinbunsha, 1978.
——. "Sakai Hōitsu to Nami zu byōbu (jō): Kōrin hitsu Hatō zu byōbu no sōzōteki hensō." *Kokka* 1109 (December 1987): 9–26.
——. "Sakai Hōitsu to Nami zu byōbu (ge): Kōrin hitsu Hatō zu byōbu no sōzōteki hensō." *Kokka* 1110 (January 1988): 26–30.
——. *Sakai Hōitsu.* Shinchō Nihon bijutsu bunko 18. Tokyo: Shinchōsha, 1997.
——. "Kōrin kan no hensen." *Bijutsu kenkyū* 371 (March 1999): 1–70.
——. "Rinpa: The Past, Present, and Future." In *Arts of Japan: An International Symposium*, 133–60. New York: Metropolitan Museum of Art, 2000.
——. *Ikitsuzukeru Kōrin: Imēji to gensetsu wo hakobu "norimono" to sono kiseki.* Tokyo: Yoshikawa Kōbunkan, 2004.
——. "Kunō ka, kendo jūrai ka: Kōrin no Edo seikatsu wo kangaeru." *Bijutsu fōramu 21* 10 (2004): 35–40.
——. *Toshi no naka no e: Sakai Hōitsu no kaiji to sono efekuto.* Tokyo: Brücke, 2004.
——. "'Kazari' to 'tsukuri' to kaiga no isō." In *Kōza Nihon bijutsushi daigokan*, 95–133. Tokyo: Tōkyō Daigaku Shuppankai, 2005.
——. "Kōrin no e no isō." In *Kōrin dezain*, 132–43. Kyoto: Tankōsha, 2005.
——. *Rinpa to dezain sōshoku kazari.* Nihon no bijutsu 464. Tokyo: Shibundō, 2005.
——. "Kōetsu sho Sōtatsu ga Hasu shita-e hyakunin isshu wakakan no denrai to fukugen ni kan suru ikkōsatsu: Shinshutsu dankan no shōkai wo kanete." *Kokka* 1403 (September 2012): 7–23.
——. *Tawaraya Sōtatsu kingin no kazari no keifu.* Tokyo: Tōkyō Daigaku Shuppankai, 2012.
——. "Shashi to tōjin he no akogare: Yatsuhashi zu no juyō to tenshō." *Shikun* 5 (2013): 73–96.
——. "Sōtatsu no me to majutsu." *Shūbi* 7 (Spring 2013): 14–37.
Tanabe, George Joji, ed. *Religions of Japan in Practice.* Princeton Readings in Religions. Princeton, N.J.: Princeton University Press, 1999.
Tanabe Saburōsuke and

Nagasaki Iwao, eds. *Kaijō nijūgo shūnen kinen Kokuritsu nōgakudō korekushon ten: Nō no ga, kyōgen no myō.* Tokyo: NHK Puromōshon, 2008.

Tanaka Eiji. "Kangeki no mukō gawa: Hōitsu hitsu Natsu aki kusa zu byōbu ni tsuite." In *Hōitsu to Edo Rinpa,* 101–9. Rinpa bijutsukan 3. Tokyo: Shūeisha, 1993.

Tanaka Ichimatsu. *Tawaraya Sotatsu.* Rutland, Vt.: Charles E. Tuttle, 1956.

———. *Kōrin.* Tokyo: Nihon Keizai Shinbunsha, 1959.

———. "Sesson hitsu Enkō zu." *Kokka* 815 (February 1960): 51–57.

Tanaka Ichimatsu and Yamane Yūzō, eds. *Tawaraya Sōtatsu ten.* Tokyo: Nihon Keizai Shinbunsha, 1961.

Tanaka Kisaku. "Tawaraya Sōtatsu hitsu Maki hinoki zu byōbu." *Bijutsu kenkyū* 2 (February 1932): 28–29.

———. "Konishi-ke kyūzō Kōrin kankei shiryō (jō)." *Bijutsu kenkyū* 56 (August 1936): 20–28.

———. "Konishi-ke kyūzō Kōrin kankei shiryō (chū)." *Bijutsu kenkyū* 57 (September 1936): 379–88.

———. "Konishi-ke kyūzō Kōrin kankei shiryō (ge no 1)." *Bijutsu kenkyū* 59 (November 1936): 31–39.

———. "Konishi-ke kyūzō Kōrin kankei shiryō (ge no 2)." *Bijutsu kenkyū* 60 (December 1936): 531–39.

———. "Shūseidōki ni tsuite." *Gasetsu* 10 (October 1937): 322–32.

———. "Shūseidō hoki." *Gasetsu* 17 (May 1938): 427–28.

Tanaka Michio. *Hachijō kadensho.* Fukuoka: Zaikyūshū Kokubun Shiryō Eiin Sōsho Kankōkai, 1981.

Tanaka Sakutarō. *Ninsei.* Tōki zenshū 24. Tokyo: Heibonsha, 1960.

Tanaka Yukihiro. "Kōrin hyakuzu ni tsuite." In *Kōrin dezain,* 198–209. Tokyo: NHK Puromōshon, 2007.

Tani Akira, ed. *Kanamori Sōwa chasho.* Chanoyu koten sōsho 4. Kyoto: Shibunkaku Shuppan, 1997.

———. *Chakaiki no kenkyū.* Kyoto: Tankōsha, 2001.

———. "Kuge no cha." *Tankō* 55, no. 8 (August 2001): 18–26.

———. "Sadōgu zenshi kara Rikyū no 'wabi' he." *Tankō* 59 (September 2005): 16–35.

Tani Shin'ichi. "Sōtatsu hitsu Akikusa zu byōbu ni tsuite." *Kokka* 505 (1932).

———. "Kōrin to sono jidai." In *Kōrin,* 5–7. Tokyo: Nihon Keizai Shinbunsha, 1959.

Tanihata Akio. "Kinsei Daimyō no cha, kizoku no cha." *Tankō* 59 (September 2005): 64–93.

———. *Kuge sadō no kenkyū.* Kyoto: Shibunkaku Shuppan, 2005.

Tanomura Tadao. "Kōrin no shi Yamamoto Soken no gaseki (jō)." *Kokka* 787 (October 1957): 311–20.

———. "Kōrin no shi Yamamoto Soken no gaseki (ge)." *Kokka* 788 (November 1957): 351–58.

———. "Soken no Teika yomi kachō waka-e (jō): Soken to Kōrin Kenzan no kankei." *Kokka* 802 (January 1959): 6–12.

———. "Soken no Teika yomi kachō waka-e (ge): Soken to Kōrin Kenzan no kankei." *Kokka* 803 (February 1959): 43–47.

———. "Ga no byōbu kō: Kinsei ni okeru gasan byōbu no yōshiki to seisaku katei." *Bijutsushi* 40 (March 1961): 133–41.

Tatara Takiko. "Kano Einō Jūnikagetsu kai zu byōbu ni tsuite: gajō no kakudai ni yoru shinki juyō e no taiō." *Bigaku* 57, no. 1 (June 2006): 56–69.

Tazawa Hiroyoshi. "Rinpa keishō to hensō no bi: Mitsu no jidai rokunin no geijutsuka." In *Dai Rinpa ten: Keishō to hensō,* 32–44. Tokyo: Yomiuri Shinbunsha, 2008.

Teishitsu Hakubutsukan, ed. *Kundaikan sōchōki.* Tokyo: Teishitsu Hakubutsukan, 1932.

Thornton, Peter. "Monomane, Yūgen, and Gender in Izutsu and Sotoba Komachi." *Asian Theatre Journal* 20, no. 2 (October 2003): 218–25.

Tokugawa Yoshinobu. "Kakitsubata zu byōbu no sanjigenteki kōzu." In *Kinkō sōsho,* 371–95. Tokyo: Shibunkaku Shuppan, 1988.

Tokugawa Yoshiyasu. *Sōtatsu no suibokuga.* Tokyo: Zayu Hankōkai, 1948.

Tōkyō Kokuritsu Hakubutsukan, ed. *Sōtatsu Kōrin-ha zuroku.* Kyoto: Benridō, 1952.

———. *Sōritsu hyakunen kinen tokubetsuten Rinpa.* Tokyo: Tōkyō Kokuritsu Hakubutsukan, 1972.

———. *Dai Rinpa ten: Keishō to hensō.* Tokyo: Yomiuri Shinbunsha, 2008.

———. *Eisai to Kenninji.* Tokyo: NHK Puromōshon, 2014.

Tōkyō Kokuritsu Kindai Bijutsukan, ed. *Rinpa.* Tokyo: Tōkyō Kokuritsu Kindai Bijutsukan, 2004.

———, ed. *Rinpa: Kokusai shinpojiumu hōkokusho.* Tokyo: Buryukke, 2006.

Toyama Bijutsukan, ed. *Genroku bunka to chatō.* Cha no bijutsu shirīzu 6. Toyama: Toyama Bijutsukan, 1988.

Trede, Melanie. "Terminology and Ideology: Coming to Terms with 'Classicism' in Japanese Art-Historical Writing." In *Critical Perspectives on Classicism in Japanese Painting, 1600–1700,* 21–52. Honolulu: University of Hawai'i Press, 2004.

Trinh, Khanh, ed. *Kamisaka Sekka: Dawn of Modern Japanese Design.* Sydney: Art Gallery of New South Wales, 2012.

Tsubaki, Andrew T. "Zeami and the Transition of the Concept of Yūgen: A Note on Japanese Aesthetics." *Journal of Aesthetics and Art Criticism* 30, no. 1 (October 1971): 55–67.

Tsuchiya Kei'ichirō. "Nō to renga: Tabi ga umidashita mono." *Kokubungaku* 43, no. 14 (December 1998): 50–56.

Tsuchiya Maki. "Heiji monogatari emaki Rokuhara gassenkan dankan." *Kokka* 1375 (May 2010): 18–21.

Tsuji Nobuo. "Kitagawa Sōsetsu hitsu Shiki kusabana zu." *Kobijutsu* 19 (October 1967): 75–80.

———. "Kitagawa Sōsetsu hitsu Shiki kusabana zu." *Kobijutsu* 26 (June 1969): 81–86.

———. "Sōtatsu-ha no kusabana zu gairon: Suibokuga kingindei-e nado no mondai mo fukumete." In *Rinpa kaiga zenshū Sōtatsu-ha,* 5–18. Tokyo: Nihon Keizai Shinbunsha, 1978.

———. "Kano Tan'yū hitsu Chōrui shasei chō mohon (Daiei hakubutsukan zō) ni tsuite." *Bijutsu kenkyū* 310 (August 1979): 25–27.

———. "Kōrin hyakuzu to genzon sakuhin." In *Rinpa kaiga zenshū Kōrin-ha ichi,* 67–72. Tokyo: Nihon Keizai Shinbunsha, 1979.

———. *Playfulness in Japanese Art.* Lawrence: Spencer Museum of Art, University of Kansas, 1986.

———. "Ogata Kōrin hitsu Kiku zu byōbu." *Kokka* 1302 (April 2004): 34–37.

Tsukamoto Maromitsu. "Frictions in Universal Contexts and Individual Values: Chinese Paintings at the Toyokan." *Orientations* 44, no. 5 (June 2013): 40–47.

Tsuneyoshi Yukiko. "Kinsei kizoku no handanryoku: Kanbun ninen Nakanoin Michishige nikki yori." *Kassui ronbunshū gendai Nihon bunka gakka hen* 53 (March 2010): 1–17.

Tsuruta Eiichi. "Ganryō no rekishi." *Shikizai kyōkaishi* 75, no. 4 (April 2002): 43–53.

Tsutsui Kōichi. "Chake to chasho: Genroku ki no chanoyu." In *Senke sadō ten Genroku ki no chanoyu*, 7–11. Kyoto: Chadō Shiryōkan, 1980.

Tyler, Royall. "The No Play Matsukaze as a Transformation of Genji Monogatari." *Journal of Japanese Studies* 20, no. 2 (July 1994): 377–422.

———, trans. *Japanese Nō Dramas*. London: Penguin Classics, 1992.

———, trans. *The Tale of Genji*. New York: Viking, 2001.

———, trans. *The Tale of the Heike*. New York: Penguin, 2012.

Uchida Takayuki. "Ogata Kōrin hitsu Kōhakubai zu byōbu ni tsuite no shiron." *Kokka* 1316 (June 2004): 35–40.

Uchida Tokugo. "Yatsuhashi maki-e suzuribako ni miru bungaku ikō." In *Kokuhō Kakitsubata zu: Kōrin Genroku no isai*, 90–96. Tokyo: Nezu Bijutsukan, 2005.

———. *Suzuribako no bi: Maki-e no seika*. Tokyo: Tankōsha, 2006.

———. "Kenzan yaki no dezain." In *Kenzan no geijutsu to Kōrin*, 174–77. Tokyo: NHK Puromōshon, 2007.

———. *Kōrin maki-e no kenkyū*. Tokyo: Chūō Kōronsha, 2012.

Uchida Tokugo, Suzuta Shigeto, Shimoyama Susumu, and Nakai Izumi. "Kokuhō Kōhakubai zu byōbu no gihō zairyō ni kan suru kōgakuteki kenkyū." *Kajima bijutsu kenkyū* 27 (November 2010): 34–46.

Uemura Masurō, ed. *Kōrin*. Tokyo: Takamizawa Mokuhansha, 1940.

———. *Sōtatsu*. Tokyo: Takamizawa Mokuhansha, 1940.

Usuda Daisuke. "Sakuhin shōkai Seki Jizōin hondō tenjōga: Kano Eikei to jūhasseiki shotō no Kyō-Gano-ke ni tsuite." *Gakushūin daigaku jinbun kagaku ronshū* 19 (2010): 65–93.

Varley, H. Paul, and Isao Kumakura, eds. *Tea in Japan: Essays on the History of Chanoyu*. Honolulu: University of Hawai'i Press, 1989.

Wakisaka Atsushi. "Fūjin Raijin zu no tenkai." In *Hōitsu to Edo Rinpa*, 110–21. Rinpa bijutsukan 3. Tokyo: Shūeisha, 1993.

———. *Kyō-Gano no kenkyū*. Tokyo: Chūō Kōron Bijutsu Shuppan, 2010.

Watanabe Daimon. "Otogishū Kodera Kyūmu no kisōteki kenkyū." *Nomura bijutsukan kenyū kiyō* 11 (2002): 1–11.

Watanabe, Masako. "Narrative Framing in the 'Tale of Genji Scroll': Interior Space in the Compartmentalized Emaki." *Artibus Asiae* 58, no. 1/2 (January 1998): 115–45.

Watsky, Andrew M. "Floral Motifs and Mortality: Restoring Numinous Meaning to a Momoyama Building." *Archives of Asian Art* 50 (January 1997): 62–92.

———. *Chikubushima: Deploying the Sacred Arts in Momoyama Japan*. Seattle: University of Washington Press, 2004.

Watson, William. "Textile Decoration in the Edo Period and Its Further Implication." *Modern Asian Studies* 18, no. 4 (January 1984): 657–66.

Wattles, Miriam. "The Life and Afterlives of Hanabusa Itchō (1652–1724)." Ph.D. diss., Institute of Fine Arts, New York University, 2005.

———. *The Life and Afterlives of Hanabusa Itchō, Artist-Rebel of Edo*. Leiden: Brill, 2013.

Weigl, Gail Capitol. "The Reception of Chinese Painting Models in Muromachi Japan." *Monumenta Nipponica* 35, no. 3 (Autumn 1980): 257–72.

Wheelwright, Carolyn. "Kano Painters of the Sixteenth Century A.D.: The Development of Motonobu's Daisen-in Style." *Archives of Asian Art* 34 (January 1981): 6–31.

———. "Tōhaku's Black and Gold." *Ars Orientalis* 16 (January 1986): 1–31.

———. "Past and Present, Text and Image." In *Word in Flower: The Visualization of Classical Literature in Seventeenth-Century Japan*, 84–108. New Haven: Yale University Art Gallery, 1989.

Wilson, Richard L. "Kenzan yaki no keifu." In *Kenzan no tōgei*, 127–48. Tokyo: Gotō Bijutsukan, 1987.

———. *The Art of Ogata Kenzan: Persona and Production in Japanese Ceramics*. New York: Weatherhill, 1991.

Wilson, Richard L., and Ogasawara Saeko. *Ogata Kenzan: zensakuhin to sono keifu*. 4 vols. Tokyo: Yūzankaku, 1992.

———. "Kenzan yaki: Gasan yōshiki to shutten no subete." *Kokusai kurisutokyō daigaku gakuhō jinbun kagaku kenkyū* 35 (March 2004): 1–47.

Word in Flower: The Visualization of Classical Literature in Seventeenth-Century Japan. New Haven, Conn.: Yale University Art Gallery, 1989.

Wu Hung. *The Double Screen: Medium and Representation in Chinese Painting*. Chicago: University of Chicago Press, 1996.

Wu, Xiaojin. "Metamorphosis of Form and Meaning: Ink Bird-and-Flower Screens in Muromachi Japan." Ph.D. diss., Princeton University, 2011.

———. "Innumerable Embodiments of Hotei: The Emergence of a Literati Persona." In *Crossing the Sea: Essays on East Asian Art in Honor of Professor Yoshiaki Shimizu*, 267–81. Princeton, N.J.: P. Y. and Kinmay W. Tang Center for East Asian Art, 2012.

Yabumoto Yūko, Ōyama Kazuya, Nakashima Mari, and Nakamura Takeshi. "Nakanoin Michishige 'Miraiki uchūgin kikigaki' honkoku (4)." *Kyoto daigaku kokubungaku ronsō* 24 (September 2010): 75–86.

Yamada Ichijirō, ed. *Enogu senryō shōkō shi*. Osaka: Ōsaka Enogu Senryō Dōgyō Kumiai, 1938.

Yamaguchi Kyōko. *Shōkadō Shōjō to Takimoto ryū no tenkai*. Kyoto: Shibunkaku Shuppan, 2011.

Yamaji Kōzō. *Kinsei geinō no taidō*. Tokyo: Yagi Shoten, 2010.

Yamamoto Masako. *Karamonoya*

kara bijutsushō he: Kyōto ni okeru bijutsu shijō wo chūshin ni. Kyoto: Kōyō Shobō, 2010.

Yamamoto Tokurō, ed. *Ise monogatari: Kyōju no tenkai*. Tokyo: Chikurinsha, 2010.

Yamanaka Reiko. "Kinsei no nō no shūdansei: Kanze Motoakira no kakushin undō." *Kokubungaku* 43, no. 14 (December 1998): 113–19.

Yamane Yūzō. "Inen in Kusabana zu fusuma-e ni tsuite." *Kokka* 701 (August 1950): 3, 268–80.

——. "Ogata Kenzan hitsu Shiki kachō zu byōbu kaisetsu." *Bijutsu kenkyū* 188 (September 1956): 42–45.

——. "Kōrin hitsu Akikusa zu byōbu ni tsuite." *Bijutsu kenkyū* 206 (September 1959): 26–35.

——. "Ogata Kōrin hitsu Shiraji akikusa moyō byakue kosode." *Kokka* 814 (January 1960): 18–25.

——. "Kōrin hitsu Senmen harimaze tebako." *Yamato bunka* 33 (September 1960): 1–14.

——, ed. *Konishi-ke kyūzō Kōrin kankei shiryō to sono kenkyū*. Tokyo: Chūō Kōron Bijutsu Shuppan, 1962.

——. *Sōtatsu*. Tokyo: Nihon Keizai Shinbunsha, 1962.

——. "Eya ni tsuite." *Bijutsushi* 48 (March 1963): 107–17.

——. "Den Sōtatsu hitsu no Kusabana zu senmen harimaze byōbu ni tsuite." *Yamato bunka* 39 (May 1963): 39–54.

——. "Ogata Sōken san Ise monogatari zu byōbu ni tsuite." *Bijutsushi* 51, no. 3 (December 1964): 91–96.

——. "Ogata Kōrin and the Art of the Genroku Era." *Acta Asiatica* 15 (1968): 69–86.

——. *Sōtatsu to Kōrin*. Genshoku Nihon no bijutsu 14. Tokyo: Shōgakukan, 1970.

——. "Utaibon Matsukaze." *Kokka* 922 (June 1970): 23–24.

——. "Den Sōtatsu hitsu Ise monogatari zu shikishi ni tsuite." *Yamato bunka* 59 (March 1974): 1–27.

——. "Tawaraya Sōtatsu to Ihon Ise monogatari-e oyobi Shu Kongōjin engi-e: Shinshutsu no Ise monogatari byōbu wo chūshin ni." *Kokka* 977 (February 1975): 11–33.

——. "Kōetsu to Sōtatsu." In *Suiboku bijutsu taikei fukyūhan daijukkan Kōetsu Sōtatsu Kōrin*, 39–52. Tokyo: Kōdansha, 1977.

——, ed. *Suiboku bijutsu taikei fukyūhan daijukkan Kōetsu Sōtatsu Kōrin*. Tokyo: Kōdansha, 1977.

——, ed. *Rinpa kaiga zenshū Sōtatsu-ha ichi*. Tokyo: Nihon Keizai Shinbunsha, 1977.

——, ed. *Rinpa kaiga zenshū Hōitsu-ha*. Tokyo: Nihon Keizai Shinbunsha, 1978.

——, ed. *Rinpa kaiga zenshū Sōtatsu-ha ni*. Tokyo: Nihon Keizai Shinbunsha, 1978.

——. "Ogata Kōrin hitsu Takarabune zu." *Kokka* 1015 (August 1978): 21–29.

——. "Ogata Kōrin hitsu Daikokuten zu." *Kokka* 1015 (August 1978): 29–32.

——. "Sōtatsu kingindei-e no seiritsu to tenkai." In *Kōetsu sho Sōtatsu kingindei-e kenkyūhen*, 7–70. Tokyo: Asahi Shinbunsha, 1978.

——. "Kōrin to Nakamura Kuranosuke: Kōrin hitsu Nakamura Kuranosuke-zō wo chūshin ni." *Kokka* 1023 (May 1979): 7–22.

——. "Kōrin no gafū tenkai ni tsuite." In *Rinpa kaiga zenshū Kōrin-ha ichi*, 7–19. Tokyo: Nihon Keizai Shinbunsha, 1979.

——. "Kōrin no jihitsu shojō to kaisetsu." In *Rinpa kaiga zenshū Kōrin-ha ichi*, 57–66. Tokyo: Nihon Keizai Shinbunsha, 1979.

——, ed. *Rinpa kaiga zenshū Kōrin-ha ichi*. Tokyo: Nihon Keizai Shinbunsha, 1979.

——, ed. *Rinpa kaiga zenshū Kōrin-ha ni*. Tokyo: Nihon Keizai Shinbunsha, 1980.

——. "Kōrin to Kenzan yaki nidai." *Kokka* 1037 (September 1980): 15–23.

——. "Fukae Roshū no funbo hakken wo megutte Misogi zu byōbu hissha kō: Sōtatsu, Kōrin, Kōrin deshi wo megutte." *Kokka* 1104 (June 1987): 31–42.

——. "Kōrin Kenzan no gassaku ni tsuite." In *Kenzan no tōgei*, 119–26. Tokyo: Gotō Bijutsukan, 1987.

——. "Ogata Kōrin Kenzan gassaku Matsunami zu futamono." *Kokka* 1127 (January 1989): 56–61.

——. "Kōrin maki-e nidai." *Kokka* 1123 (May 1989): 11–28.

——. "Kōrin bannen no maki-e ni tsuite." *Kokka* 1136 (July 1990): 11–28.

——. "Shinshutsu no Kōrin jihitsu shojō santsū." *Kokka* 1135 (June 1990): 38–42.

——. "Sōtatsu geijutsu no kaika." In *Tawaraya Sōtatsu: Ryōshi sōshoku to senmenga wo chūshin ni*, 4–9. Nara: Yamato Bunkakan, 1990.

——. "Ogata Kōrin hitsu Ryūsui zu hyōshi kaisetsu." *Kokka* 1162 (September 1992): 37–38.

——. "Zoku Kōrin to Nakamura Kuranosuke: Kōrin no kōhansei, Hōei, Shōtoku nenkan wo chūshin ni." *Kokka* 1167 (February 1993): 19–42.

——. "Kōrin no uchiwaga ni tsuite." *Kokka* 1167 (February 1993): 43–48.

——. "Tōmorokoshi (shika, yūka) zu, shika kōyō zu." *Kokka* 1167 (February 1993): 52–53.

——. "Ogata Kōrin hitsu Sōgi-zō." *Kokka* 1173 (August 1993): 18–25.

——. *Sōtatsu kenkyū ichi*. Yamane Yūzō chosakushū 1. Tokyo: Chūō Kōron Bijutsu Shuppan, 1994.

——. *Sōtatsu kenkyū ni*. Yamane Yūzō chosakushū 2. Tokyo: Chūō Kōron Bijutsu Shuppan, 1994.

——. *Kōrin kenkyū ichi*. Yamane Yūzō chosakushū 3. Tokyo: Chūō Kōron Bijutsu Shuppan, 1995.

——. "Sakai Hōitsu hitsu Yatsuhashi zu byōbu." *Kokka* 1190 (January 1995): 19–26.

——. "Ogata Kōrin hitsu Ebon." *Kokka* 1195 (June 1995): 14–20.

——. "Yōgen'in zō Asai-shi kankei hōzō ga ni tsuite." *Yamato bunka* 96 (September 1996): 14–29.

——. *Kōrin kenkyū ni*. Yamane Yūzō chosakushū 4. Tokyo: Chūō Kōron Bijutsu Shuppan, 1997.

——. "Ogata Kōrin hitsu Ume zu chōshi." *Kokka* 1257 (July 2000): 17–20.

Yamane Yūzō, Naitō Masato, and Timothy Clark. *Rimpa Art from the Idemitsu Collection, Tokyo*. London: British Museum Press, 1998.

Yamasaki K. and K. Nishikawa. "Polychromed Sculptures in Japan." *Studies in Conservation* 15, no. 4 (November 1970): 278–93.

Yamasaki Kazuo and Yoshimichi Emoto. "Pigments Used on Japanese Paintings from the Protohistoric Period through the 17th Century." *Ars Orientalis* 11 (January 1979): 1–14.

Yamashita Yūji and Asano

Shūgō, eds. *Sesson ten: Sengoku jidai no sūpā ekisentorikku.* Tokyo: Asano Kenkyūjo, 2002.

Yamato Bunkakan, ed. *Tawaraya Sōtatsu: Ryōshi sōshoku to senmenga wo chūshin ni.* Nara: Yamato Bunkakan, 1990.

——, ed. *Yamato Bunkakan shozōhin zuhan mokuroku kaiga shoseki (Nihon hen).* Nara: Yamato Bunkakan, 1990.

——, ed. *Tokubetsuten Shōkadō Shōjō: Chanoyu no kokoro to hitsuboku.* Nara: Yamato Bunkakan, 1993.

Yamazaki Hiroshi. "Shōsō yogin ni arawareru Kōrin to Kenzan (jō)." *Kobijutsu* 81 (January 1987): 58–65.

——. "Shōsō yogin ni arawareru Kōrin to Kenzan (ge)." *Kobijutsu* 82 (April 1987): 84–90.

Yamazaki Masakazu. *On the Art of Noh Drama: The Major Treatises of Zeami.* Translated by J. Thomas Rimer. Princeton, N.J.: Princeton University Press, 1984.

Yashiro Yukio. "Zuihitsu Kōrin." *Yamato bunka* 33 (September 1960): 18–27.

Yasuda Atsuo. "Edo jidai ni okeru Kōrin-zō no hensen ni tsuite (jō): Shōtoku-Hōreki." *Aichi kyōiku daigaku kenkyū hōkoku* 50 (March 2001): 106–97 (reverse numbering).

——. "Edo jidai ni okeru Kōrin-zō no hensen ni tsuite (chū): Meiwa-Kyōwa." *Aichi kyōiku daigaku kenkyū hōkoku* 50 (March 2003): 96–86 (reverse numbering).

Yasumura Toshinobu. "Karasumaru Mitsuhiro to Tawaraya Sōtatsu." In *Karasumaru Mitsuhiro to Tawaraya Sōtatsu.* Tokyo: Itabashi Kuritsu Bijutsukan, 1982.

——. "Kibatsuna kōzu to tamashi no shikake." In *Hōitsu to Edo Rinpa,* 122–30. Rinpa bijutsukan 3. Tokyo: Shūeisha, 1993.

——. "Rinpa kankaku no tenkai." In *Kōgei to Rinpa kankaku no tenkai,* 5–12. Rinpa bijutsukan 4. Tokyo: Shūeisha, 1993.

——, ed. *Nihon bijutsu zenshū Edo jidai II.* Tokyo: Shōgakukan, 2013.

Yasumura Toshinobu, Okudaira Shunroku, Nagaoka Yumiko, and Arakawa Masaaki. *Kōgei to Rinpa kankaku no tenkai.* Rinpa bijutsukan 4. Tokyo: Shūeisha, 1993.

Yasumura Toshinobu, Tanaka Eiji, and Wakisaka Atsushi. *Hōitsu to Edo Rinpa.* Rinpa bijutsukan 3. Tokyo: Shūeisha, 1993.

Yawata Shiritsu Shōkadō Bijutsukan, ed. *Shōkadō Shōjō to furusato Yawata no hōmotsu: Uketsugareta kaiga.* Yawata-shi: Yawata Shiritsu Shōkadō Bijutsukan, 2010.

——, ed. *Shōjō to Tokugawa-ke yukari no hitobito.* Yawata-shi: Yawata Shiritsu Shōkadō Bijutsukan, 2011.

Yazaki Itaru. "Shōkadō Shōjō no gadai: Hotei zu to Kanzan Jittoku zu." *Museum* 401 (August 1984): 27–34.

——. "Shōkadō Shōjō no shōgai to geijutsu." *Sadō bunka kenkyū* 4 (October 1998): 1–43.

Yazaki Itaru and Masuda Takashi. "Shōkadō Shōjō nenpu." *Sadō bunka kenkyū* 4 (October 1998): 121–25.

Yip, Leo Shing Chi. "Reinventing China: Cultural Adaptation in Medieval Japanese Nō Theatre." Ph.D. diss., Ohio State University, 2004.

Yokota, Toshiko. "Buson as Bunjin: The Literary Field of Eighteenth-Century Japan." Ph.D. diss., University of California, Irvine, 2000.

Yonezawa Yoshio. "Chūgoku no kingindeiga." In *Kōetsu sho Sōtatsu kingindei-e kenyūhen,* 143–65. Tokyo: Asahi Shinbunsha, 1978.

Yoshida Kōichi, ed. *Kōshoku fumi denju Kōshoku nishikigi.* Koten bunko 604. Tokyo: Koten Bunko, 1997.

Yoshioka Akemi. "Kogire to shifuku Rikyū to shiraji kinran: Bizen chaire Hotei no shifuku." *Shūbi* 6 (Winter 2013): 112–14.

Zaitsu Eiji. "Chanoyu to kohitsu." In *Sadō shūkin,* 9:129–37. Tokyo: Shōgakukan, 1984.

INDEX

Page numbers in italics indicate illustrations.